D0793352

200 FARMHOUSE & COUNTRY HOME PLANS

BLUE RIBBON DESIGNER SERIES™

Classic And Modern Farmhouses
From 1299 To 4890 Square Feet

HOME PLANNERS, INC.
TUCSON, ARIZONA

Published by Home Planners, Inc.
Editorial and Corporate Offices:
3275 West Ina Road, Suite 110
Tucson, Arizona 85741

Distribution Center:
29333 Lorie Lane
Wixom, Michigan 48393

Charles W. Talcott, Chairman
Rickard D. Bailey, President and Publisher
Cindy J. Coatsworth, Publications Manager
Paulette Mulvin, Editor
Paul D. Fitzgerald, Book Designer

Photo Credits
Front Cover: © John R. Dillon, Photographer
Back Cover: © Carl Socolow

First Printing, September 1992
10 9 8 7 6 5 4 3 2 1

Printed in the United States of America.

ISBN softcover: 0-918894-96-4
ISBN hardback: 1-881955-00-1

On the front cover: A beautifully configured Classic Farmhouse, Design Q9242, the home of Rick and Kathy Slivka, was built by Christopher Semenza of Semenza Homes. For additional information about this design, see page 20.

On the back cover: Classic Farmhouse design at its best! Our Design Q2774, the home of John and Janie Deardorff, is a popular and practical family plan. For more information about this design, see page 7.

TABLE OF CONTENTS

Editor's Note
Everyone loves Farmhouse design—maybe because it evokes such a sense of warmth and security. From rustic exterior to cozy interior, the country style is a favorite from Mid-West plains to East and West Coast urban centers. This collection draws its inspiration from the simple honesty of country living, while actually providing the most popular features in residential housing. Filled with the spirit of the country life, this book brings together recognizable rural style and efficient, amenity-laden architectural floor planning for a selection of homes that tugs at the heart.

About The Designers

The Blue Ribbon Designer Series™ is a collection of books featuring the home plans of a diverse group of outstanding home designers and architects known as the Blue Ribbon Network of Designers. This group of companies is dedicated to creating and marketing the finest possible plans for home construction on a regional and national basis. Each of the companies exhibits superior work and integrity in all phases of the stock-plan business including modern, trendsetting floor planning, a professionally executed blueprint package and a strong sense of service and commitment to the consumer.

Design Basics, Inc.

For nearly a decade, Design Basics, a nationally recognized home design service located in Omaha, has been developing plans for custom home builders. Since 1987, the firm has consistently appeared in *Builder* magazine, the official magazine of the National Association of Home Builders, as the top-selling designer. The company's plans also regularly appear in numerous other shelter magazines such as *Better Homes and Gardens*, *House Beautiful* and *Home Planner*.

Design Traditions Atlanta

Design Traditions was established by Stephen S. Fuller with the tenets of innovation, quality, originality and uncompromising architectural techniques in traditional and European homes. Especially popular throughout the Southeast, Design Traditions' plans are known for their extensive detail and thoughtful design. They are widely published in such shelter magazines as *Southern Living* magazine and *Better Homes and Gardens*.

Alan Mascord Design Associates, Inc.

Founded in 1983 as a local supplier to the building community, Mascord Design Associates of Portland, Oregon, began to successfully publish plans nationally in 1985. With plans now drawn exclusively on computer, Mascord Design Associates quickly received a reputation for homes that are easy to build yet meet the rigorous demands of the buyers' market, winning local and national awards. The company's trademark is creating floor plans that work well and exhibit excellent traffic patterns. Their motto is: "Drawn to build, designed to sell."

Larry W. Garnett & Associates, Inc.

Starting as a designer of homes for Houston-area residents, Garnett & Associates has been marketing designs nationally for the past ten years. A well-respected design firm, the company's plans are regularly featured in *House Beautiful*, *Country Living*, *Home* and *Professional Builder*. Numerous accolades, including several from the Texas Institute of Building Design and the American Institute of Building Design, have been awarded to the company for excellence in architecture.

Home Planners, Inc.

Headquartered in Tucson, Arizona, with additional offices in Detroit, Home Planners is one of the longest-running and most successful home design firms in the United States. With over 2,500 designs in its portfolio, the company provides a wide range of styles, sizes and types of homes for the residential builder. All of Home Planners' designs are created with the care and professional expertise that fifty years of experience in the home-planning business affords. Their homes are designed to be built, lived in and enjoyed for years to come.

Donald A. Gardner, Architect, Inc.

The South Carolina firm of Donald A. Gardner was established in response to a growing demand for residential designs that reflect constantly changing lifestyles. The company's specialty is providing homes with refined, custom-style details and unique features such as passive-solar designs and open floor plans. Computer-aided design and drafting technology resulting in trouble-free construction documents places the firm at the leading edge of the home plan industry.

CLASSIC FARMHOUSES

The Classic American Farmhouse is the very essence of country-style living. It evokes images of Sunday-afternoon picnics on rolling green lawns, cold lemonade served on wide covered porches and gatherings around a cozy fireplace on wintery evenings. Its floor plans cater to family living with roomy living spaces, large kitchens and plenty of bedrooms.

Easily recognizable, the Classic Farmhouse has a number of characteristics that make it a standout. Probably most noticeable is its tall, upright, stately appearance coupled with a covered front porch or wrapping porch. The porch usually has simple, square columns with square, dimensioned railings.

The home itself is almost always two-stories, or at least 1½-stories, with the porch being either raised or at grade. The Classic Farmhouse will support a straight gabled roof that is usually steeply pitched. In some instances, the roof may have cross gables over a garage or a living area extension. It is not unusual to find a cupola or a weathervane at the rooftop or over the garage.

Covered on the exterior with horizontal wood siding, the Classic Farmhouse is trimmed with wood and sports a wood fascia. Other exterior details include a prominent chimney stack at one or both ends of the home and paned, shuttered windows in a symmetrical fenestration. Some versions may have round, half-round or Palladian windows and entry doors with fan lights. Though not common, some Classic Farmhouses have two or three dormer windows at the second floor.

Design Q2774 is the quintessential Classic Farmhouse, bringing together a rustic charm and comfortable livability. The wraparound covered porch, raised-hearth fireplace in the family room and exterior enhancements such as the shuttered, multi-pane windows and the steeply gabled roofline herald its popular interior layout. In two stories, the plan accommodates formal and informal living spaces, four bedrooms and 2½ baths. Attic space on the unfinished third floor makes a great storage area or can be developed into additional bedrooms at a later time.

This home is just one of many in the Classic Farmhouse section that draws design flavor from rustic predecessors, yet provides a comfortable, convenient home for today's family.

Design Q2694

First Floor: 2,026 square feet
Second Floor: 1,386 square feet
Total: 3,412 square feet

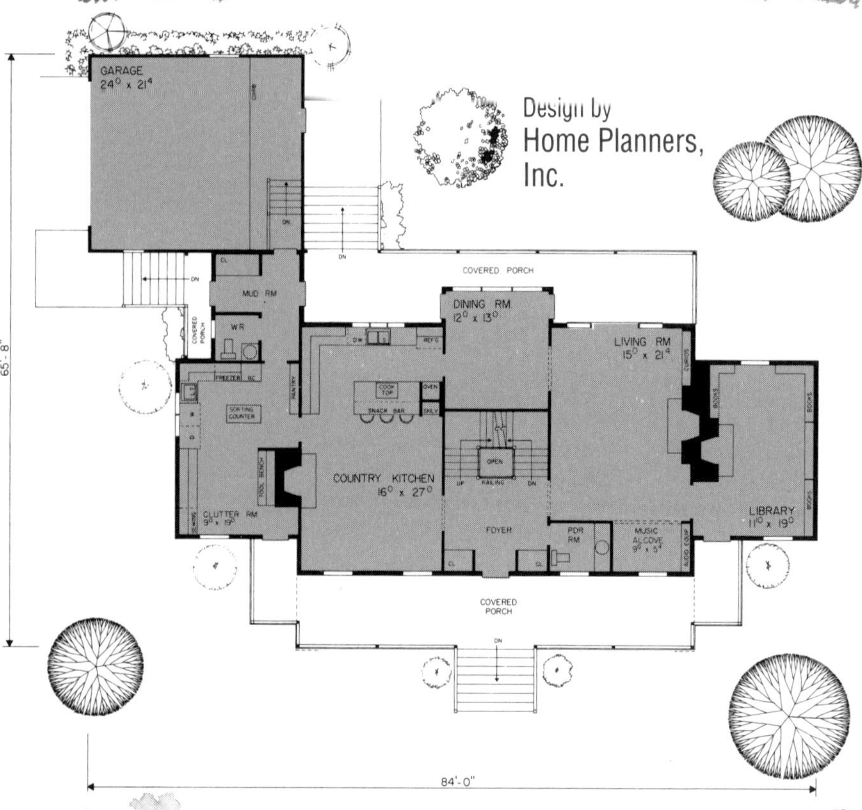

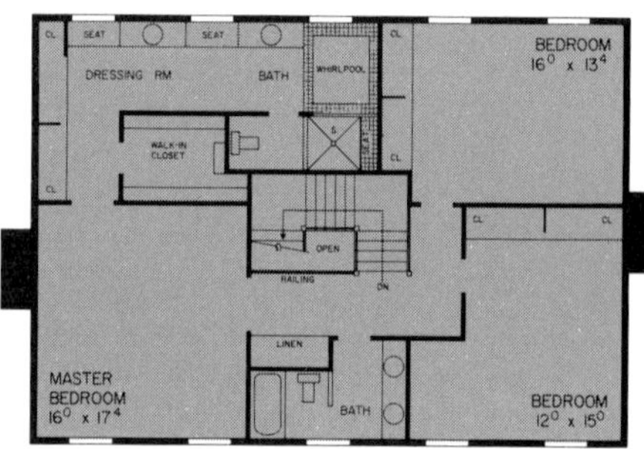

● This two-story design faithfully recalls the 18th-Century homestead of Sec. of Foreign Affairs John Jay. Downstairs features include a large country kitchen, clutter room, music alcove, and library wing. Upstairs are three sizable bedrooms, including a master suite with whirlpool.

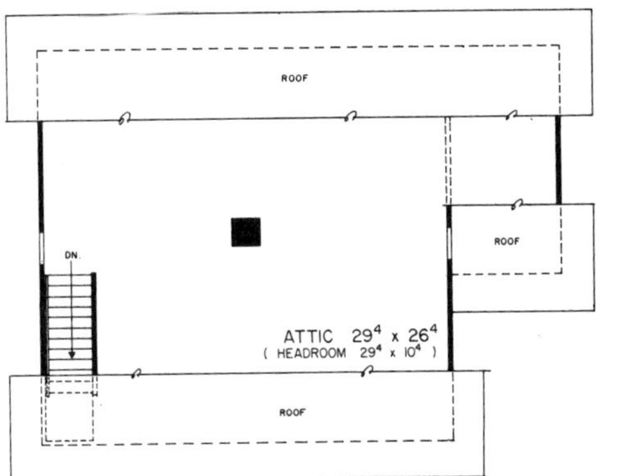

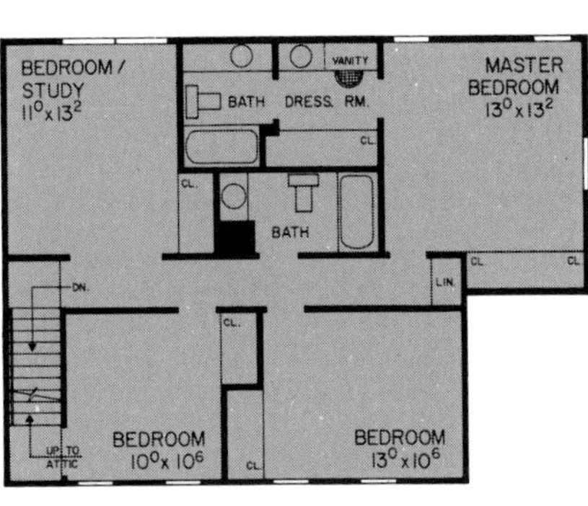

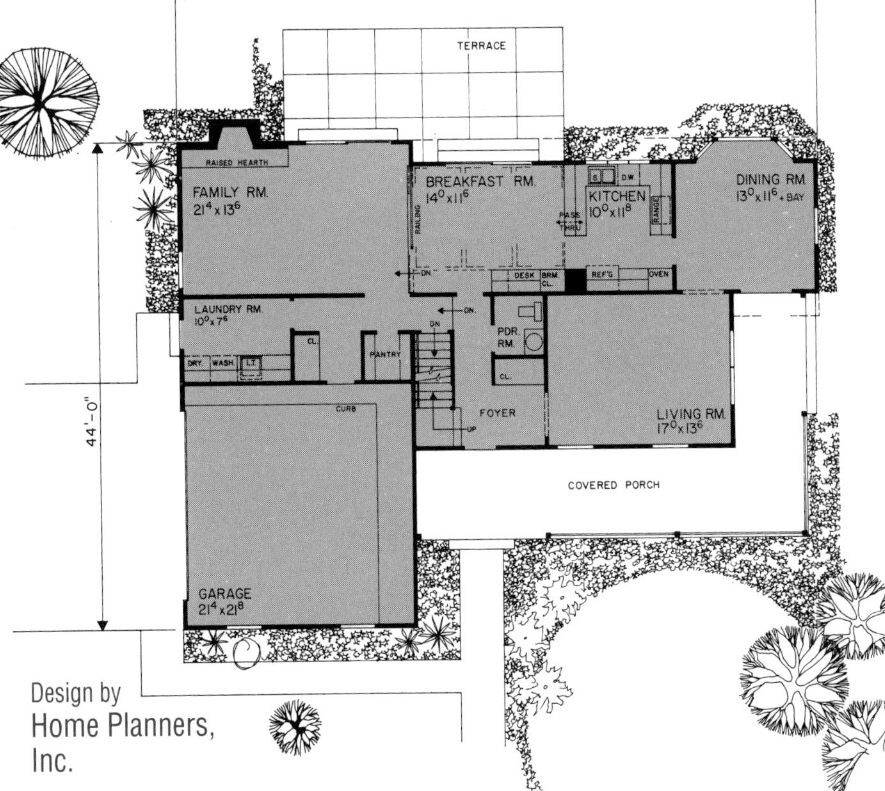

Design by
Home Planners,
Inc.

Design Q2774

First Floor: 1,370 square feet
Second Floor: 969 square feet
Total: 2,339 square feet

● Another farmhouse adaptation with all the most up-to-date features expected in a new home. Beginning with the formal areas, this design offers pleasures for the entire family. There is the quit corner living room which has an opening to the sizable dining room. This room will enjoy plenty of natural light from the delightful bay window overlooking the rear yard. It is also conveniently located with the efficient U-shaped kitchen just a step away. The kitchen features many built-ins with pass-through to the beam-ceiling nook. Sliding glass doors to the terrace are fine attractions in both the sunken family room and nook. The service entrance to the garage has a storage closet on each side. There is extra storage in the large attic, with expansion possibilities there also. Recreational activities and hobbies can be pursued in the basement area, where there is more bulk storage space. Note four bedrooms with two baths upstairs.

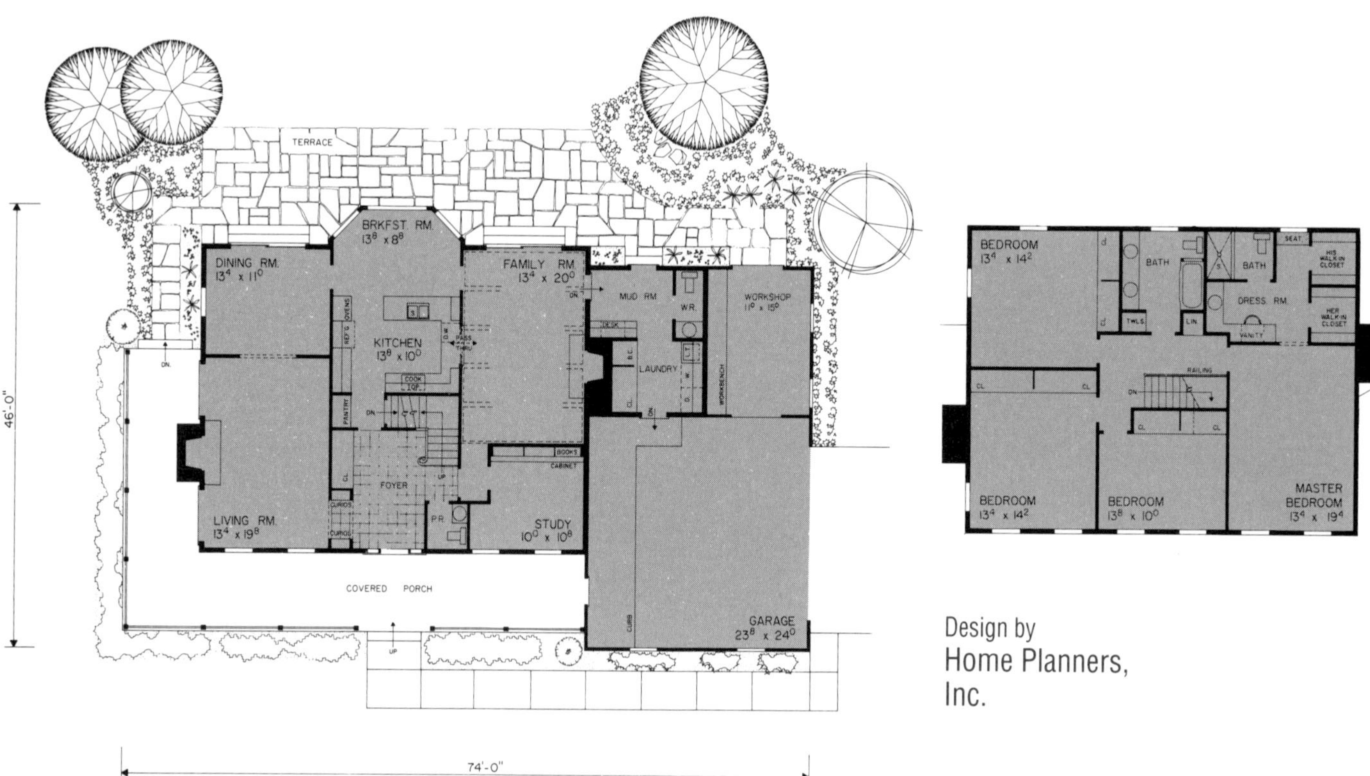

Design by
Home Planners,
Inc.

Design Q2946 First Floor: 1,590 square feet
Second Floor: 1,344 square feet
Total: 2,934 square feet

● Here's a traditional design that's made for down-home hospitality, the pleasures of casual conversation, and the good grace of pleasant company. The star attractions are the large covered porch and terrace, perfectly relaxing gathering points for family and friends. Inside, though, the design is truly a hard worker; separate living room and family room, each with its own fireplace; formal dining room; large kitchen and breakfast area with bay windows; separate study; workshop with plenty of room to maneuver; mud room; and four bedrooms up, including a master suite. Not to be overlooked are the curio niches, the powder room, the built-in bookshelves, the kitchen pass-through, the pantry, the planning desk, the workbench, and the stairs to the basement.

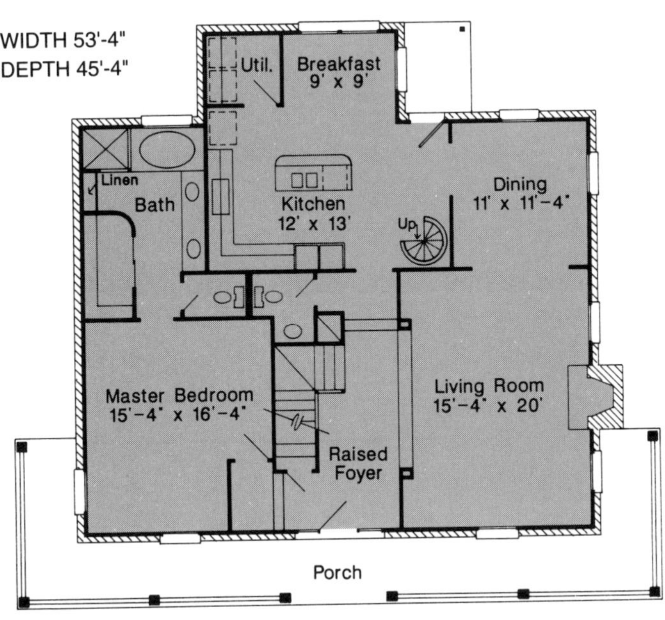

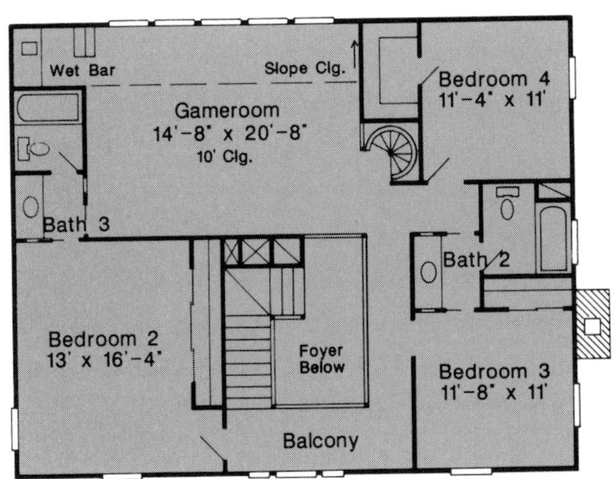

Design Q9076

First Floor: 1,576 square feet
Second Floor: 1,242 square feet
Total: 2,818 square feet

● From Palladian window in the upstairs balcony to the covered front porch, this design is pure delight. The first floor contains a formal living area with attached dining room and fireplace. To the rear is an L-shaped kitchen with breakfast nook. A spiral staircase leads to the second-floor game room. The master suite is separated from secondary bedrooms with its location on the first floor. It holds a large walk-in closet, compartmented commode and double vanity. There are three bedrooms on the second floor—one with a private bath. Bedrooms 3 and 4 share a full bath. Note the wetbar and counter in the game room. Other special features of this home include a powder room for guests, a coat closet and an open stairwell in the raised foyer.

Design by
Larry W.
Garnett &
Associates, Inc.

Design Q9677

First Floor: 1,584 square feet
Second Floor: 867 square feet
Total: 2,451 square feet

● Flexibility is the key to the appeal of this country-style plan. The dining room/great room can be built as one great room with the dining room relocated to the family room. The master suite has a large walk-in closet, a fireplace and a master bath with shower, whirlpool tub and double-bowl vanity. Both the sun room and master bath have access to a uniquely shaped deck. Note that there is space available on the deck for a hot tub. The screened porch offers the best in outdoor living space. Three bedrooms on the second level are joined by two full baths for convenience. Dormer windows on the second floor project out from two of the bedrooms, allowing room for window seats or storage.

BED RM. 11-10 x 11-4
BED RM. 13-0 x 12-0
BED RM. 13-4 x 12-0
DECK
SUN RM. 15-4 x 9-6
KITCHEN 13-4 x 13-8
MASTER BED RM. 15-0 x 14-4
DINING/ GREAT RM. 15-4 x 23-8
FAMILY RM. 13-4 x 14-4
SCREENED PORCH 10-4 x 16-0
GARAGE 21-8 x 21-0
PORCH 33-6 x 7-0

Design by
Donald A. Gardner, Architect, Inc.

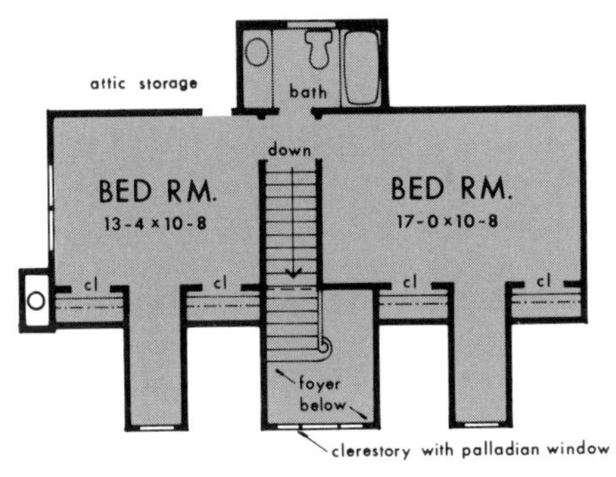

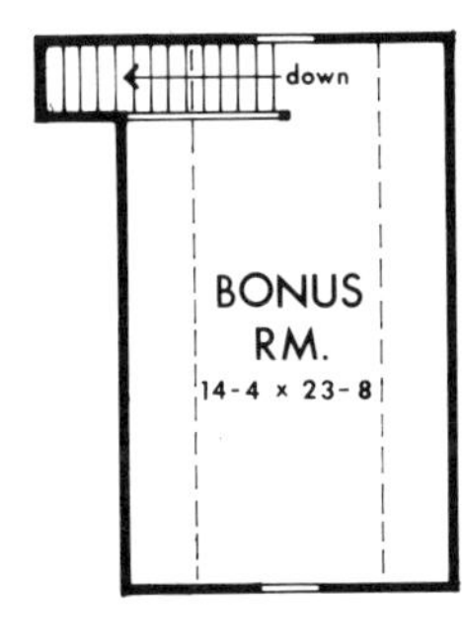

Design by
Donald A.
Gardner,
Architect, Inc.

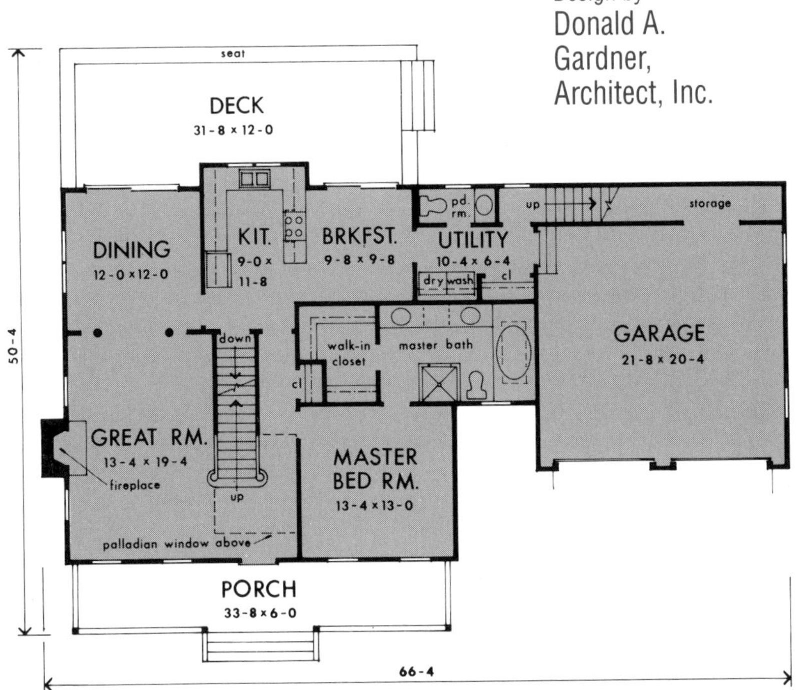

Design Q9606

First Floor: 1,289 square feet
Second Floor: 542 square feet
Total: 1,831 square feet

● This cozy country cottage is perfect for the growing family —offering both an unfinished basement option and a bonus room. Enter through the two-story foyer with a Palladian window in a clerestory dormer above. The master suite is on the first floor for privacy and accessibility. Its accompanying bath boasts a whirlpool tub with skylight above and double-bowl vanity. The second floor contains two bedrooms, a full bath, and plenty of storage. Note that all first-floor rooms except the kitchen and utility room boast 9-foot ceilings. For crawl-space foundation, order Design Q9606; for basement foundation, order Design Q9606A.

Design Q9421

First Floor: 1,157 square feet
Second Floor: 980 square feet
Total: 2,137 square feet

● This great looking farmhouse home comes complete with covered front porch, varied roof lines and shuttered windows. The dramatic two-story foyer contains an angled stairway that forms the circulation hub for the floor plan. The dining room lies to one side; the formal parlor to the other (don't miss the beautiful bay window that lights this living space). The back of the plan is dominated by the family room with fireplace and island kitchen with attached nook. A large pantry makes kitchen duty a breeze. There's even a well-placed utility area at the entrance to the garage. Upstairs are four bedrooms. Three are family bedrooms, sharing a full bath. The master suite includes a spa tub, large shower and walk-in closet.

Design by
Alan Mascord
Design Associates, Inc.

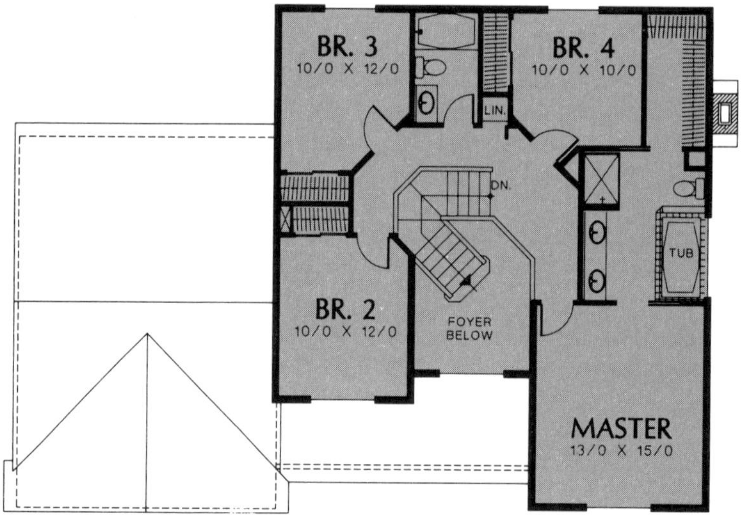

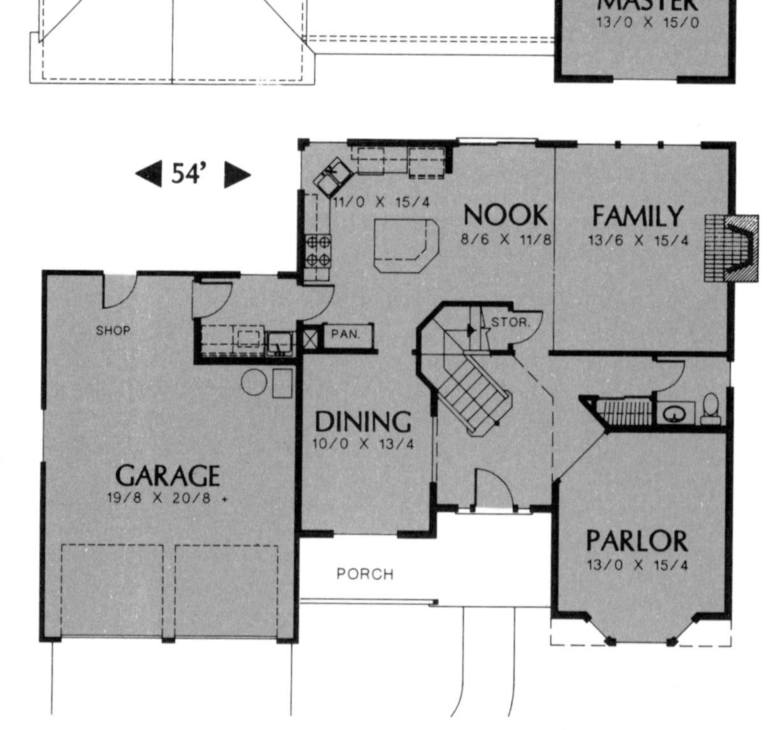

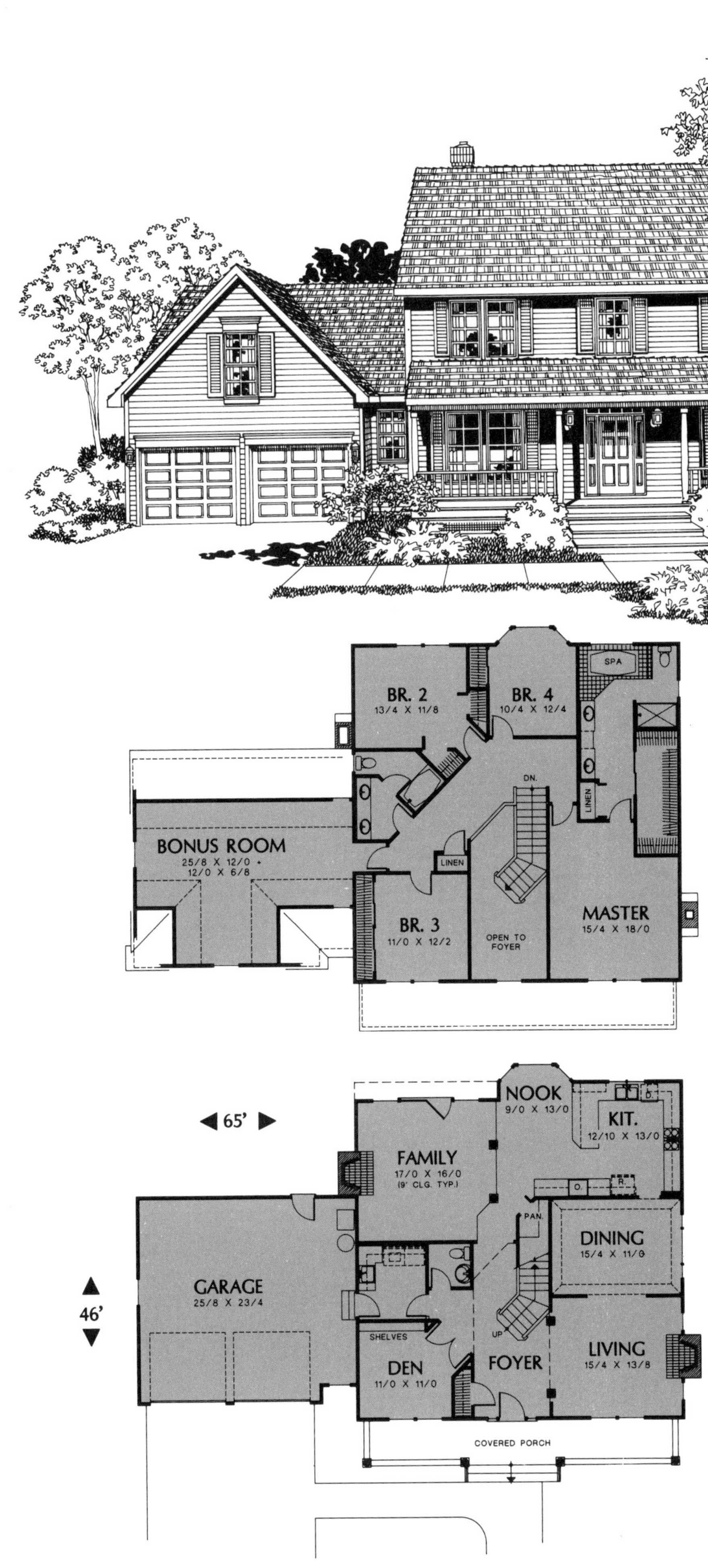

Design Q9419

First Floor: 1,501 square feet
Second Floor: 1,341 square feet
Total: 2,842 square feet

● Totally country-styled, this home boasts a full-width porch across the front. The two-story foyer opens up to the living room on one side and through a pair of French doors to the den on the other. A large family room, nook and kitchen sweep across the back of the home overlooking the outdoor living area. An extra-large garage includes space ideal for a work bench. Four good-sized bedrooms and a large bonus room are found on the upper floor.

Design by
Alan Mascord
Design Associates, Inc.

Design Q9644

First Floor: 943 square feet
Second Floor: 840 square feet
Total: 1,783 square feet

● Roundtop windows and an inviting covered porch offer an irresistible appeal for this three-bedroom plan. A two-story foyer provides a spacious feeling to this well-organized open layout. Round columns between the great room and kitchen add to the impressive quality of the plan. An expansive deck promotes casual outdoor living to its fullest. The master suite with walk-in closet and complete master bath is on the second floor along with two additional bedrooms and a full bath. The bonus room over the garage offers room for expansion.

Design by
Donald A.
Gardner,
Architect, Inc.

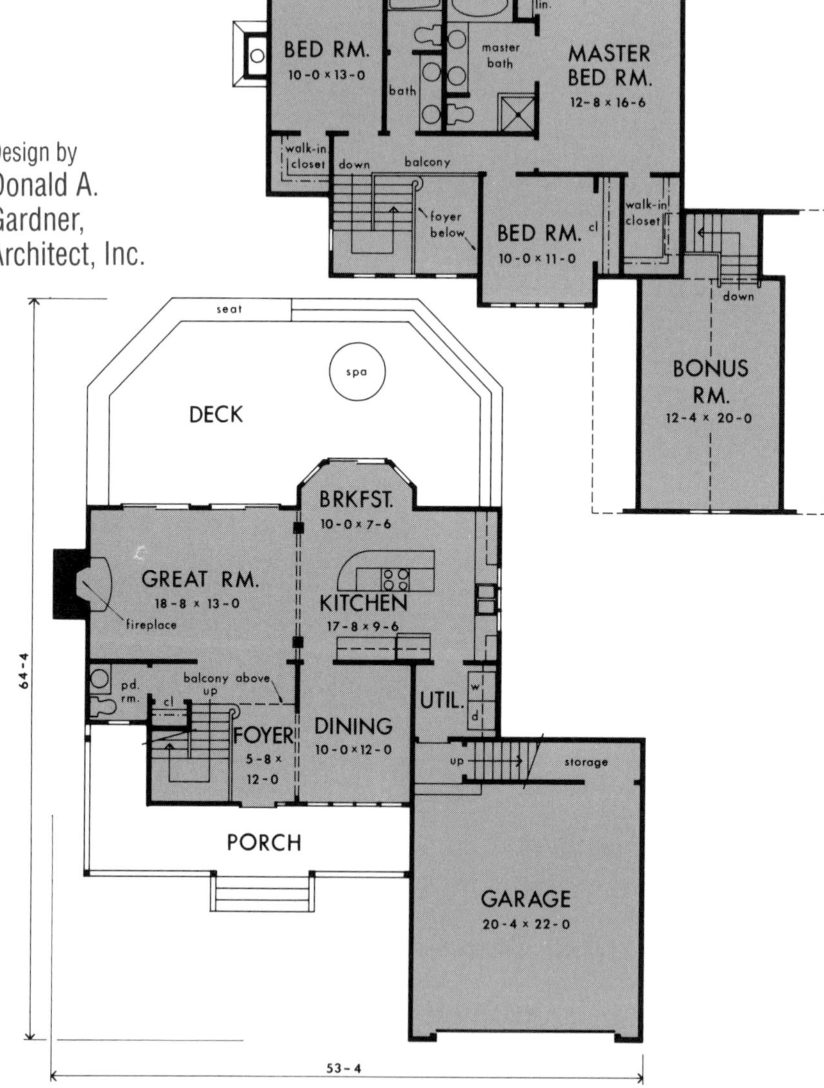

Design Q9643

First Floor: 1,152 square feet
Second Floor: 1,040 square feet
Total: 2,192 square feet
Bonus Room: 282 square feet

● The beauty of the exterior of this four-bedroom plan is enhanced by the use of arched windows, dormers and a wraparound front porch. The entrance foyer is partially open to the second level, allowing a balcony to pass over the center and generate visual excitement. Both the living and family rooms have fireplaces. The U-shaped kitchen is centrally located between the breakfast area and dining room for maximum efficiency. A large rear deck enhances outdoor living. A master suite with a generous master bath shares the second floor with three other bedrooms and a bonus room.

Design by
Donald A.
Gardner,
Architect, Inc.

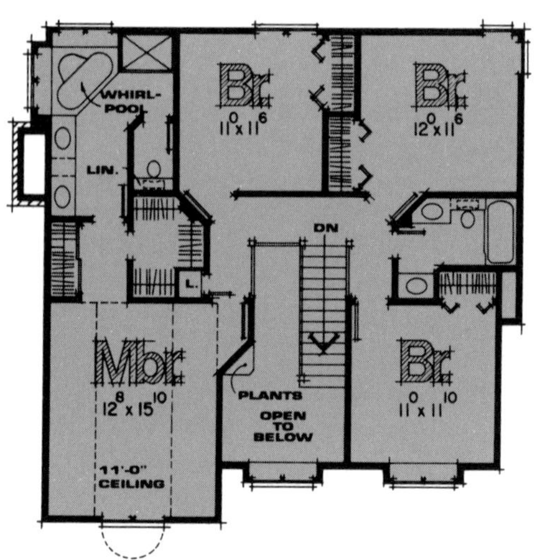

● It's hard to get beyond the covered front porch of this home, but doing so reveals a bright two-story entry open to the central hall. Just to the left, an enticing bay window enlivens the living room, featuring French doors which connect to the family room. The efficient kitchen with snack bar and pantry is open to the bay-windowed breakfast area with planning desk. The salad sink and counter space double as a service for the formal dining room. The master bedroom features a raised ceiling and arched window. Its adjoining bath contains a walk-through closet/transition area and a corner whirlpool.

Design Q9230

First Floor: 1,303 square feet
Second Floor: 1,084 square feet
Total: 2,387 square feet

Design by
Design
Basics,
Inc.

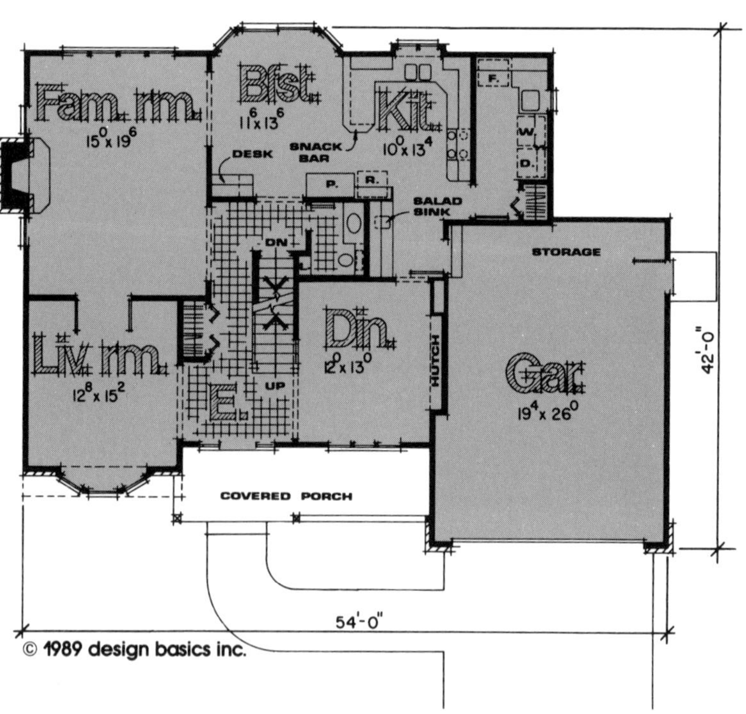

Design Q9214

First Floor: 1,188 square feet
Second Floor: 1,172 square feet
Total: 2,360 square feet

● Beginning with the interest of a wraparound porch, there's a feeling of country charm in this two-story plan. Formal dining and living rooms, visible from the entry, offer ample space for gracious entertaining. The large family room is truly a place of warmth and welcome with its gorgeous bay window, fireplace and French doors to the living room. The kitchen, with island counter, pantry and desk, makes cooking a delight. Upstairs, the secondary bedrooms share an efficient compartmented bath. The expansive master suite has its own luxury bath with double vanity, whirlpool, walk-in closet and dressing area.

Design by
Design Basics, Inc.

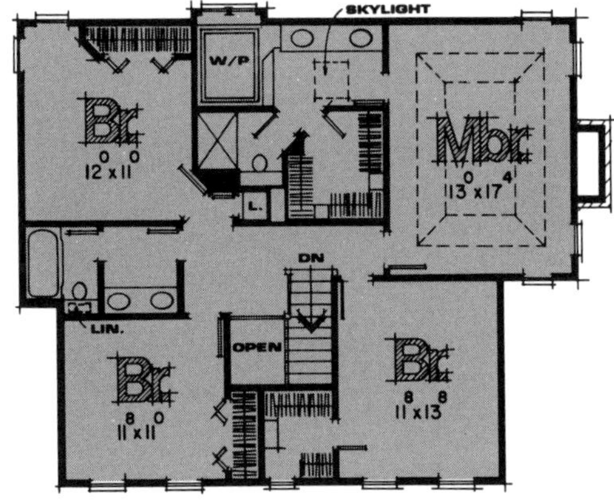

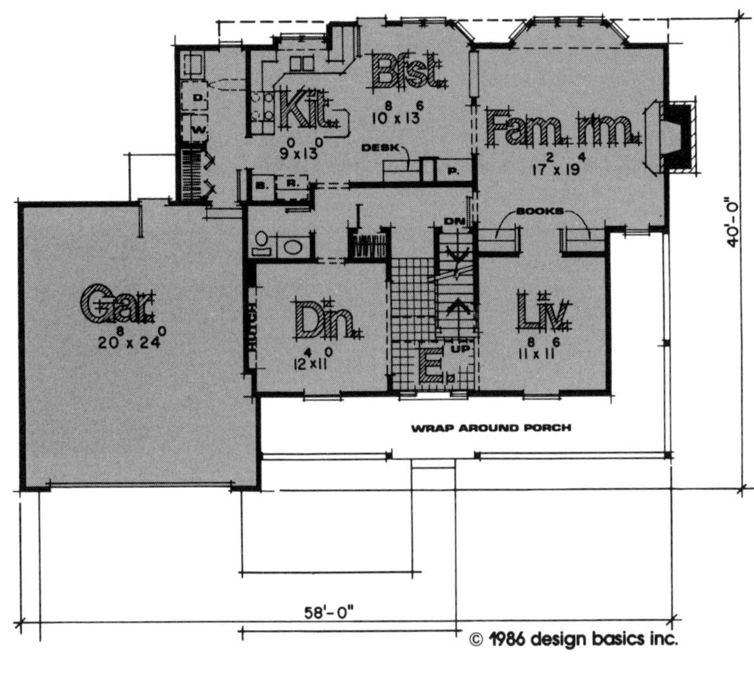

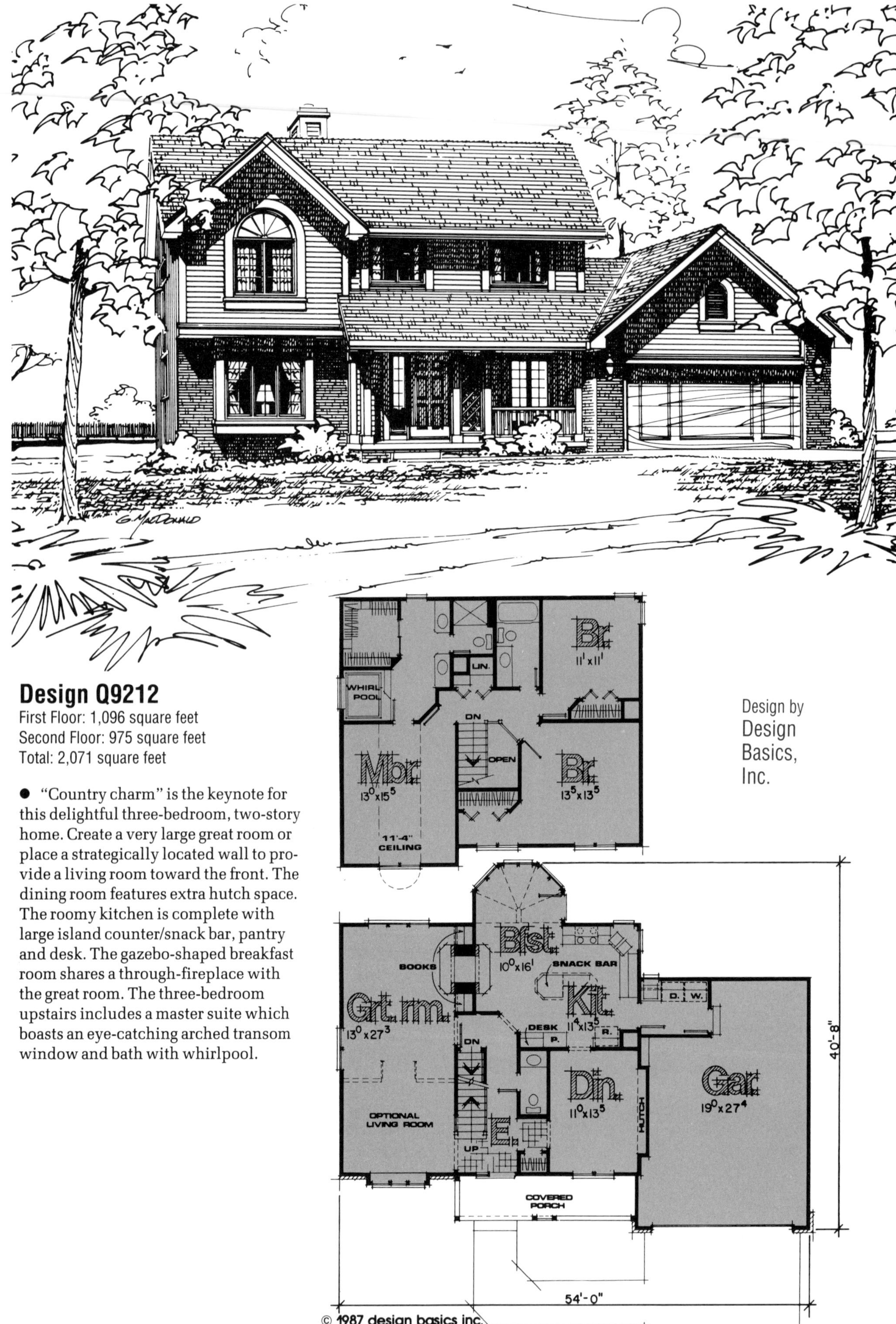

Design Q9212

First Floor: 1,096 square feet
Second Floor: 975 square feet
Total: 2,071 square feet

● "Country charm" is the keynote for this delightful three-bedroom, two-story home. Create a very large great room or place a strategically located wall to provide a living room toward the front. The dining room features extra hutch space. The roomy kitchen is complete with large island counter/snack bar, pantry and desk. The gazebo-shaped breakfast room shares a through-fireplace with the great room. The three-bedroom upstairs includes a master suite which boasts an eye-catching arched transom window and bath with whirlpool.

Design by
Design Basics, Inc.

Design Q9289

First Floor: 927 square feet
Second Floor: 1,163 square feet
Total: 2,090 square feet

● If you've ever dreamed of living in a country home, you'll love the wrapping porch on this four-bedroom, two-story home. Comfortable living begins in the great room with windows and nearby staircase. Just off the entry, a formal dining room was designed to make entertaining a pleasure. The large kitchen includes a pantry, island counter, roll-top desk and Lazy Susan. A private door accesses the wraparound porch from the kitchen. Be sure to take a good look at the bright dinette. Upstairs, secondary bedrooms share a centrally located bath with double vanity. For convenience, the laundry room is located on the same level as the bedrooms. The deluxe master bedroom is accessed by double doors. In the master bath, you'll enjoy the whirlpool, transom window and sloped ceiling.

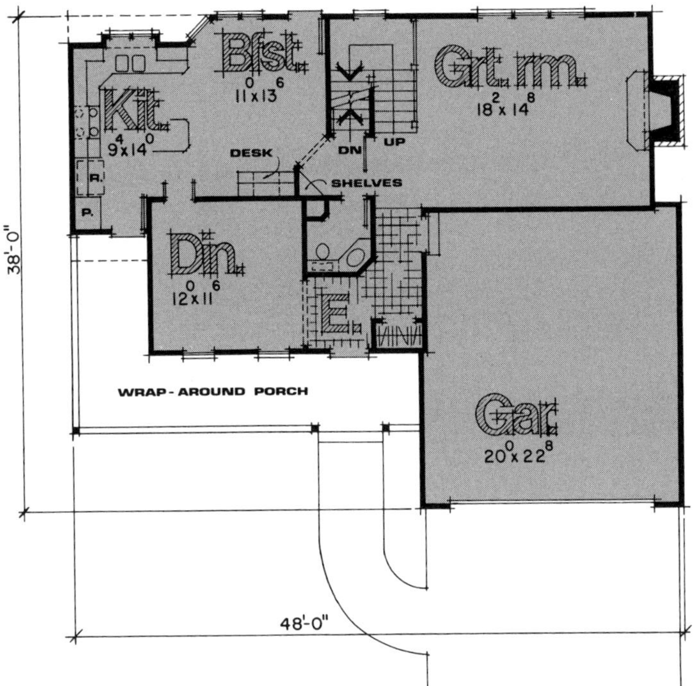

Design by
Design
Basics,
Inc.

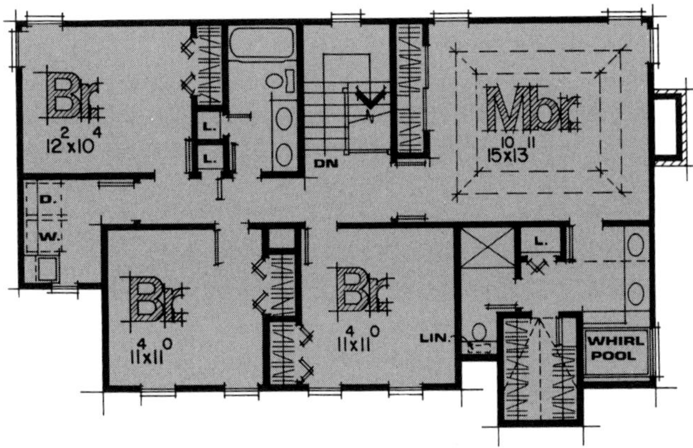

Design Q9242

First Floor: 1,322 square feet
Second Floor: 1,272 square feet
Total: 2,594 square feet

● Here's the luxury you've been looking for—from the wraparound covered front porch to the bright sun room at the rear off the breakfast room. A sunken family room with fireplace serves everyday casual gatherings, while the more formal living and dining rooms are reserved for special entertaining situations. The kitchen has a central island with snack bar and is located most conveniently for serving and cleaning up. Upstairs are four bedrooms, one a lovely master suite with French doors into the master bath and a whirlpool tub in a dramatic bay window. A double vanity in the shared bath easily serves the three family bedrooms.

Design by
Design
Basics,
Inc.

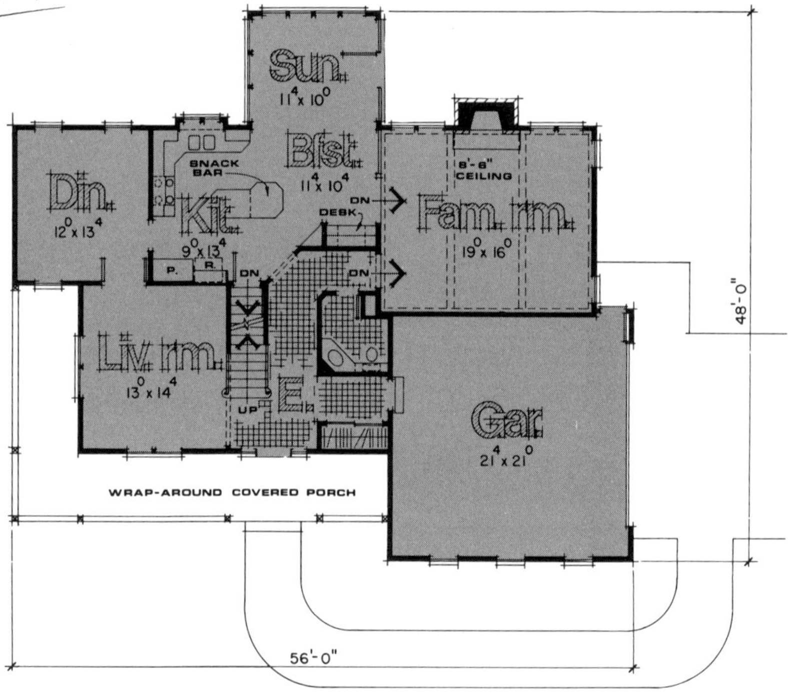

Sun $11^{4} \times 10^{0}$
Bfst. $11^{4} \times 10^{4}$
SNACK BAR
Din. $12^{0} \times 13^{4}$
Kit. $9^{0} \times 13^{4}$
P. R.
DESK
DN
8'-6" CEILING
Fam. rm. $19^{0} \times 16^{0}$
DN
Liv. rm. $13^{0} \times 14^{4}$
UP
E.
Gar. $21^{4} \times 21^{0}$
WRAP-AROUND COVERED PORCH
48'-0"
56'-0"

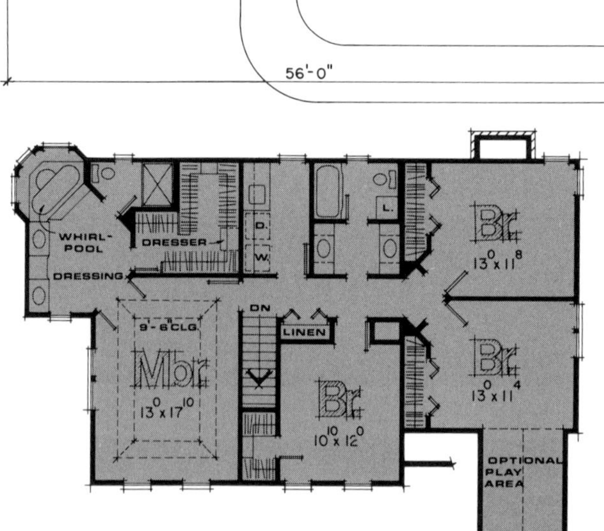

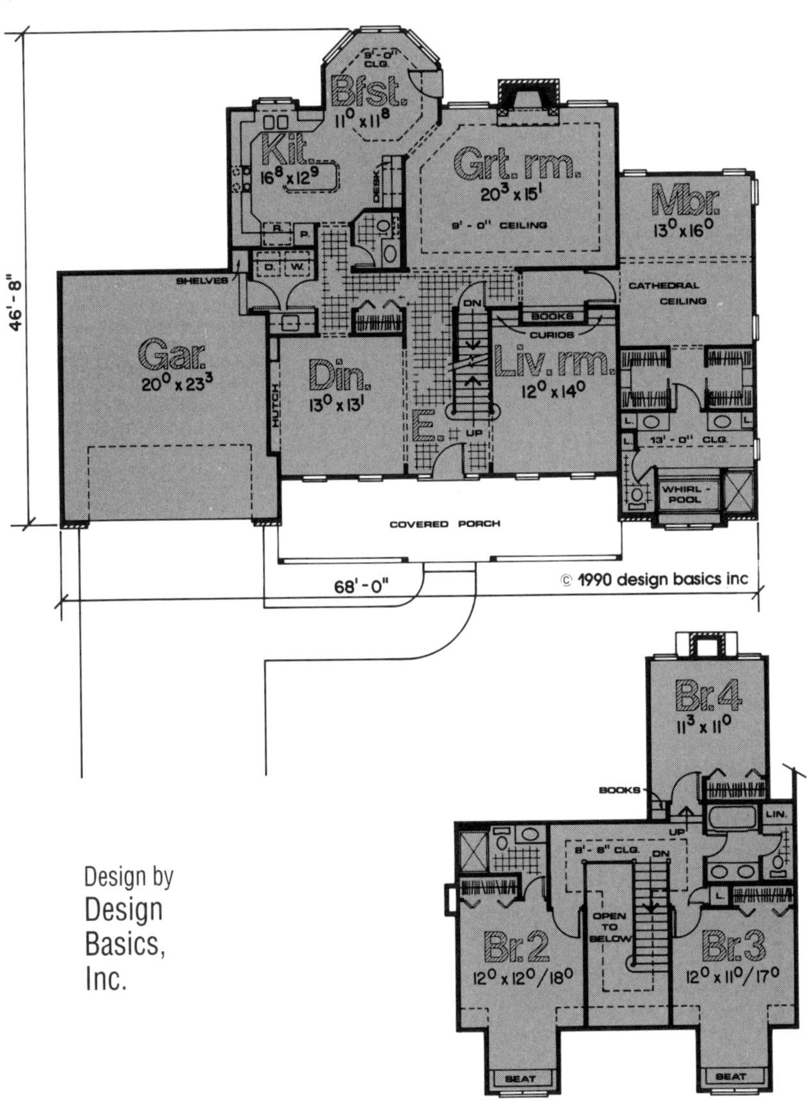

Design by
Design
Basics,
Inc.

Design Q9274

First Floor: 1,780 square feet
Second Floor: 815 square feet
Total: 2,595 square feet

● A large covered front porch welcomes visitors to this home. The entrance hall opens to a formal dining room with hutch space and a living room with built-in curio cabinets. The volume great room features a handsome fireplace flanked by windows. A large kitchen provides an island counter, pantry, dual Lazy Susans and a desk. A private hall with built-in bookcase leads to the first-floor master suite. The extravagant master bath features two walk-in closets, His and Hers vanities and a whirlpool tub. Upstairs, two of the three bedrooms feature decorator window seats.

Design by
Donald A. Gardner, Architect, Inc.

● Enjoy outdoor living with a covered front porch at the front of this home and an expansive deck to the rear. The floor plan allows for great livability and features split-bedroom styling with the master suite on the first floor. Upstairs bedrooms share a full bath. There is also bonus space above the garage for a studio, study or play room. For a crawl-space foundation, order Plan Q9654; for a basement foundation, order Q9654-A.

Design Q9654

First Floor: 1,578 square feet
Second Floor: 554 square feet
Total: 2,132 square feet

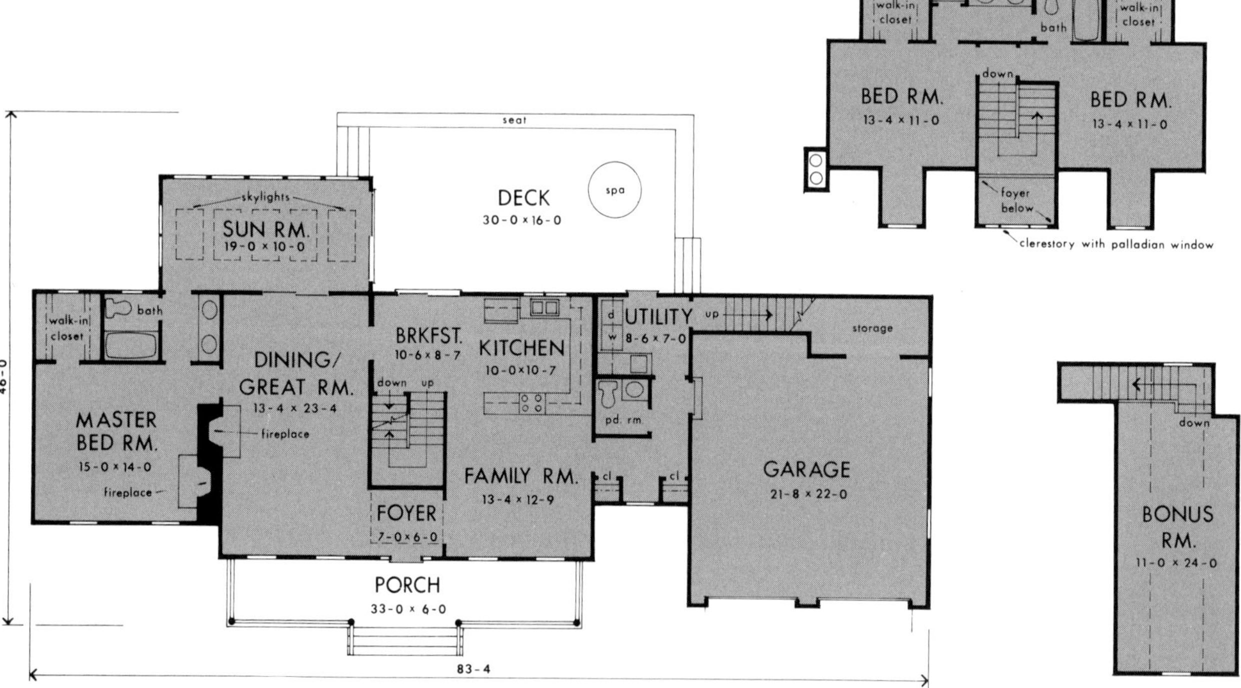

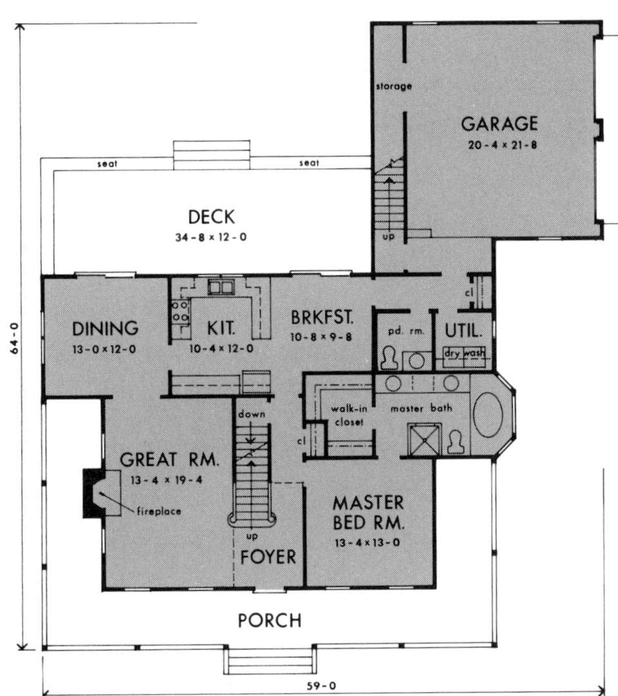

Design Q9645

First Floor: 1,356 square feet
Second Floor: 542 square feet
Total: 1,898 square feet

● The welcoming charm of this country farmhouse is expressed by its many windows and its covered wraparound porch. A two-story entrance foyer is enhanced by a Palladian window in a clerestory dormer above to allow natural lighting. A first-floor master suite allows privacy and accessibility. The master bath includes a whirlpool tub, shower, and double-bowl vanity along with a walk-in closet. The first floor features a nine-foot ceiling throughout with the exception of the kitchen area, which features an eight-foot ceiling. The second floor provides two additional bedrooms, a full bath, and plenty of storage space. An unfinished basement and bonus room provide room to grow. Order Design Q9645 for crawl-space foundation; order Design Q9645-A for basement foundation.

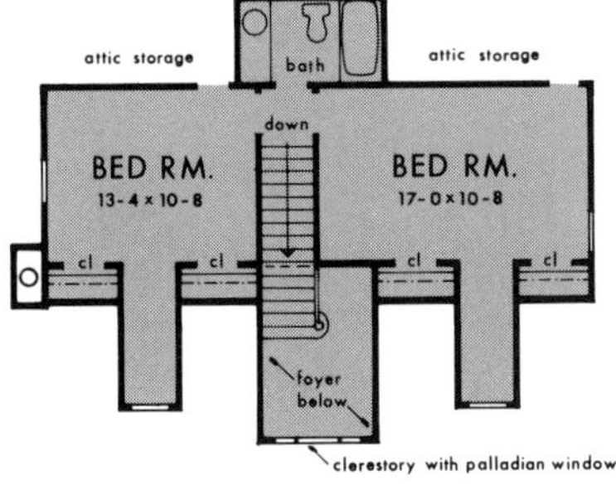

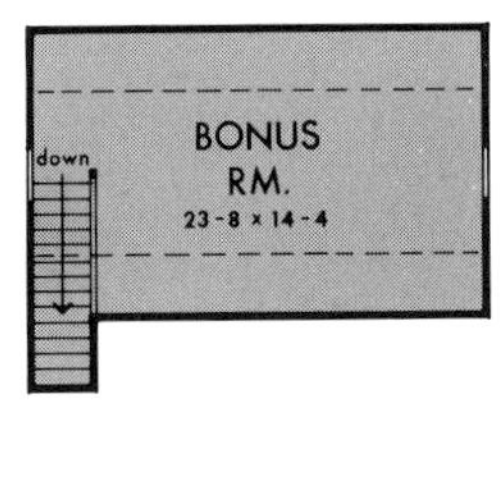

Design by
Donald A.
Gardner,
Architect, Inc.

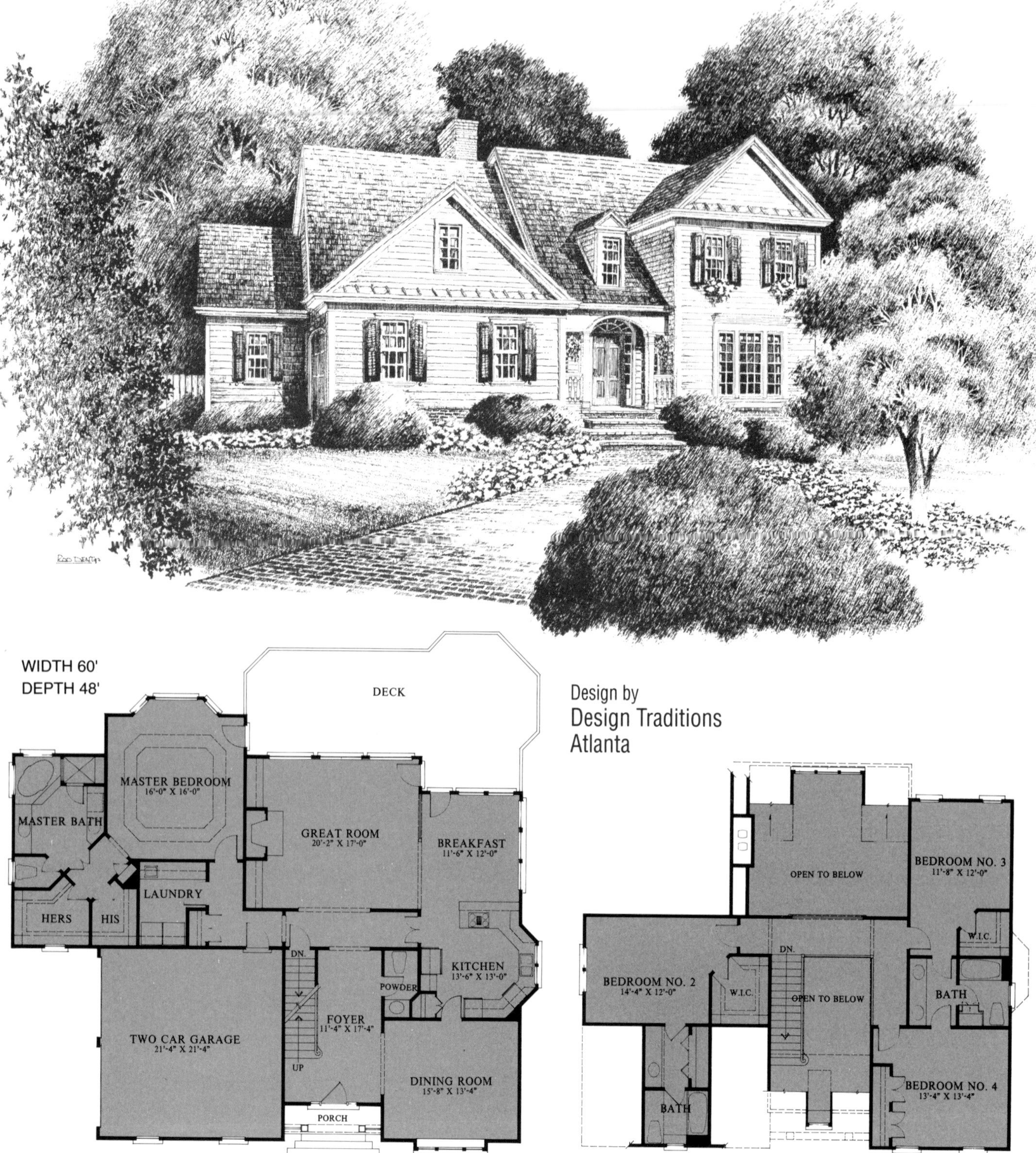

Design by
Design Traditions
Atlanta

Design Q9863 First Floor: 1,940 square feet
Second Floor: 987 square feet
Total: 2,927 square feet

● Some of the most charming features of Traditional design are revealed as one approaches this home. Wood siding, window shutters, flower boxes and a classic elliptical entranceway bring this architectural tradition to life. The open foyer with tray ceiling and powder room leads to the dining room. The adjacent kitchen with an octagonal counter top gives way to a spacious breakfast area with access to the deck and vaulted great room complete with fireplace. The great room hall leads to a very private master suite with bay window overlooking the back yard and easy access to the out-of-doors. The master bath with separate shower, garden tub, His and Hers vanities and a spacious walk-in closet completes the master suite. Overlooking the great room, the upper level stairway landing leads to two additional bedrooms that share a full bath. A fourth bedroom offers more privacy, with a walk-in closet and a private bath.

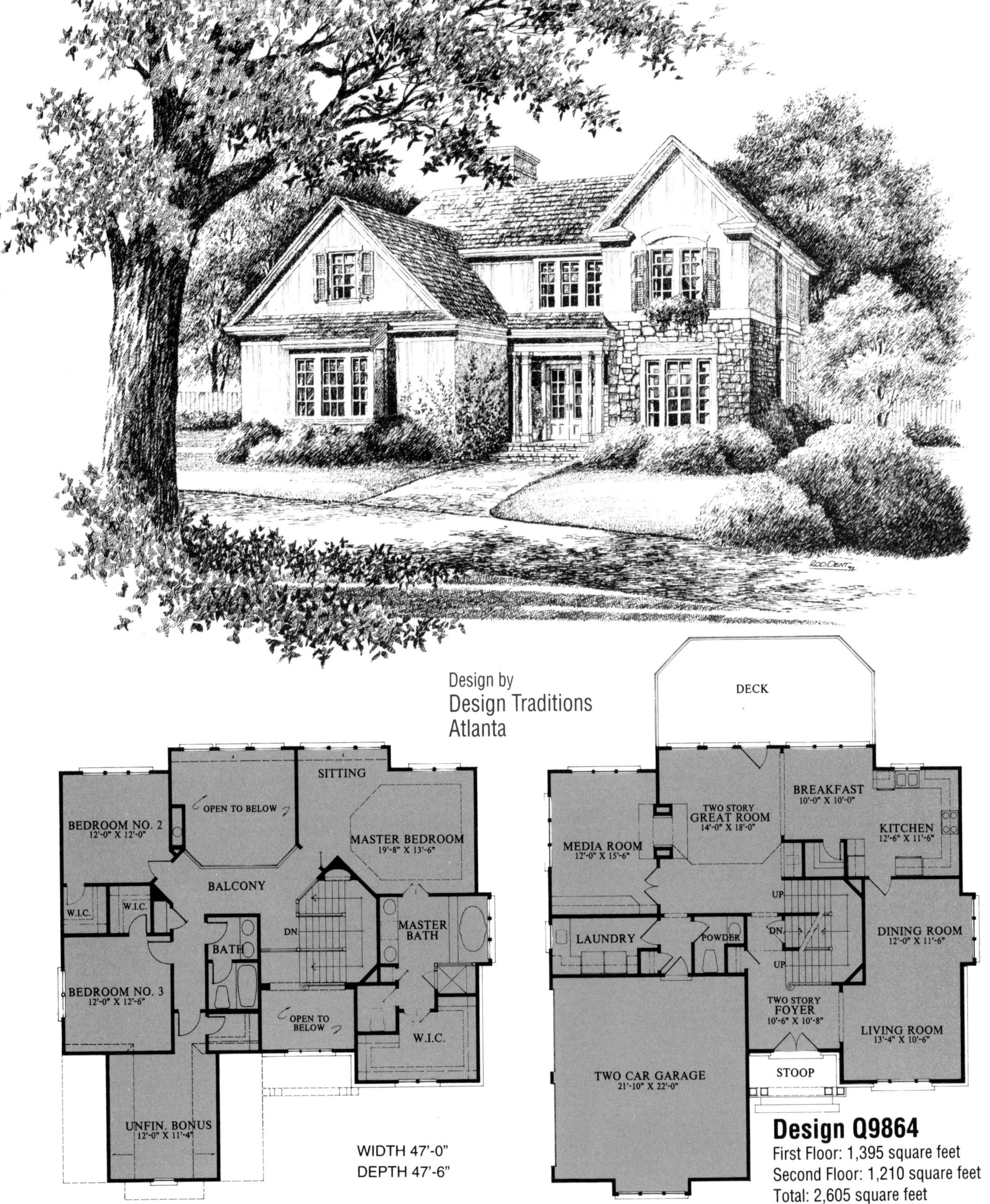

Design Q9864

First Floor: 1,395 square feet
Second Floor: 1,210 square feet
Total: 2,605 square feet

● The well-balanced use of stucco and stone combined with box bay window treatments and a covered entry make this English country home especially inviting. The two-story foyer opens on the right to the attractive living and dining rooms with large windows. The step-saving kitchen and breakfast areas flow easily into the two-story great room and a media room with a see-through fireplace. The upper level offers a pleasing combination of open design and privacy. To the right of the foyer stairs, the balcony overlooks the great room. The master bedroom has a modified tray ceiling and is complete with a sitting area. The master bath with a double vanity and separate shower leads to a large walk-in closet. Double vanities are also found in the full bath off the hall. Bedrooms 2 and 3 are ample in size and feature walk-in closets. The unfinished bonus room completes this level and provides further storage space.

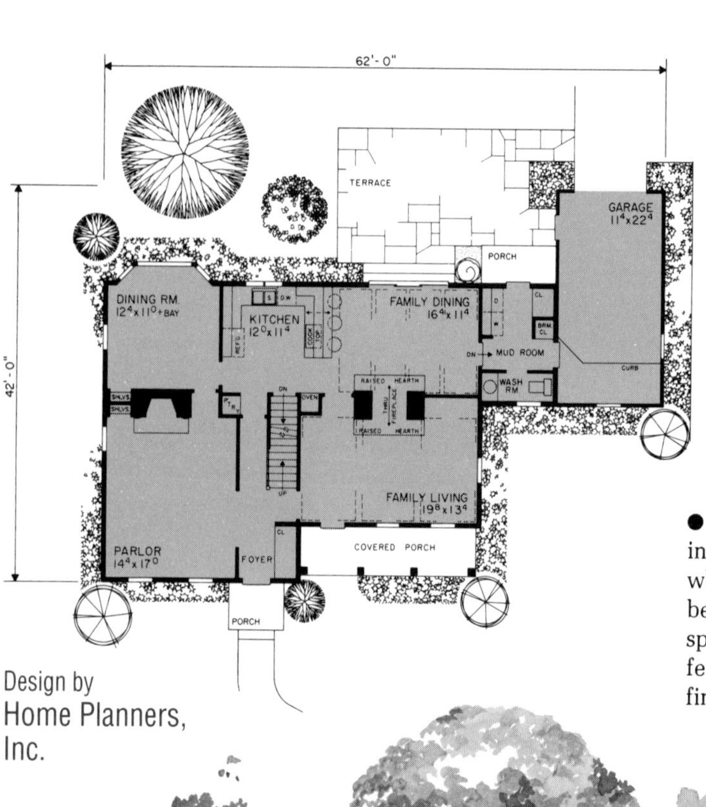

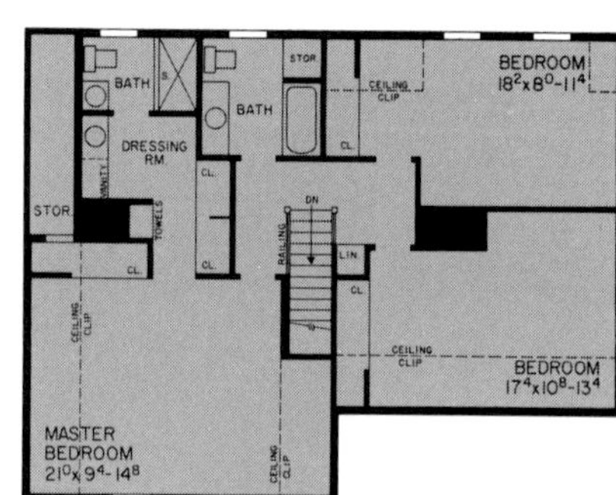

Design Q2681

First Floor: 1,350 square feet
Second Floor: 1,224 square feet
Total: 2,574 square feet

● The charm of Early America is exemplified in this delightful design. Note the three areas which are highlighted by a fireplace. The three-bedroom second floor is nicely planned. Make special note of the master bedroom's many fine features. Study the rest of this design's many fine qualities.

Design by
Home Planners, Inc.

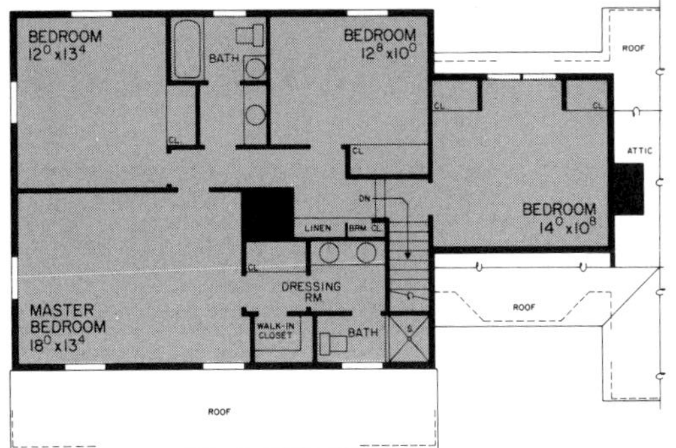

Design by
Home Planners, Inc.

Design Q2908

First Floor: 1,427 square feet
Second Floor: 1,153 square feet
Total: 2,580 square feet

● This Early American farmhouse offers plenty of modern comfort with its covered front porch with pillars and rails, double chimneys, building attachment, and four upstairs bedrooms. The first floor attachment includes a family room with bay window. It leads from the main house to a two-car garage. The family room certainly is the central focus of this fine design, with its own fireplace and rear entrance to a laundry and sewing room behind the garage. Disappearing stairs in the building attachment lead to attic space over the garage. The upstairs also is accessible from stairs just off the front foyer. Included is a master bedroom suite. Downstairs one finds a modern kitchen with breakfast room, dining room, and front living room.

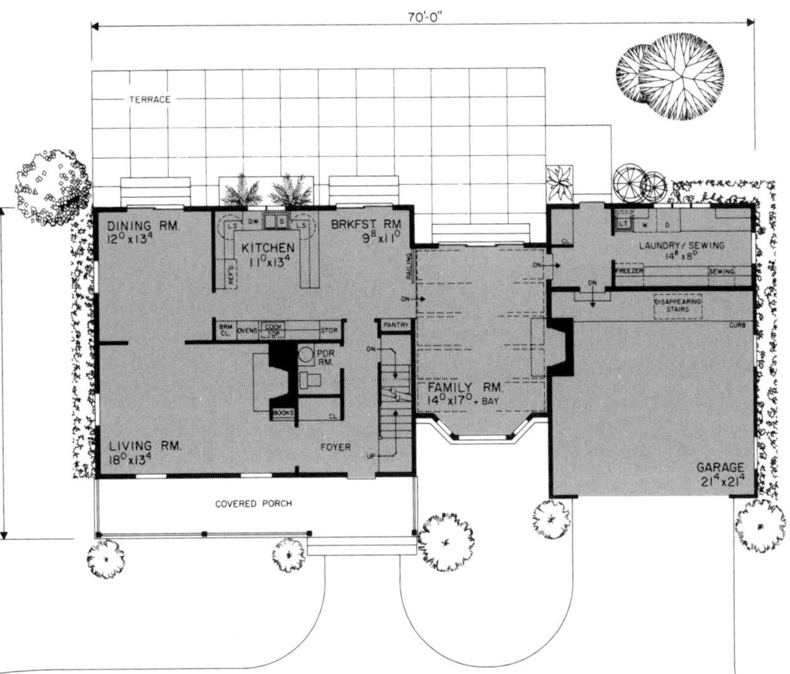

Design Q9314

First Floor: 1,679 square feet
Second Floor: 1,990 square feet
Total: 3,669 square feet

● Designed to be a country estate residence, this two-story home combines a sophisticated floor plan with a charming elevation. Throughout the home, beautiful windows bring the outdoors in. From the covered front porch, move inside to view a spectacular two-story entry with curving staircase. French doors lead into the library with a bayed window, built-in desk and bookcases. To the right, note the formal dining room. A great room benefits from the 10-foot spider-beamed ceiling, plus a wet bar and built-in entertainment center. Home owners will relish the combination breakfast/hearth room and kitchen concept. Upstairs, a balcony between the bedrooms overlooks the entry below. Segregation of the secondary bedrooms with walk-in closets provides privacy. Special finishing touches include the formal ceiling and bayed sitting area in the master suite. The master dressing/bath area is enhanced by His and Hers vanities, an oval whirlpool beneath the arched window and a deluxe walk-in closet with windows.

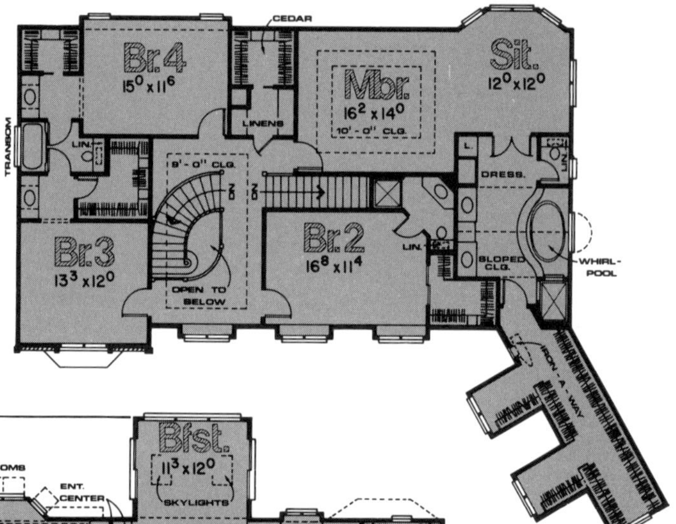

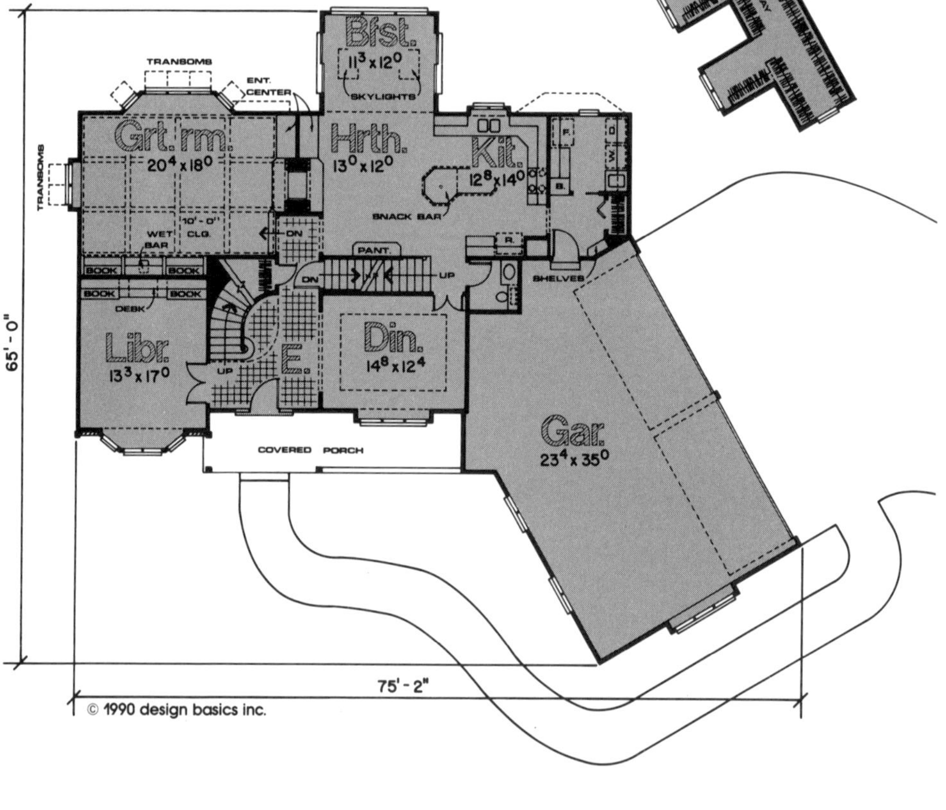

Design by Design Basics, Inc.

Design by
Design
Basics,
Inc.

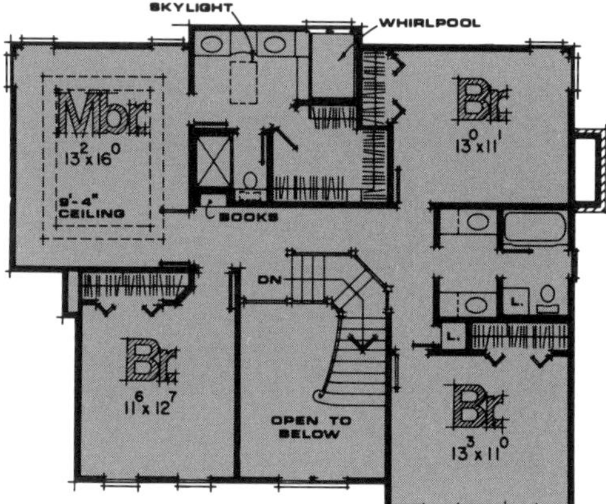

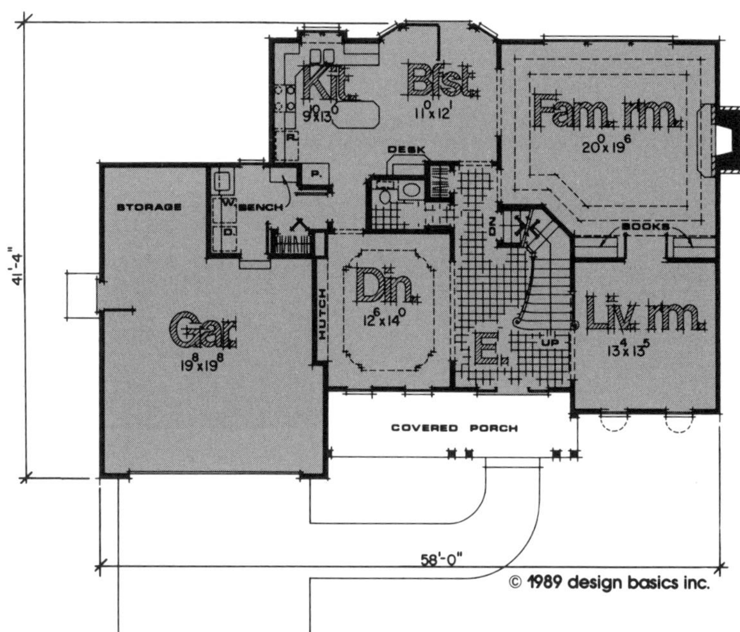

Design Q9215

First Floor: 1,386 square feet
Second Floor: 1,171 square feet
Total: 2,557 square feet

● Amenities for casual family living and entertaining abound in this attractive Colonial. A charming covered front porch makes for an inviting exterior. Inside, the two-story entry with flared staircase opens into the formal dining and living rooms. French doors connect the living room with the more informal family room for expanded entertaining space. A spacious kitchen handily serves both the family and dining rooms. Also note the bay-windowed breakfast area. The first floor features nine-foot ceilings throughout. Upstairs are four bedrooms, one a master suite with a skylit bath with whirlpool and large walk-in closet.

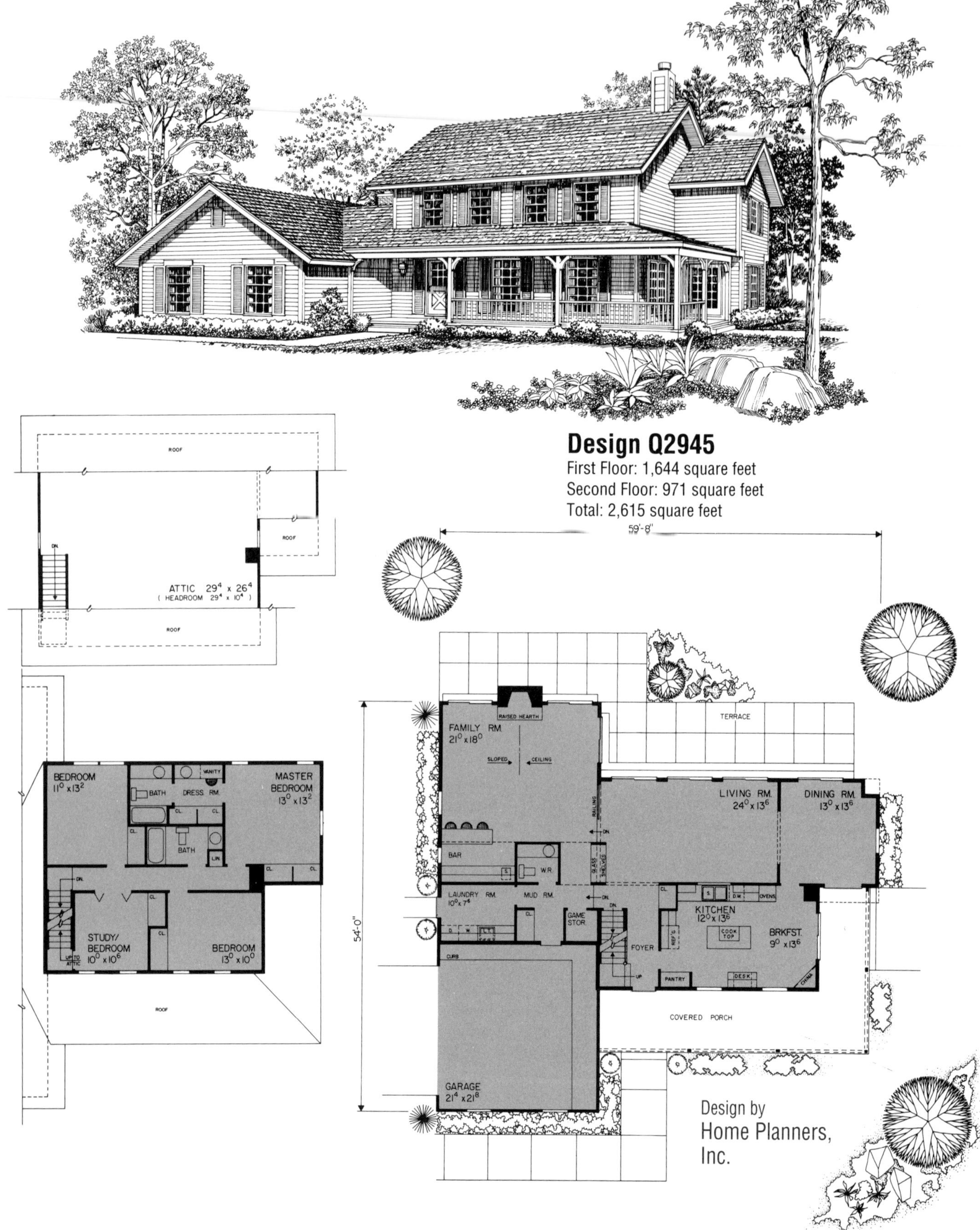

● Here is a new floor plan designed to go with the almost identical exterior of one of Home Planners' most popular houses. A masterfully affordable design, this plan manages to include all the basics - and then adds a little more. Note the wraparound covered porch, large family room with raised-hearth fireplace and wet bar, spacious kitchen with island cook top, formal dining room, rear terrace, and extra storage on the first floor. Upstairs, the plan's as flexible as they come: three or four bedrooms (the fourth could easily be a study or playroom) and lots of unfinished attic just waiting for you to transform it into living space. This could make a fine studio, sewing room, home office, or just a place for the safe, dry storage of the family's paraphernalia, Christmas decorations, etc.

Plains or Prairie-Type Farmhouses

In the days of Western expansion, homes on the plains and prairies were, for the most part, utilitarian structures erected quickly and with little fuss. They were usually built from available materials — often sod or hay — because of the scarcity of wood or brick. Practical in form, though not especially architecturally appealing, these home were constructed to withstand the fierce winds, harsh winters and burning summer sun so prevalent in that part of the country.

Today's versions of the Plains or Prairie Farmhouse take all the best features of those sturdy ancestors and incorporate them into a much more charming and livable rendition. Their tremendous appeal derives from their nostalgic nod to pioneer beginnings and timeless endurance. Maintaining a low-slung, ground-hugging appearance (to shrug off prairie winds), the modern Prairie Farmhouse almost always has a covered front porch that wraps around at least three sides to shield the house from the sun. Some examples carry the covered porch on all four sides. This porch is usually an at-grade-level element, in keeping with the low profile of the whole house. Porch columns and railings are normally square though some turned spindles and other simple decoration may appear, echoing Colonial and Victorian influences.

The roof of these prairie homes is the most obvious design element. The entire structure of the home is dominated by a roof that is double-pitched from gable to porch covering. Looking somewhat like a large hat, these roofs function as sun-deflectors in areas of the country known for warm, dry summer seasons.

Sometimes two-story, more often 1½-story, in nature, the Prairie Farmhouse boasts upper-level dormer windows that protrude from the roof. Two or three dormer windows to a set seems to be the general rule; however, four or even five may appear on some examples. On more dramatic examples, a Palladian window may appear at the center of the second floor. The windows themselves are symmetrically set, paned and often shuttered.

Horizonal wood siding is the facing of choice, with brick and occasionally stone complementing as the exterior detailing. Chimneys generally have no regular placement but may be seen anywhere (or not at all) from the front.

Design Q9004 is a fine example of the Prairie-Type Farmhouse. Its sweeping, wide porch wraps around three sides of an exterior sided in wood and it supports a prominent roofline that is double-pitched. Three dormers grace the facade, while two chimneys (one to the left front and one to the right rear) allow for hearths throughout the house. Like others in this section, this Prairie-Type Farmhouse includes a luxurious floor plan within its rustic, countrified exterior.

Design Q9004

First Floor: 2,166 square feet
Second Floor: 1,169 square feet
Total: 3,335 square feet

● This farmhouse design, with its expansive wraparound porch and spacious interior, will suit the needs of any large, active family. The foyer opens directly to the formal living room with an elegant fireplace. The family room offers a unique brick wall with built-in fireplace and a French door opening onto a covered porch. The well planned kitchen overlooks a breakfast area with full-length windows that allow an uninterrupted view of the rear yard. The large utility room, with plenty of storage space, leads to an attached two-car garage. The master bedroom has access to a private study with built-in bookshelves. A third fireplace further enhances the master area. His and Hers walk-in closets, along with a garden tub and glass-enclosed shower, complete this secluded master suite. Upstairs, three bedrooms and two baths offer plenty of space and convenience for the children. A game room with an alcove that is perfect for exercise equipment provides a versatile family activity area.

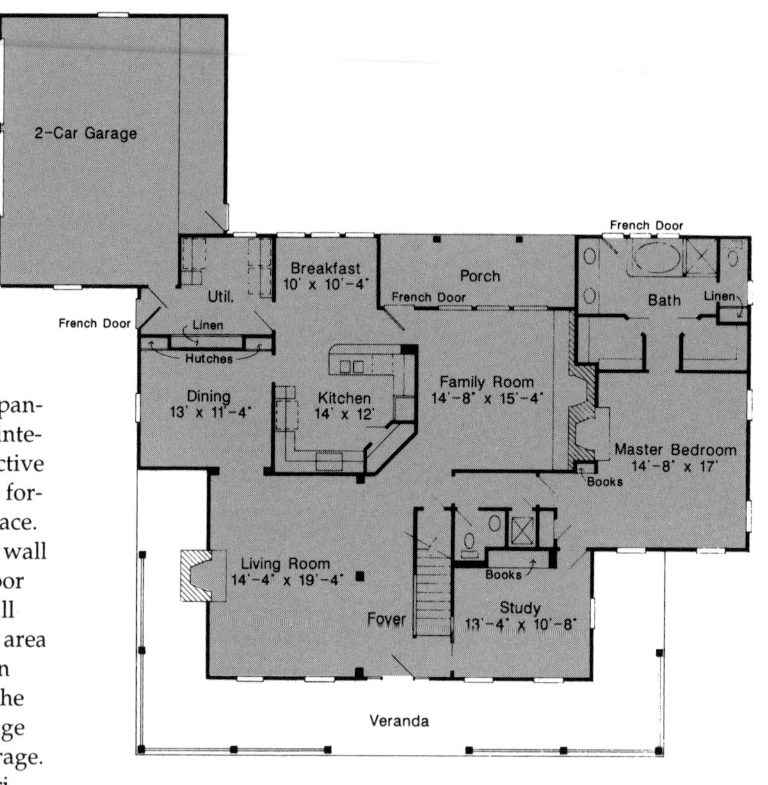

Width 74' - 8"
Depth 71' - 8"

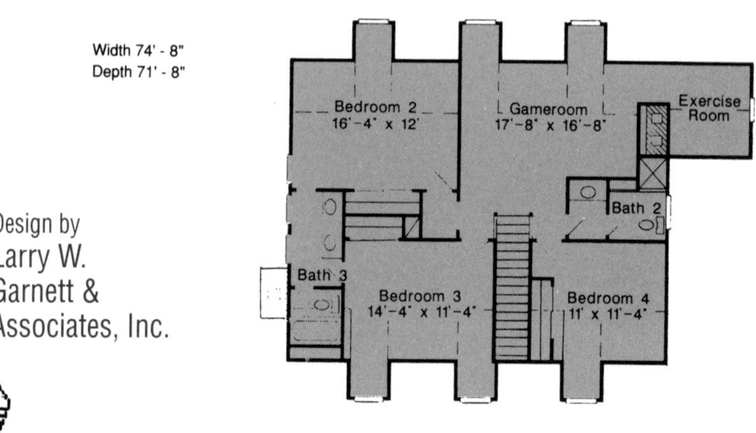

Design by
Larry W. Garnett & Associates, Inc.

Design Q9002

First Floor: 1,504 square feet
Second Floor: 690 square feet
Total: 2,194 square feet

● The symmetry and grace of the turn-of-the-century farmhouse is captured in this design. The veranda provides plenty of shade for outdoor activities. Inside, the kitchen with center-island work counter opens to the breakfast area with a full-length bay window. The master bedroom features a walk-in closet and abundant linen storage. A corner tub and glass-enclosed shower highlight the bath. An optional French door allows access to a swimming pool, or possibly a private spa. Upstairs, the balcony overlooks the living room below. Two bedrooms each have walk-in closets and private dressing areas. Plans for a detached two-car garage are included.

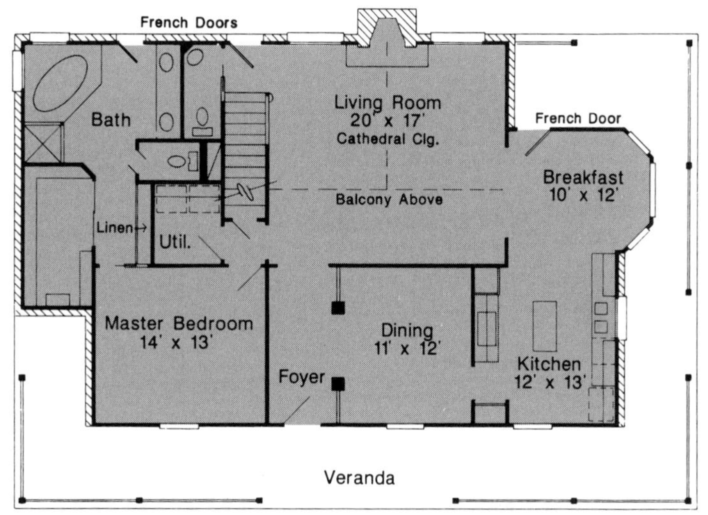

Design by
Larry W.
Garnett &
Associates, Inc.

Width 57' - 4"
Depth 37' - 8"

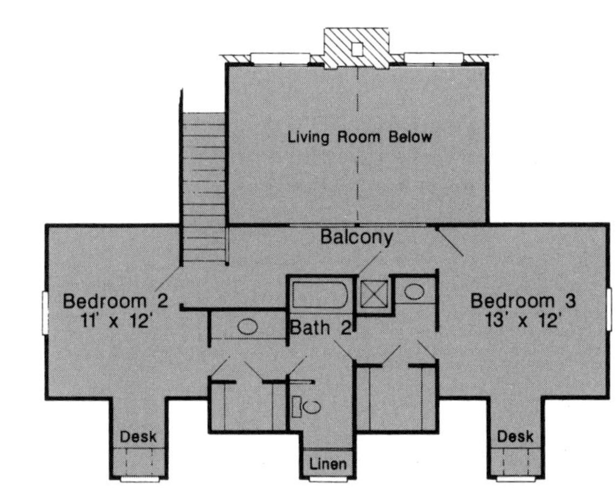

Design Q9000

First Floor: 1,669 square feet
Second Floor: 780 square feet
Total: 2,449 square feet

● The wraparound veranda of this farmhouse design offers a shaded outdoor living area. Inside, an efficient floor plan provides plenty of open living areas. The foyer and formal dining room are separated by a thirty-two-inch high wall, while the kitchen opens directly to a spacious breakfast area. The convenient utility room has plenty of space for a freezer and extra storage. A small rear porch can be connected by a breezeway to the de-tached garage (plans included). The highlight of this home is the living room. A center fireplace with tall glass on each side soars to the top of the cathedral ceiling, while a balcony opens from the game above. A French door opens to the rear porch. Each upstairs bedroom offers a built-in desk or window seat. The master bath features His and Hers walk-in closets and abundant linen storage.

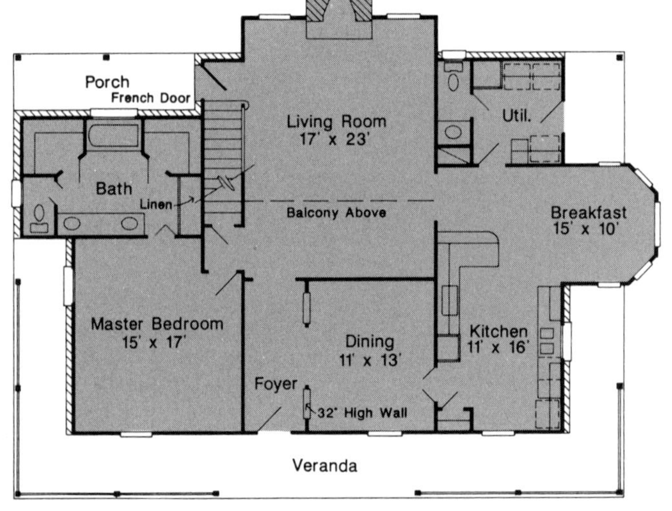

Design by
Larry W.
Garnett &
Associates, Inc.

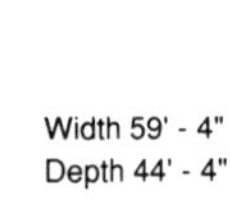

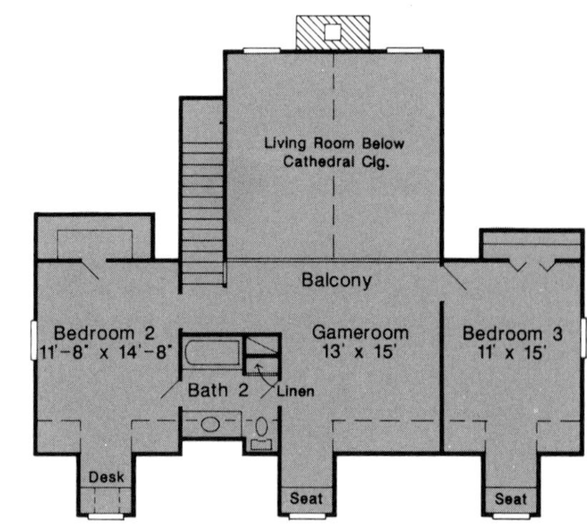

Design Q9005

First Floor: 1,995 square feet
Second Floor: 1,077 square feet
Total: 3,072 square feet

● A wraparound front porch and dormer windows give this home a casual and comfortable appearance. A leaded-glass transom above the front door, along with the dormer window in the sloped ceiling, fill the foyer with natural light. The large living area features French doors on each side of an elegant fireplace, and a built-in wet bar. An island cooktop, along with a walk-in pantry are part of the well-planned kitchen. The utility room, with extra work space, leads to an attached two-car garage and storage area. The master bedroom has generous closet space and a two-way fireplace opening into the master bath. His and Hers lavatories, an oversized tub and glass-enclosed shower complete this elegant master bath. The balcony has French doors opening into a large game room. Bedroom 3 has a private bath, while Bedroom 2 shares access to a bath with the game room. Each bedroom has a sloped ceiling and a cozy alcove created by the dormer window.

Design by
Larry W. Garnett & Associates, Inc.

2-Car Garage
Bath
Porch
2-Way Fireplace
French Doors
Breakfast 10' x 10'
Util.
Storage
Master Bedroom 15'-8" x 16'
Living Room 22'-8" x 16'-8"
Kitchen 12'-4" x 12'
Bedroom 4 10' x 12'-8"
Foyer
Dining 16' x 13'-4"
Porch

Width 79'
Depth 60' - 6"

Slope Clg.
Slope Clg.
Gameroom 22'-4" x 13'
Bath 4
Bath 3
French Door
Bedroom 3 16' x 14'-4"
Bedroom 2 16' x 14'-4"
Foyer Below
Slope Clg.

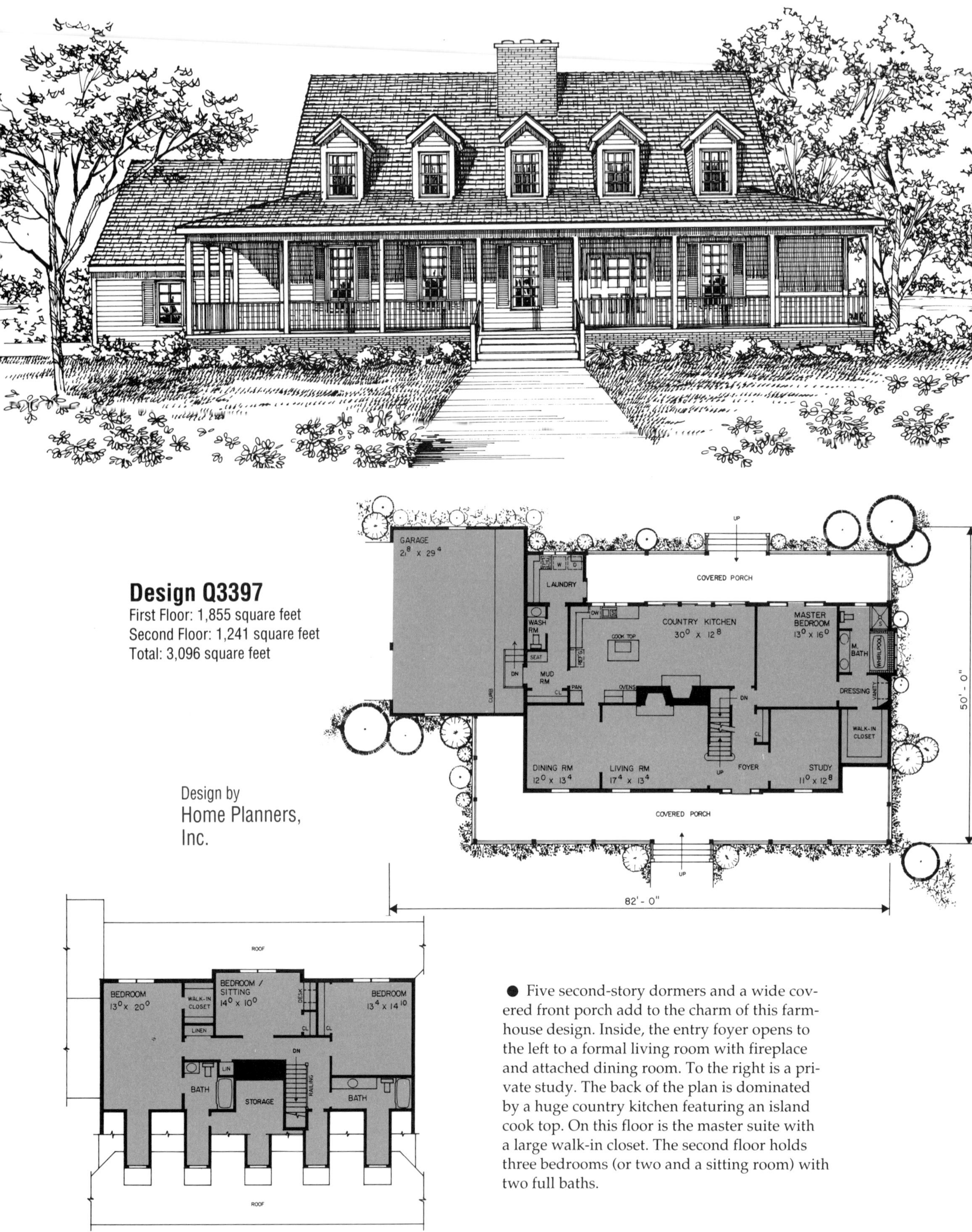

Design Q3397

First Floor: 1,855 square feet
Second Floor: 1,241 square feet
Total: 3,096 square feet

Design by
Home Planners, Inc.

● Five second-story dormers and a wide covered front porch add to the charm of this farmhouse design. Inside, the entry foyer opens to the left to a formal living room with fireplace and attached dining room. To the right is a private study. The back of the plan is dominated by a huge country kitchen featuring an island cook top. On this floor is the master suite with a large walk-in closet. The second floor holds three bedrooms (or two and a sitting room) with two full baths.

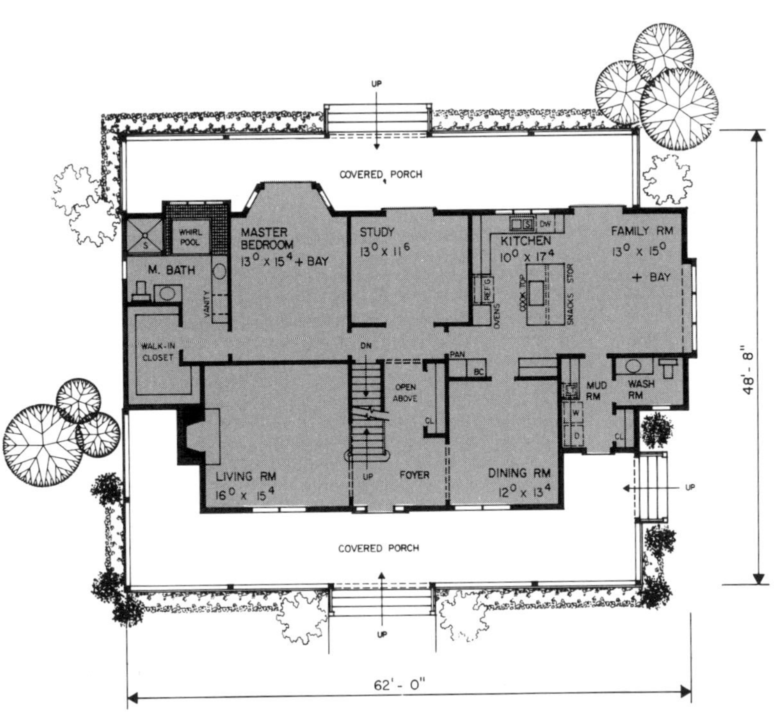

Design Q3396

First Floor: 1,829 square feet
Second Floor: 947 square feet
Total: 2,776 square feet

● Rustic charm abounds in this pleasant farmhouse rendition. Covered porches to the front and rear enclose living potential for the whole family. Flanking the entrance foyer are the living and dining rooms. To the rear is the L-shaped kitchen with island cook top and snack bar. A small family room/breakfast nook is attached. A private study is tucked away on this floor next to the master suite. On the second floor are three bedrooms and a full bath. Two of the bedrooms have charming dormer windows.

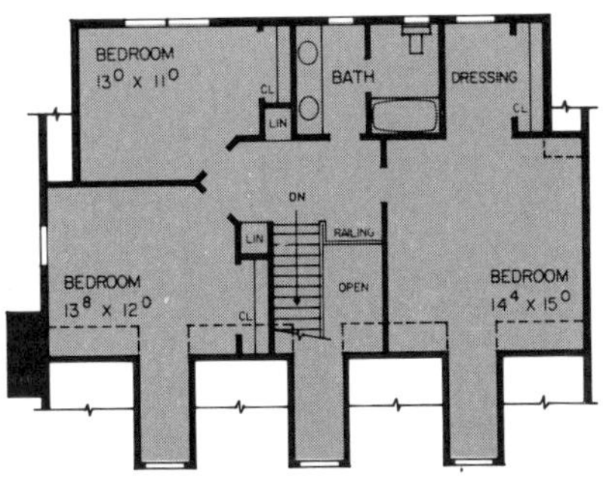

BEDROOM 13^{0} x 11^{0}
BATH
DRESSING
LIN
CL
DN
RAILING
OPEN
BEDROOM 13^{8} x 12^{0}
BEDROOM 14^{4} x 15^{0}

Design by
Home Planners, Inc.

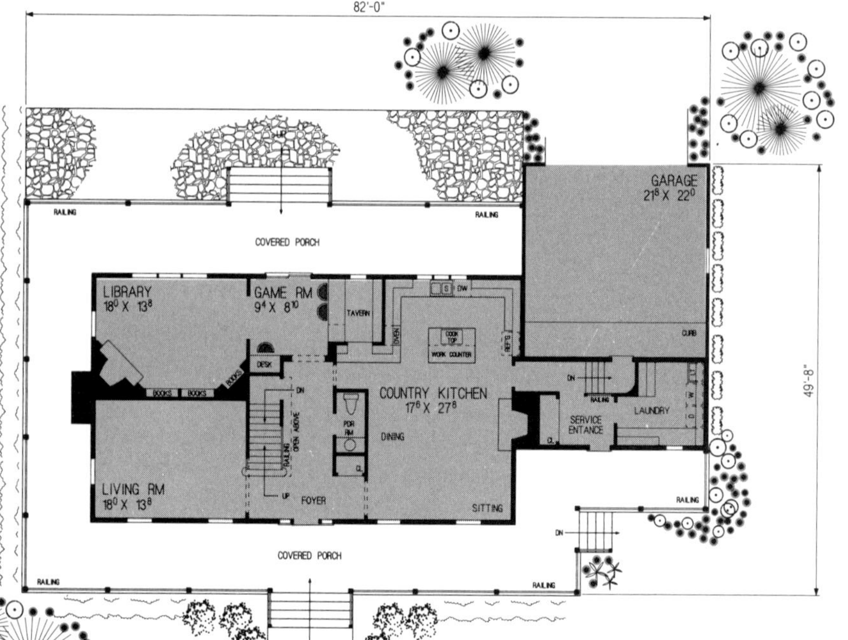

Design Q3399

First Floor: 1,716 square feet
Second Floor: 2,102 square feet
Total: 3,818 square feet

Design by
Home Planners, Inc.

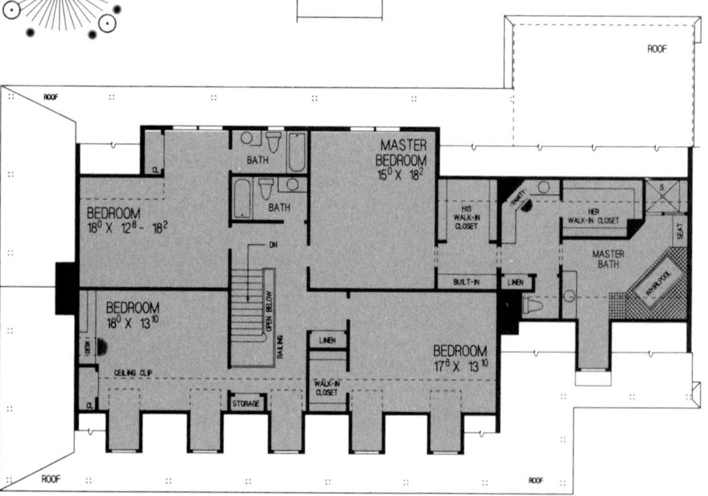

● This is the ultimate in farmhouse living — six dormer windows and a porch that stretches essentially around the entire house. Inside, the plan is open and inviting. Besides the large country kitchen with fireplace, there is a small game room with attached tavern, a library with built-in bookshelves and a fireplace, and a formal living room. The second floor has four bedrooms and three full baths. The service entrance features a laundry area conveniently just off the garage.

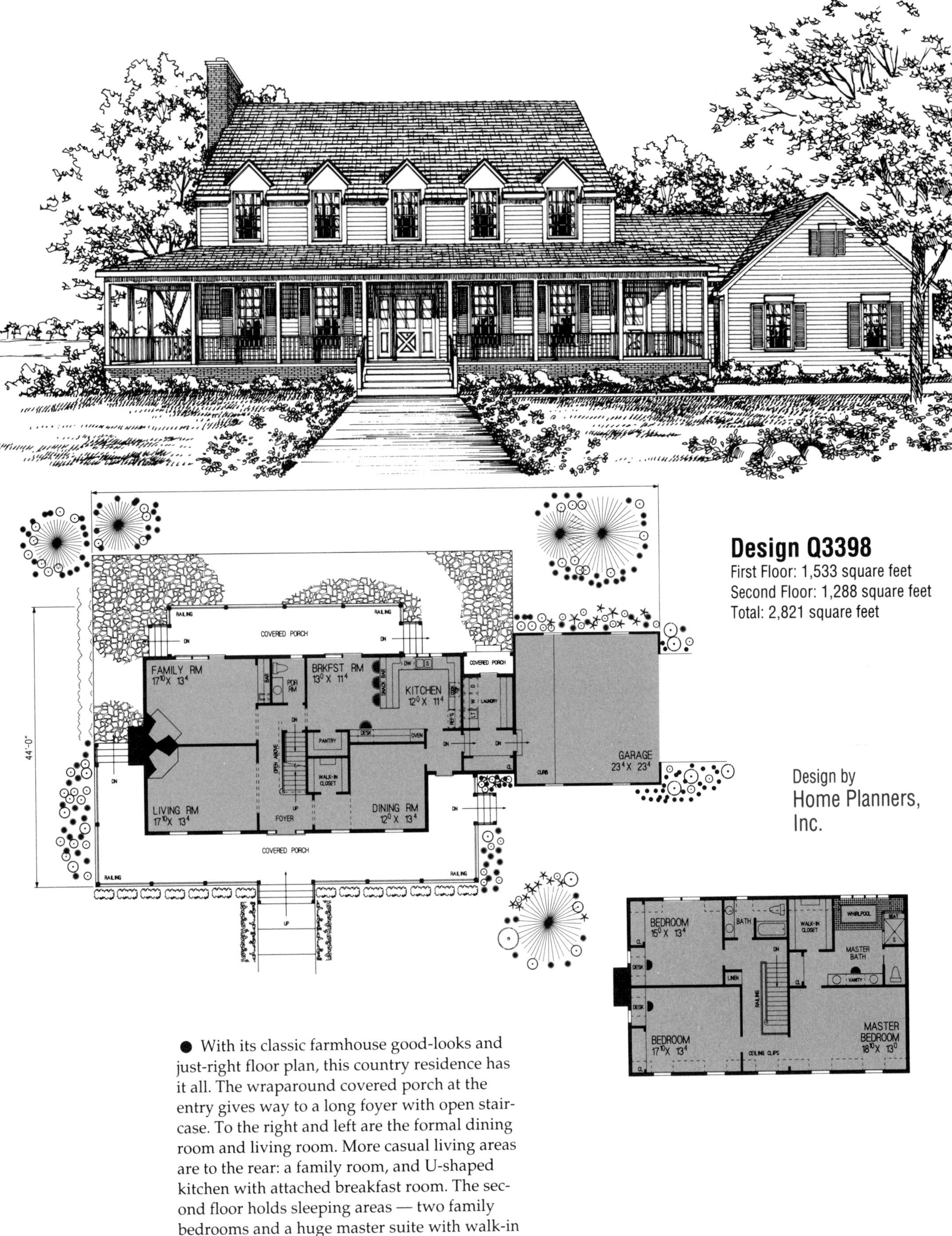

Design Q3398

First Floor: 1,533 square feet
Second Floor: 1,288 square feet
Total: 2,821 square feet

Design by
Home Planners, Inc.

● With its classic farmhouse good-looks and just-right floor plan, this country residence has it all. The wraparound covered porch at the entry gives way to a long foyer with open staircase. To the right and left are the formal dining room and living room. More casual living areas are to the rear: a family room, and U-shaped kitchen with attached breakfast room. The second floor holds sleeping areas — two family bedrooms and a huge master suite with walk-in closet and pampering master bath.

Design Q9067

First Floor: 1,999 square feet
Second Floor: 933 square feet
Total: 2,932 square feet

● The wraparound veranda and simple lines give this home an unassuming elegance that is characteristic of its Folk Victorian heritage. Opening directly to the formal dining room, the two-story foyer offers extra space for large dinner parties. Double French doors lead to the study with raised paneling and a cozy fireplace. Built-in bookcases conceal a hidden security vault. The private master suite features a corner garden tub, glass-enclosed shower and a walk-in closet. Overlooking the family room and built-in breakfast nook is the central kitchen. A rear staircase provides convenient access to the second floor from the family room. The balcony provides a view of the foyer below and the Palladian window. Three additional bedrooms complete this exquisite home.

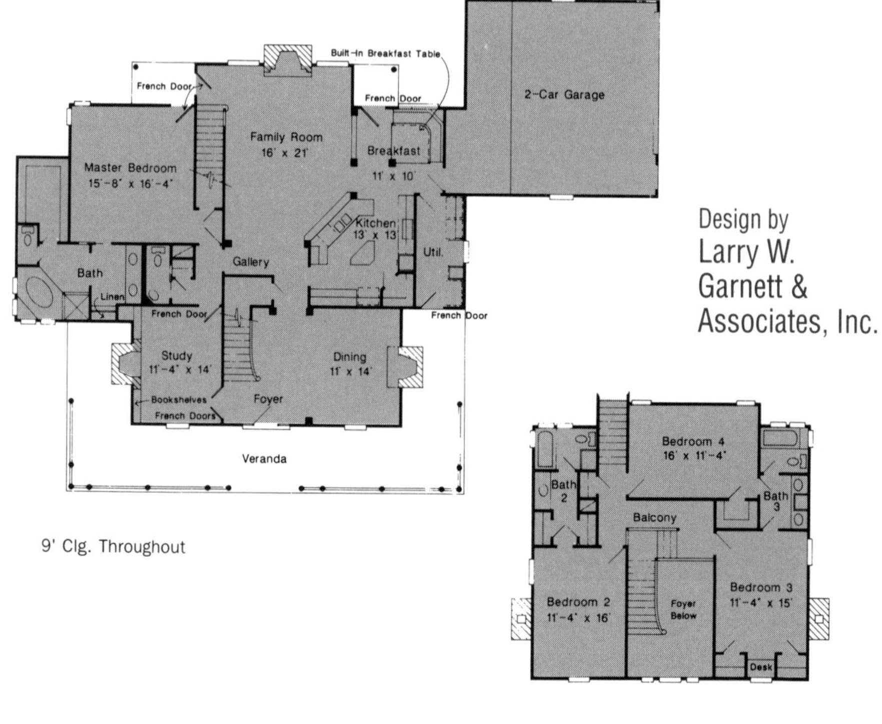

Design by
Larry W. Garnett & Associates, Inc.

REAR VIEW

WIDTH 79' 8"
DEPTH 59'

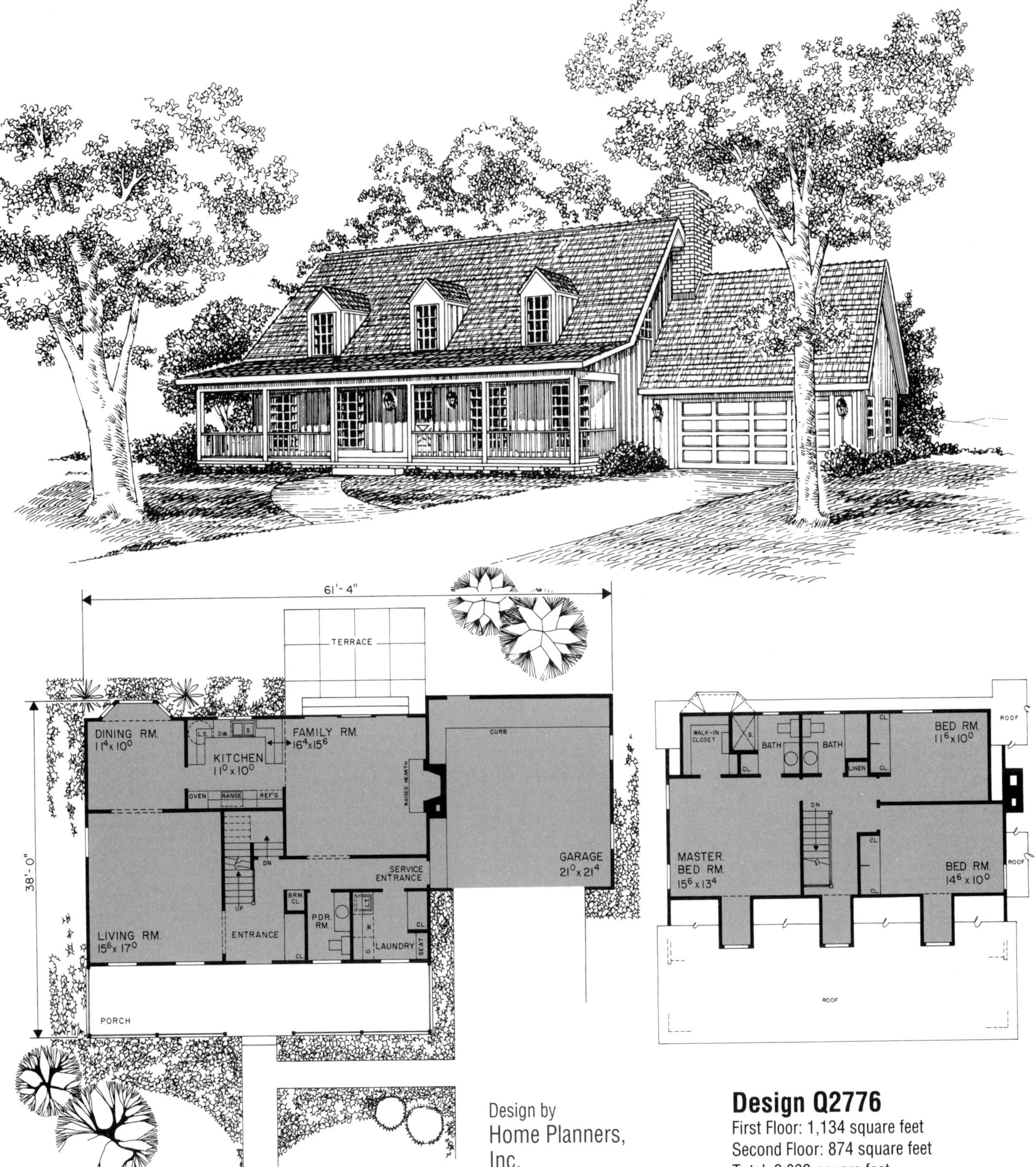

Design by
Home Planners,
Inc.

Design Q2776

First Floor: 1,134 square feet
Second Floor: 874 square feet
Total: 2,008 square feet

● This board-and-batten farmhouse design has all of the country charm of New England. The large front covered porch surely will be appreciated during the beautiful warm weather months. Immediately off the front entrance is the delightful corner living room. The dining room with bay window will be easily served by the U-shaped kitchen. Informal family living enjoyment will be obtained in the family room which features a raised hearth fireplace, sliding glass doors to the rear terrace and easy access to the work center of powder room, laundry and service entrance. The second floor houses all of the sleeping facilities. There is a master bedroom with a private bath and walk-in closet. Two other bedrooms share a bath. This is an excellent one-and-half story design.

Design Q9298

First Floor: 1,881 square feet
Second Floor: 814 square feet
Total: 2,695 square feet

● Oval windows and an appealing covered porch lend character to this 1½-story home. Inside, a volume entry views the formal living and dining rooms. Three large windows and a raised-hearth fireplace flanked by bookcases highlight a volume great room. An island kitchen with huge pantry and two Lazy Susans serves a captivating gazebo dinette. In the master suite, a cathedral ceiling, corner whirlpool and roomy dressing area deserve careful study. A gallery wall for displaying family mementos and prized heirlooms graces the upstairs corridor. Each secondary bedroom has convenient access to the bathrooms. This home's charm and blend of popular amenities will fit your lifestyle.

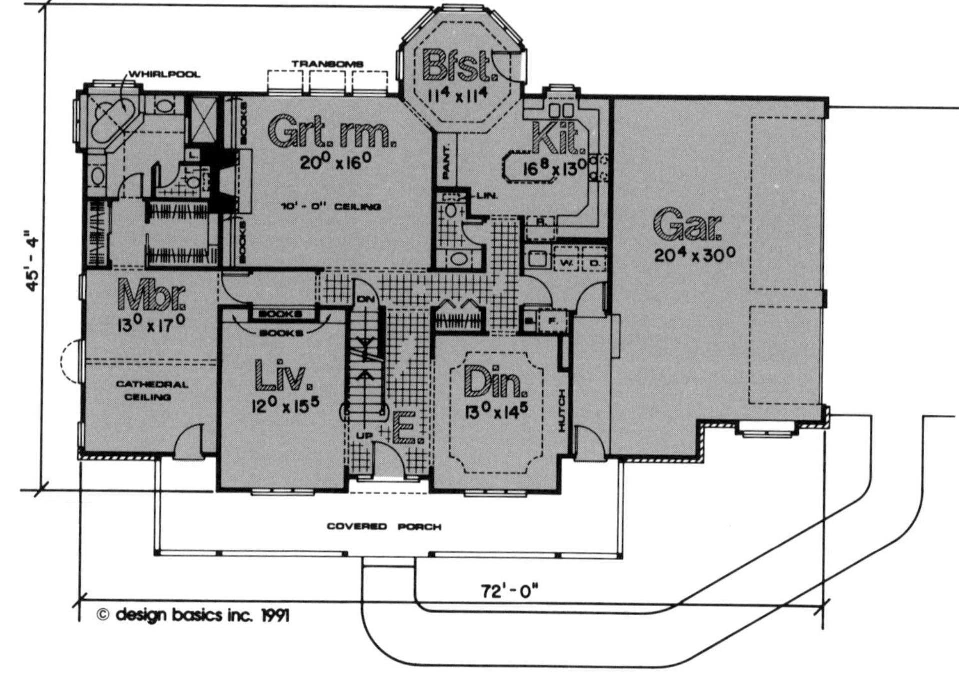

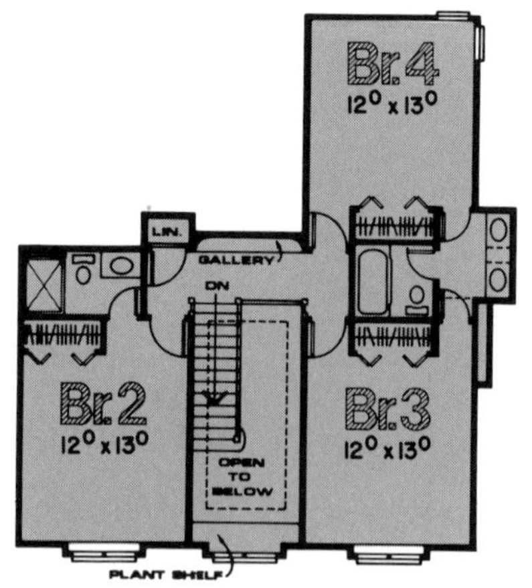

Design by
Design Basics, Inc.

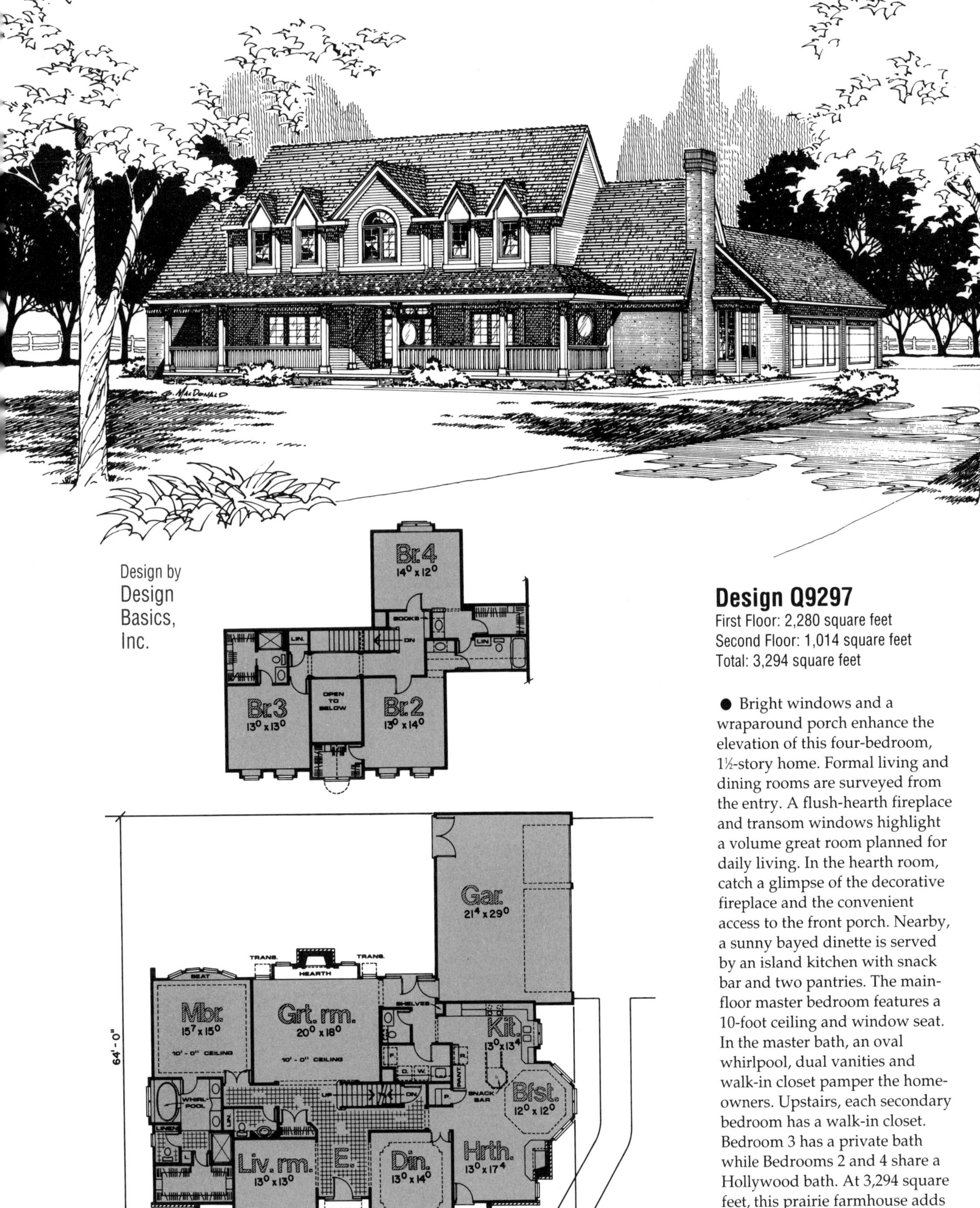

Design by
Design
Basics,
Inc.

Design Q9297

First Floor: 2,280 square feet
Second Floor: 1,014 square feet
Total: 3,294 square feet

● Bright windows and a wraparound porch enhance the elevation of this four-bedroom, 1½-story home. Formal living and dining rooms are surveyed from the entry. A flush-hearth fireplace and transom windows highlight a volume great room planned for daily living. In the hearth room, catch a glimpse of the decorative fireplace and the convenient access to the front porch. Nearby, a sunny bayed dinette is served by an island kitchen with snack bar and two pantries. The main-floor master bedroom features a 10-foot ceiling and window seat. In the master bath, an oval whirlpool, dual vanities and walk-in closet pamper the homeowners. Upstairs, each secondary bedroom has a walk-in closet. Bedroom 3 has a private bath while Bedrooms 2 and 4 share a Hollywood bath. At 3,294 square feet, this prairie farmhouse adds distinction to any location.

Design Q9603

First Floor: 1,377 square feet
Second Floor: 536 square feet
Total: 1,913 square feet

● One of the most outstanding characteristics of this plan is its flexibility — turn the great room/dining room combination into one large great room and relocate the dining room to the family room. The cheery sun room with its soothing hot tub provides access through sliding glass doors to the deck and great room and access to the master bedroom through French doors. (Don't overlook the fireplace, walk-in closet and twin vanity in the master suite.) Two second-floor bedrooms share a full bath with twin vanity and linen closet. Both bedrooms have dormer windows and walk-in closets. Other grand features include the screened porch with skylights and the sheltered front porch. For a crawlspace foundation, order plan Q9603, for a basement foundation order Q9603-A.

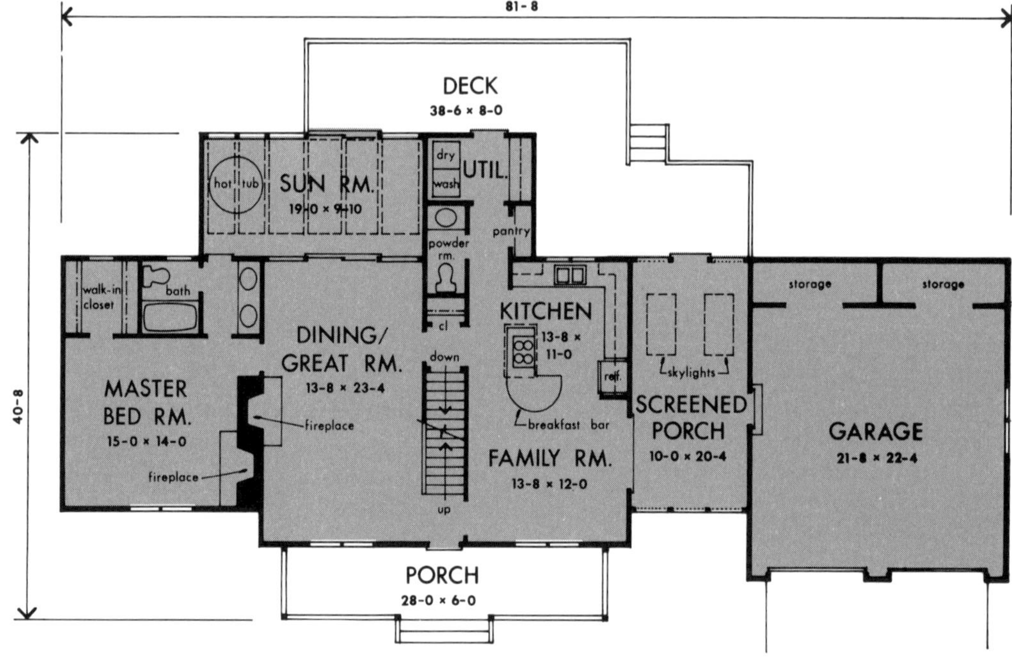

Design by
Donald A.
Gardner,
Architect, Inc.

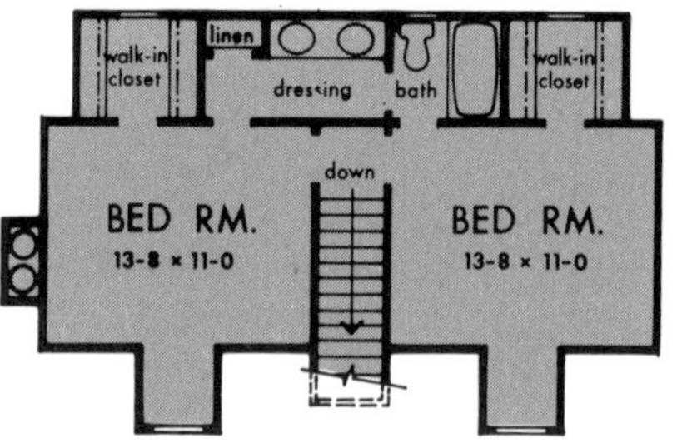

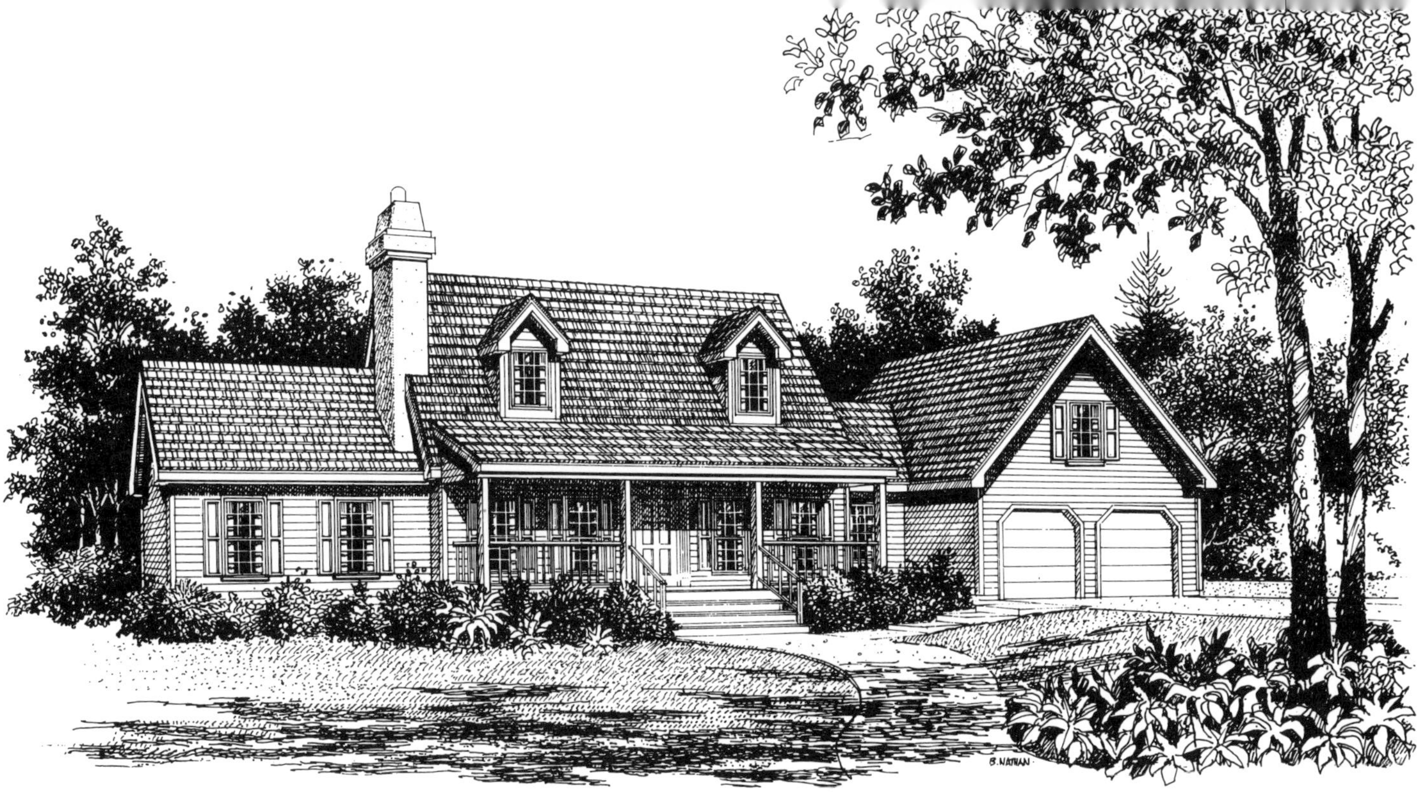

Design Q9625

First Floor: 1,436 square feet
Second Floor: 549 square feet
Sun Room: 145 square feet
Bonus Room: 334 square feet
Total: 2,319 square feet

● Great flexibility is available in this plan—the great room/dining room can be reworked into one large great room with the dining room relocated to the family room. A sun room with cathedral ceiling and sliding glass door to the deck is accessible from both the breakfast and dining rooms. A large kitchen boasts a convenient cooking island. The master bedroom has a fireplace, walk-in closet and spacious master bath. Two second-level bedrooms are equal in size and share a full bath with double-bowl vanity. Both bedrooms have a dormer window and a walk-in closet. A large bonus room over the garage is accessible from the utility room below. For a crawl-space foundation order Plan Q9625; for a basement foundation order Plan Q9625-A.

Design by
Donald A.
Gardner,
Architect, Inc.

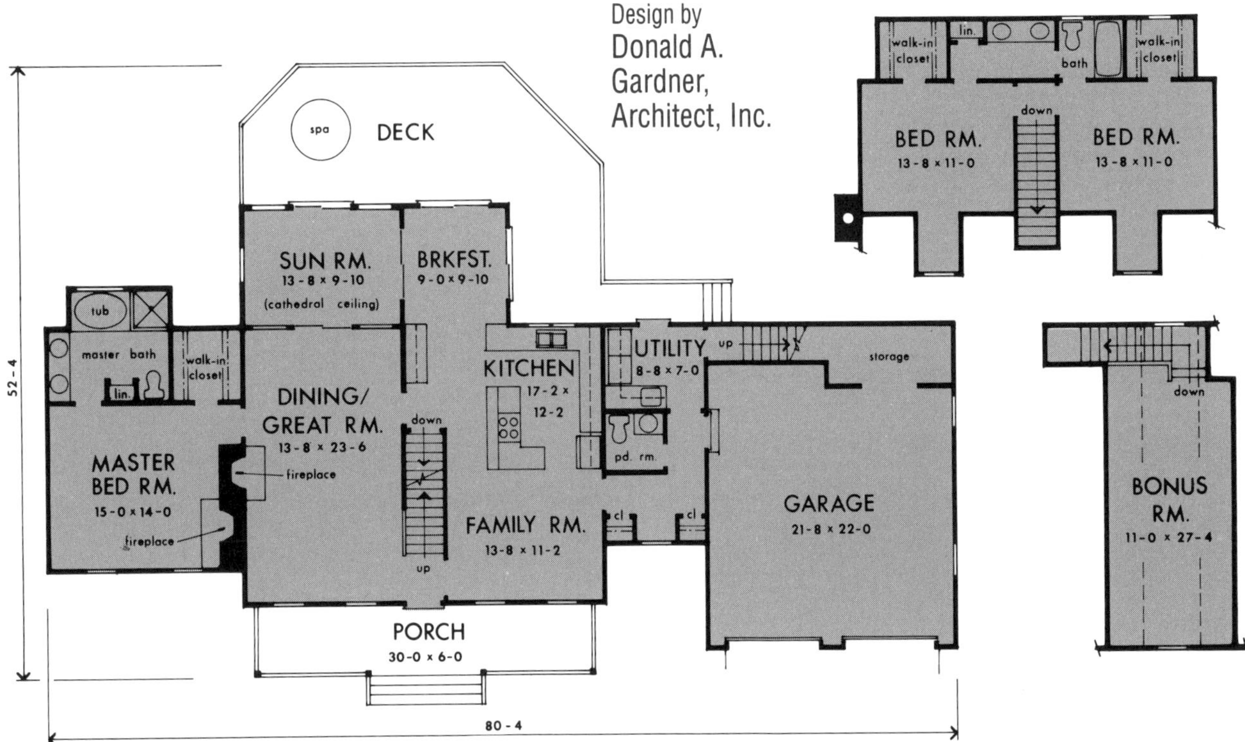

Design Q9001

First Floor: 1,308 square feet
Second Floor: 751 square feet
Total: 2,059 square feet

● A wraparound veranda and simple, uncluttered lines give this home an unassuming elegance that is characteristic of its farmhouse heritage. The kitchen overlooks an octagon-shaped breakfast room with full-length windows. The master bedroom features plenty of closet space and an elegant bath. Located within an oversized bay window is a garden tub with adjacent planter and glass-enclosed shower. Upstairs, two bedrooms share a bath with separate dressing and bathing areas. The balcony sitting area is perfect as a playroom or study. Plans for a detached two-car garage are included.

Design by
Larry W.
Garnett &
Associates, Inc.

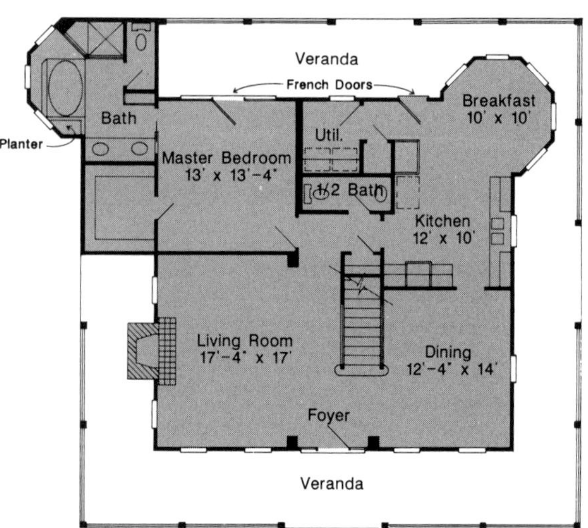

Width 53'
Depth 45' - 4"

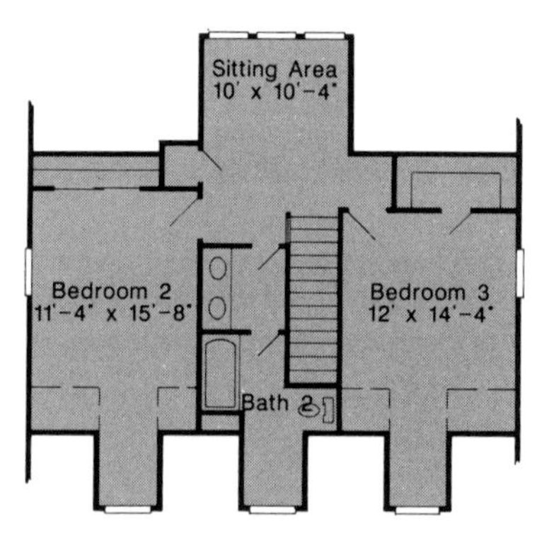

Design Q9624

First Floor: 1,659 square feet (Including Sun Room)
Second Floor: 674 square feet
Total: 2,333 square feet

Design by
Donald A.
Gardner,
Architect, Inc.

● Outdoor living takes a beautiful turn in this lovely home. The interior is just as great: bay windows in breakfast room and master bath, dormers and arched rear windows, sun room. The spacious great room has a fireplace, cathedral ceiling and clerestory with arched window. The master bath complements the master bedroom with a garden tub, separate shower, double-bowl vanity and walk-in closet. Two bedrooms share the upper level with a study/loft area overlooking the great room. This study area could be converted to a fourth bedroom.

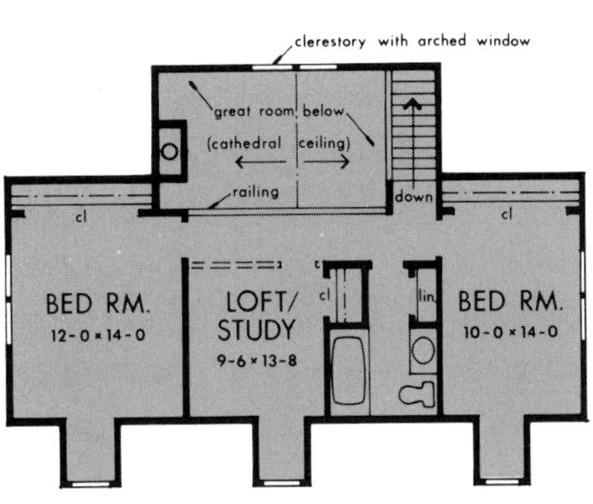

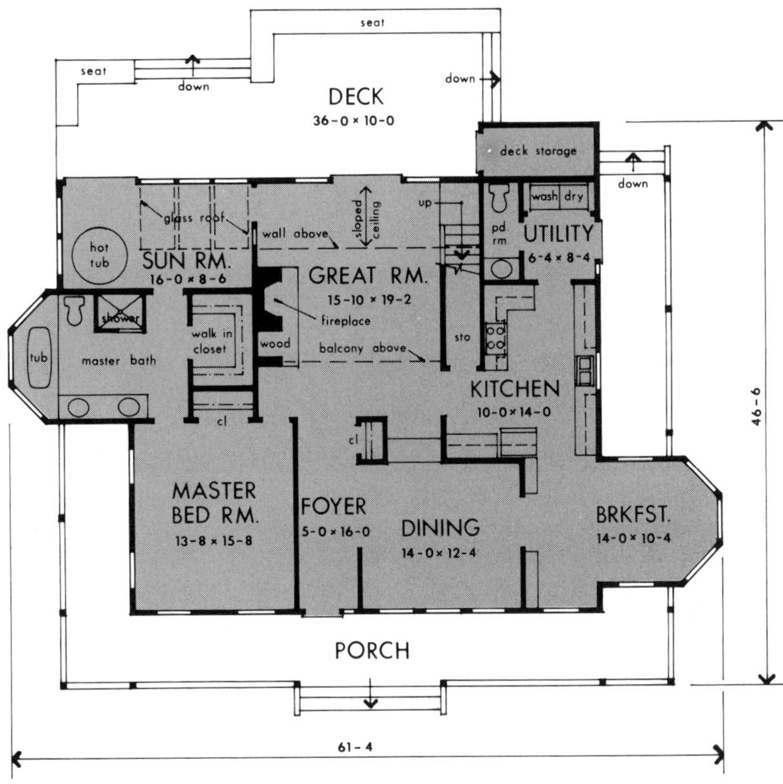

Design Q9003

First Floor: 1,244 square feet
Second Floor: 551 square feet
Total: 1,795 square feet

● The timeless beauty and practicality of the wraparound veranda give this farmhouse a casual, yet distinctive appearance. The efficiently designed kitchen opens to a light-filled breakfast area with full-length windows and a French door that leads to the veranda. The master suite offers His and Hers lavatories and a large walk-in closet. Upstairs, optional skylights provide plenty of natural light to the balcony. Two bedrooms share a bath that has separate bathing and dressing areas. Plans for a two-car detached garage are included.

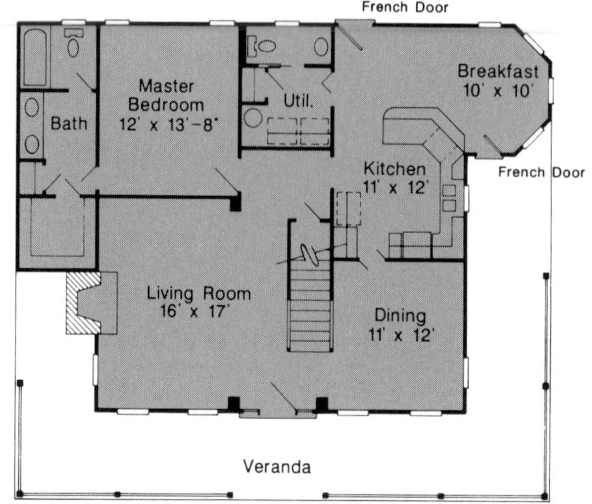

Width 46'
Depth 38' - 8"

Design by
Larry W.
Garnett &
Associates, Inc.

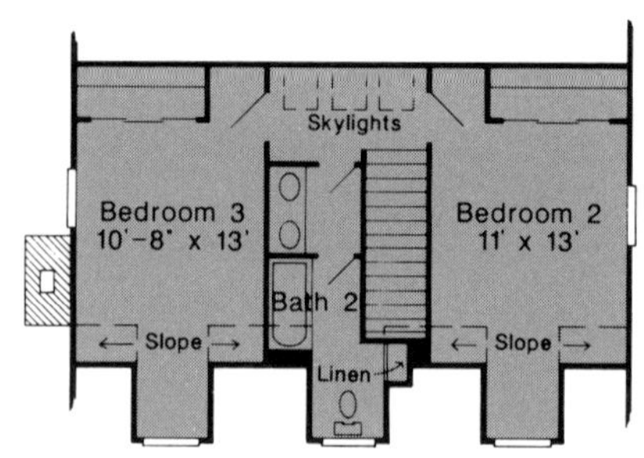

Design Q9605

First Floor: 1,562 square feet
Second Floor: 537 square feet
Total: 2,099 square feet

● Outdoor living is realized in a wraparound covered porch at the front and sides of this house, as well as the open deck with storage to the rear. Also notice how the country feel is updated with arched rear windows and a sun room. Inside find the spacious great room with fireplace, cathedral ceiling and clerestory with arched windows. The kitchen occupies a central location between the dining room and the great room for equally convenient formal and informal occasions. A generous master suite has a fireplace and access to the sun room and covered porch. On the second level are two more bedrooms, a full bath and storage space.

Design by
Donald A. Gardner, Architect, Inc.

FRONT

REAR

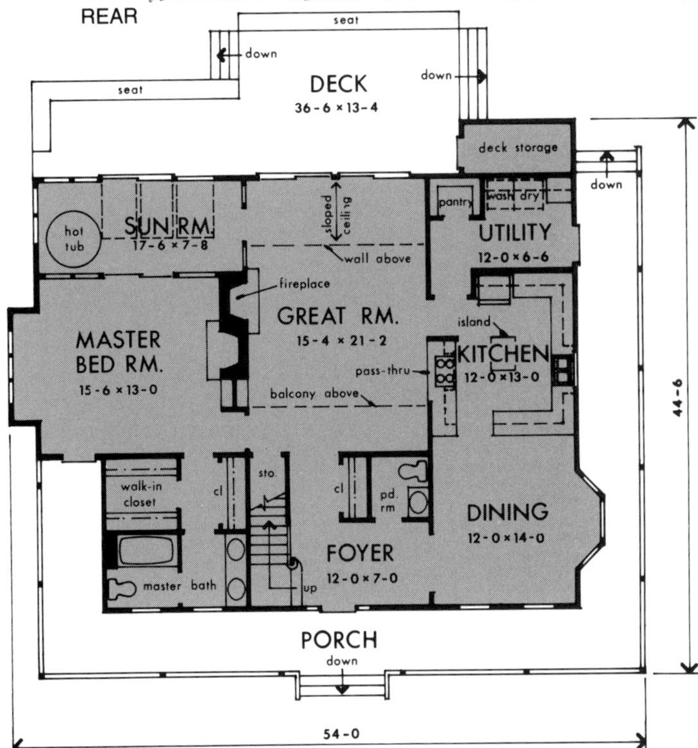

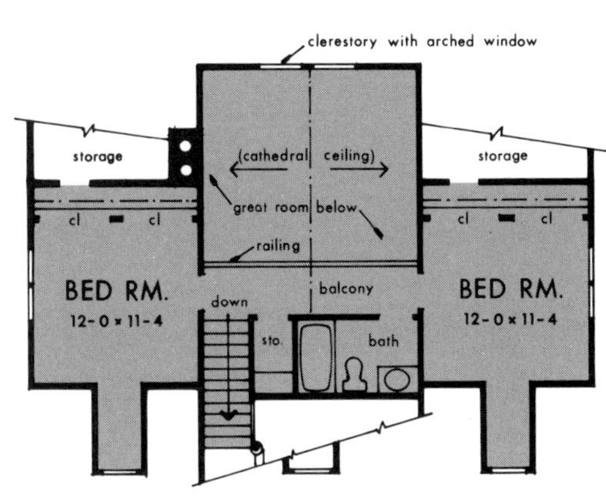

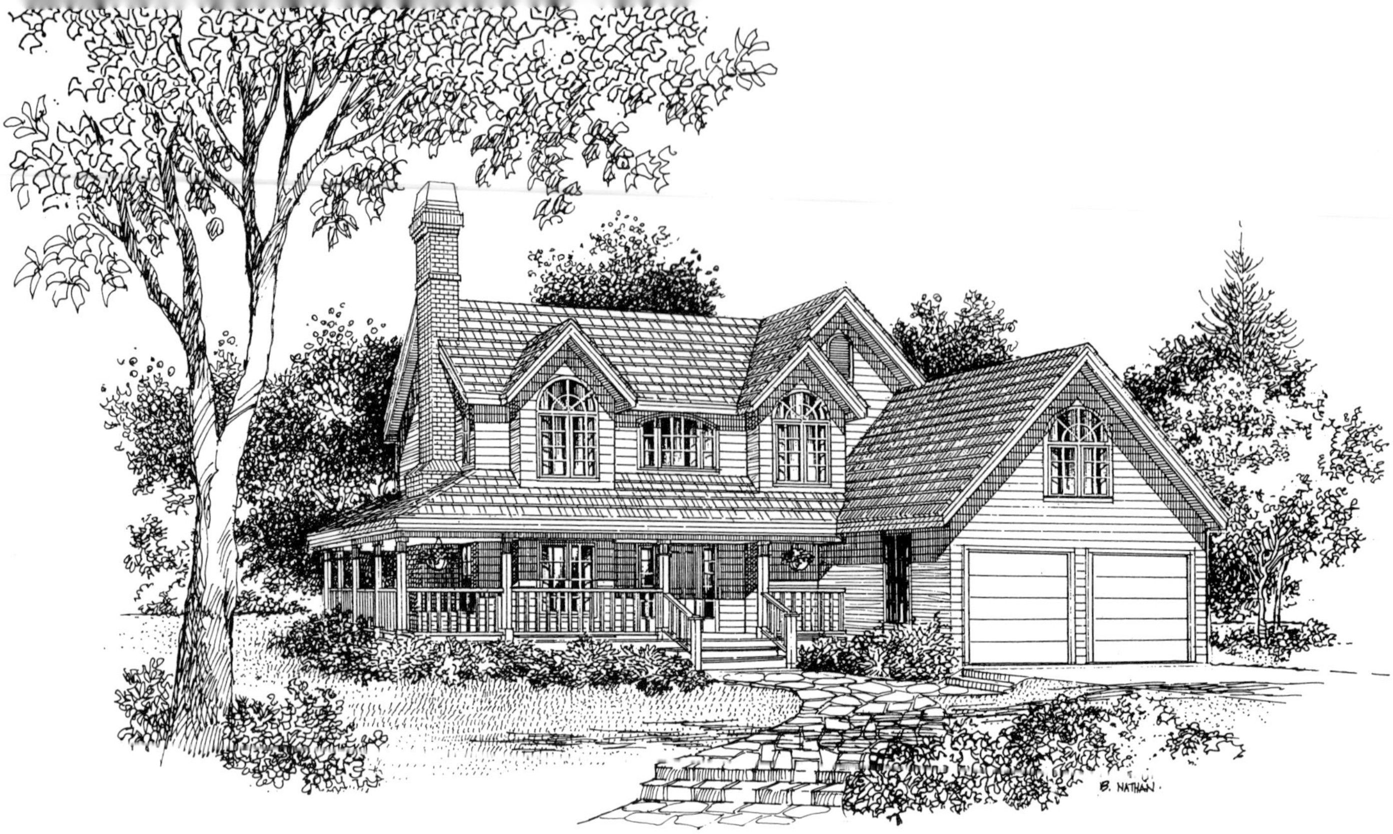

B. NATHAN

Design by
Donald A.
Gardner,
Architect, Inc.

Design Q9662

First Floor: 1,025 square feet
Second Floor: 911 square feet
Total: 1,936 square feet

● The exterior of this three-bedroom home is enhanced by its many gables, arched windows and wraparound porch. A large great room with impressive fireplace leads to both the dining room and screened porch with access to the deck. An open kitchen offers a country-kitchen atmosphere. The second-level master suite has two walk-in closets and an impressive bath. There is also bonus space over the garage. The plan is available with a crawl-space foundation.

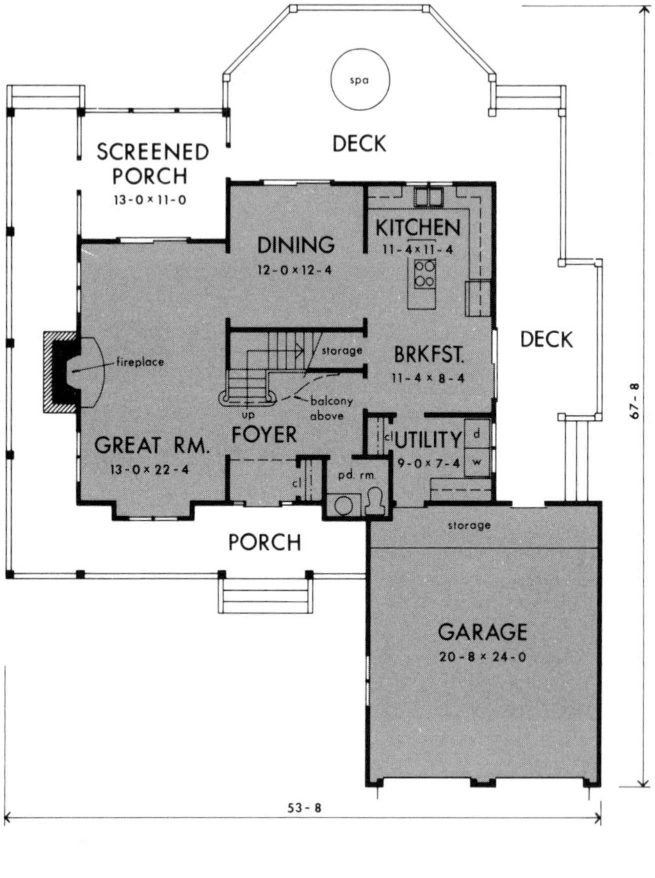

spa
DECK
SCREENED
PORCH
13-0 × 11-0
DINING
12-0 × 12-4
KITCHEN
11-4 × 11-4
DECK
fireplace
storage
BRKFST.
11-4 × 8-4
balcony
above
up
GREAT RM.
13-0 × 22-4
FOYER
UTILITY
9-0 × 7-4
cl
pd. rm.
d
w
storage
PORCH
GARAGE
20-8 × 24-0
67-8
53-8

master bath
BED RM.
11-0 × 12-4
BED RM.
10-0 × 12-4
closet
closet
cl
walk-in
closet
down
sto.
storage
MASTER
BED RM.
13-0 × 14-4
balcony
foyer
below
bath
sto.
BONUS
RM.
12-4 × 24-0

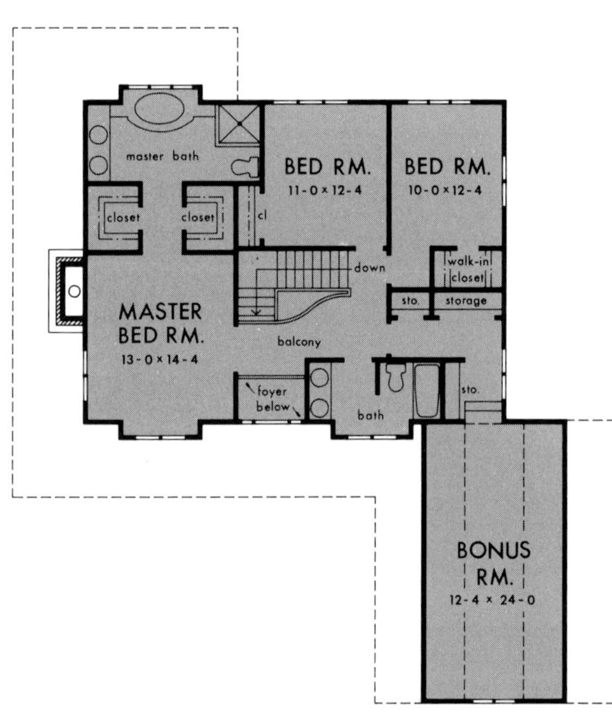

SOUTHERN OR PLANTATION-STYLE FARMHOUSES

Catering to a life filled with richness and grace, the historic homes of the Southern plantations were true showpieces. Replete with generous space for dining and entertaining, they mirrored the warm hospitality for which the South became famous. Rooms were large, ornate and filled with amenities geared toward comfort. Kitchens were the focal points around which daily life flowed. Porches, verandas and balconies were plentiful; numerous wide windows were in grand supply to catch any hint of breeze in the stifling Southern summers.

Today's Plantation-Style Farmhouse resembles the Prairie Farmhouse with its double-pitched, sprawling roofline; however, it is overall taller and more upright. The porches on these Southern belles are grand, wrapping structures that are often raised to lift the house out of wet or soggy ground. In fact, in some locations in the South, houses are built on piers to allow water to seep harmlessly beneath the level of the house. Porch columns are often round, in reminiscence of Southern Georgians or columned Colonials. The railings can be square, dimensioned lumber or round, turned spindles.

Plantation-Style homes may be either 1½ or two stories, though the most common examples are 1½-story renditions with secondary living quarters upstairs. Two-story versions may have a full, second-story balcony in the best Southern ante-bellum style. Often, secondary bedrooms are contained on the second floor with the master suite holding court on the first — a split sleeping arrangement agreeable to both children and parents.

Windows are strongly symmetrical with the second-story windows being dormers that protrude from the roof. The center unit is often larger and may have a circle-head on some more modern models. Ornate fan lights may flank entry doors.

Other exterior details include horizontal wood siding and strong, tall chimney stacks often capped with a curved masonry piece to protect the hearth from rain and spark-summoning wind. This once-only-practical design item has grown to be a style statement.

Design Q9623 incorporates some of the best details of the Southern-Style Farmhouse. Its wide covered porch extends around three sides of the design and is complemented by a beautiful deck with room for a spa to the rear. Three dormers appear at the second-story facade — the center one is a lovely Palladian-style. The characteristic protective, curved masonry piece caps the chimney which is just off center of the house. The floor plan is open and airy and contains a great room with cathedral ceiling for entertaining in high style.

Other plans in this section represent the gracious expression of Southern style. Together they provide a grand collection of homes for commodious living.

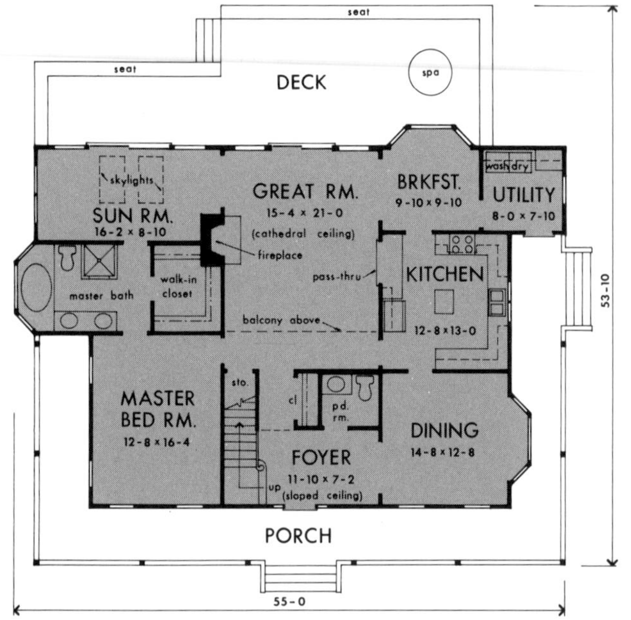

Design Q9623

First Floor: 1,651 square feet
Second Floor: 567 square feet
Total: 2,218 square feet

● A wonderful wraparound covered porch at the front and sides of this house and the open deck with spa at the back provide plenty of outside living area. Inside, the spacious great room has a fireplace, cathedral ceiling and clerestory with arched window. The kitchen is centrally located for maximum flexibility in layout and has a food preparation island for convenience. Besides the master bedroom with access to the sun room, there are two second-level bedrooms that share a full bath. For a crawl-space foundation, order Design Q9623; for a basement foundation, order Design Q9623-A.

clerestory with arched window
(cathedral ceiling)
great room below
storage
storage
railing
BED RM.
12-8 × 12-0
balcony
BED RM.
12-8 × 12-0
down
cl
cl
bath
cl
cl
foyer below
clerestory with palladian window

B. NATHAN

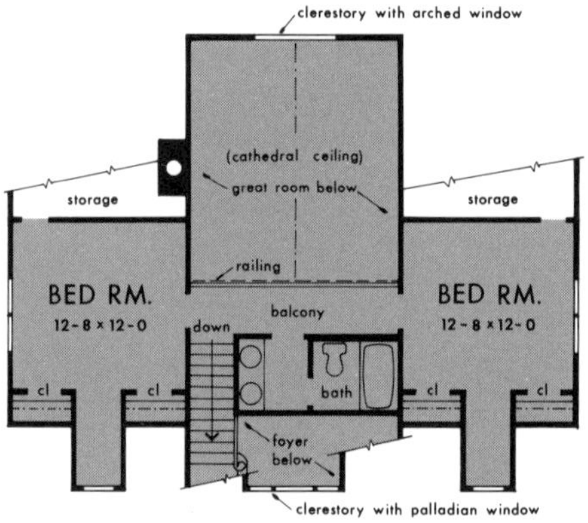

Design by
Donald A.
Gardner,
Architect, Inc.

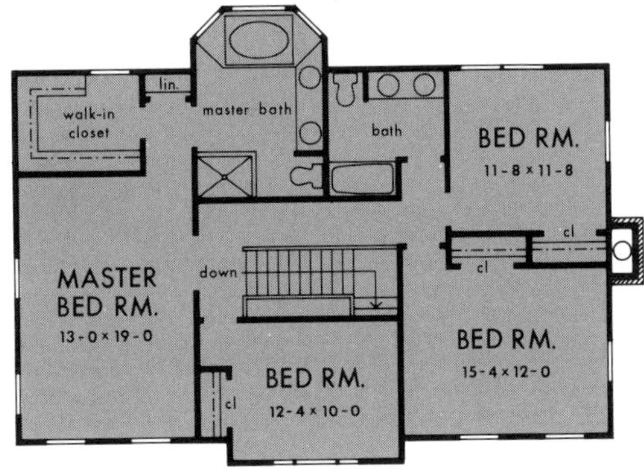

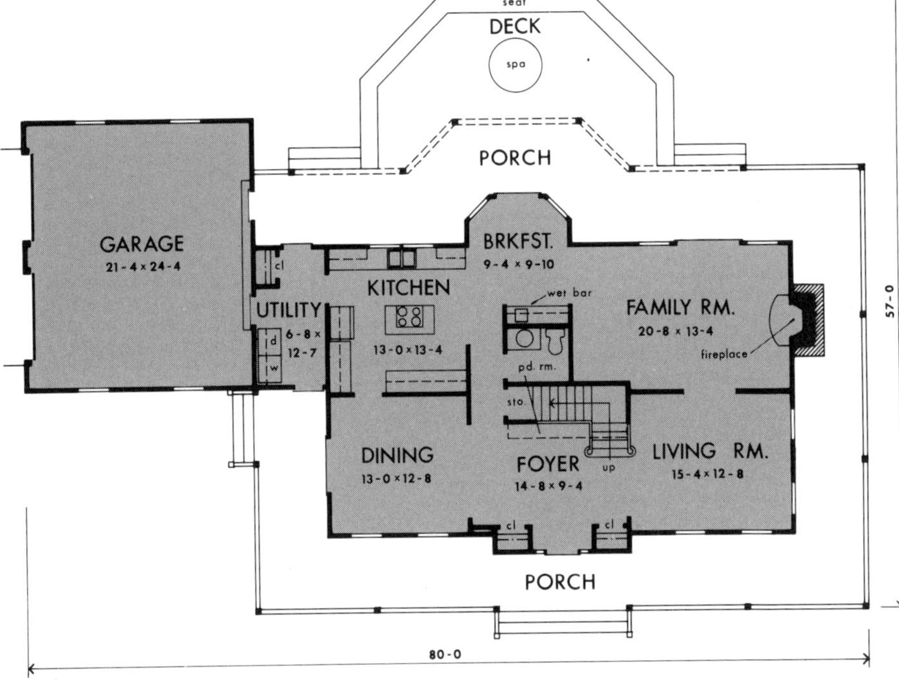

Design Q9667

First Floor: 1,357 square feet
Second Floor: 1,204 square feet
Total: 2,561 square feet

● This grand four-bedroom farmhouse with wraparound porch has eye-catching features: a double-gabled roof, Palladian window at the upper level, arched window on the lower level and intricately detailed brick chimney. Entry to the home reveals a generous foyer with direct access to all areas. The living room opens to the foyer and provides a formal entertaining area. The exceptionally large family room allows for more casual living. Look for a fireplace, wet bar and direct access to a porch and deck here. The lavish kitchen boasts a cooking island and serves the dining room, breakfast and deck areas. The master suite on the second level has a large walk-in closet and master bath with a whirlpool tub, shower and double-bowl vanity. Three additional bedrooms share a full bath.

Design Q9632

First Floor: 1,756 square feet
Second Floor: 565 square feet
Total: 2,321 square feet

Design by
Donald A. Gardner, Architect, Inc.

● A wraparound covered porch at the front and sides of this house and an open deck at the back provide plenty of outside living area. The spacious great room features a fireplace, cathedral ceiling, and clerestory with an arched window. The first-floor master bedroom contains a generous closet and a master bath with garden tub, double-bowl vanity, and shower. The second floor sports two bedrooms and a full bath with double-bowl vanity. This plan includes a crawl-space foundation.

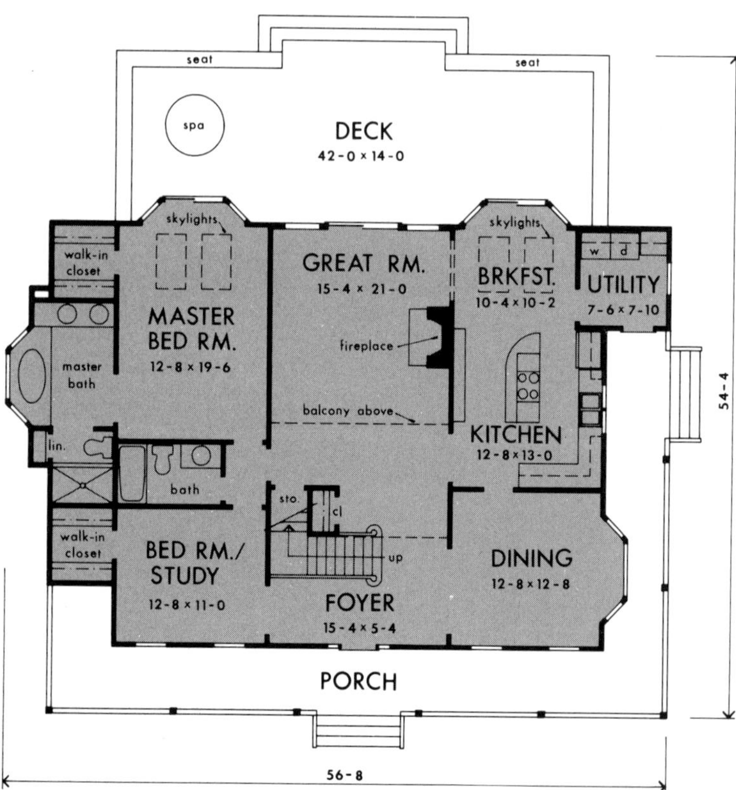

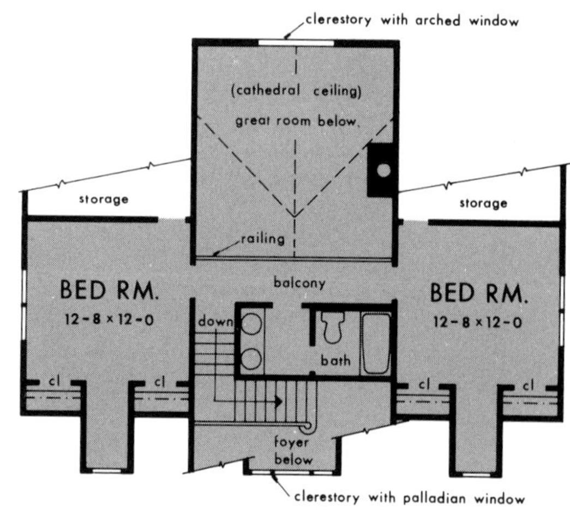

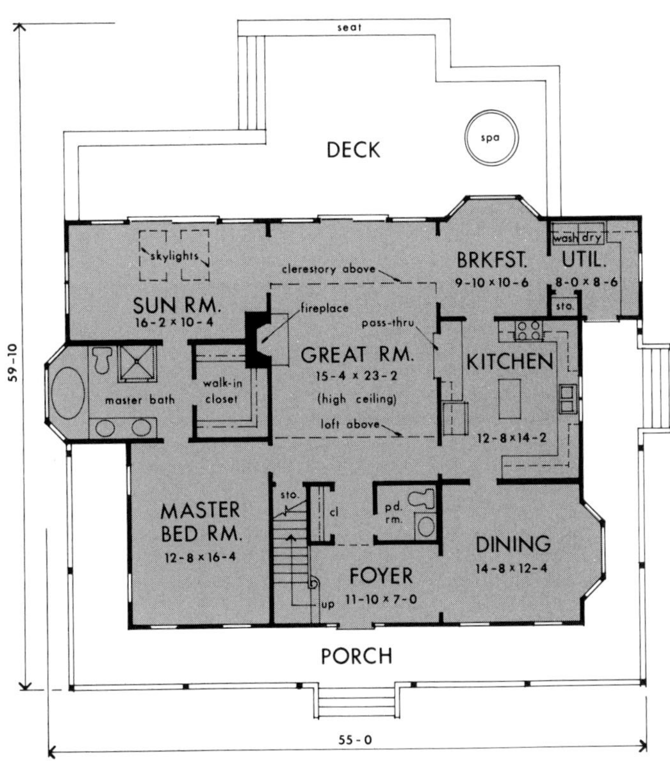

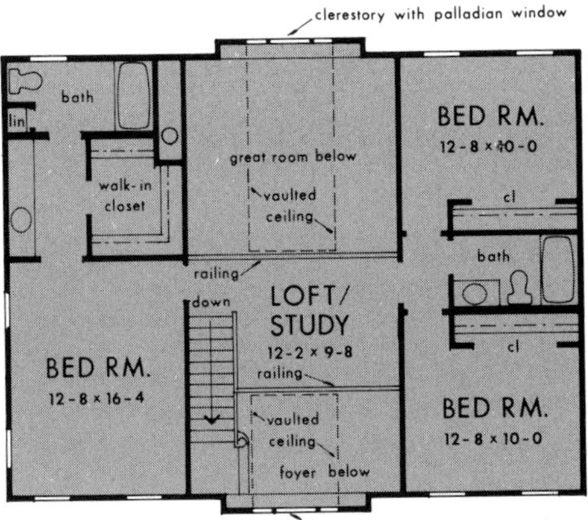

Design Q9616

First Floor: 1,734 square feet
Second Floor: 958 square feet
Total: 2,692 square feet

● A wraparound covered porch at the front and sides of this home and the open deck with spa and seating provide plenty of outside living area. A central great room features a vaulted ceiling, fireplace and clerestory windows above. The loft/study on the second floor overlooks this gathering area. Besides a formal dining room, kitchen, breakfast room and sun room on the first floor, there is also a generous master suite with garden tub. Three second-floor bedrooms complete sleeping accommodations. The plan includes a crawl-space foundation.

Design by
Donald A. Gardner, Architect, Inc.

FRONT

REAR

Design Q9621

First Floor: 1,325 square feet
Second Floor: 453 square feet
Total: 1,778 square feet

● For the economy-minded family desiring a wraparound covered porch, this compact design has all the amenities available in larger plans with little wasted space. In addition, a front Palladian window, dormer and rear arched windows provide exciting visual elements to the exterior. The spacious great room has a fireplace, cathedral ceiling and clerestory arched windows. A second-level balcony overlooks this gathering area. The kitchen is centrally located for maximum flexibility in layout and features a pass-through to the great room. Besides the generous master suite with well-appointed full bath, there are two family bedrooms located on the second level sharing a full bath with double vanity. Note the ample attic storage space. For a crawlspace foundation, order Design Q9621; for a basement foundation, order Design Q9621-A.

FRONT

REAR

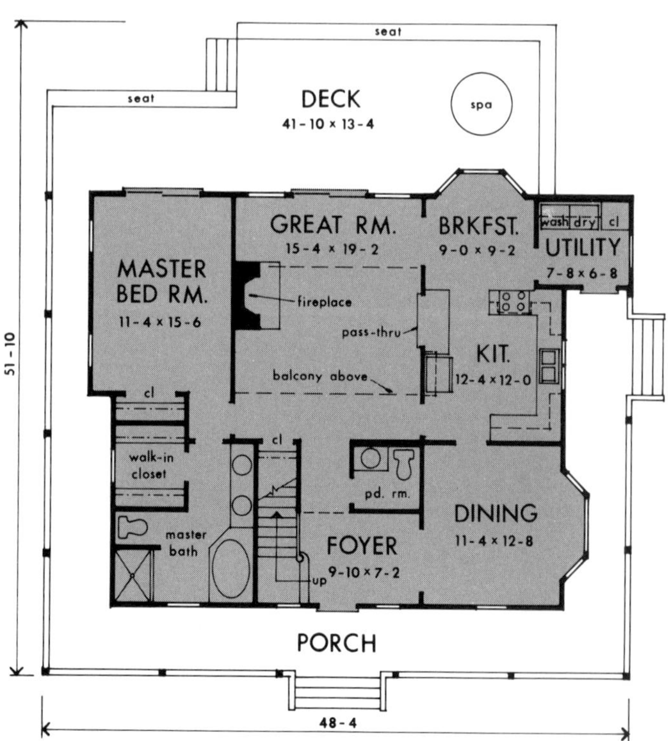

Design by
Donald A.
Gardner,
Architect, Inc.

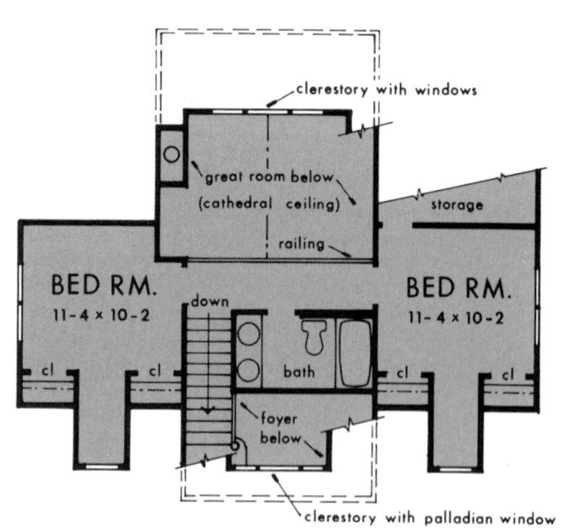

Design Q9668

First Floor: 1,254 square feet
Second Floor: 1,060 square feet
Total: 2,314 square feet

Design by
Donald A.
Gardner,
Architect, Inc.

● This stylish country farmhouse shows off its good looks both front and rear. A wraparound porch allows sheltered access to all first-level areas along with a covered breezeway to the garage. On the first floor, the spacious, open layout has all the latest features. The master bedroom on the second level has a fireplace, large walk-in closet and a master bath with shower, whirlpool tub and double-bowl vanity. Three additional bedrooms share a full bath with double-bowl vanity.

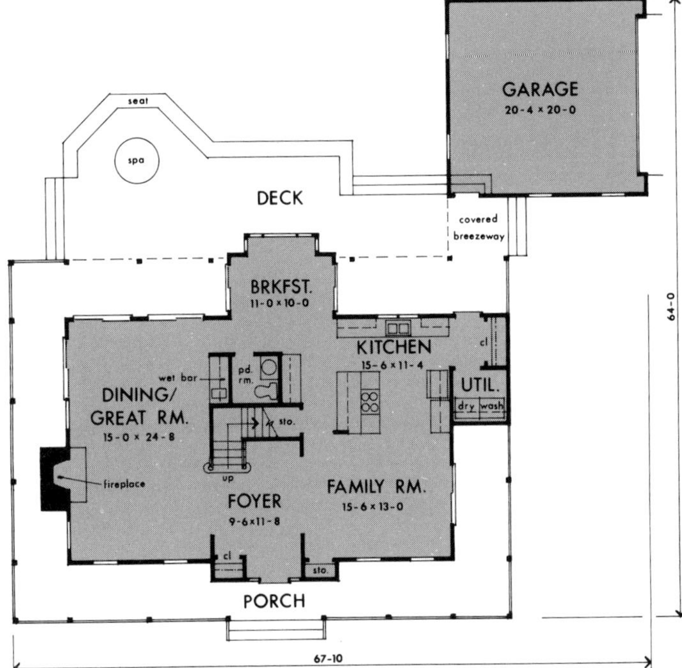

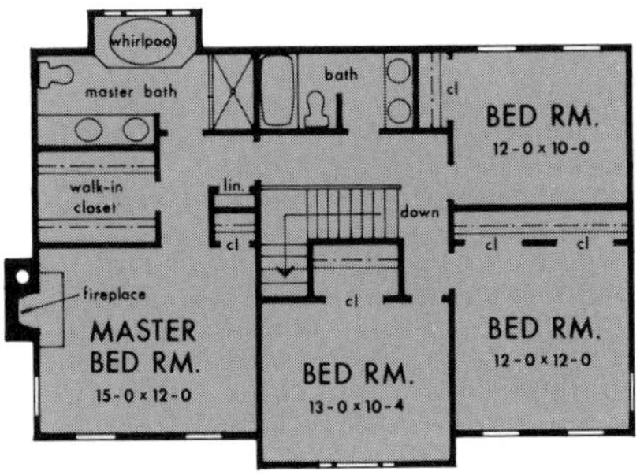

Design Q2650

First Floor: 1,451 square feet
Second Floor: 1,091 square feet; Total: 2,542 square feet

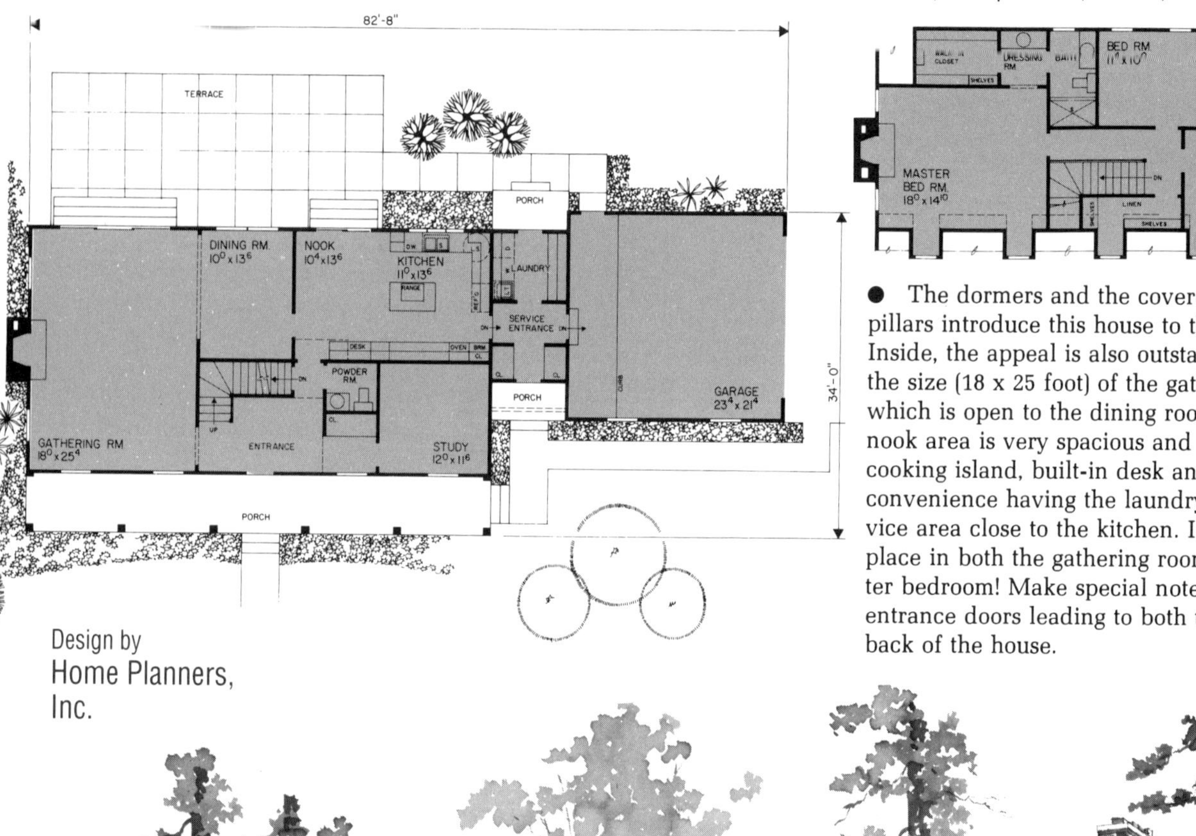

Design by
Home Planners, Inc.

● The dormers and the covered porch with pillars introduce this house to the on-lookers. Inside, the appeal is also outstanding. Note the size (18 x 25 foot) of the gathering room which is open to the dining room. Kitchen-nook area is very spacious and features a cooking island, built-in desk and more. Great convenience having the laundry and the service area close to the kitchen. Imagine, a fireplace in both the gathering room and the master bedroom! Make special note of the service entrance doors leading to both the front and back of the house.

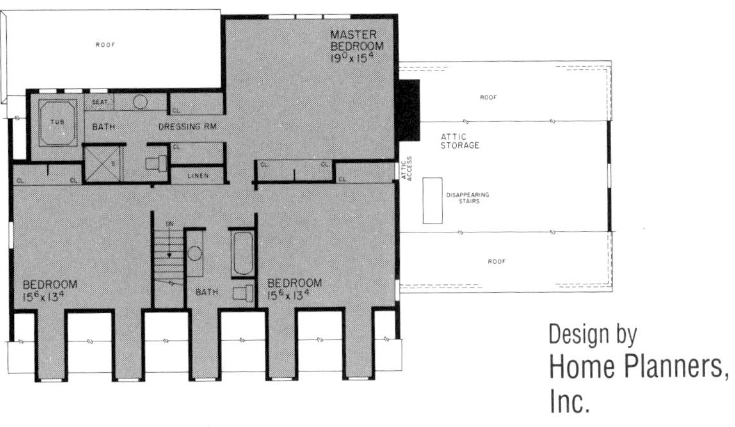

Design by
Home Planners,
Inc.

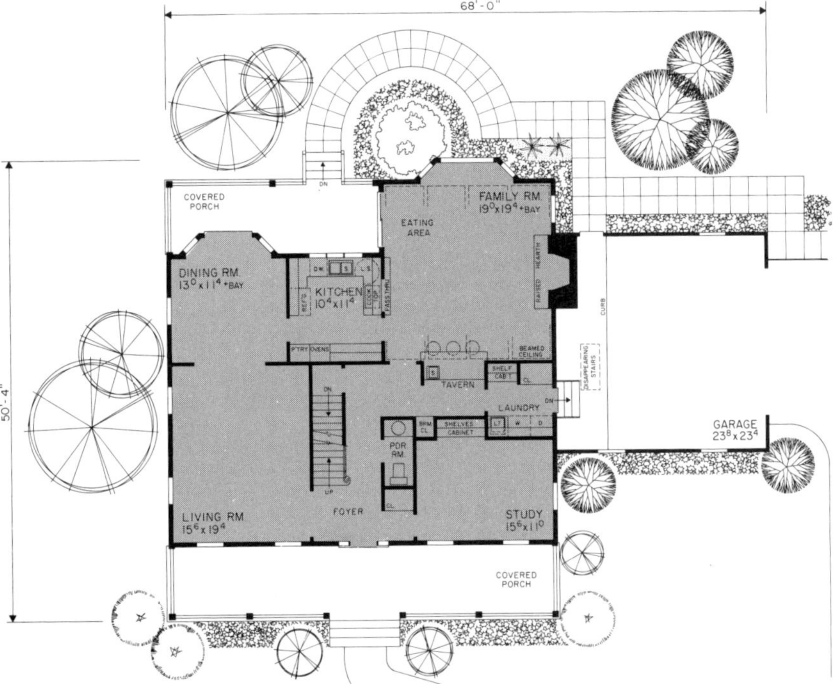

Design Q2890

First Floor: 1,612 square feet
Second Floor: 1,356 square feet
Total: 2,968 square feet

● An appealing Farmhouse that is complimented by an inviting front porch. Many memorable summer evenings will be spent here. Entering this house, you will notice a nice-sized study to your right and spacious living room to the left. The adjacent dining room is enriched by an attractive bay window. Just a step away, an efficient kitchen will be found. Many family activities will be enjoyed in the large family room. The tavern/snack bar will make entertaining guests a joy. A powder room and laundry are also on the first floor. Upstairs you'll find a master bedroom suite featuring a bath with an oversized tub and shower and a dressing room. Also on this floor; two bedrooms, full bath and a large attic.

Design Q2981

First Floor: 2,104 square feet
Second Floor: 2,015 square teet
Total: 4,119 square feet

Design by
Home Planners, Inc.

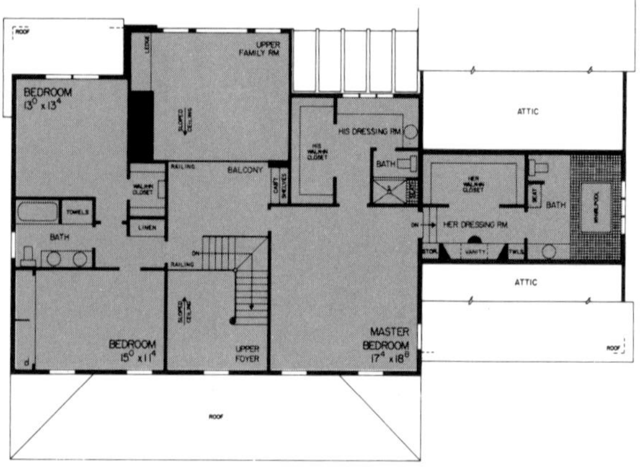

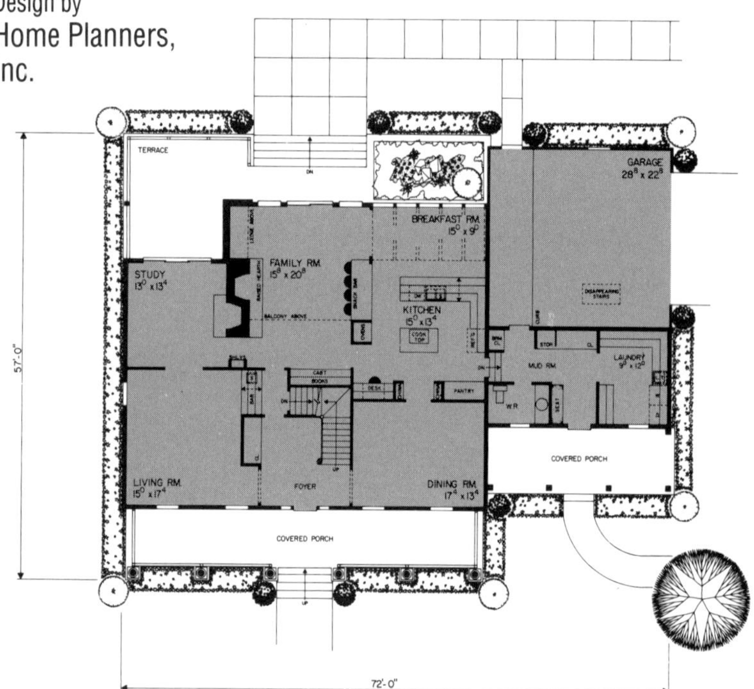

● This formal two-story recalls a Louisiana plantation house, Land's End, built in 1857. The Ionic columns of the front porch and the pediment gable echo the Greek Revival style. Highlighting the interior is the bright and cheerful spaciousness of the informal family room area. It features a wall of glass stretching to the second story sloping ceiling. Enhancing the drama of this area is the adjacent glass area of the breakfast room. Note the "His/Her" areas of the master bedroom.

Design by
Home Planners,
Inc.

● The exterior of this full two-story is highlighted by the covered porch and balcony. Many enjoyable hours will be spent at these outdoor areas. The interior is highlighted by a spacious country kitchen. Be sure to notice its island cook-top, fireplace and the beamed ceiling. A built-in bar is in the family room.

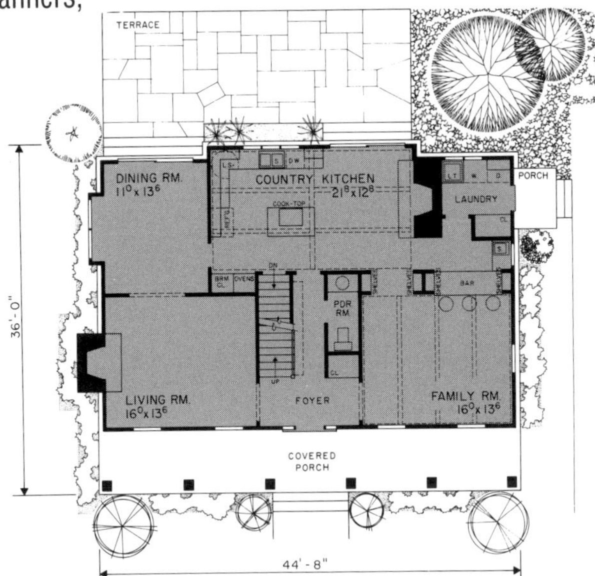

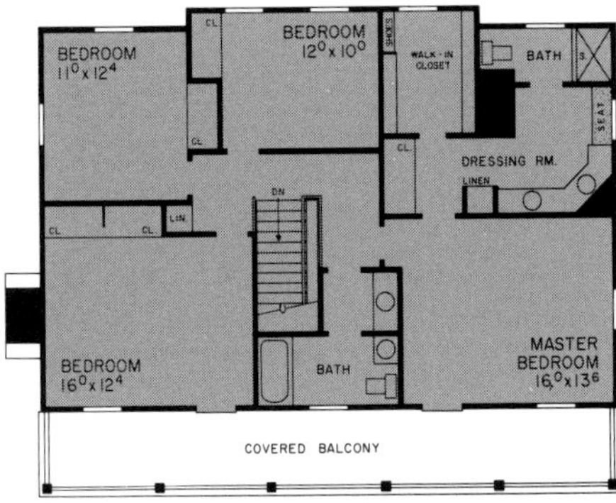

Design Q2664 First Floor: 1,308 square feet
Second Floor: 1,262 square feet; Total: 2,570 square feet

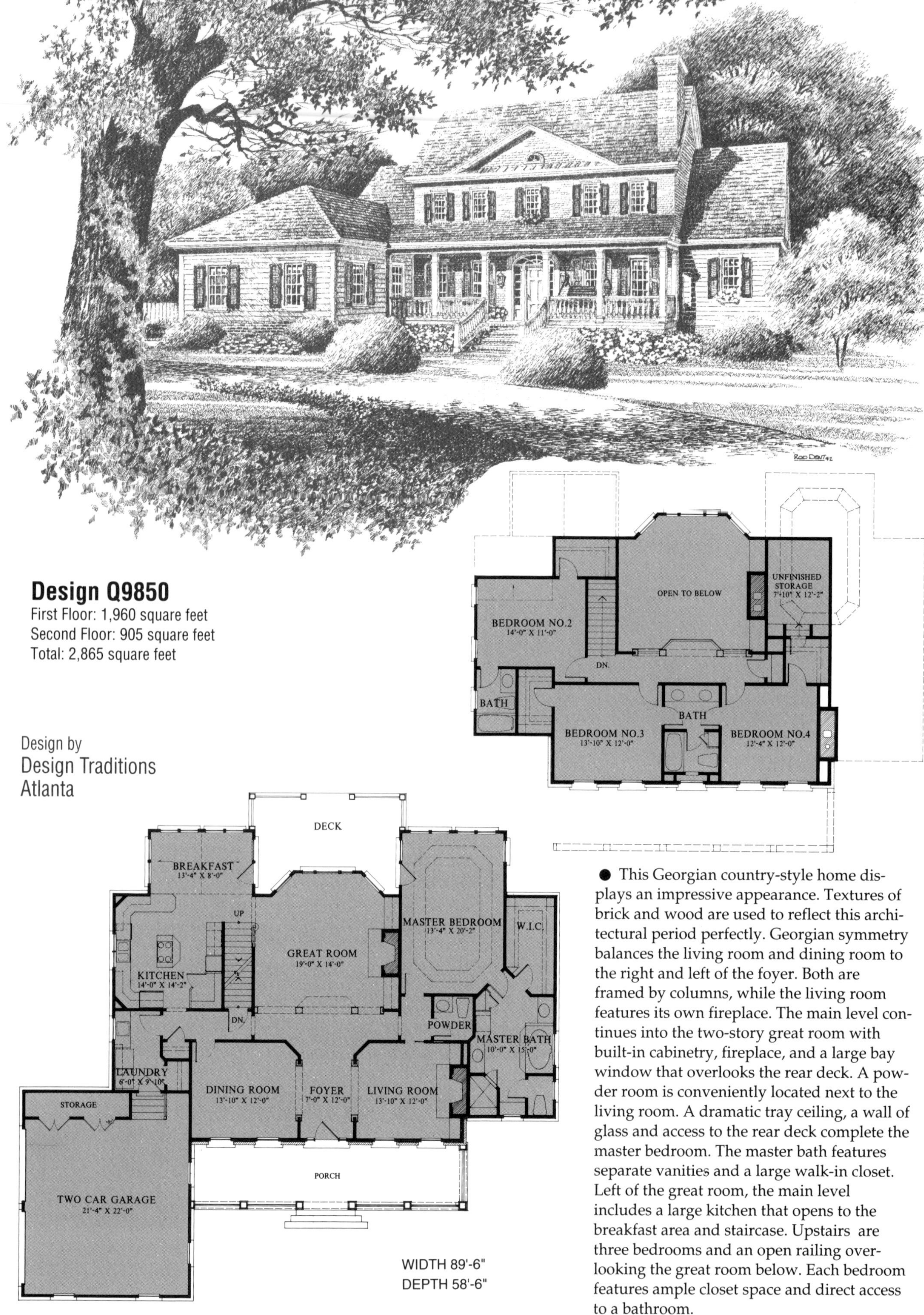

Design Q9850

First Floor: 1,960 square feet
Second Floor: 905 square feet
Total: 2,865 square feet

Design by
Design Traditions
Atlanta

WIDTH 89'-6"
DEPTH 58'-6"

● This Georgian country-style home displays an impressive appearance. Textures of brick and wood are used to reflect this architectural period perfectly. Georgian symmetry balances the living room and dining room to the right and left of the foyer. Both are framed by columns, while the living room features its own fireplace. The main level continues into the two-story great room with built-in cabinetry, fireplace, and a large bay window that overlooks the rear deck. A powder room is conveniently located next to the living room. A dramatic tray ceiling, a wall of glass and access to the rear deck complete the master bedroom. The master bath features separate vanities and a large walk-in closet. Left of the great room, the main level includes a large kitchen that opens to the breakfast area and staircase. Upstairs are three bedrooms and an open railing overlooking the great room below. Each bedroom features ample closet space and direct access to a bathroom.

Design Q9851

First Floor: 2,208 square feet
Second Floor: 1,250 square feet
Total: 3,458 square feet

● A generous front porch enhances the living area of this home with its sheltering welcome and Americana detailing. The classic style is also echoed in the use of wood siding, shuttered windows and stone finish work on two chimneys. The main level begins with a two-story foyer with tray ceiling. Double doors open into the study with an exposed beam ceiling and fireplace. Left of the foyer lies the dining room drenched in natural sunlight. Across the hall, the great room with fireplace, wet bar and two sets of French doors provides a great gathering place. A hall powder room is to the right rear of the foyer. The master suite is located at the end of the main hallway. It features a tray ceiling and a complete master bath with separate shower, walk-in closet and dual vanities. The two-car garage is at the rear of the home, with convenient access from the expansive kitchen and breakfast area. Staircases from the family room and foyer lead to the upper level. Two additional bedrooms, each having walk-in closets and vanities, share the tub area. A third bedroom has a generous walk-in closet and private bath.

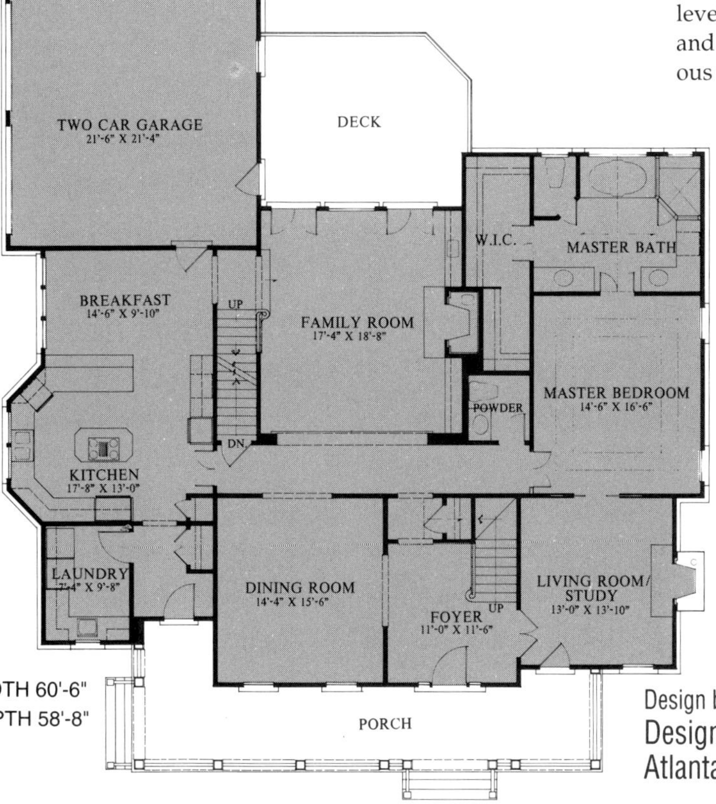

TWO CAR GARAGE 21'-6" X 21'-4"
DECK
W.I.C.
MASTER BATH
BREAKFAST 14'-6" X 9'-10"
UP
FAMILY ROOM 17'-4" X 18'-8"
POWDER
MASTER BEDROOM 14'-6" X 16'-6"
DN.
KITCHEN 17'-8" X 13'-0"
LAUNDRY 7'-4" X 9'-8"
DINING ROOM 14'-4" X 15'-6"
FOYER 11'-0" X 11'-6"
UP
LIVING ROOM/ STUDY 13'-0" X 13'-10"
PORCH

WIDTH 60'-6"
DEPTH 58'-8"

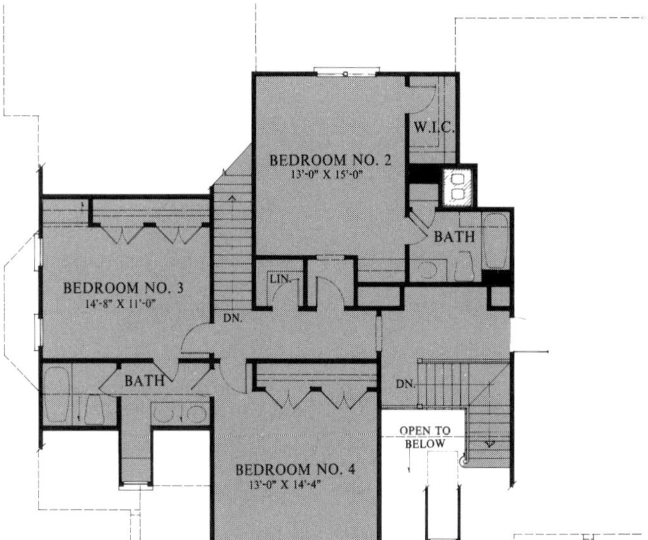

W.I.C.
BEDROOM NO. 2 13'-0" X 15'-0"
BATH
BEDROOM NO. 3 14'-8" X 11'-0"
LIN.
DN.
BATH
DN.
OPEN TO BELOW
BEDROOM NO. 4 13'-0" X 14'-4"

Design by
Design Traditions
Atlanta

Design Q9669

First Floor: 1,759 square feet
Second Floor: 888 square feet
Total: 2,647 square feet

● This complete four-bedroom country farmhouse ignites a passion for both indoor and outdoor living with the well-organized open layout and the continuous flowing porch and deck encircling the house. Front and rear Palladian window dormers allow natural light to penetrate the foyer and family room below as well as adding exciting visual elements to the exterior. The dramatic family room with sloped ceiling envelopes a curved balcony. The master suite includes a large walk-in closet, a special sitting area, and a master bath with whirlpool tub, shower and double bowl vanity. A bonus room over the garage adds to the completeness of this house.

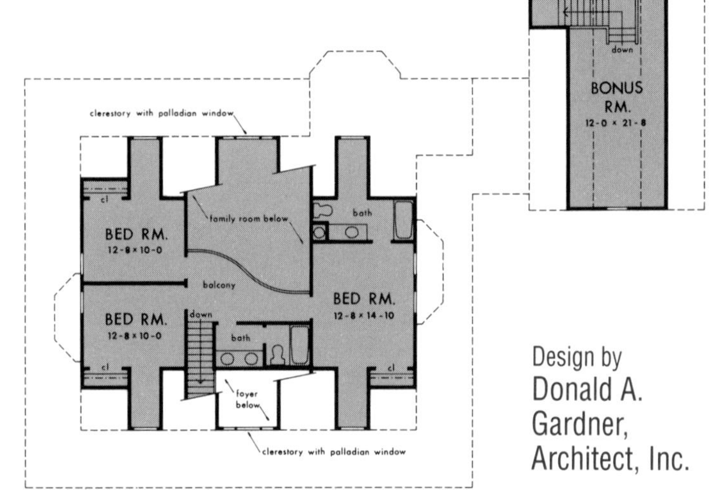

Design by
Donald A. Gardner, Architect, Inc.

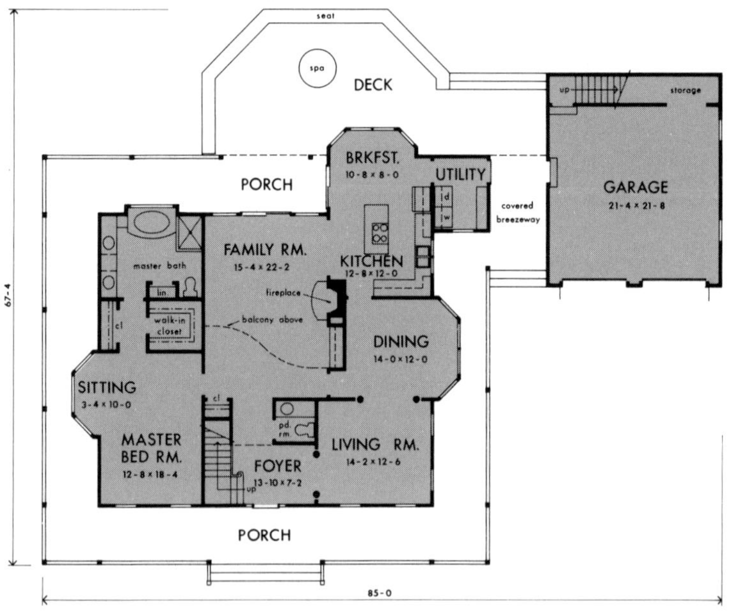

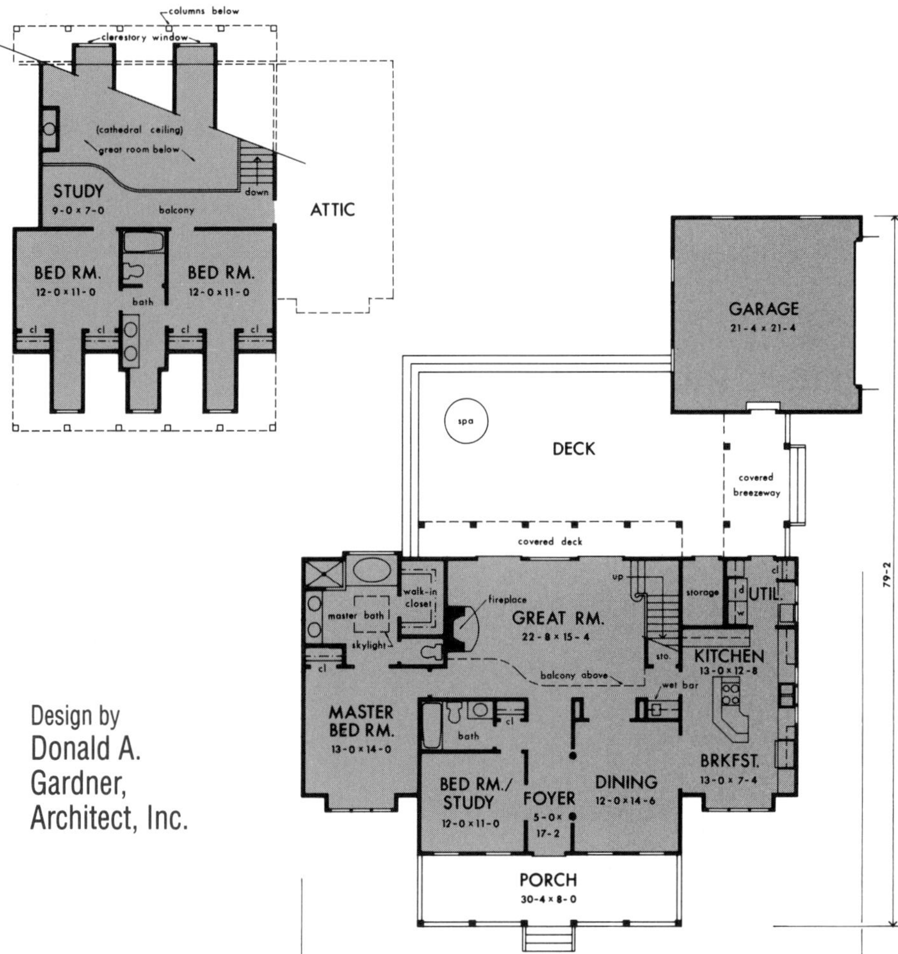

Design by
Donald A.
Gardner,
Architect, Inc.

Design Q9636

First Floor: 1,714 square feet
Second Floor: 651 square feet
Total: 2,365 square feet

● The elegance of this four-bedroom plan is reinforced by the symmetry of the front elevation with arched windows and intricately detailed square columns. The interior offers a wealth of architectural excitement: great room with cathedral ceiling, kitchen with large island, wet bar, bedroom/study on the first level and gorgeous master suite with amenity-laden bath. Two bedrooms sharing a full bath are on the second level along with ample attic space for storage. The large front porch and rear deck offer maximum outdoor living potential. For a crawl-space foundation, order Design Q9636; for a basement foundation, order Design Q9636-A.

Design by
Larry W.
Garnett &
Associates, Inc.

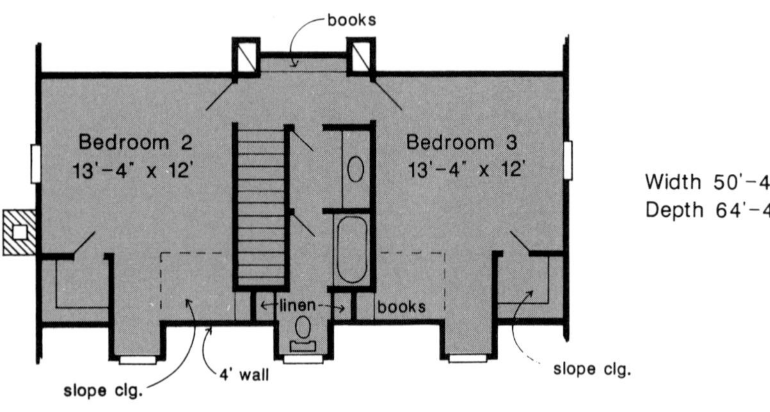

Width 50'-4"
Depth 64'-4"

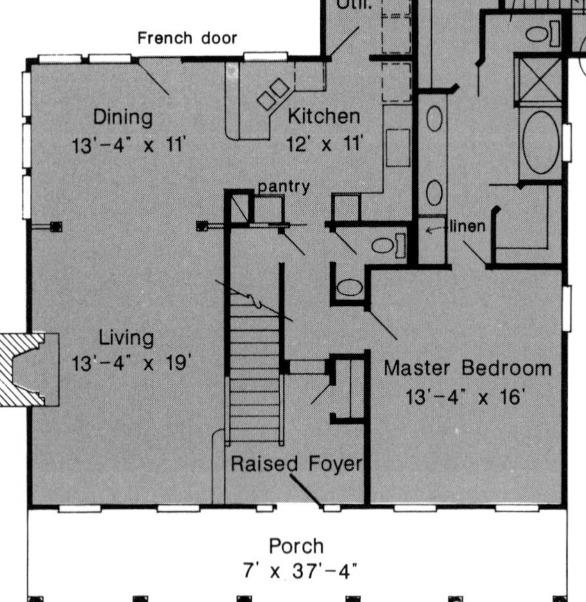

Design Q9121

First Floor: 1,266 square feet
Second Floor: 639 square feet
Total: 1,905 square feet

● Complete with dormers and a covered front porch, the facade details of this home are repeated at the side-loaded garage, making it a perfectly charming plan from any angle. From the raised foyer, step down into the living room with fireplace. This area opens to a dining room which has a French door to the rear yard. Close by is a kitchen with pantry and access to a utility room and the garage. The master suite is on the first floor for convenience. Note the two large walk-in closets here. Upstairs there are two secondary bedrooms and a full compartmented bath. An entry near the garage contains a staircase to an optional storage room. This space could be developed later as a mother-in-law suite or home office.

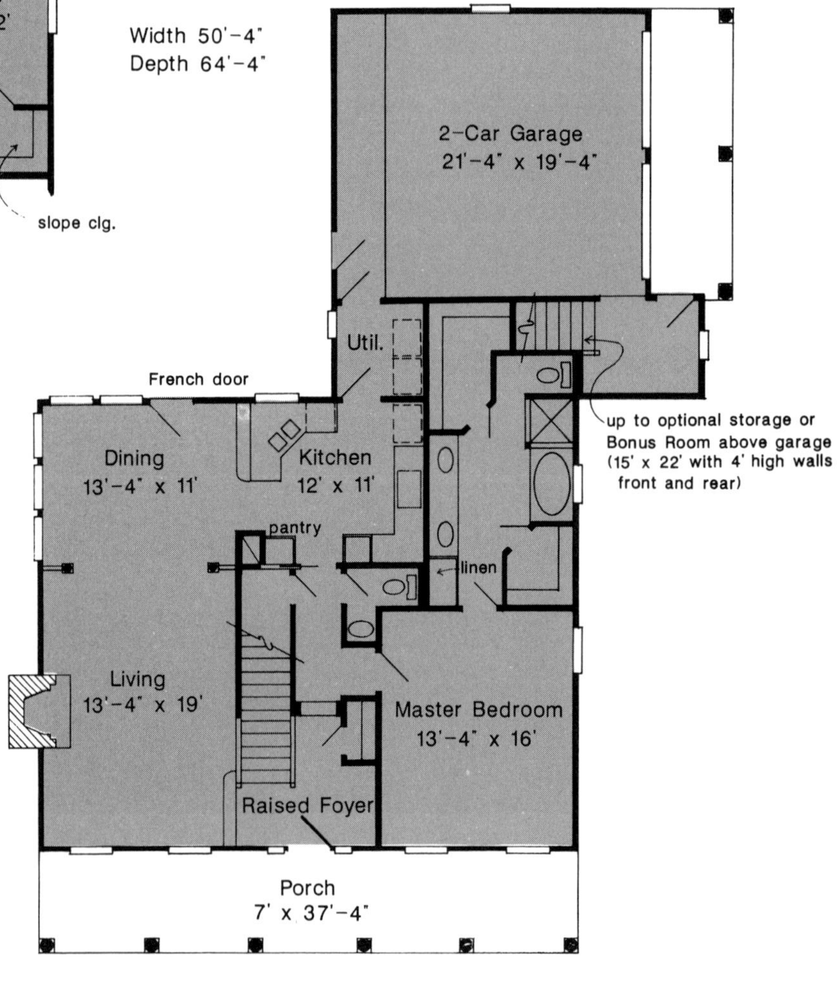

Design by
Larry W.
Garnett &
Associates, Inc.

Width 69'
Depth 78'-1"

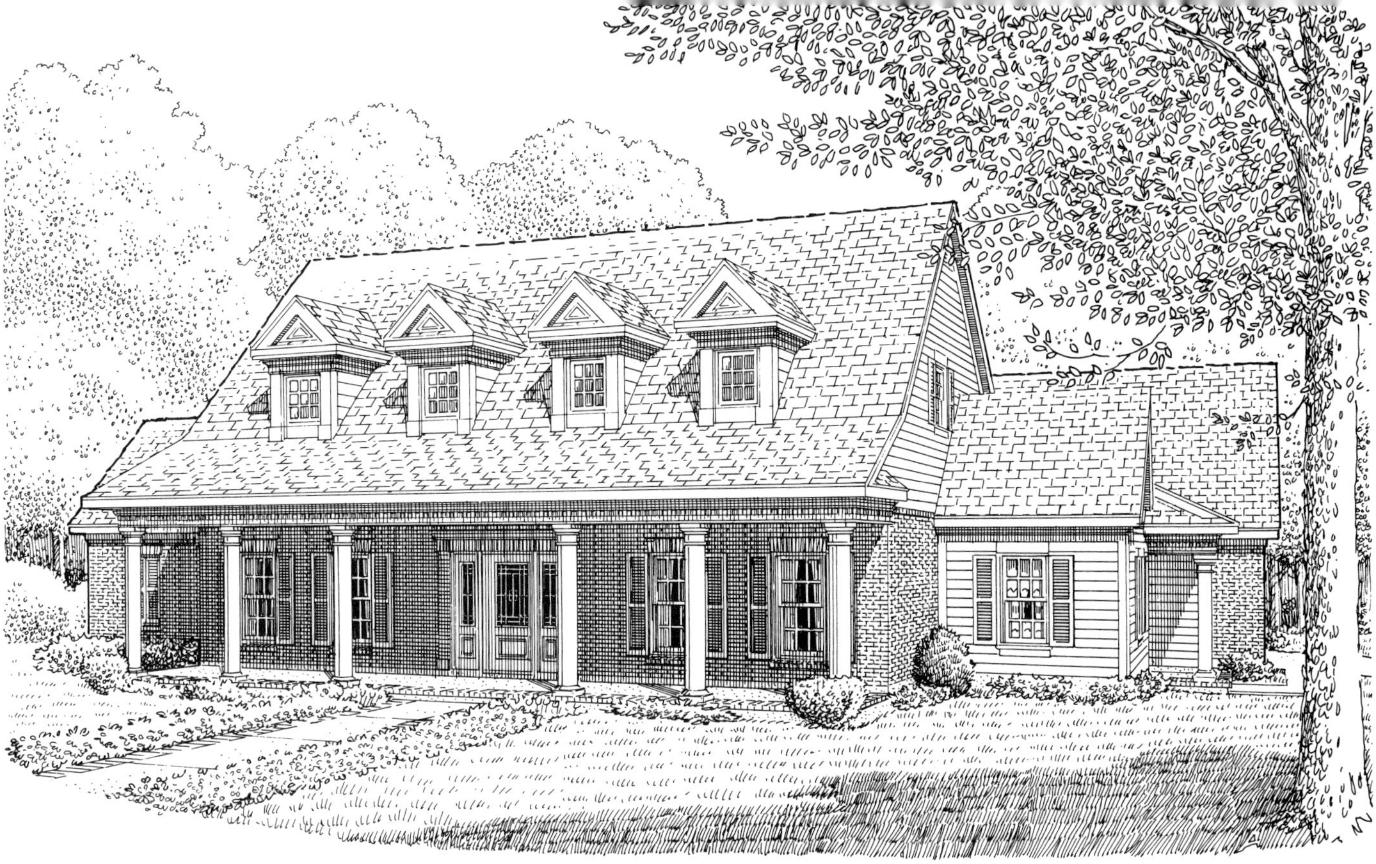

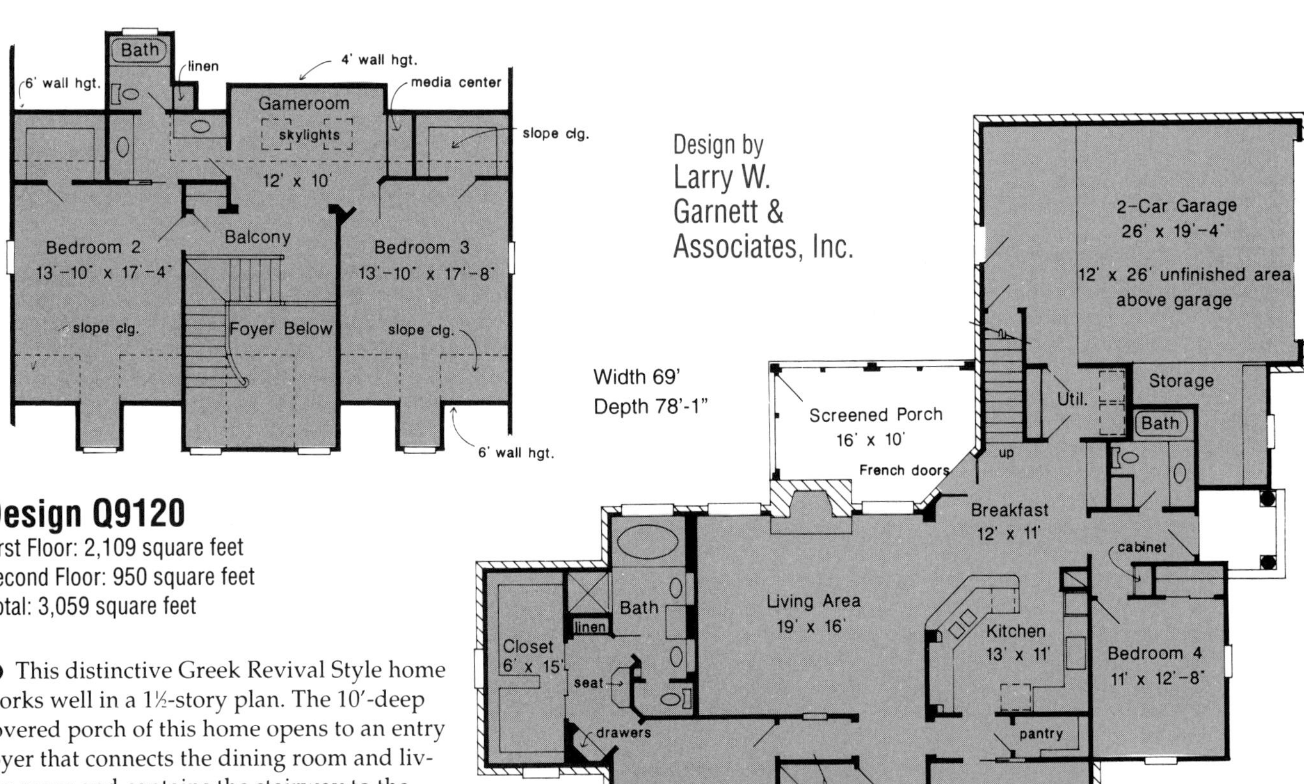

Design Q9120

First Floor: 2,109 square feet
Second Floor: 950 square feet
Total: 3,059 square feet

● This distinctive Greek Revival Style home works well in a 1½-story plan. The 10'-deep covered porch of this home opens to an entry foyer that connects the dining room and living room and contains the stairway to the second floor. Stairs at the breakfast room provide access to a 12' x 26' future room. The master bedroom is complemented by a bath with many amenities. Tucked away to the right of the plan is a bedroom that works well as guest quarters or could hold a home office or study. For additional sleeping space, there are two bedrooms with dormer windows and walk-in closets, plus a full bath on the second floor.

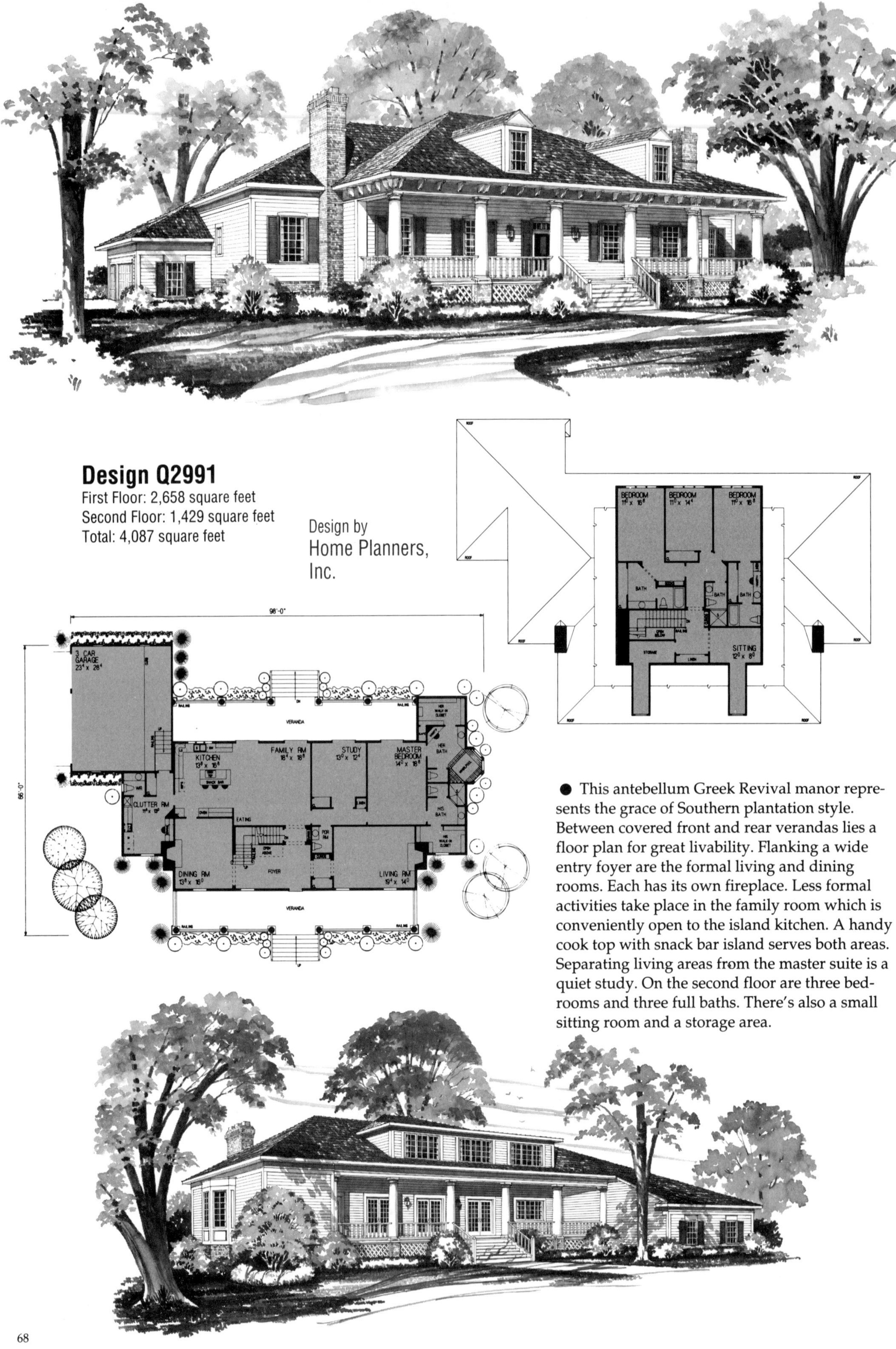

Design Q2991

First Floor: 2,658 square feet
Second Floor: 1,429 square feet
Total: 4,087 square feet

Design by
Home Planners, Inc.

● This antebellum Greek Revival manor represents the grace of Southern plantation style. Between covered front and rear verandas lies a floor plan for great livability. Flanking a wide entry foyer are the formal living and dining rooms. Each has its own fireplace. Less formal activities take place in the family room which is conveniently open to the island kitchen. A handy cook top with snack bar island serves both areas. Separating living areas from the master suite is a quiet study. On the second floor are three bedrooms and three full baths. There's also a small sitting room and a storage area.

VICTORIAN-INFLUENCED FARMHOUSES

In a time defined by freedom of expression, the Romantic ideals of architecture helped bring about Victorian style. For 70 years, from 1840 to 1910, people embraced the style and developed its various shapes and forms. So popular were the features of Victoriana that many of its more prominent, ornate characteristics began appearing on otherwise plain facades. Simple, unadorned farmhouses were seen sporting Queen-Anne-Style porch rails and posts, decorative corner brackets, spindlework friezes and other "gingerbread" details. This was possible (and practical) because of the availability of pre-cut Victorian trim pieces obtained through local lumber yards. The long-lasting appeal of Victorian detailing is evident, as the features appear on myriads of homes built throughout the country.

The Victorian Farmhouse today presents many of the same properties as the Classic Farmhouse — tall, upright proportions with wood siding and covered porches. However, the Victorian era influenced these rural residences by enhancing the plainness of Farmhouse style with detailing. Special features that became part of this newly integrated design include round or square double porch columns, spindled railings and friezes, spiderweb decoration at gables, shingle scallops, and cornice and dentil ornamentation.

Structural modifications were also accomplished to the basic Farmhouse design that make these simpler homes much more appealing. Plain, symmetrical windows became metal-clad, French-style bays or dormer windows. Even circle-head and fan-type windows were added. Wings and appendages were attached and took the shape of hexagons or octagons. Shingles took the place of horizontal wood siding in many instances.

In the following collection of Victorian Farmhouses, two designs are able representatives of the style: Design Q9015 and Design Q2970. Though obviously descended from stolid farmhouse roots, Design Q9015 is a model of exquisite detailing. Turned posts and delicate spindles adorn the covered front porch; eave brackets and lacy cornice trim grace the exterior. Of special note is the metal-clad roof over the porch and the decorative work on the pediments at the dormer windows. Design Q2970 presents many of the same details and also adds shingle scallops and a hexagonal bump-out that holds the dining room on the first floor and a sitting room on the second floor.

Displayed in both one- and two-story versions, the Victorian Farmhouses in this section are filled with the charm and delight that has always made Victorian styling so popular.

Design Q9420

First Floor: 1,587 square feet
Second Floor: 716 square feet
Bonus Room: 427 square feet
Total: 2,730 square feet

Design by
Alan Mascord
Design Associates, Inc.

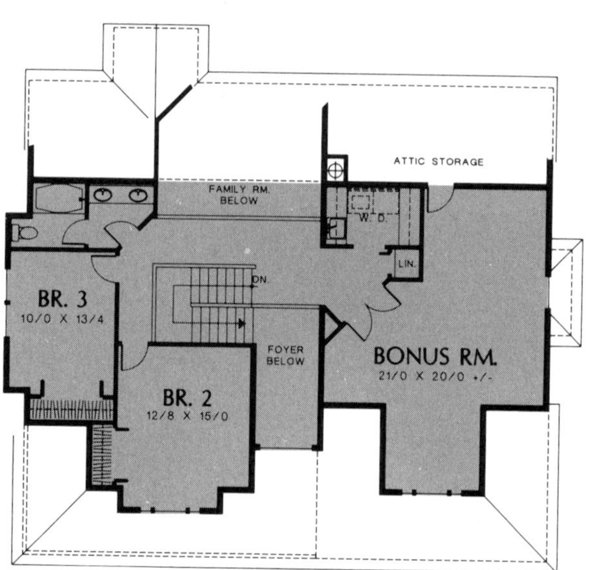

● This compact Victorian home has its fully featured master bedroom on the main floor. A wraparound porch with a pair of French doors leading from the dining room complements the facade. The upper hallway overlooks the vaulted family room on one side and the two-story foyer on the other. A bonus room over the garage allows some expansion space to either add another bedroom or a game room.

Design Q9475

First Floor: 1,085 square feet
Second Floor: 1,110 square feet
Total: 2,195 square feet

● Farmhouse design is popular throughout the country—this plan is an outstanding example. The corner entry leads to a formal parlor on the left and dining room on the right. To the rear of the first floor are the family room with fireplace and island kitchen with nook. The stairs are centrally located and a nearby powder room will be appreciated by guests. Upstairs are four bedrooms (or three and a den). The master bedroom has a vaulted ceiling and lovely private bath.

Design by
Alan Mascord
Design Associates, Inc.

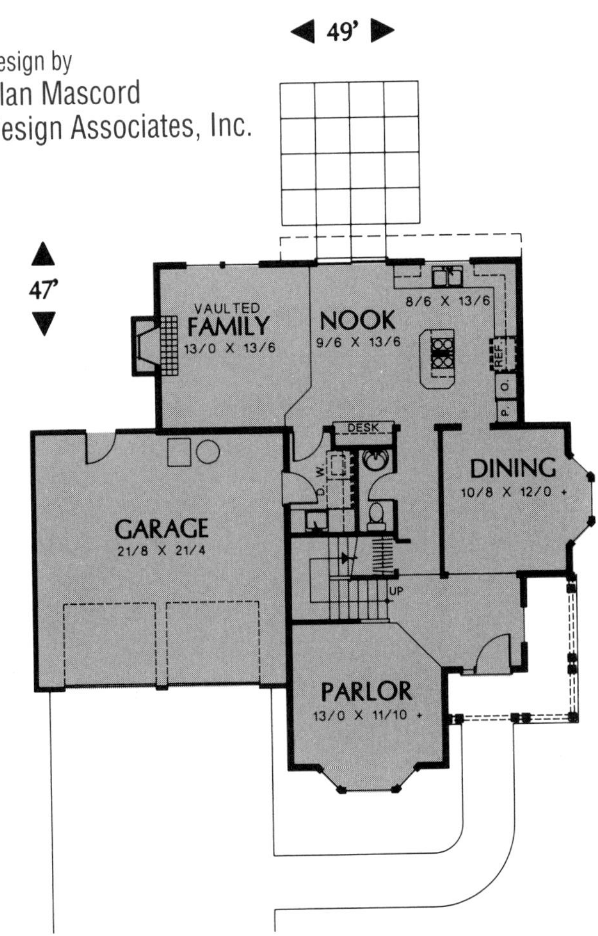

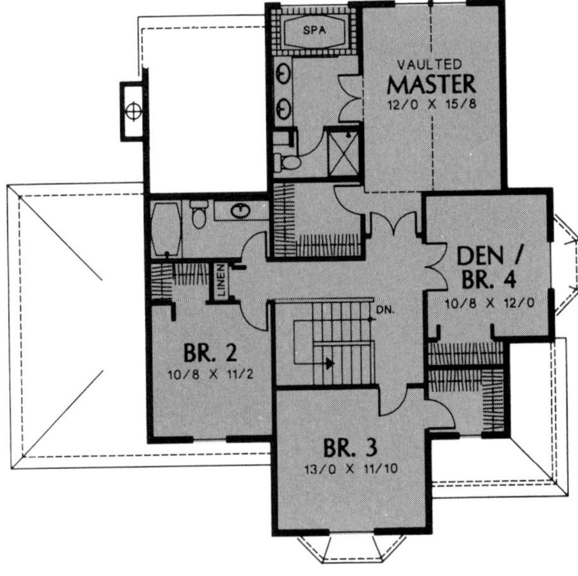

Design Q9054

First Floor: 860 square feet
Second Floor: 818 square feet
Total: 1,678 square feet

● Taking its cue from Victorian design, this two-story home allows for a great deal of livability in a smaller square footage. Downstairs are the living and dining areas, plus full work areas in a galley kitchen, utility room, and powder room. The wraparound veranda provides lovely indoor/outdoor living potential. Upstairs are three bedrooms with large closets. The master bedroom has a bay window and bath with double-bowl vanity. Secondary bedrooms share a full bath. Thoughtful extras like the fireplace in the living room, coat closet in the foyer and dividing wall between the living room and dining room make this a very special plan.

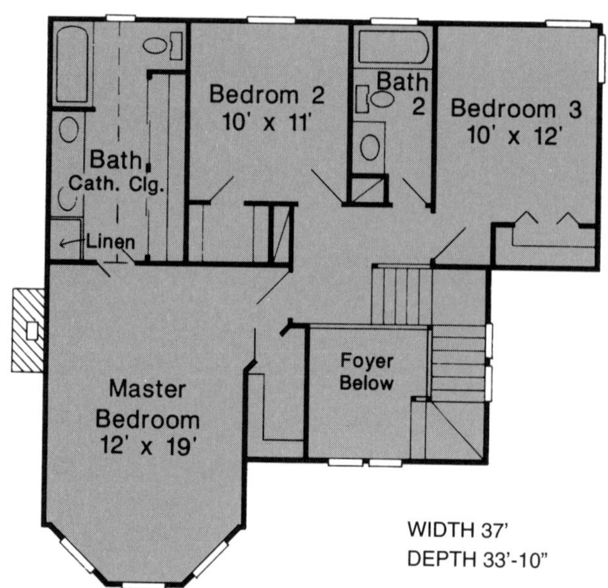

WIDTH 37'
DEPTH 33'-10"

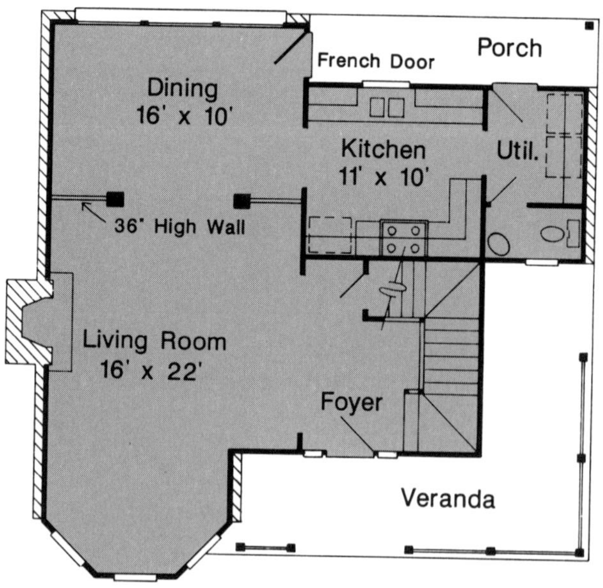

Design by
Larry W. Garnett & Associates, Inc.

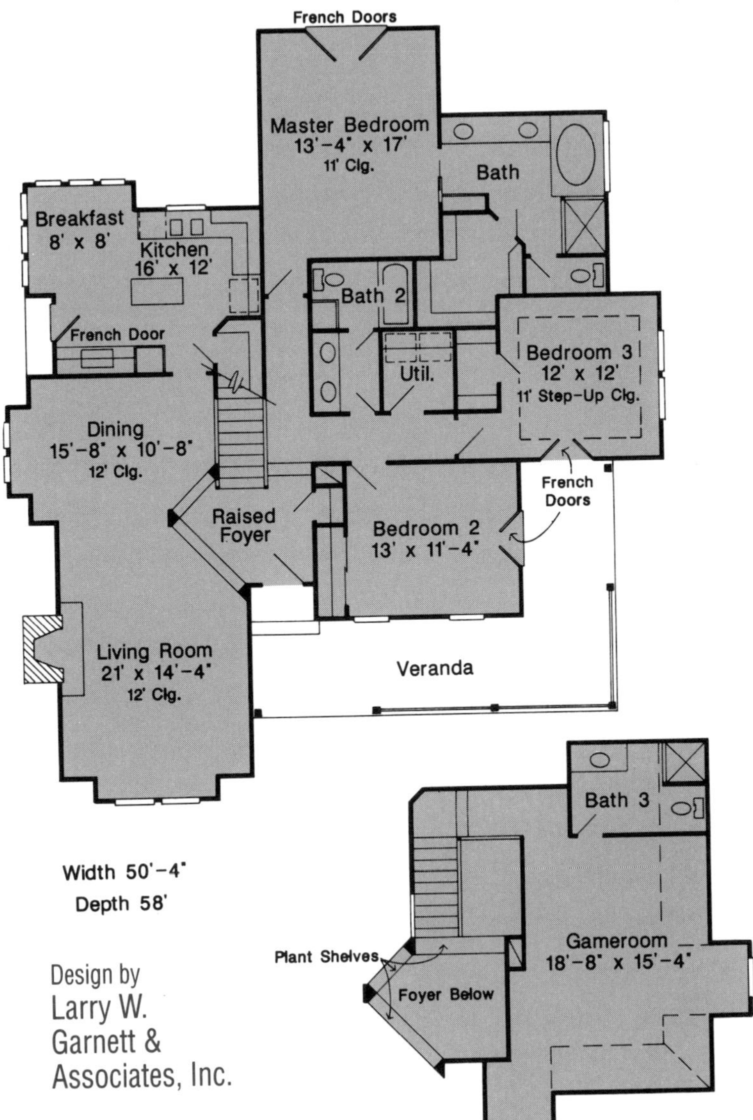

Design by
Larry W.
Garnett &
Associates, Inc.

Design Q9030

First Floor: 1,837 square feet
Second Floor: 445 square feet
Total: 2,282 square feet

● A seven-foot wide veranda with ornate fretwork, porch railing and intricate post brackets, along with a copper-topped box window provide this home with old-fashioned charm and romance. Inside, the raised foyer opens into living and dining areas that are perfect for family activities or formal entertaining. Stairs lead to the second floor gameroom and bath. Bedrooms 2 and 3 each have French doors that open to the front veranda. The secluded master bedroom has an eleven-foot ceiling and French doors, while the spacious master bath features a garden tub with adjacent glass-enclosed shower, along with a large walk-in closet. The kitchen combines both form and function with ample cabinet space, a center work island, and a magnificent view through the breakfast area to the rear yard. Plans for a detached two-car garage are included with this design.

Design Q3384 First Floor: 1,399 square feet
Second Floor: 1,123 square feet
Total: 2,522 square feet

● Classic Victorian styling comes to the forefront in this Queen Anne two-story. Complementary fishscale-adorned pediments top the bayed tower to the left and garage to the right. Smaller versions are found at the dormer windows above a spindlework porch. The interior boasts comfortable living quarters for the entire family. On opposite sides of the wide foyer are the formal dining and living rooms. To the rear, is a country-style island kitchen with attached family room (don't miss the fireplace here). A small library shares a covered porch with this informal gathering area and also has its own fireplace. Three bedrooms on the second floor include a master suite with grand bath. The two family bedrooms share a full bath. Take special note of the service area conveniently attached to the two-car garage.

Design by
Home Planners, Inc.

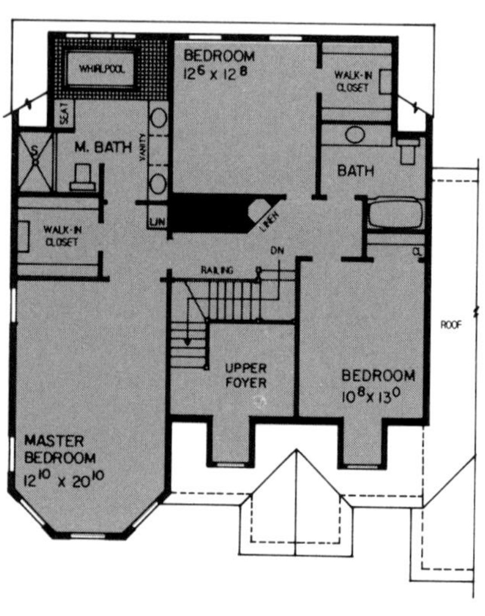

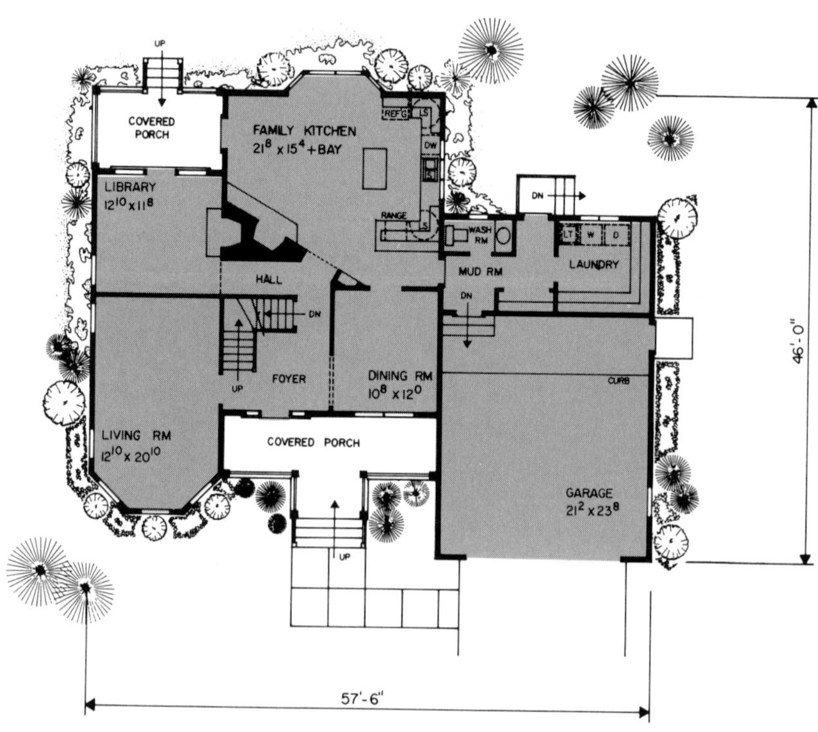

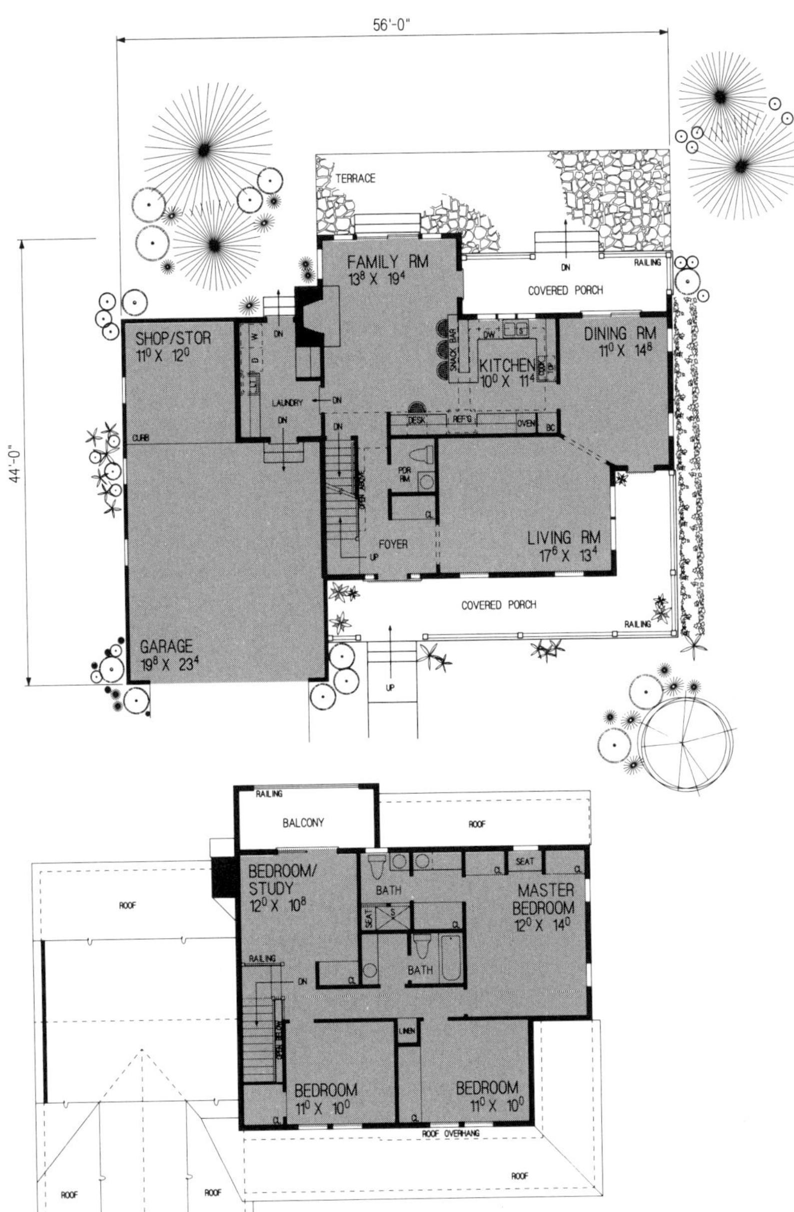

Design Q3385

First Floor: 1,096 square feet
Second Floor: 900 square feet
Total: 1,996 square feet

● Covered porches front and rear are the first signal that this is a fine example of Folk Victorian styling. Complementing the exterior is a grand plan for family living. A formal living room and attached dining room provide space for entertaining guests. The large family room with fireplace is a gathering room for everyday. Both areas have access to outdoor spaces. Four bedrooms occupy the second floor. The master suite features two lavatories, a window seat and three closets. One of the family bedrooms has its own private balcony and could be used as a study. Note the open staircase and convenient linen storage.

Design by
Home Planners, Inc.

Design Q3391

First Floor: 1,230 square feet
Second Floor: 991 square feet
Total: 2,221 square feet

Design by
Home Planners, Inc.

● Detailing is one of the characteristic features of Queen Anne Victorians and this home has no lack of it. Interior rooms add special living patterns. Features include a powder room for guests in the front hallway, a through-fireplace between the ample gathering room and cozy study, an efficient U-shaped kitchen with pantry, and a full-width terrace to the rear. On the second floor are three bedrooms — one a master suite with walk-in closet and amenity-filled bath. An open balcony overlooks the gathering room.

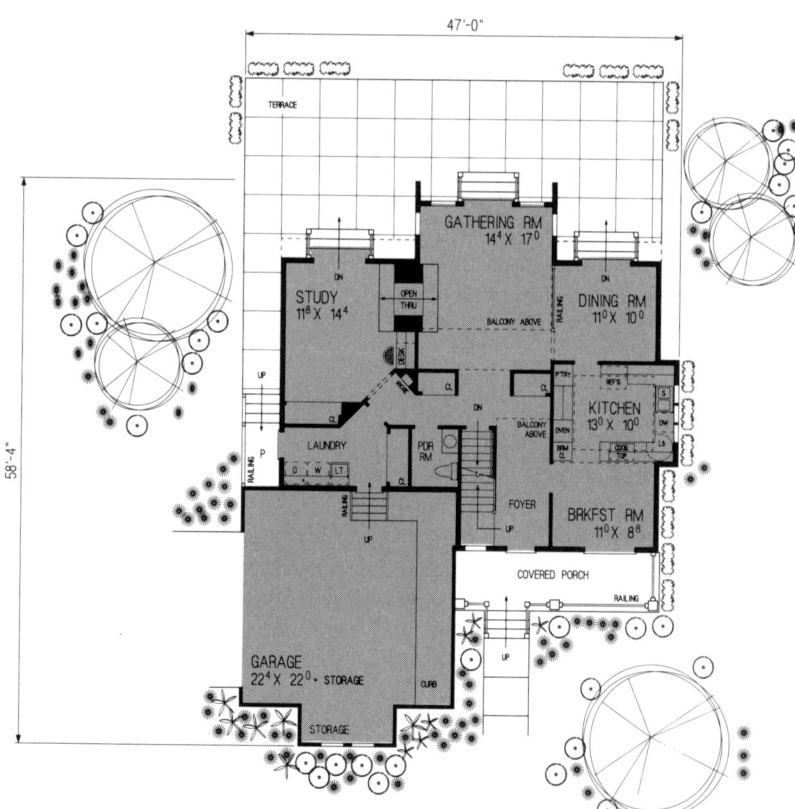

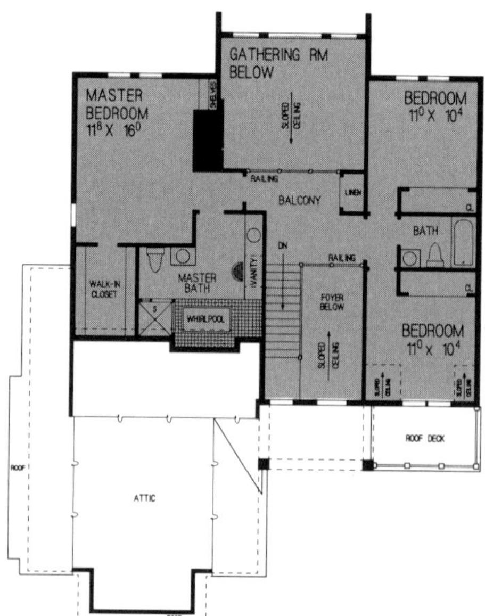

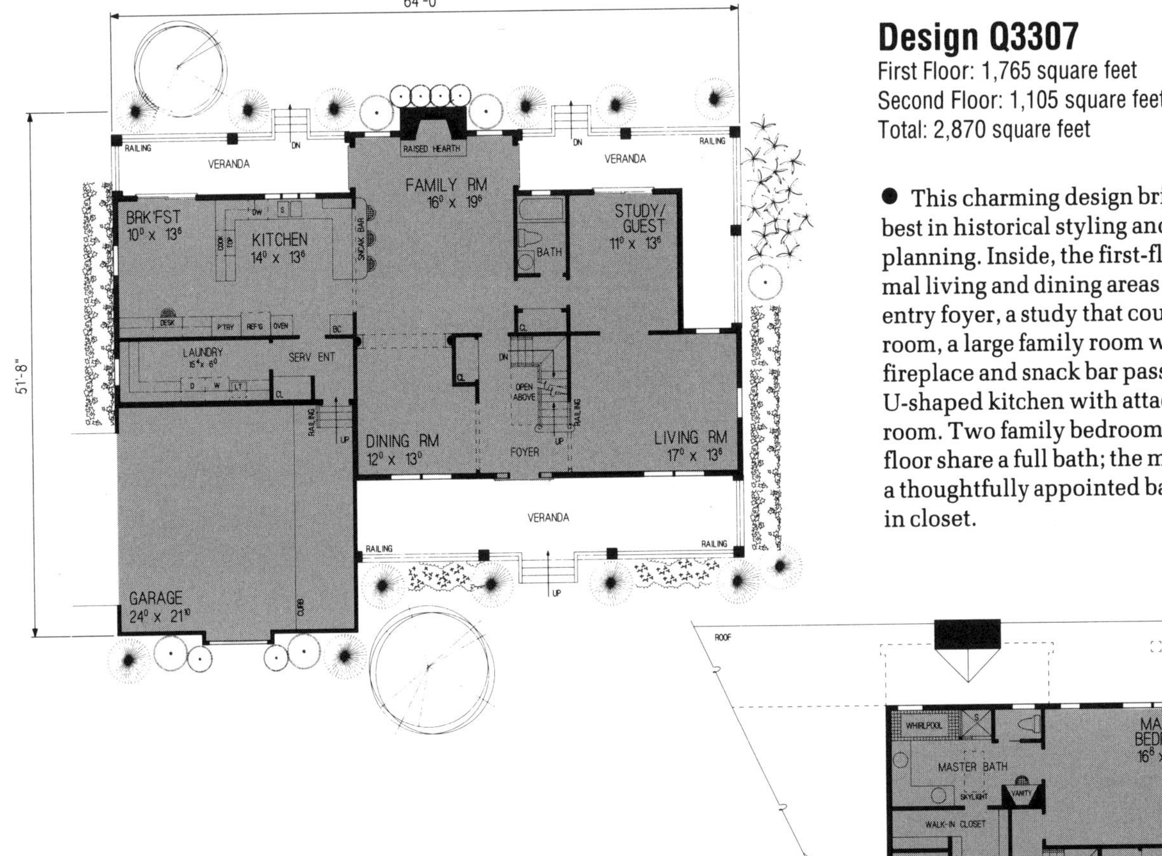

Design Q3307

First Floor: 1,765 square feet
Second Floor: 1,105 square feet
Total: 2,870 square feet

● This charming design brings together the best in historical styling and modern floor planning. Inside, the first-floor plan boasts formal living and dining areas on either side of the entry foyer, a study that could double as a guest room, a large family room with raised-hearth fireplace and snack bar pass-through, and a U-shaped kitchen with attached breakfast room. Two family bedrooms on the second floor share a full bath; the master bedroom has a thoughtfully appointed bath and large walk-in closet.

ROOF
WHIRLPOOL
MASTER BATH
SKYLIGHT
VANITY
MASTER BEDROOM
16⁸ x 13⁴
WALK-IN CLOSET
CL
DN
OPEN BELOW
LINEN
RAILING
BEDROOM
12⁰ x 11⁰
BEDROOM
12¹⁰ x 13⁶
BATH

Design by
Home Planners, Inc.

Design Q9854

Square Footage: 2,770

● This English cottage with cedar shake exterior displays the best qualities of a traditional design. With the bay window and recessed entry visitors feel warmly welcomed. The foyer opens to both the dining room with vaulted ceiling and great room with fireplace and built-in cabinetry. Surrounded by windows, the breakfast room opens to a gourmet kitchen and laundry room conveniently located near the garage entrance. To the right of the foyer is a hall powder room. Two bedrooms with large closets are joined by a full bath with individual vanities and window seat. Through double doors at the end of a short hall, the master suite awaits with tray ceiling and adjoining sunlit sitting room. The master bath has His and Hers closets, separate vanities, individual shower and a garden tub with bay window.

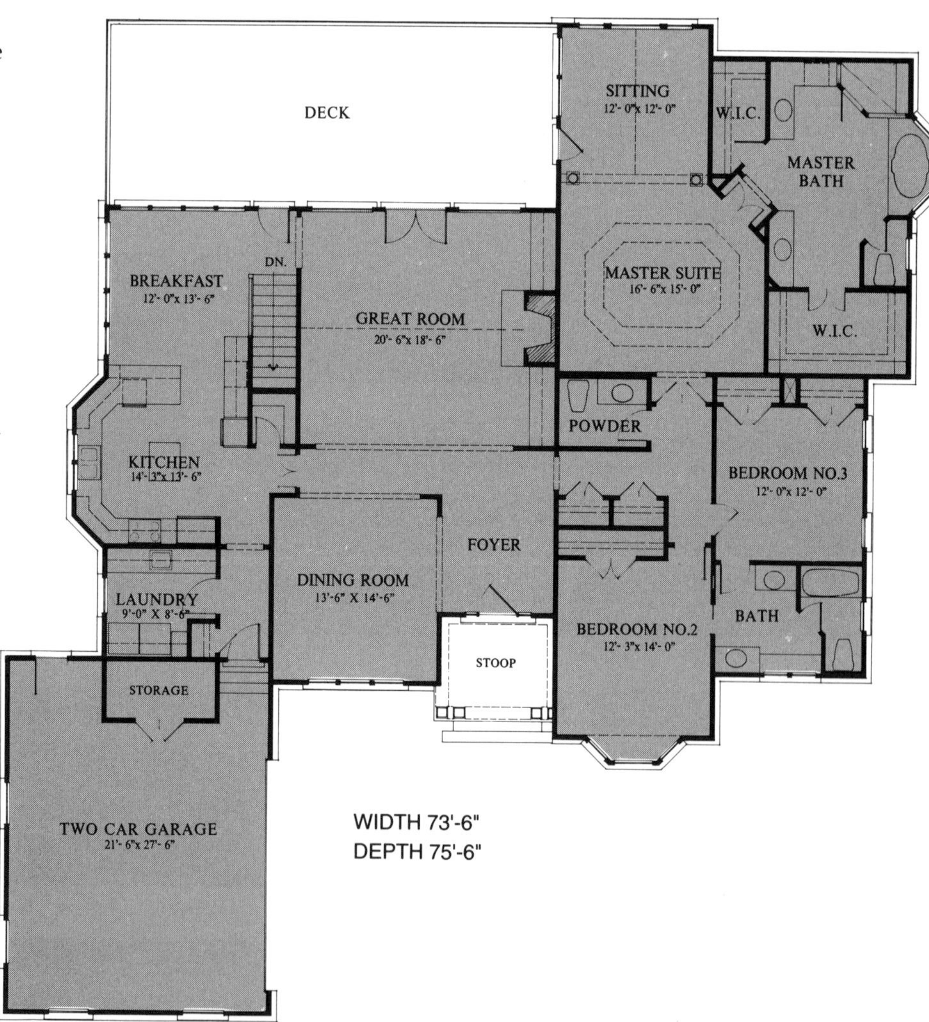

Design by
Design Traditions
Atlanta

Design by
Design Traditions
Atlanta

Design Q9853

Square Footage: 2,090

● This traditional home features board and batten and cedar shingles in an attractively proportioned exterior. Finishing touches include a covered entrance and porch with column detailing and arched transom, flower boxes and shuttered windows. The foyer opens to both the dining room and great room beyond with French doors opening onto the porch. Through the double doors to the right of the foyer is the combination bedroom/study. A short hallway leads to a full bath and a secondary bedroom with ample closet space. The master bedroom is spacious, with walk-in closets on both sides of the entrance to the master bath. With separate vanities, shower and toilet, the master bath is of symmetrical design, and forms a private retreat at the rear of the home. Convenient to both the great room and dining room, the kitchen opens to an attractive breakfast area featuring a bay window. An additional room is remotely located off the kitchen, providing a retreat for today's at-home office or guest.

Design Q9852

First Floor: 1,840 square feet
Second Floor: 950 square feet
Total: 2,790 square feet

Design by
Design Traditions
Atlanta

● The appearance of this early American home brings the past to mind with its wraparound porch, wood siding and flower-box detailing. The uniquely shaped foyer leads to the dining room accented by columns, vaulted ceiling and bay window. Columns frame the great room as well, while a ribbon of windows creates a wall of glass at the back of the house from the great room to the breakfast area. The asymmetrical theme continues through the kitchen as it leads back to the hallway, accessing the laundry and two-car garage. Left of the foyer lies the living room with a warming fireplace. The master suite begins with double doors that open to a space with octagonal tray ceiling and bay window. The spacious master bath and walk-in closet complete the suite. Stairs to the second level lead from the breakfast area to an open landing overlooking the great room. Three additional bedrooms with large walk-in closets and a variety of bath arrangements complete this level.

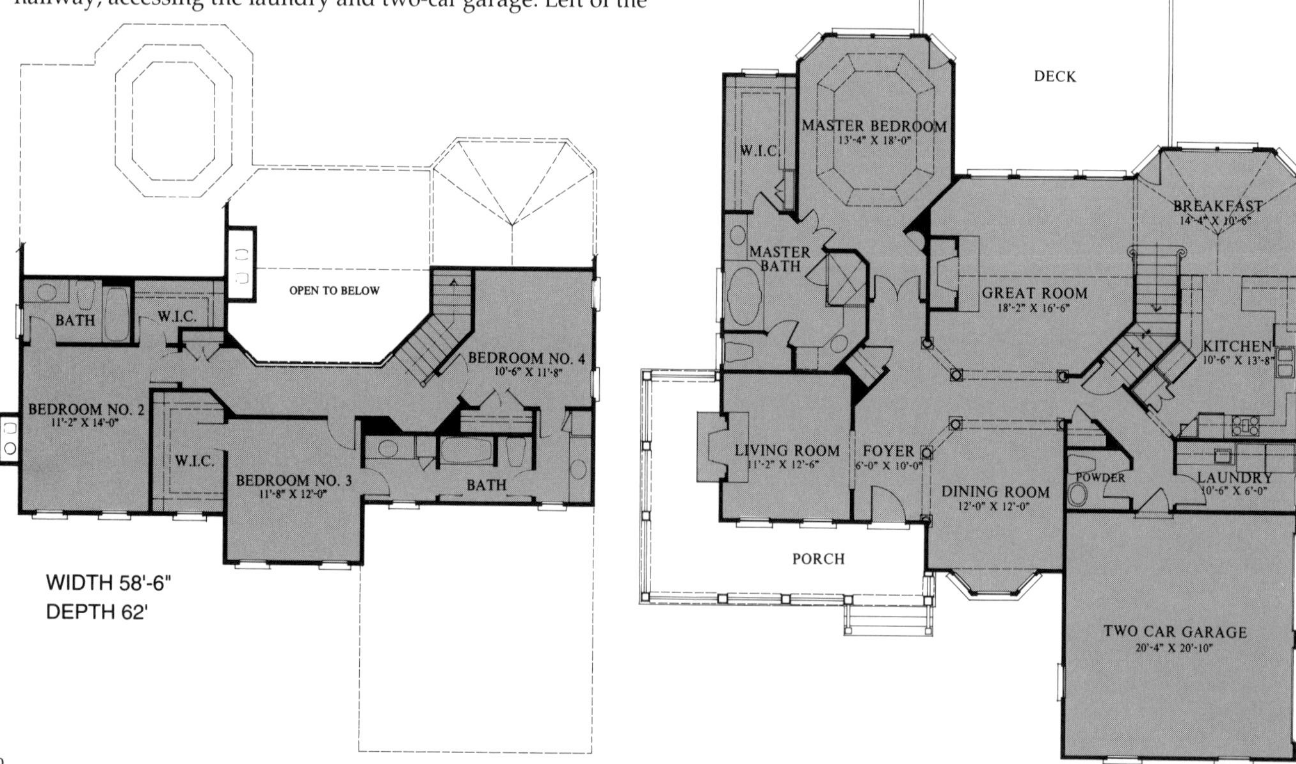

Design Q9868

First Floor: 1,725 square feet
Second Floor: 650 square feet
Total: 2,375 square feet

● This example of Classic American architecture features a columned front porch and wood framing. Bay window detailing and an arched dormer above the porch complete the picture. The foyer includes a closet and an open staircase to the upper level. Straight ahead, the great room is largely glass, and opens to the vaulted breakfast area which leads outdoors to the patio. The octagonal kitchen is designed for ease of movement and to promote the flow of family traffic. The dining room and living room share a hearth and an open design with bay window treatments for interest and natural light. The master bedroom at the right rear of the home features a tray ceiling and large bay window. The master bath with dual vanities, individual shower and walk-in closets completes the master suite. The upper level is comprised of a gallery and loft open to the great room and foyer below, which is warmed by the natural light from the dormer windows. Beyond the loft are two bedrooms that share a bath and an unfinished bonus room. Upper level attic storage is spacious and convenient with an entrance just at the top of the stairs.

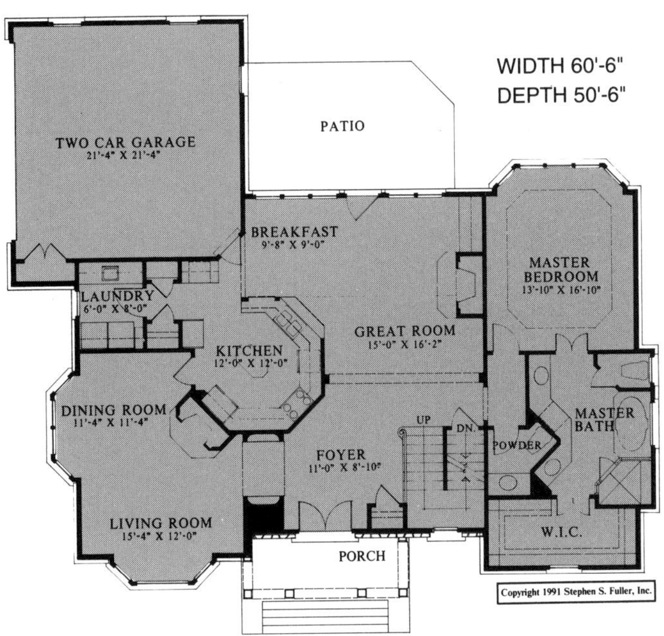

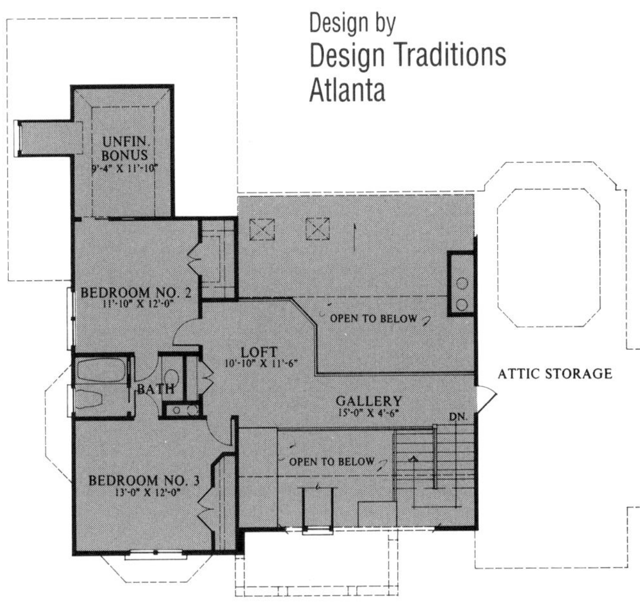

Design Q9232

First Floor: 1,551 square feet
Second Floor: 725 square feet
Total: 2,276 square feet

● This narrow-lot plan features a wraparound porch at the two-story entry, which opens to the formal dining room with beautiful bay windows. The great room features a handsome fireplace and a ten-and-a-half foot ceiling. A well-equipped island kitchen with pantry and built-in desk is available for the serious cook. The large master bedroom has a vaulted ceiling and a luxury master bath with two-person whirlpool, skylight and large walk-in closet. Three secondary bedrooms with ample closet space share a compartmented bath including double vanity and a large linen closet.

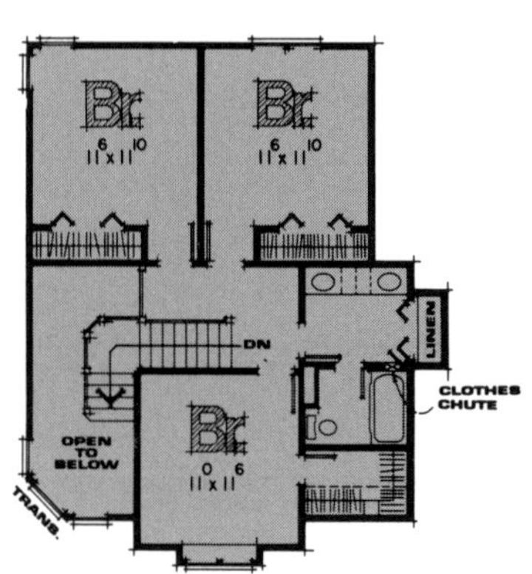

Design by
Design
Basics,
Inc.

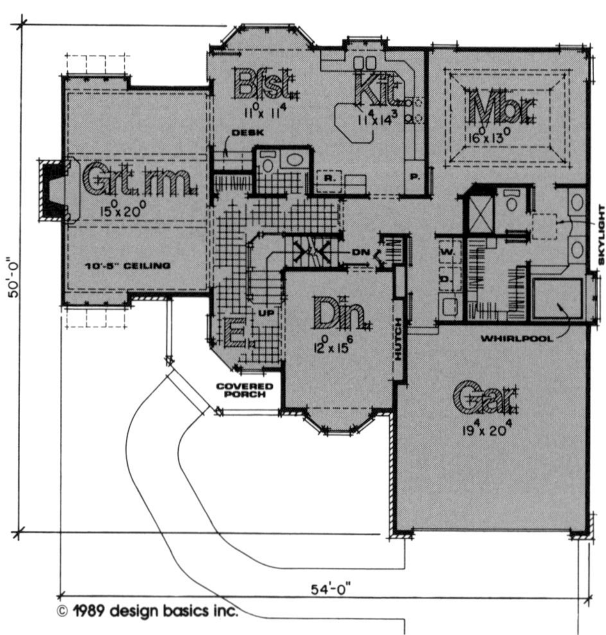

Design Q9252

First Floor: 1,113 square feet
Second Floor: 965 square feet
Total: 2,078 square feet

● Elegant detail, a charming veranda and a tall brick chimney make a pleasing facade on this four-bedroom, two-story Victorian home. Yesterday's simpler life-style is reflected throughout this plan. From the large bayed parlor with sloped ceiling to the sunken gathering room with fireplace, there's plenty to appreciate about the floor plan. The formal dining room opens to the parlor for convenient entertaining. An L-shaped kitchen with attached breakfast room is nearby. Upstairs quarters include a master suite with private dressing area and whirlpool, and three family bedrooms.

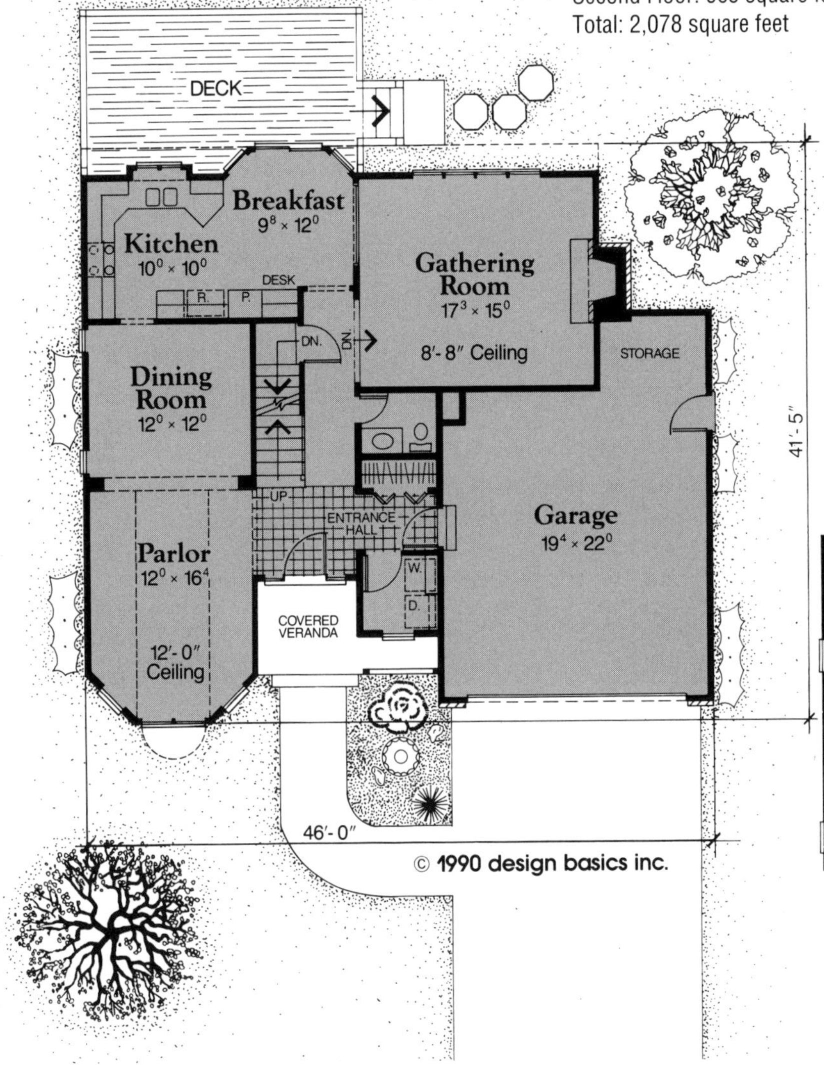

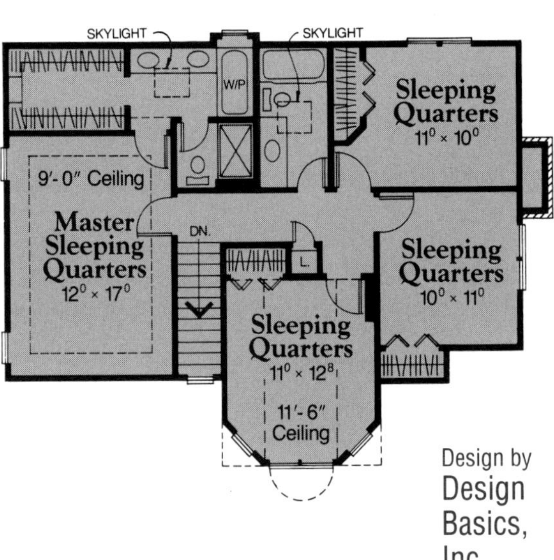

Design by Design Basics, Inc.

Design Q9008

First Floor: 1,653 square feet
Second Floor: 613 square feet
Total: 2,266 square feet

● While much less elaborate than other Victorian styles, the intersecting roof lines, arch-top windows with shutters, and detailed corner pilasters give this home a casual, yet distinctive appearance. An eight-foot-wide veranda provides plenty of room for outdoor entertaining. Inside, the large foyer opens to the formal dining area. A thirteen-foot raised ceiling with blocked panel trim and crown molding adds interest to the living room. French doors lead to a private library with built-in bookcases and a window seat. The secluded master suite offers a walk-in closet and an elegant bath with garden tub and glass-enclosed shower. Upstairs, the balcony features a built-in bookcase. Two large bedrooms each have walk-in closets and ceilings that slope from six feet to nine feet in height. Plans for a detached garage are included.

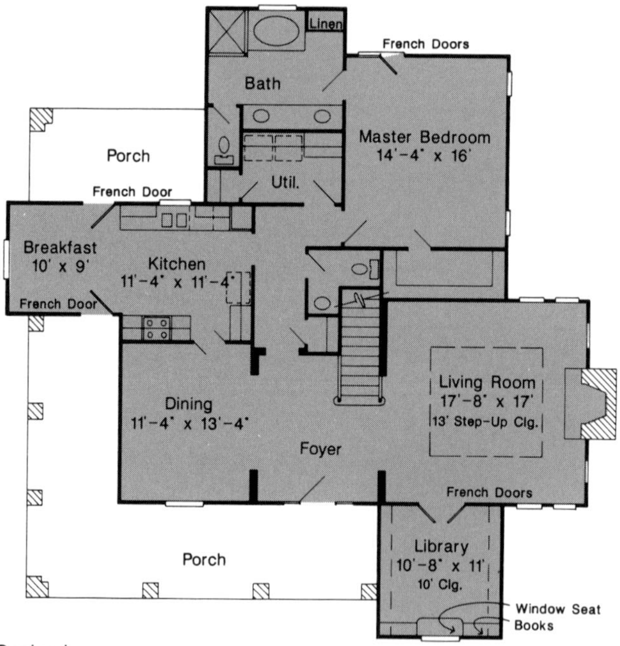

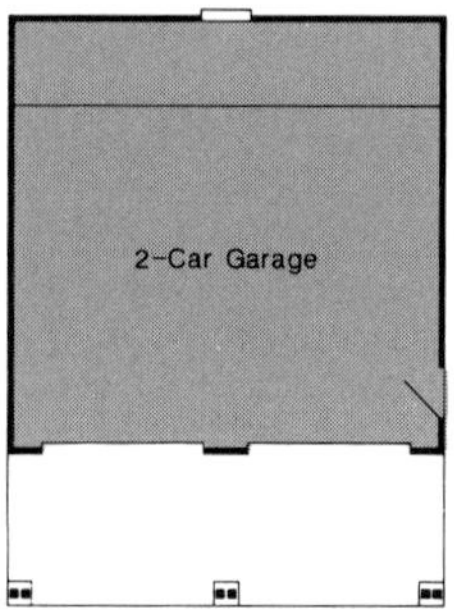

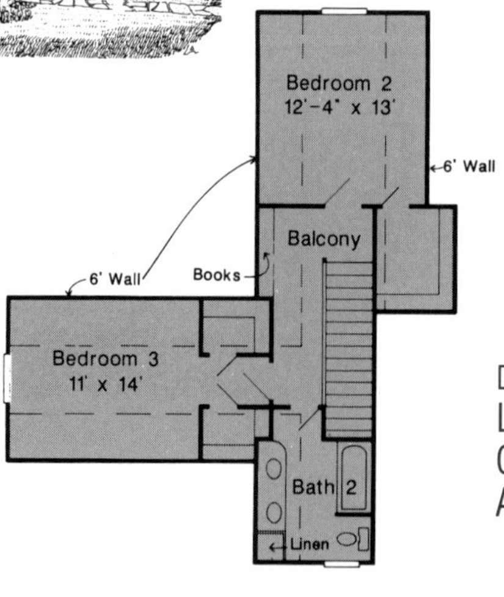

2-Car Garage

Bedroom 2
12'-4" x 13'
6' Wall
Balcony
Books
6' Wall
Bedroom 3
11' x 14'
Bath 2
Linen

Linen
French Doors
Bath
Master Bedroom
14'-4" x 16'
Porch
Util.
French Door
Breakfast
10' x 9'
Kitchen
11'-4" x 11'-4"
French Door
Dining
11'-4" x 13'-4"
Living Room
17'-8" x 17'
13' Step-Up Clg.
Foyer
French Doors
Porch
Library
10'-8" x 11'
10' Clg.
Window Seat
Books

Design by
Larry W. Garnett & Associates, Inc.

Width 54'
Depth 53' - 8"

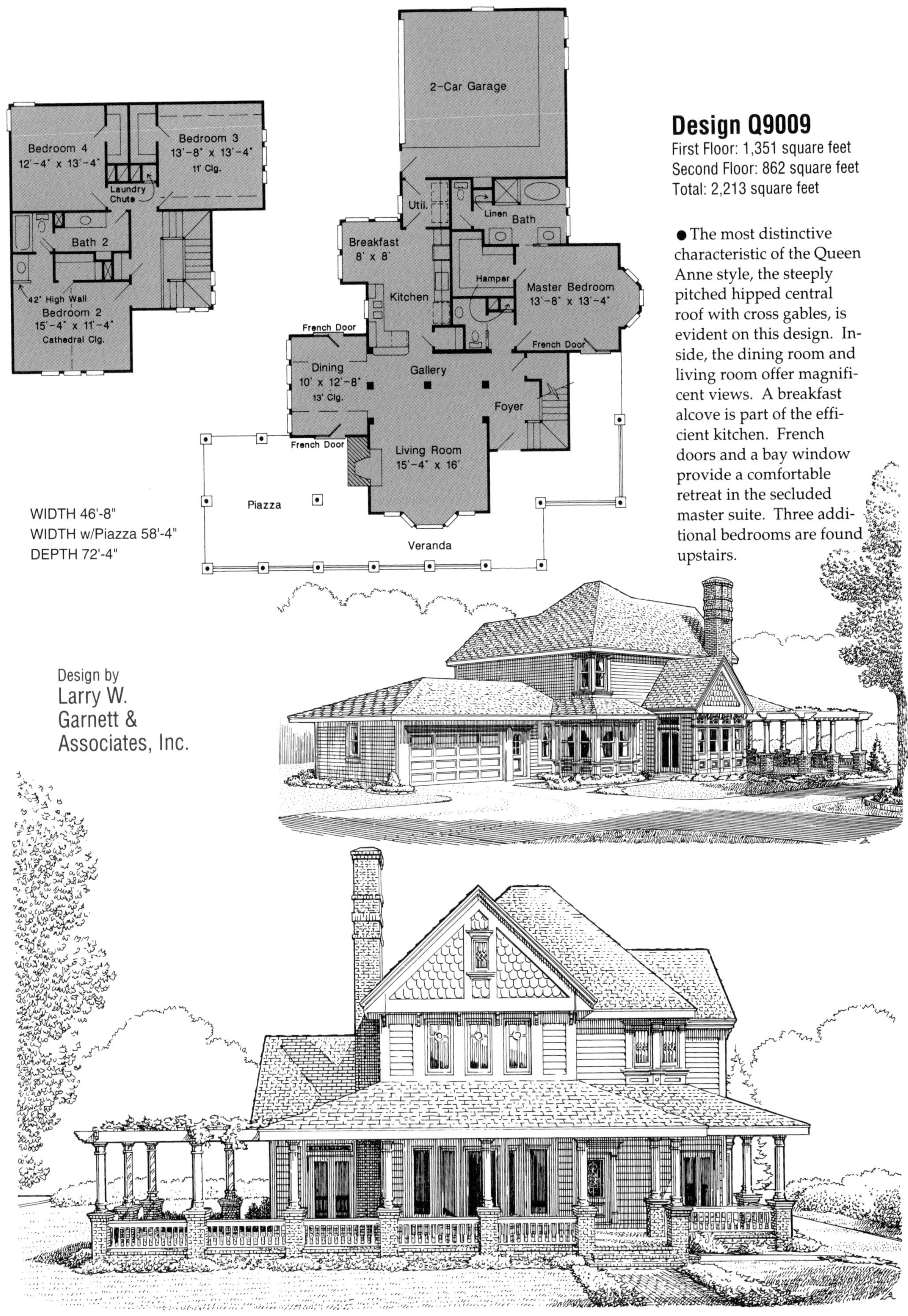

Design Q9009

First Floor: 1,351 square feet
Second Floor: 862 square feet
Total: 2,213 square feet

● The most distinctive characteristic of the Queen Anne style, the steeply pitched hipped central roof with cross gables, is evident on this design. Inside, the dining room and living room offer magnificent views. A breakfast alcove is part of the efficient kitchen. French doors and a bay window provide a comfortable retreat in the secluded master suite. Three additional bedrooms are found upstairs.

WIDTH 46'-8"
WIDTH w/Piazza 58'-4"
DEPTH 72'-4"

Design by
Larry W. Garnett & Associates, Inc.

Design Q9053 First Floor: 811 square feet; Second Floor: 1,067 square feet; Total: 1,878 square feet

● Elaborate spindlework and ornate porch posts, along with detailed block-paneled trim at the symmetrical gables, give this Queen Anne Style two-story charm and elegance. The living room has a fireplace as its focal point, while at the same time providing a view of the built-in media center. The large kitchen opens to the dining area, and also has access to the garage and laundry room. The master bedroom is truly a luxurious private retreat. The sitting area has a built-in media center for audio and video equipment. The master bath contains a glass-enclosed shower and His and Hers lavatories. Two additional bedrooms, each with a walk-in closet, share a hall bath.

Width 45'
Depth 53'

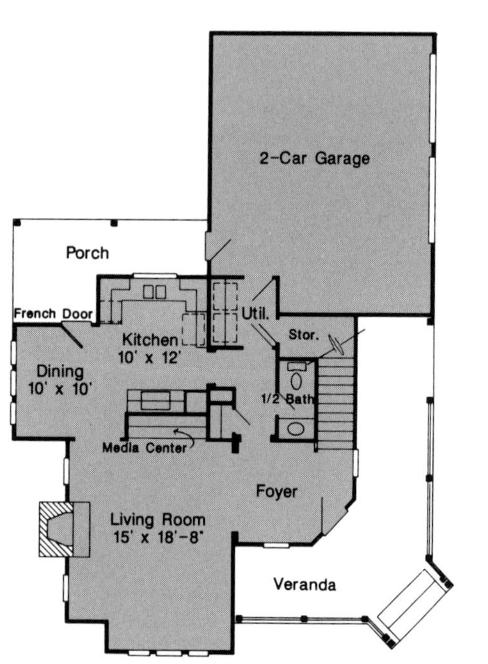

9' Clg. Throughout First and Second Floors

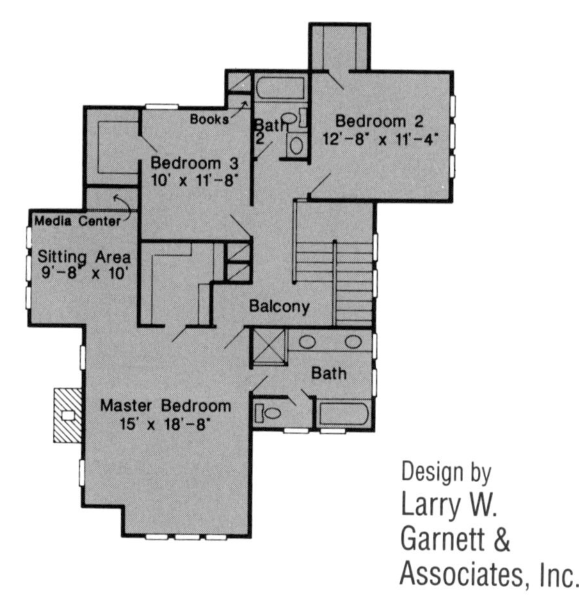

Design by
Larry W.
Garnett &
Associates, Inc.

Design Q9015

First Floor: 1,948 square feet
Second Floor: 1,891 square feet
Total: 3,839 square feet

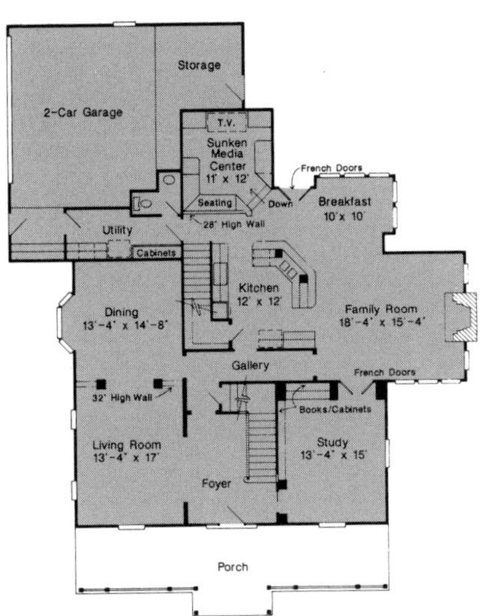

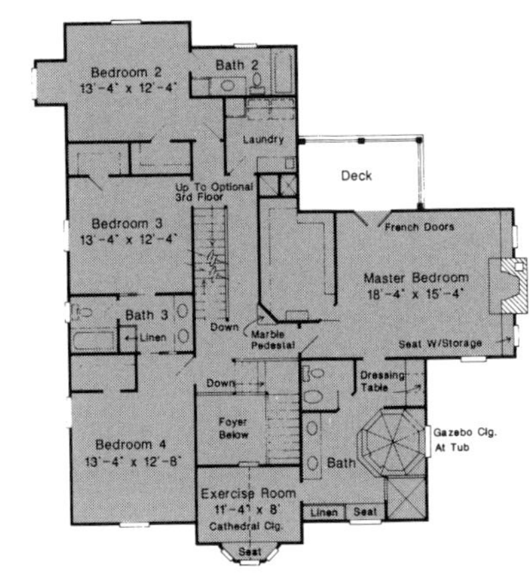

Width 59' - 4"
Depth 72' - 8"

● As authentic as the exterior of this design is, the interior offers all the luxury and elegance that today's homeowners could desire. The formal living and dining rooms are separated by detailed wood columns. Built-in bookcases and cabinets highlight the block-paneled study. The centrally located kitchen becomes the focal point of a truly outstanding family living center which includes a sunken media area, breakfast alcove, and a family room with a fireplace. Adjacent to the kitchen is a large hobby room with a built-in desk, a space for a freezer, and generous cabinet storage. A rear staircase provides convenient access to the second floor. The secluded master suite is beyond compare, with such extras as a fireplace with flanking window seats and cabinets, an enormous walk-in closet, and a private deck. The luxurious bath features a dressing table, a whirlpool tub with a gazebo-shaped ceiling above, and an oversized shower. Finally, there is a private exercise room with a bay-window seat. Three additional bedrooms and a laundry room complete the second floor. A staircase leads to an optional third floor area.

Design by
Larry W. Garnett & Associates, Inc.

Design Q2970 First Floor: 1,538 square feet
Second Floor: 1,526 square feet; Third Floor: 658 square feet
Total: 3,722 square feet

● A porch, is a porch, is a porch. But, when it wraps around to a side, or even two sides, of the house, we have called it a veranda. This charming Victorian features a covered outdoor living area on all four sides! It even ends at a screened porch which features a sun deck above. This interesting plan offers three floors of livability. And what livability it is! Plenty of formal and informal living facilities to go along with the potential of five bedrooms. The master suite is just that. It is adjacent to an interesting sitting room. It has a sun deck and excellent bath/personal care facilities. The third floor will make a wonderful haven for the family's student members.

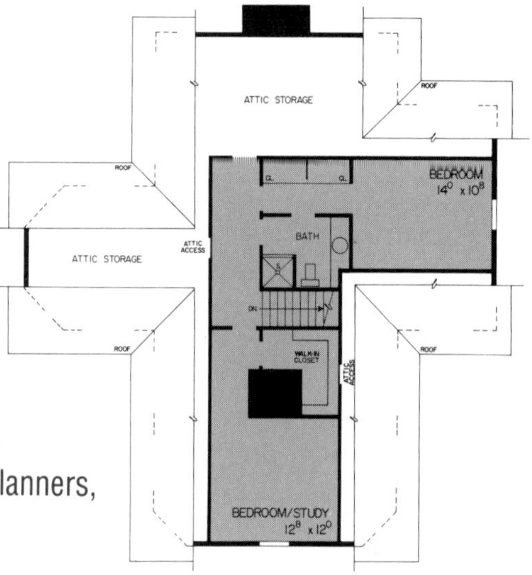

Design by
Home Planners, Inc.

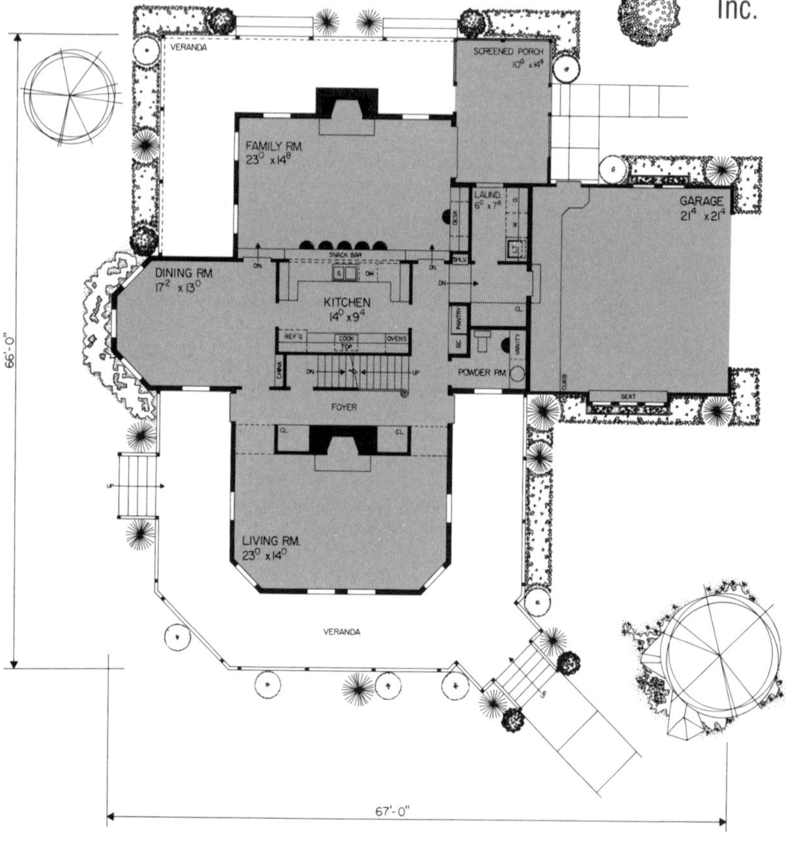

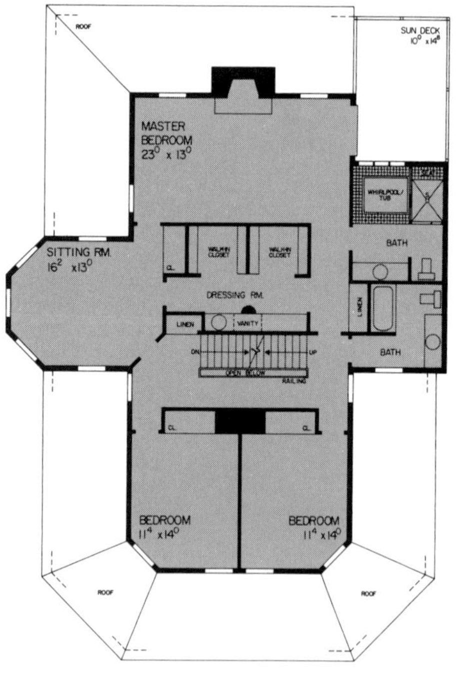

Design Q2974 First Floor: 911 square feet
Second Floor: 861 square feet; Total: 1,772 square feet

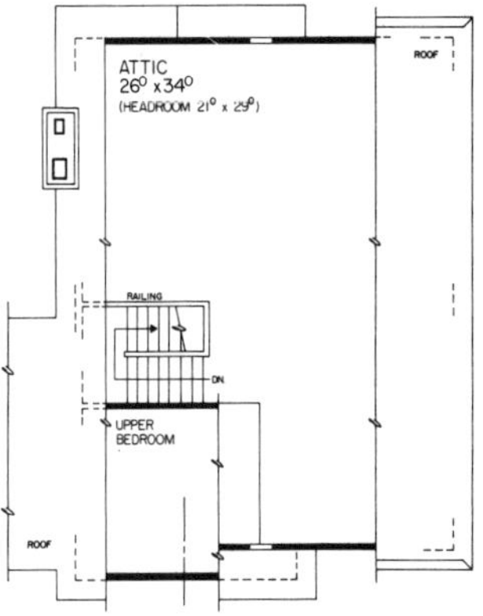

● Victorian houses are well known for their orientation on narrow building sites. And when this occurs nothing is lost to captivating exterior styling. This house is but 38 feet wide. Its narrow width belies the tremendous amount of livability found inside. And, of course, the ubiquitous porch/veranda contributes mightily to style as well as livability. The efficient, U-shape kitchen is flanked by the informal breakfast room and formal dining room. The rear living area is spacious and functions in an exciting manner with the outdoor areas. Bonus recreational, hobby and storage space is offered by the basement and the attic.

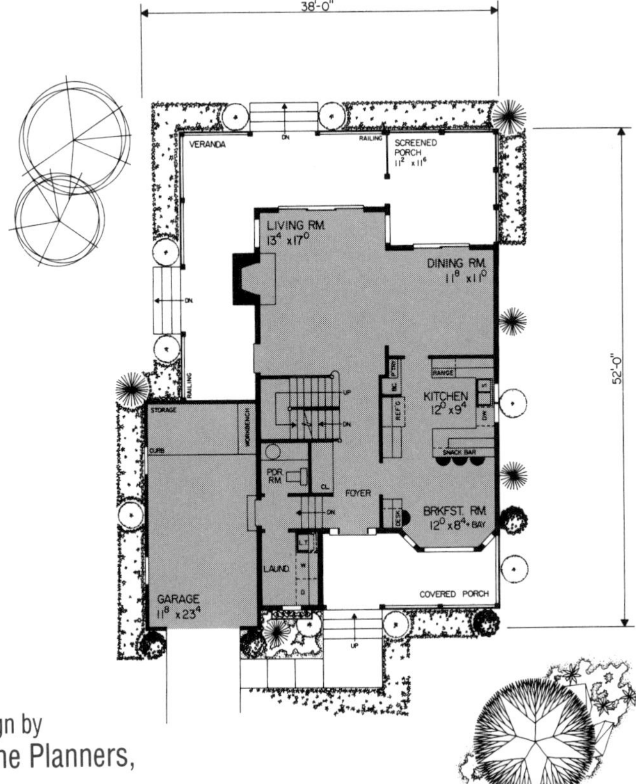

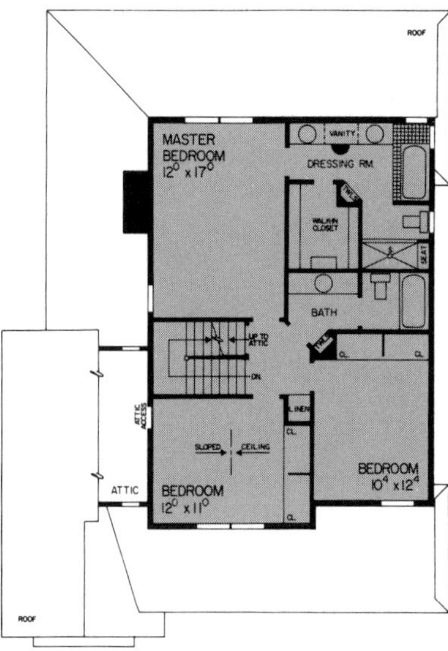

Design by
Home Planners, Inc.

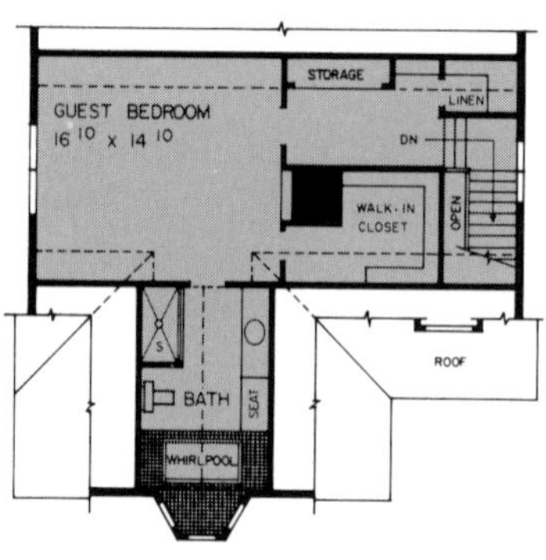

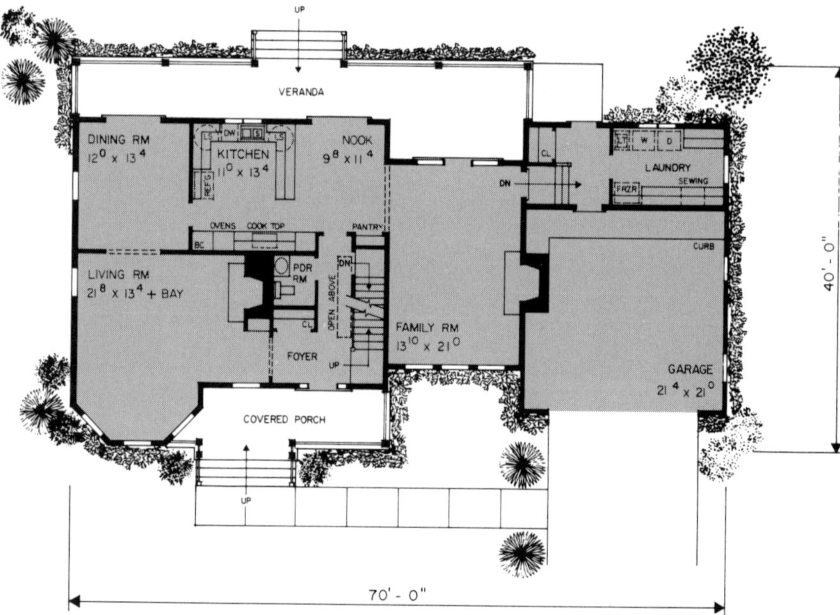

Design Q3394

First Floor: 1,531 square feet
Second Floor: 1,307 square feet
Third Floor: 664 square feet
Total: 3,502 square feet

● Though somewhat less elaborate than other Victorian types, the Folk Victorian is nevertheless an important and delightful interpretation as evidenced by this three-story example. From lovely covered front porch to classic rear veranda, it offers the finest in modern floor plans. The formal living areas are set off by a family room which connects the main house to the service areas. The laundry has room for not only a washer and dryer but also a freezer and sewing area. The second floor holds three bedrooms and two full baths. A sitting area in the master suite separates it from family bedrooms. On the third floor is a guest bedroom with gracious bath and large walk-in closet. Note the large storage area in the third-floor hall.

Design by
Home Planners, Inc.

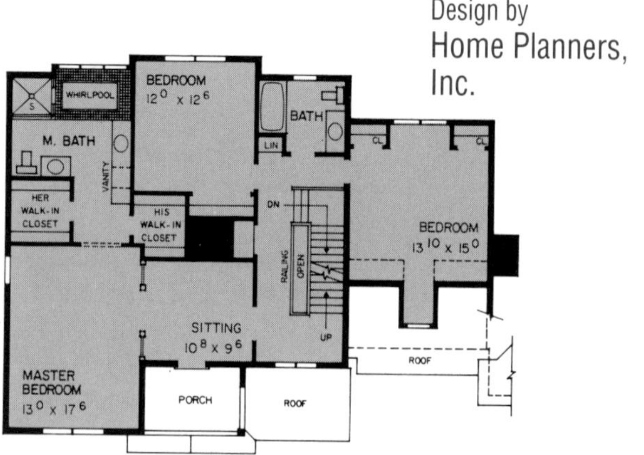

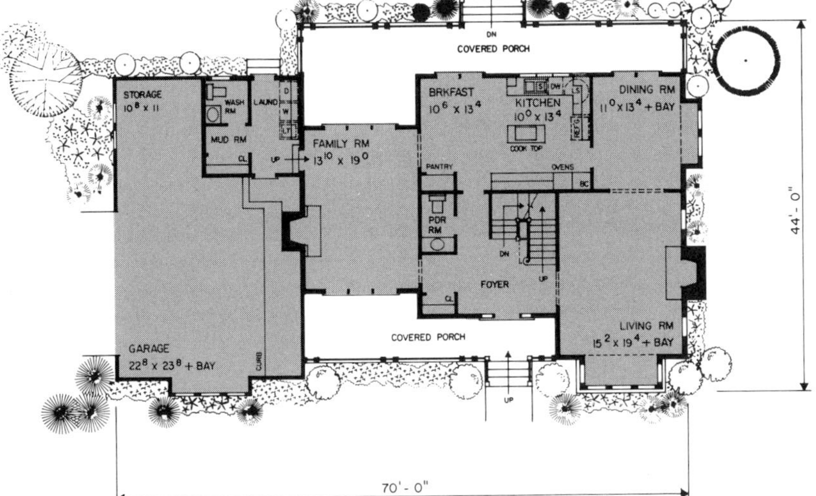

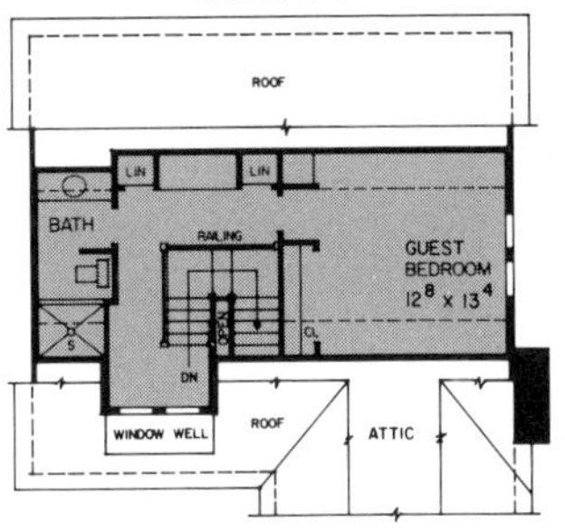

Design Q3388

First Floor: 1,517 square feet
Second Floor: 1,267 square feet
Third Floor: 480 square feet
Total: 3,264 square feet

Design by
Home Planners, Inc.

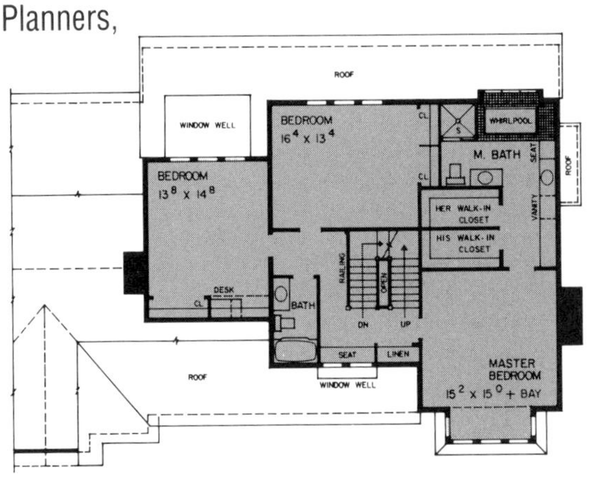

● A testament to real Folk Victorian styling, this delightful home offers the best in thoughtful floor planning. From the covered front porch the home opens to a well-executed entry foyer. To the left is the casual family room with fireplace and proximity to the laundry and mud rooms. To the right is the formal living room with bay window and fireplace. This room connects to the formal dining area, also with bay window. The kitchen/breakfast room combination features sliding glass doors to the rear covered porch, an island cook top and large pantry. Second-floor bedrooms include a well-planned master suite and two family bedrooms served by a full bath. A guest room dominates the third floor and features its own private bath.

Design Q9251

First Floor: 1,653 square feet
Second Floor: 700 square feet
Total: 2,353 square feet

● Beautiful arches and elaborate detail give the elevation of this four-bedroom, 1½-story home an unmistakable elegance. Inside the floor plan is equally appealing. Note the formal dining room with bay window, visible from the entrance hall. The large great room has a fireplace and a wall of windows out the back. A hearth room, with bookcase, adjoins the kitchen area with walk-in pantry. The master suite on the first floor features His and Hers wardrobes, a large whirlpool and double lavatories. Upstairs quarters share a full bath with compartmented sinks.

Design by
Design Basics, Inc.

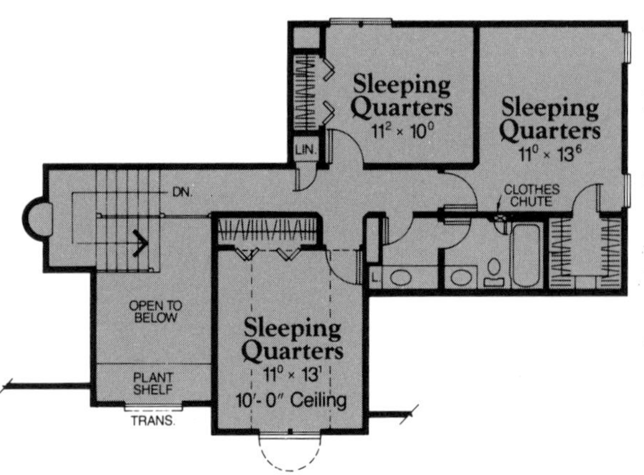

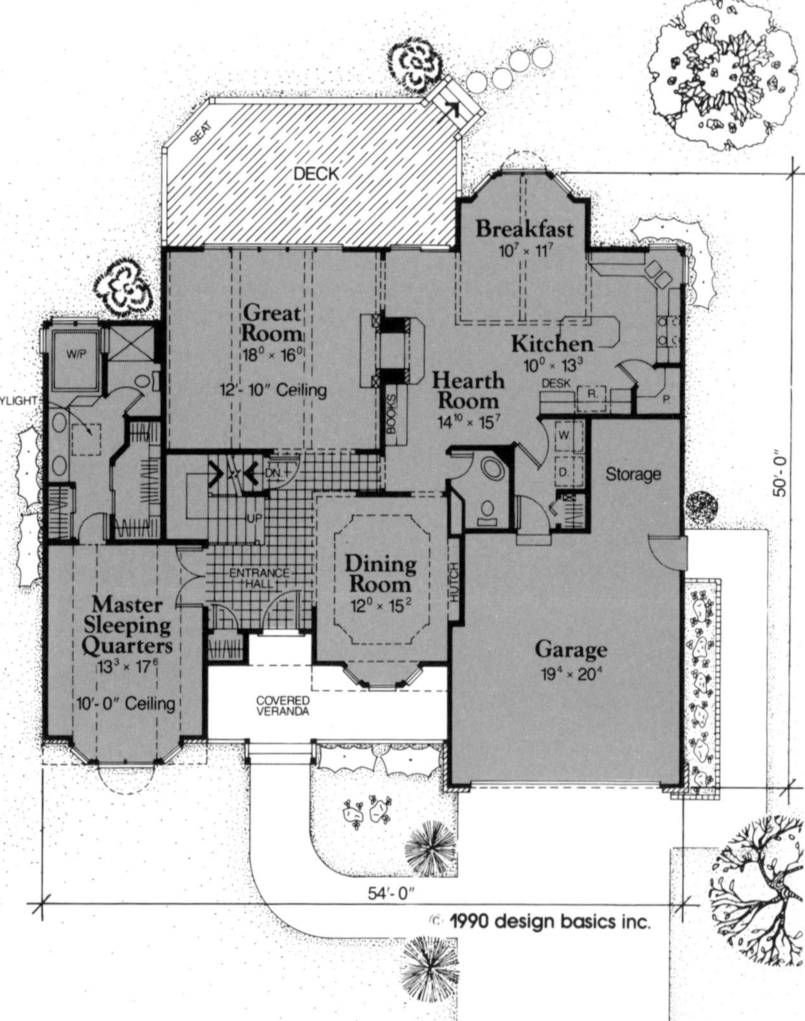

Design Q3386

First Floor: 1,683 square feet
Second Floor: 1,388 square feet
Third Floor: 808 square feet
Total: 3,879 square feet

● This beautiful Folk Victorian has all the properties of others in its class. Living areas include a formal Victorian parlor, a private study and large gathering room. The formal dining room has its more casual counterpart in a bay-windowed breakfast room. Both are near the well-appointed kitchen. Five bedrooms serve family and guest needs handily. Three bedrooms on the second floor include a luxurious master suite. For outdoor entertaining, there is a covered rear porch leading to a terrace.

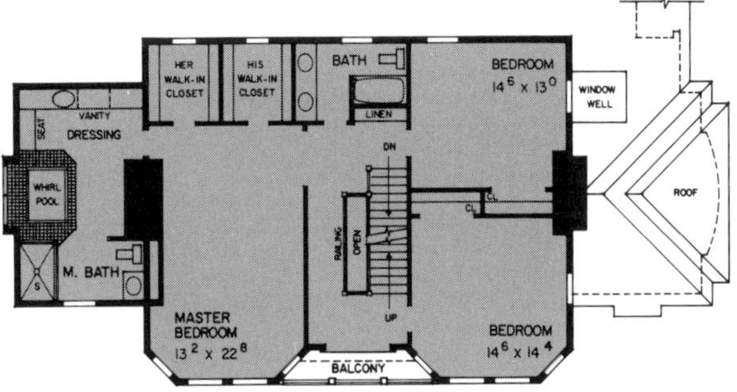

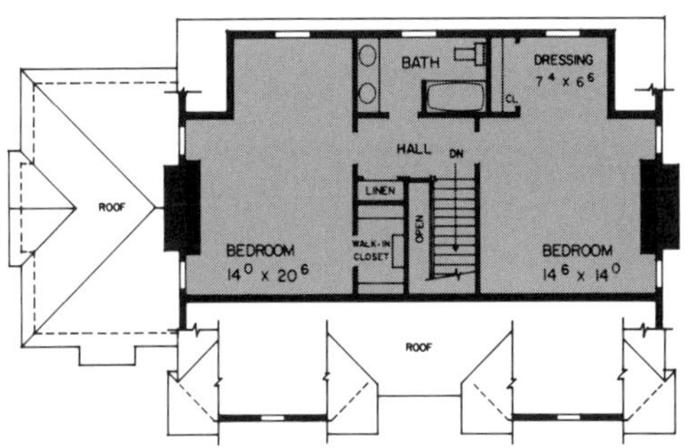

Design by
Home Planners, Inc.

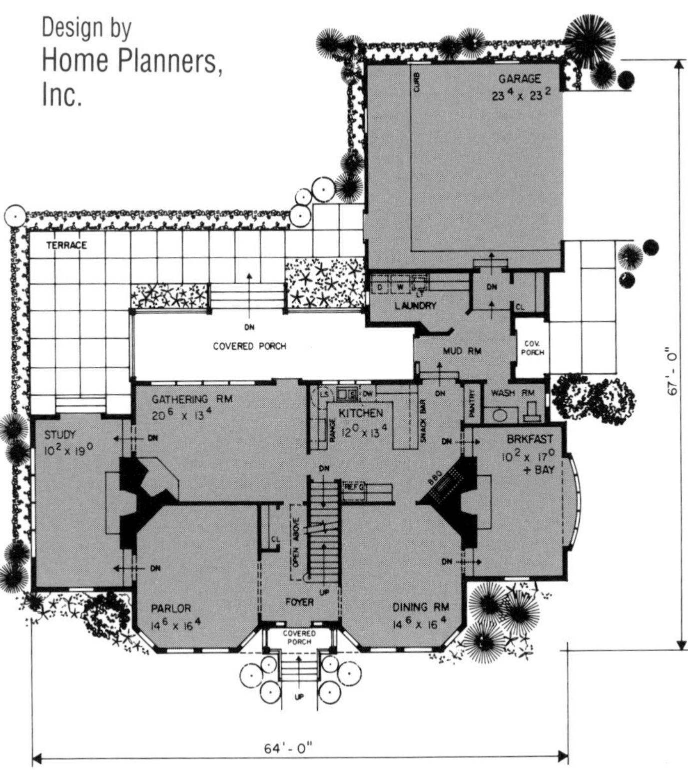

Design Q9269

First Floor: 1,081 square feet; Second Floor: 1,136 square feet
Total: 2,217 square feet

● Victorian charm and detailing radiate from the elevation of this four-bedroom, two-story design. Inside, formal living spaces, visible from the entry, begin with a dining room with hutch space and a parlor highlighted by a bayed window and alluring angles. the T-shaped staircase allows quick access to the informal spaces at the rear, such as the comfortable gathering room with a fireplace, built-in bookcase and many windows. Casual traffic patterns flow through a sunny, open breakfast area and island kitchen. Upstairs, a compartmented bath is shared by the secondary sleeping quarters. Gracing the master sleeping quarters is an elegant vaulted ceiling and private dressing/bath area offering an oval whirlpool, angled vanity and walk-in wardrobe.

Design by
Design
Basics,
Inc.

CENTER-HALL COLONIAL FARMHOUSES

Colonial architecture is a reflection of a period of dedication to hard work, simple pleasures and solid virtues. As such, it brought together design characteristics that speak of symmetry and regularity of form. Straight lines and design details that were practical as well as ornamental took precedence over frivolous decoration. Floor plans featured square or rectangular rooms and stacked livability.

Popular today in the Northeastern region, particularly New England, the Center-Hall Colonial Farmhouse is an adaptation of the early homes built in the region and, as such, is a testament to symmetry and rigid adherence to traditional values. It is a classic, upright structure with a straight roof gable. The entry may be the only indication of ornamentation and can be detailed with a decorative frieze, pediment or portico over the front door. These details derive from Colonial and Georgian influences.

The characteristic central door opens to a center hall, from which all first-story rooms flow. This is usually where the stairwell to the second floor is found as well. These homes incorporate full two-story construction usually with all bedrooms found on the second floor.

Windows are regular, symmetrical and usually multi-paned and shuttered. Fireplace stacks are large, constructed of brick and may be placed centrally or to one end of the home. Horizontal wood siding is the most common exterior choice, but it is not unusual to see Center-Hall Colonials constructed in brick or part brick and part stone.

Garages and service areas tend to be appended to the main house with a service wing or entrance. In some cases, the connecting piece may be a family room or study.

Two fine examples of the Center-Hall Colonial Farmhouse are Design Q2188 and Design Q2610. Both have the symmetrical facade and straight-gabled roof that is common to Colonial architecture.

Design Q2188 features a strong center, brick chimney stack, a transommed double-door entry and a garage attached to the main house by a service entry. Added details include a weathervane at the end of the garage and symmetrical, shuttered windows.

Design Q2610 has two imposing brick chimneys and a front entry with transom and side lights. The garage on this plan attaches directly to the house and the windows remain unshuttered.

The fine grouping of Center-Hall Colonial Farmhouses offered in this section are apt reminders of America's architectural heritage. Large enough for virtually any family, they bring modern livability to a cherished historic style.

Design Q2654

First Floor: 1,152 square feet
Second Floor: 844 square feet
Total: 1,006 square feet

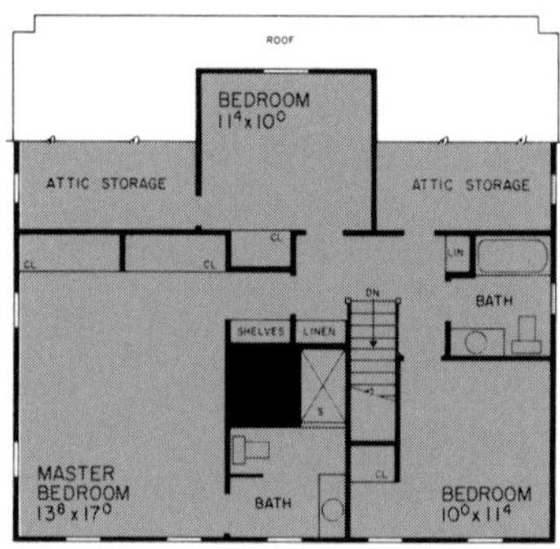

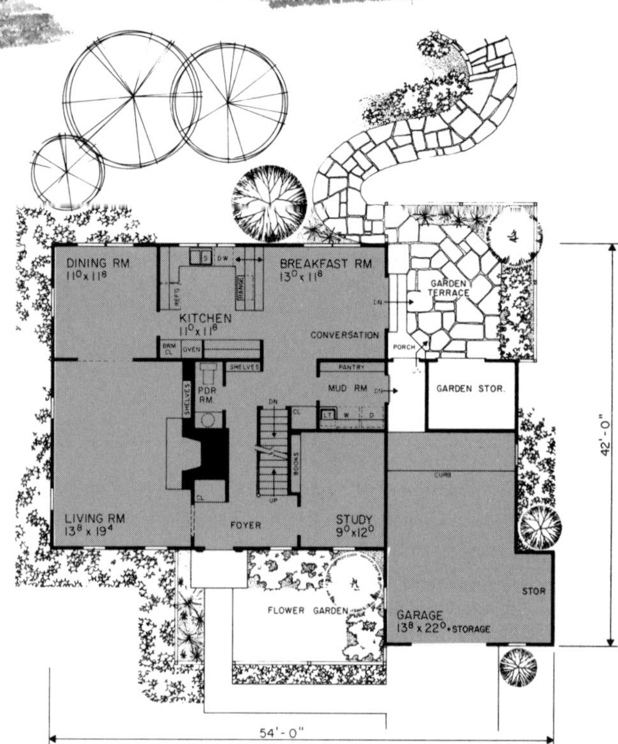

● This is certainly an authentic traditional saltbox. It features a symmetrical design with a center fireplace, a wide, paneled doorway and multi-paned, double-hung windows. Tucked behind the one-car garage is a garden shed which provides work and storage space. The breakfast room features French doors which open onto a flagstone terrace. The U-shaped kitchen has built-in counters which make efficient use of space. The upstairs plan houses three bedrooms.

Design by
Home Planners,
Inc.

Design by
Home Planners,
Inc.

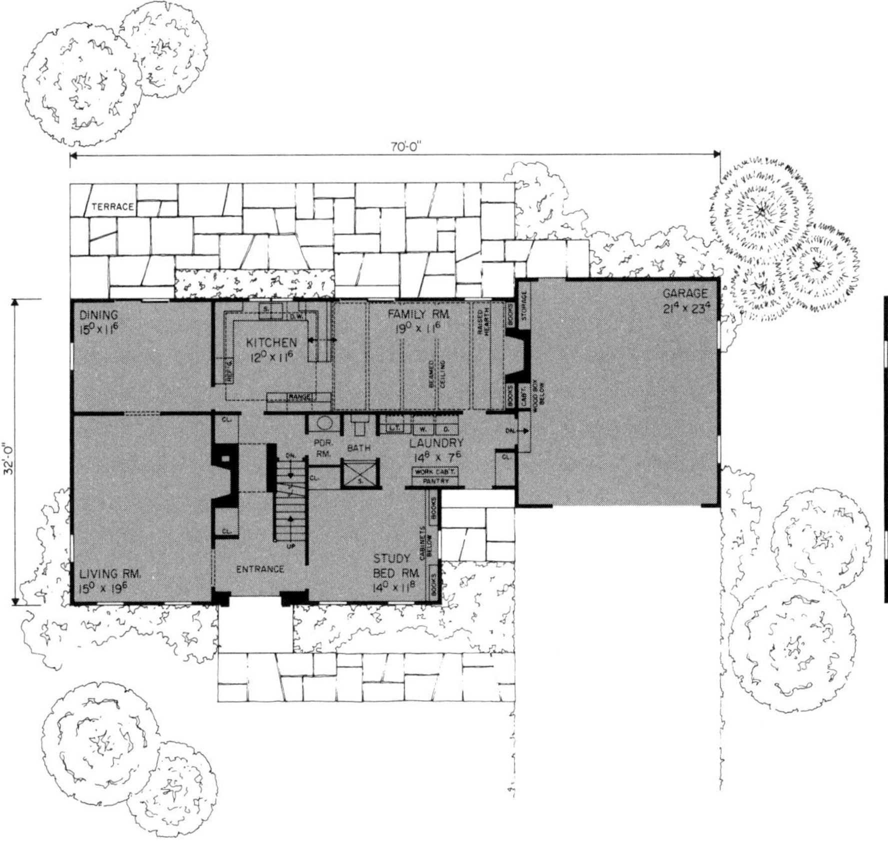

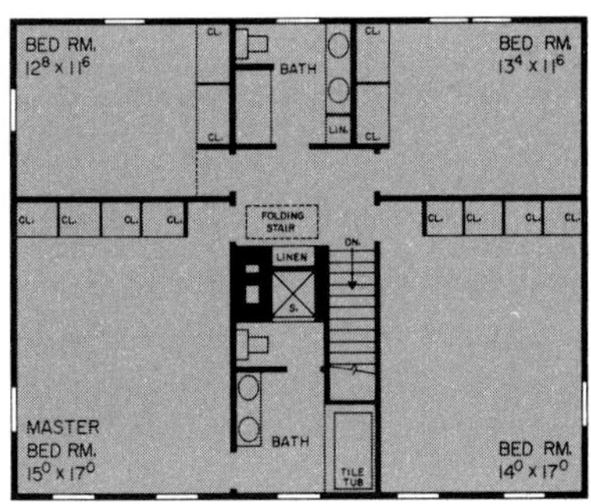

Design Q2188

First Floor: 1,440 square feet
Second Floor: 1,280 square feet
Total: 2,720 square feet

● This design is characteristic of early America and its presence will create an atmosphere of that time in our heritage. However, it will be right at home wherever located. Along with exterior charm, this design has outstanding livability to offer its occupants. Beginning with the first floor, there are formal and informal areas plus the work centers. Note the center bath which has direct access from three adjacent areas. Built-in book shelves are the feature of both the family room and the study/bedroom. Built-ins are also featured in the garage. Ascending up to the second floor, one will be in the private sleeping area. This area consists of the master suite, three bedrooms and full bath. Folding stairs are in the upstairs hall for easy access to the attic.

Design Q9300

First Floor: 1,137 square feet
Second Floor: 917 square feet
Total: 2,054 square feet

● Colonial detailing and gracious amenities makes this home ideal for a variety of lifestyles. A bright dining room opens to a hard-surfaced entry. Access the private den with bookcase via French doors. Family gatherings are comfortable in the great room with fireplace, built-in bookcase and large bayed windows at the rear. An island kitchen benefits from a pantry, desk and sunny breakfast area with outdoor access. The upstairs landing is brightened by a skylight. In the master bedroom there is a vaulted ceiling, plus a dressing area featuring a walk-in closet with mirrored bi-pass doors and window seat. Secondary bedrooms share a hall bath with window seat while the front bedroom has its own window seat. Truly, this is a delightful home inside and out!

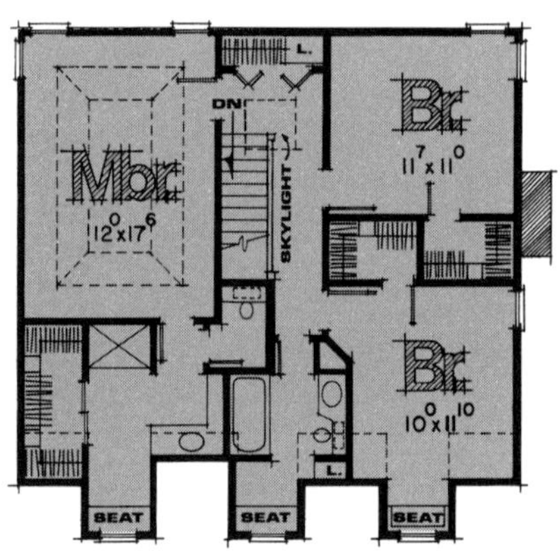

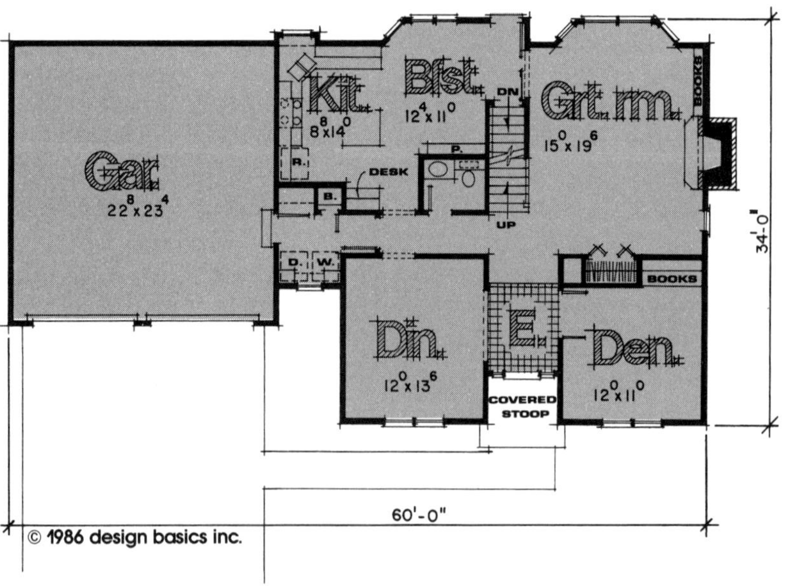

Design by
Design
Basics,
Inc.

Design Q9301

First Floor: 1,279 square feet
Second Floor: 1,241 square feet
Total: 2,520 square feet

● Colonial flavor is evident on the elevation of this four-bedroom, two-story home. A separate service entry with a closet directly accesses the laundry/mud room. Entertaining will be enjoyable in the formal dining and living rooms. In the large family room, there is a beautiful segmented arched transom window and fireplace. Nearby is the island kitchen with snack bar, built-in desk, two generous pantries and sunny dinette. On the second level, two front secondary bedrooms feature window seats. Adjacent to a third secondary bedroom is an unfinished storage area. Two lavs grace the large hall bath. A vaulted master bedroom with His and Hers closets has double doors leading into a dressing room. This area contains a large whirlpool and two lavs. At 2,520 square feet, many family-style amenities are designed into this home.

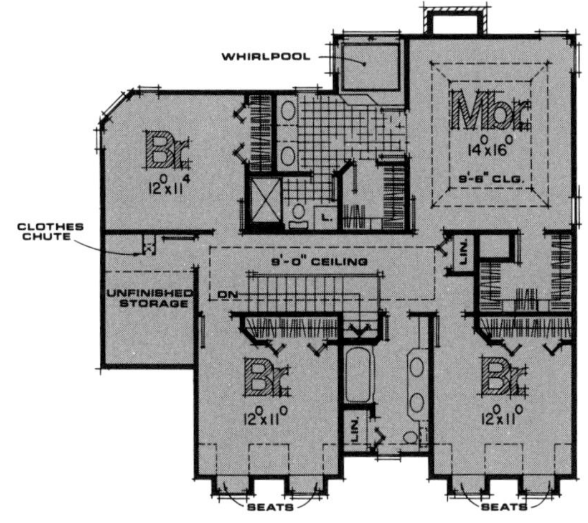

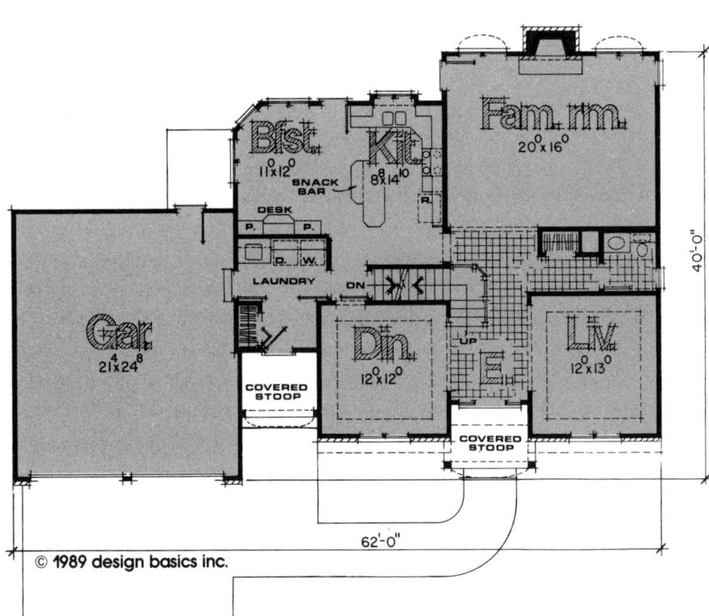

Design by
Design
Basics,
Inc.

Design Q2657

First Floor: 1,217 square feet
Second Floor: 868 square feet
Total: 2,085 square feet

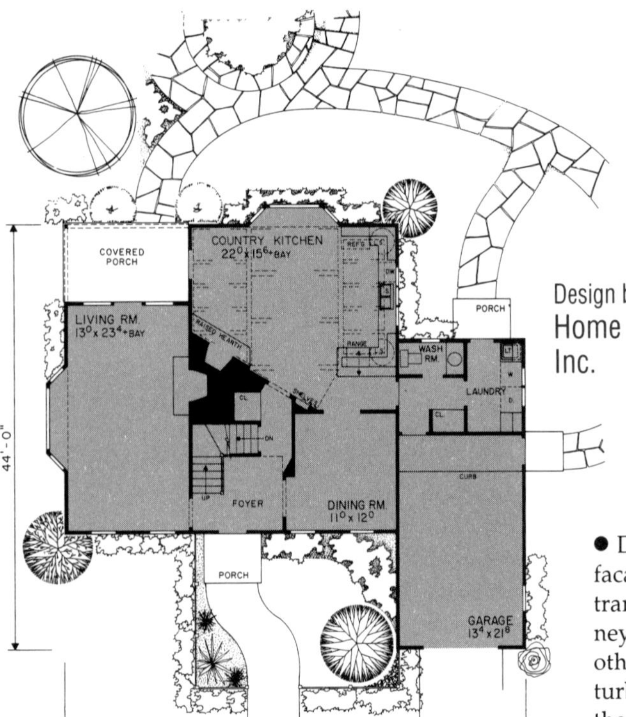

Design by
Home Planners, Inc.

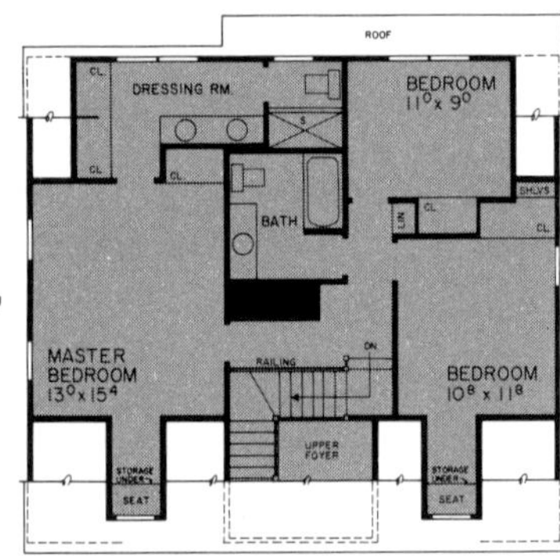

● Deriving its design from the traditional Cape Cod style, this facade features clapboard siding, small-paned windows and a transom-lit entrance flanked by carriage lamps. A central chimney services two fireplaces, one in the country-kitchen and the other in the formal living room which is removed from the disturbing flow of traffic. The master suite is located to the left of the upstairs landing. A full bathroom services two additional bedrooms on the second floor.

Design Q1701

First Floor: 1,344 square feet
Second Floor: 948 square feet
Total: 2,292 square feet

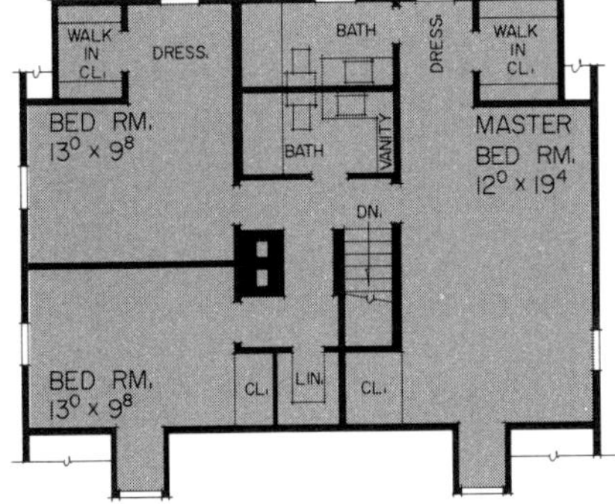

● The garage wing of this Cape closely resembles the main dwelling: narrow clapboards, shutters and lintels over the multi-paned windows all match exactly. A narrow, shaded porch leads into the family room, which has twin bookcases framing the raised hearth as well as a rustic beamed ceiling. The study downstairs easily converts to a guest bedroom and is conveniently served by a bath that boasts its own shower. This bath opens to the back hall so that it can be reached easily from the back rooms in the house. Two of the upstairs bedrooms have both dressing rooms and walk-in closets. The secondary bedrooms can, like the master bedroom, be opened up into one commodious room by removing the wall in between them.

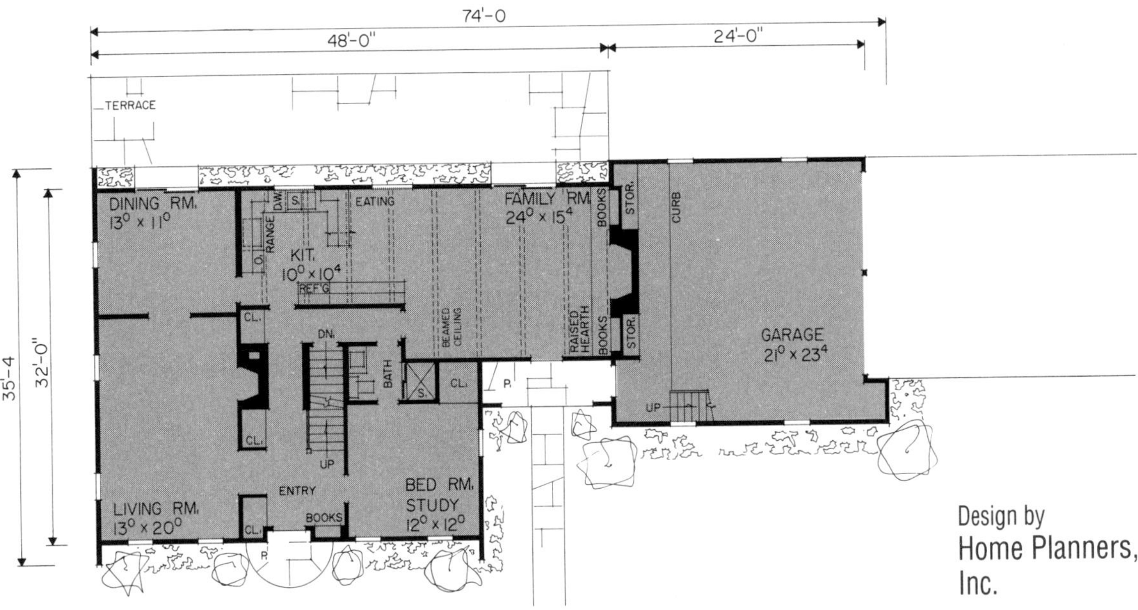

Design by
Home Planners, Inc.

Design Q1870

First Floor: 1,136 square feet
Second Floor: 936 square feet
Total: 2,072 square feet

● Besides an enchanting exterior, this home has formal dining and living rooms, plus informal family and breakfast rooms. Built-ins are located in both of these informal rooms. U-shaped, the kitchen will efficiently serve both of the dining areas. For outdoor living, a full width terrace graces the back of the home. It is accessed through sliding glass doors in the family room and the dining room, and is overlooked by the kitchen and breakfast room. The second floor holds three bedrooms or two bedrooms and a study. The master suite has its own bath with dressing room and walk-in closet. The other two bedrooms share a full bath.

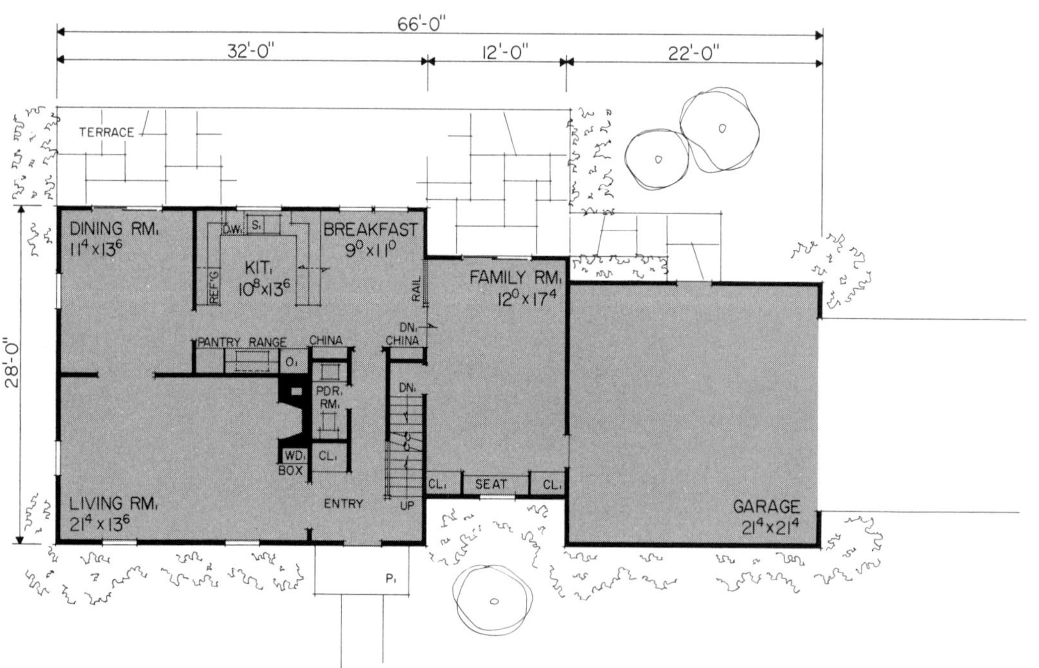

Design by
Home Planners, Inc.

Design Q1791

First Floor: 1,157 square feet
Second Floor: 875 square feet
Total: 2,032 square feet

● This moderately sized home speaks of Cape Cod styling on the outside and modern living on the inside. Charming dormers, shuttered windows and a side-lit front entry are delightful exterior details. The inside holds a formal living room, bay windowed dining room and family room with beamed ceiling. The efficient kitchen is a cook's delight. Besides the bedroom (or study) on the first floor, there are three bedrooms on the second floor. The master features its own bath with dressing room and double lavs. Two family bedrooms share a full bath. One of these bedrooms has a large walk-in closet.

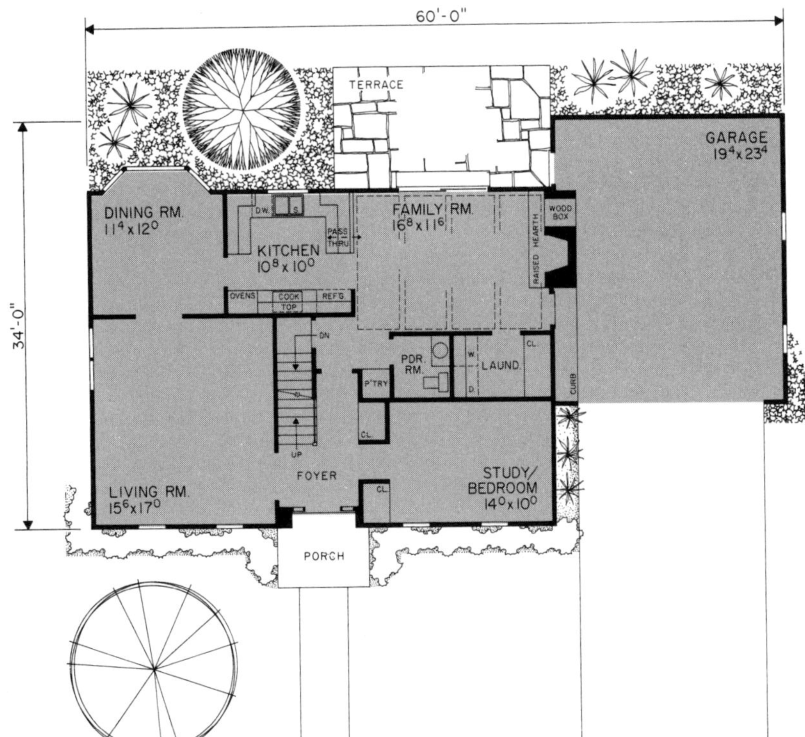

Design by
Home Planners,
Inc.

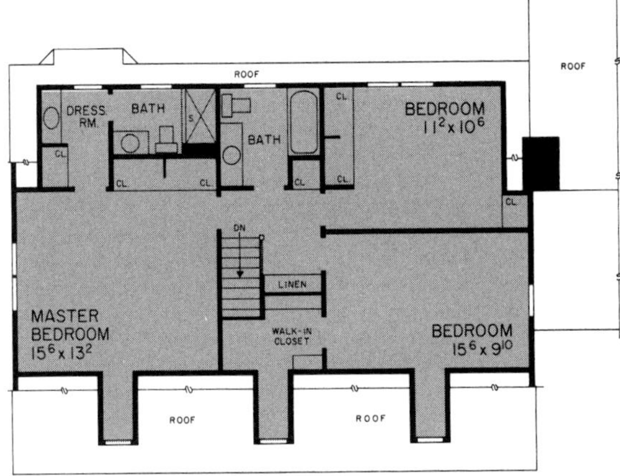

Design Q1956 First Floor: 990 square feet
Second Floor: 728 square feet; Total: 1,718 square feet

Design by
Home Planners, Inc.

● This classic Folk-Style Farmhouse design has the double advantage of good looks and a hardworking floor plan. On the outside, a brick first floor is complemented by wood siding on the second floor. Through the double front doors is a long foyer with coat closet and half bath for guests. To the right is the formal living area with dining room to the rear. The grand kitchen has a pass-through counter to the breakfast room. The sunken family room features a beamed ceiling, built-in bookshelves and warm hearth. Sliding glass doors lead to a full-width rear terrace. Upstairs are four bedrooms (or choose the three-bedroom option included in the blueprint package) and two full baths.

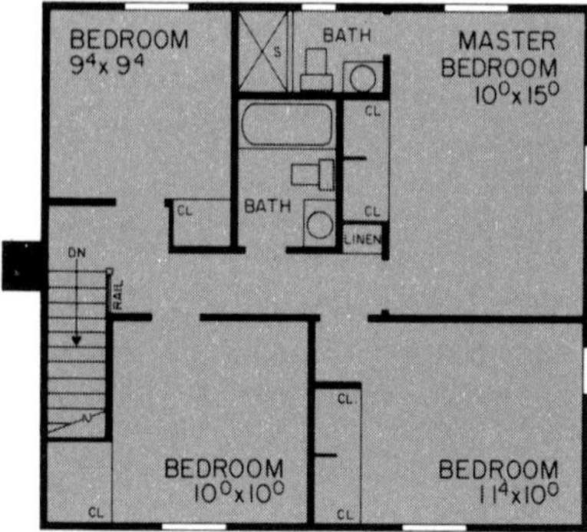

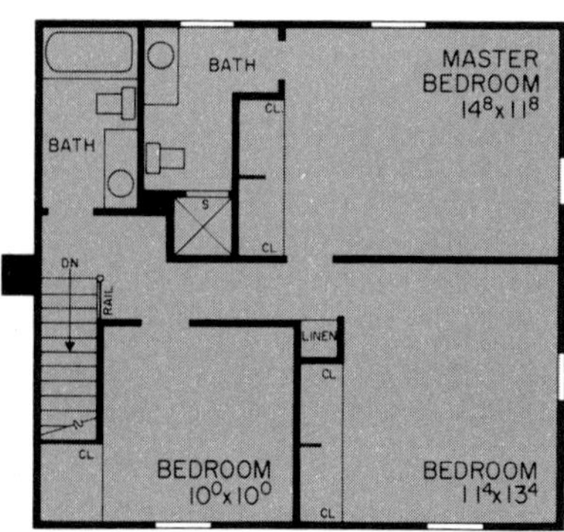

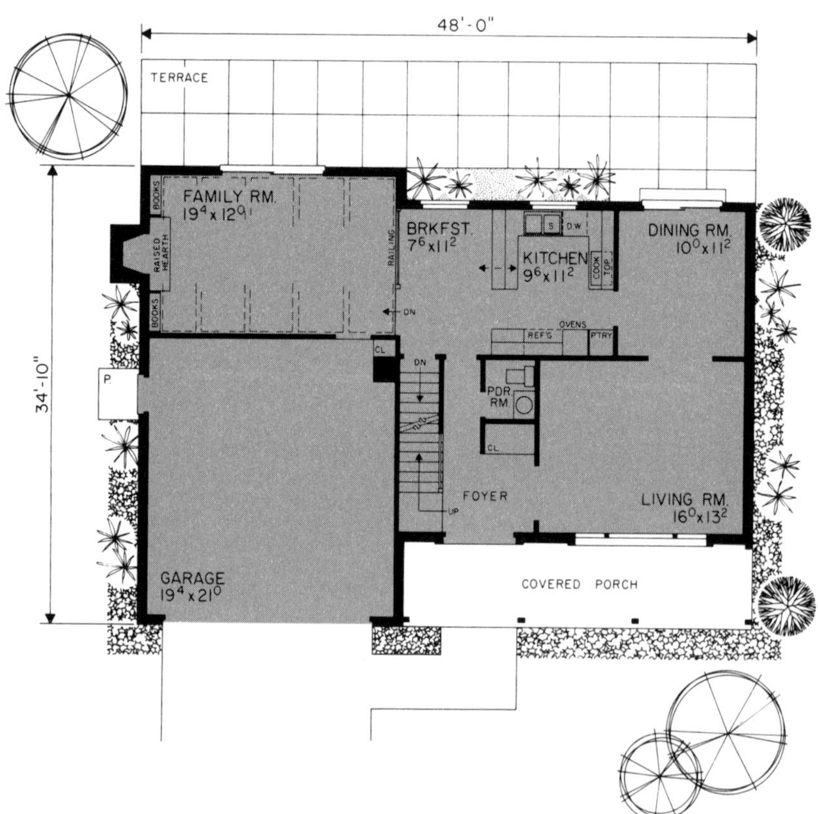

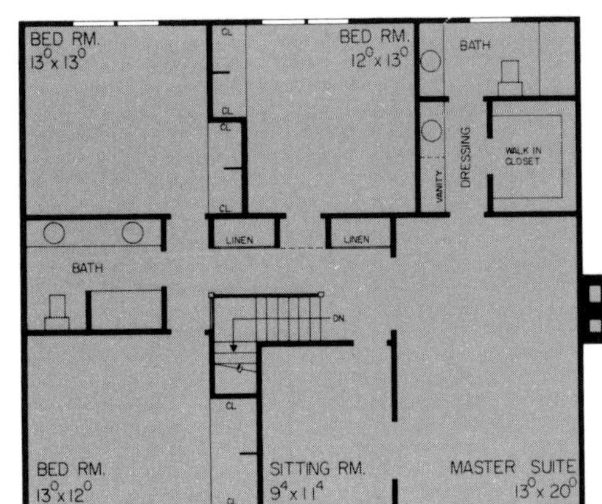

Design Q2540

First Floor: 1,306 square feet
Second Floor: 1,360 square feet
Total: 2,666 square feet

● This comfortable Colonial home puts a good foot forward in family living. The entry hall is wide and gracious to receive guests (and comes complete with a powder room for convenience). Flanking it are the family room with fireplace and the formal living room. A dining room has sliding glass doors to a rear terrace and leads directly to the L-shaped kitchen with island range. A handy utility area features washer/dryer space and storage and has an exterior door to the two-car garage. Upstairs are four bedrooms with two full baths. The master bedroom has a sitting room, dressing area, walk-in closet and bath with dual vanities.

Design by
Home Planners, Inc.

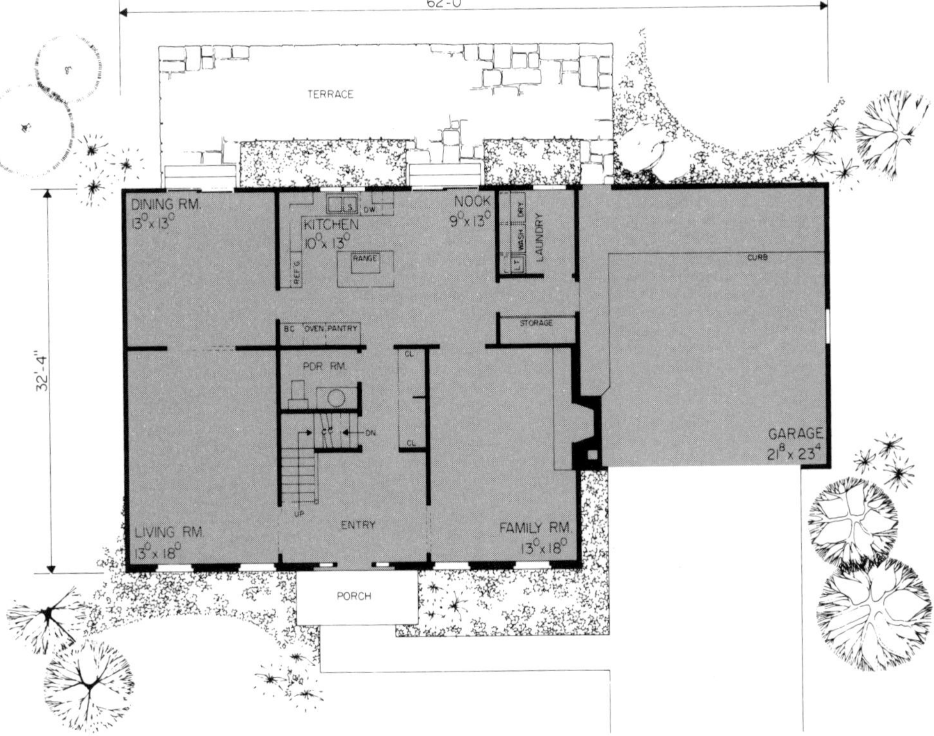

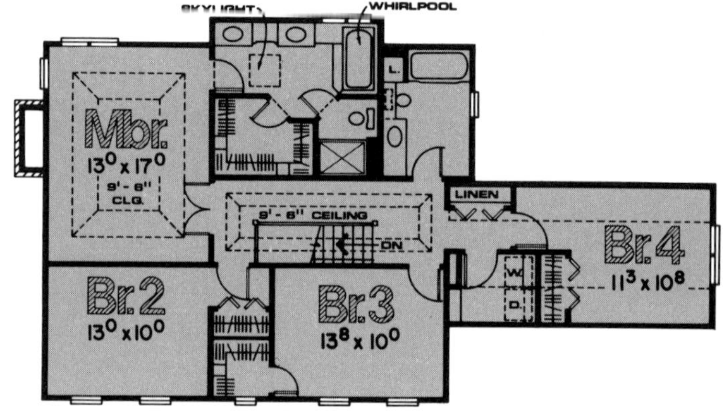

Design Q9239

First Floor: 998 square feet
Second Floor: 1,206 square feet
Total: 2,204 square feet

● The bright entry of this two-story home opens to formal living and dining space. To the back is the more informal family room with fireplace and built-in bookshelves. An island kitchen features a corner sink, pantry and convenient planning desk. Upstairs, the master bedroom has a vaulted ceiling and sumptuous master bath with skylit dressing area, whirlpool tub, and walk-in closet. Three family bedrooms and a full bath round out sleeping accommodations. Note the laundry area on the second floor as well.

Design by Design Basics, Inc.

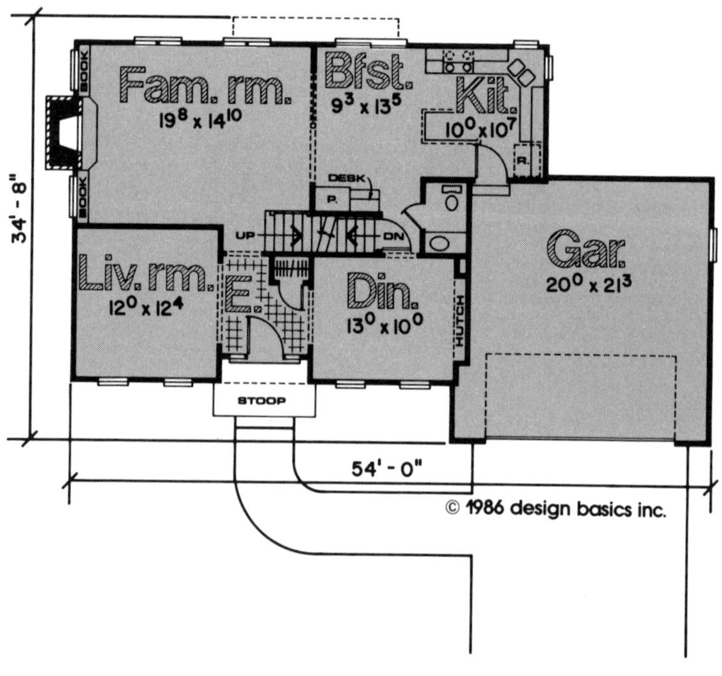

Design Q2659 First Floor: 1,023 square feet
Second Floor: 1,008 square feet; Third Floor: 476 square feet
Total: 2,507 square feet

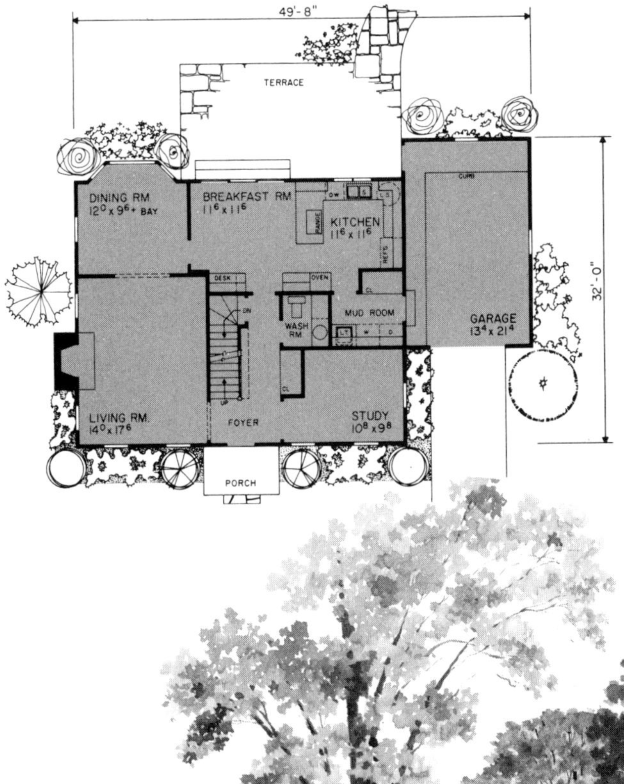

● The facade of this three-storied, pitch-roofed house has a symmetrical placement of windows and a restrained but elegant central entrance. The central hall, or foyer, expands midway through the house to a family kitchen. Off the foyer are two rooms, a living room with fireplace and a study. The windowed third floor attic can be used as a study and studio. Three bedrooms are housed on the second floor.

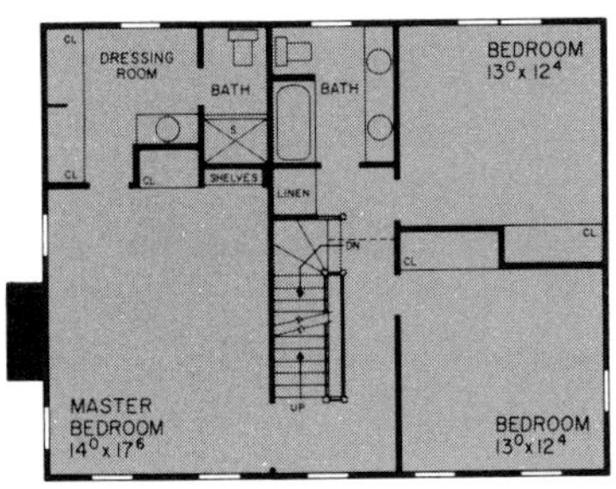

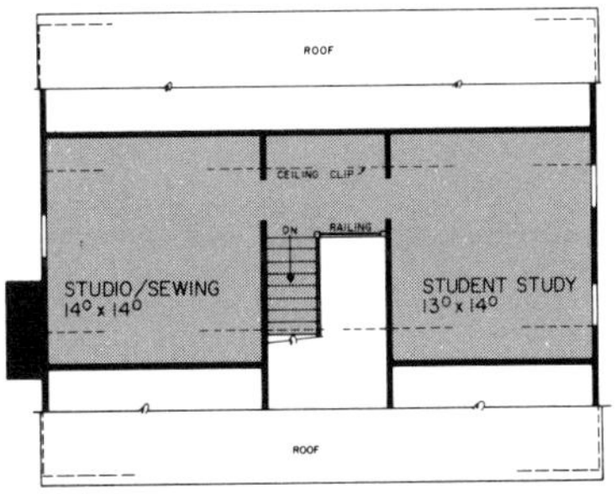

Design by
Home Planners, Inc.

Design Q2322

First Floor: 1,480 square feet
Second Floor: 1,172 square feet
Total: 2,652 square feet

Design by
Home Planners, Inc.

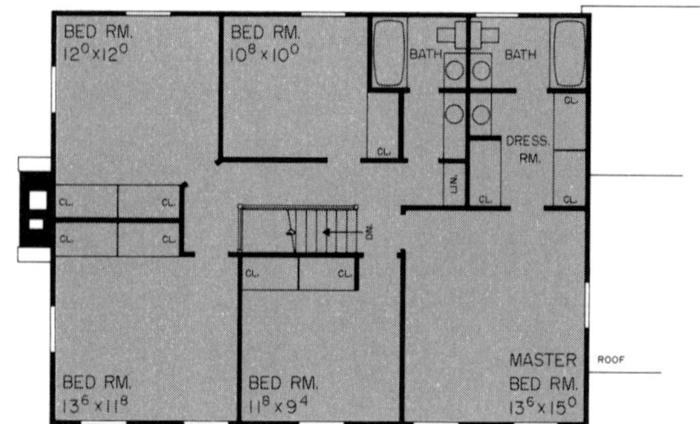

● Angular in configuration, this home offers loads of livability. There are five bedrooms on the second floor as well as two full baths. The first floor has a 27-foot living room with fireplace and a formal dining room with bay window. The U-shaped kitchen features eating space and is located nearby the informal family room with beamed ceiling. For quiet times, there is a study off the front foyer. The garage is angled and features a quaint covered porch. It has a large storage area plus smaller closet for holding all the necessities.

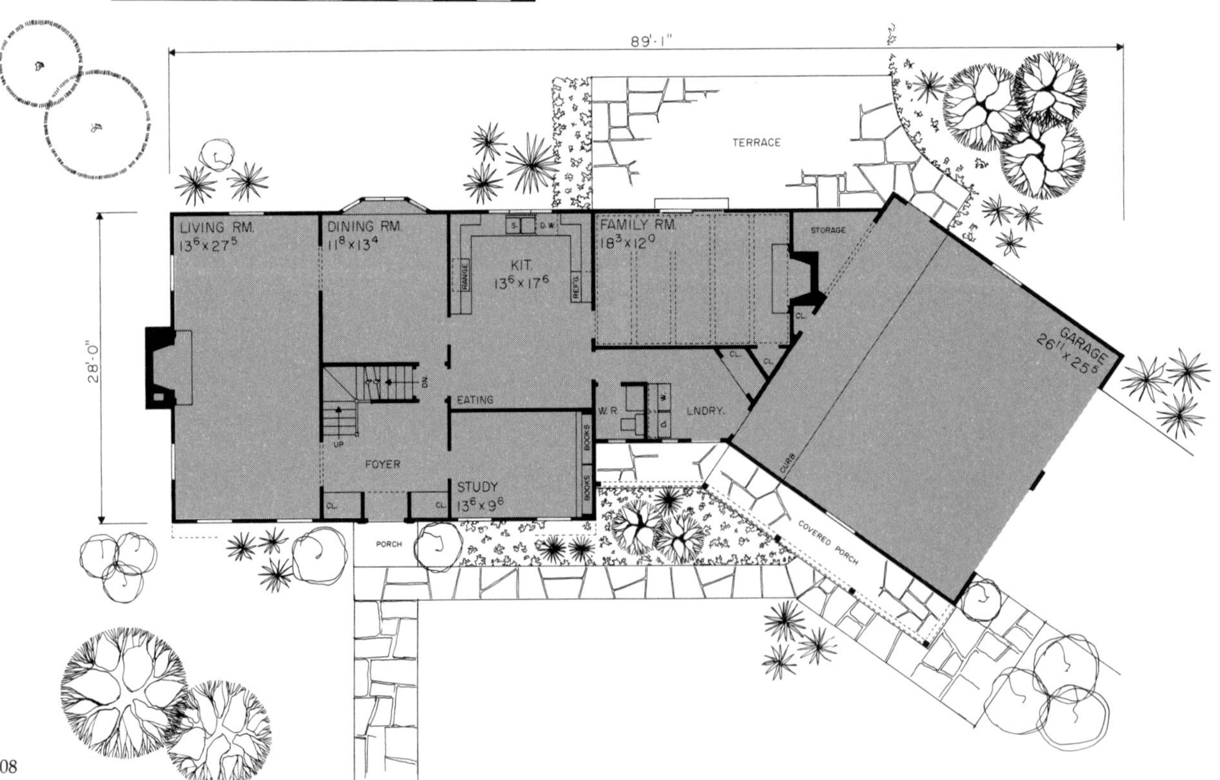

Design Q2610

First Floor: 1,505 square feet
Second Floor: 1,344 square feet
Total: 2,849 square feet

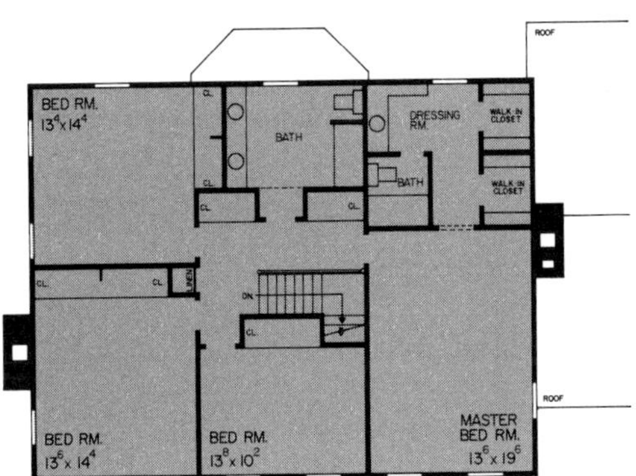

● This full two-story traditional will be worthy of note wherever built. It strongly recalls images of a New England of yesteryear. And well it might; for the window treatment is delightful. The front entrance detail is inviting. The narrow horizontal siding and the corner boards are appealing as are the two massive chimneys. The center entrance hall is large with a handy powder room nearby. The study has built-in bookshelves and offers a full measure of privacy. The interior kitchen has a pass-through to the family room and enjoys all that natural light from the bay window of the nook. A beamed ceiling, fireplace and sliding glass doors are features of the family room. The mud room highlights a closet, laundry equipment and an extra wash room. Study the upstairs with those four bedrooms, two baths and plenty of closets. An excellent arrangement for all.

Design by
Home Planners, Inc.

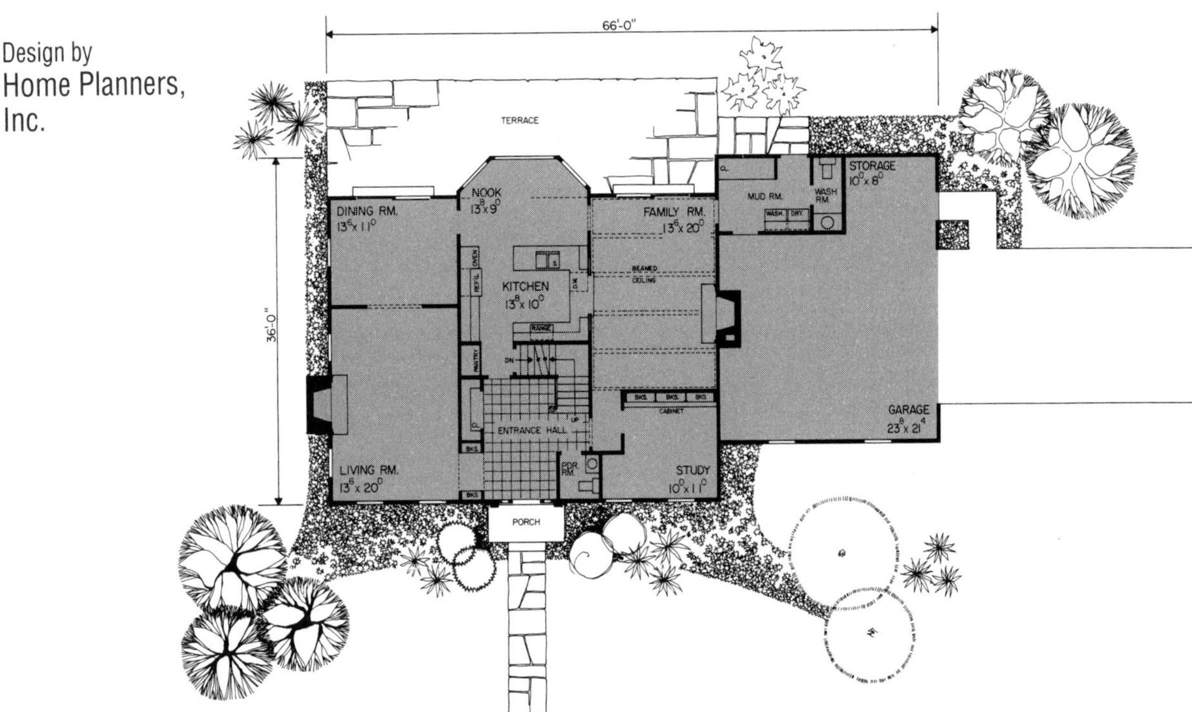

Design Q9303

First Floor: 1,428 square feet
Second Floor: 1,304 square feet
Total: 2,732 square feet

● Nine-foot main level walls are a nice feature not readily apparent in the design of this popular Colonial home. Comfortable traffic patterns segregate formal and informal living spaces. To the left of the spacious two-story entry is a formal dining room with hutch space. Sunny windows bring light into the living room and throughout the whole home. The built-in bookcases in a generous family room can easily be converted to a wet bar. Highlights of the island kitchen/breakfast area are a wraparound counter, planning desk, walk-in pantry and a butler pantry. Upstairs, secondary bedrooms are served by a compartmented hall bath with double lavs. The large master suite sports a vaulted ceiling, His and Hers closets, corner whirlpool and double vanity with makeup counter.

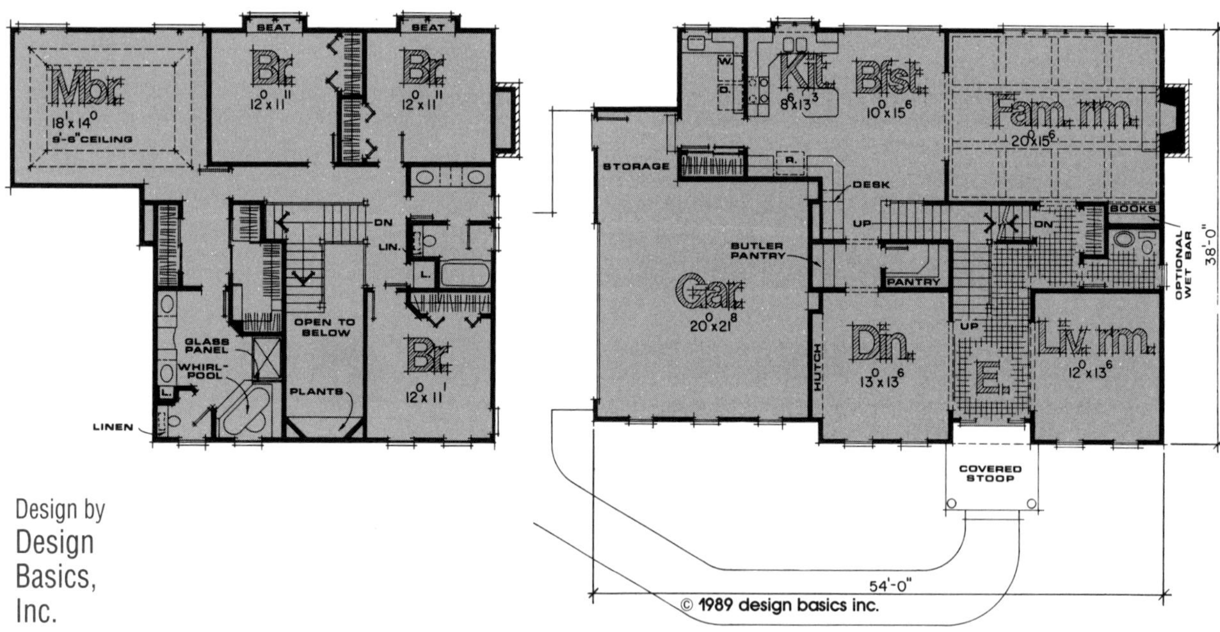

Design by
Design Basics, Inc.

Design Q9302

First Floor: 1,536 square feet
Second Floor: 1,343 square feet
Total: 2,879 square feet

● A delightful elevation will be appreciated by anyone aspiring to live in Colonial comfort. Three arches encompass the covered porch at the service entry to mud/laundry room. Inside, bright windows shed sunlight into the formal dining room with serving buffet. To the right of the elegant two-story entry is the living room. Sparkling French doors access the private den with bookcases from the spacious great room. In the roomy island kitchen, cooks will enjoy the built-in pantry and breakfast area. Be sure to notice the fireplace in the spacious master suite with three closets and a built-in dresser. A sophisticated skylit master bath has a two-person whirlpool and plant shelf. The compartmented bath upstairs has a separate tub and shower for the secondary bedrooms.

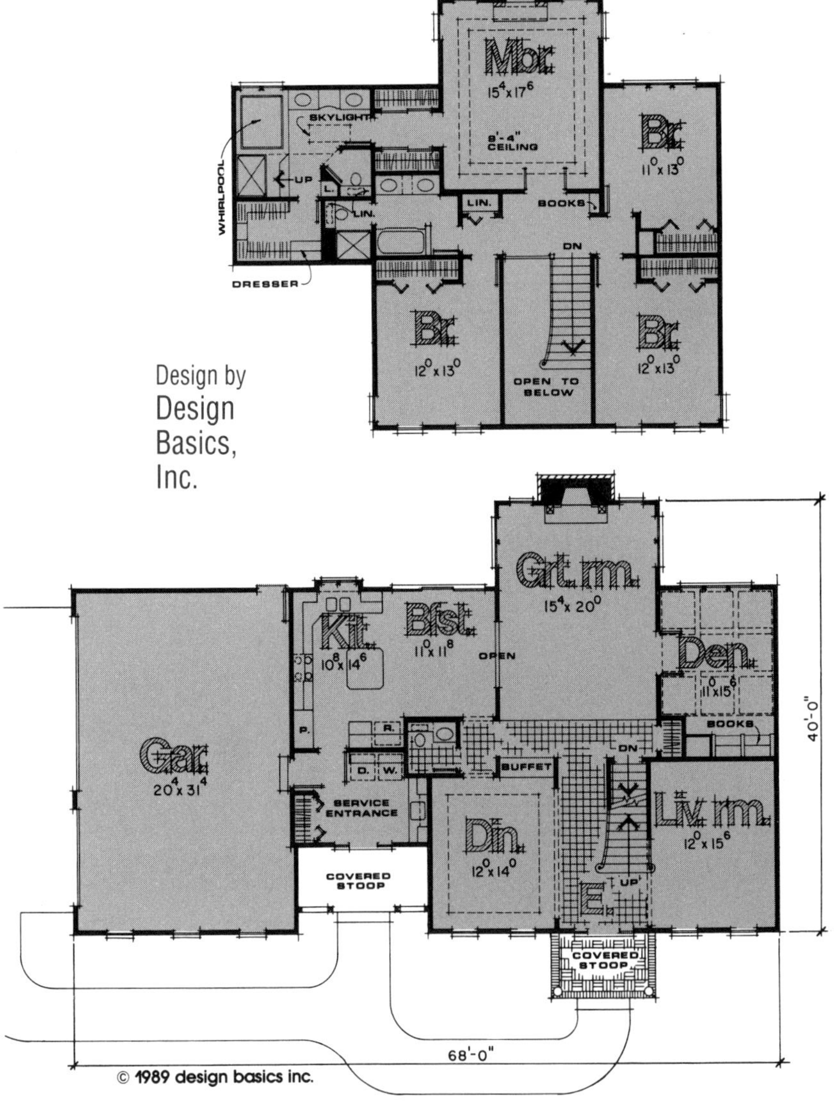

Design by Design Basics, Inc.

Design Q2687 First Floor: 1,819 square feet
Second Floor: 1,472 square feet; Total: 3,291 square feet

● Exterior styling of this home is reminiscent of the past but its floor plan is as up-to-date as it can get. Its many unique features include: a greenhouse, 78 square feet, off the country kitchen, a media room for all the modern electronic equipment, a hobby/laundry room with a washroom and a deluxe master bath.

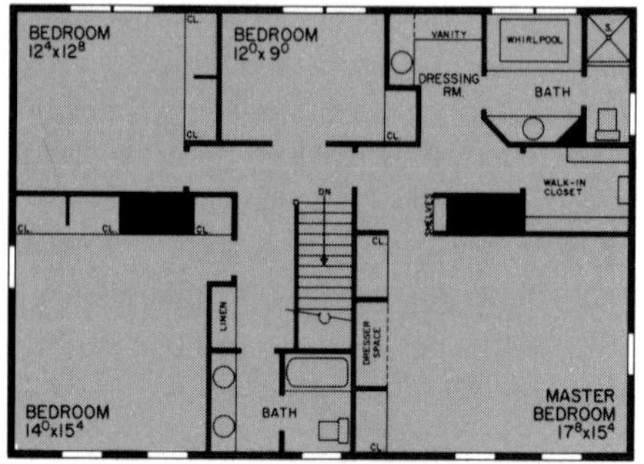

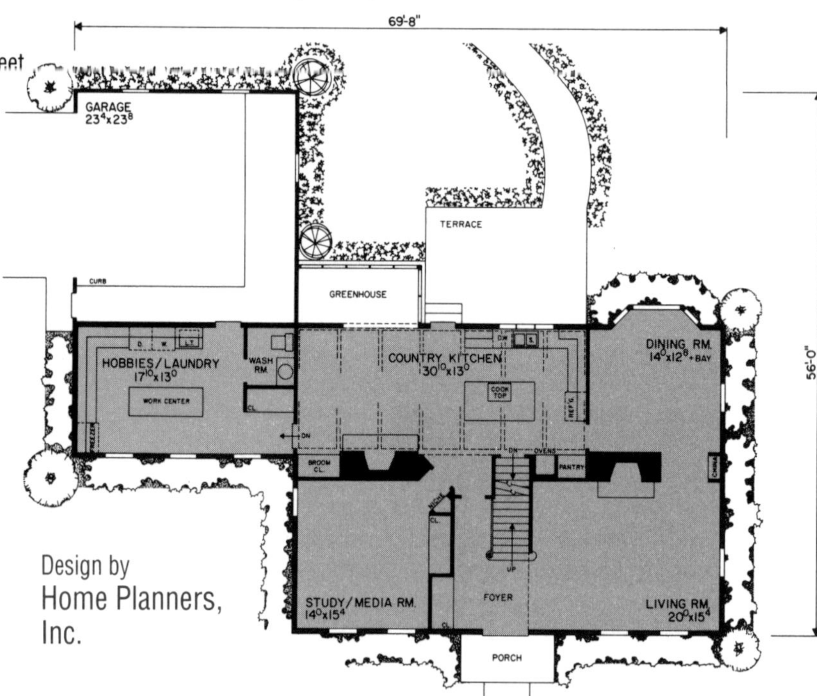

Design by
Home Planners, Inc.

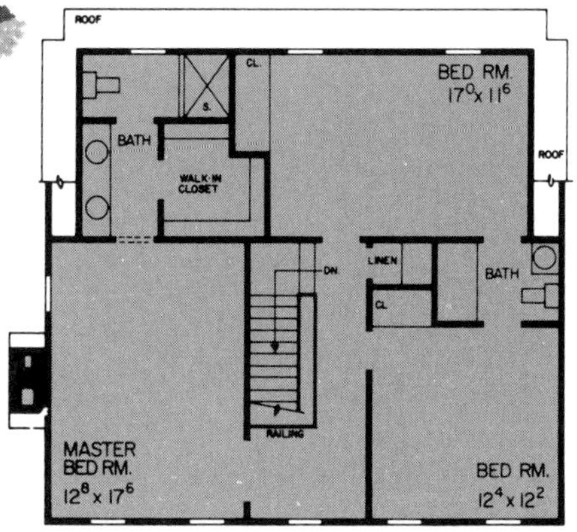

Design by
Home Planners,
Inc.

ROOF
CL.
S.
BED RM.
$17^{0} \times 11^{6}$
BATH
WALK-IN CLOSET
ROOF
DN.
LINEN
BATH
CL.
RAILING
MASTER BED RM.
$12^{8} \times 17^{6}$
BED RM.
$12^{4} \times 12^{2}$

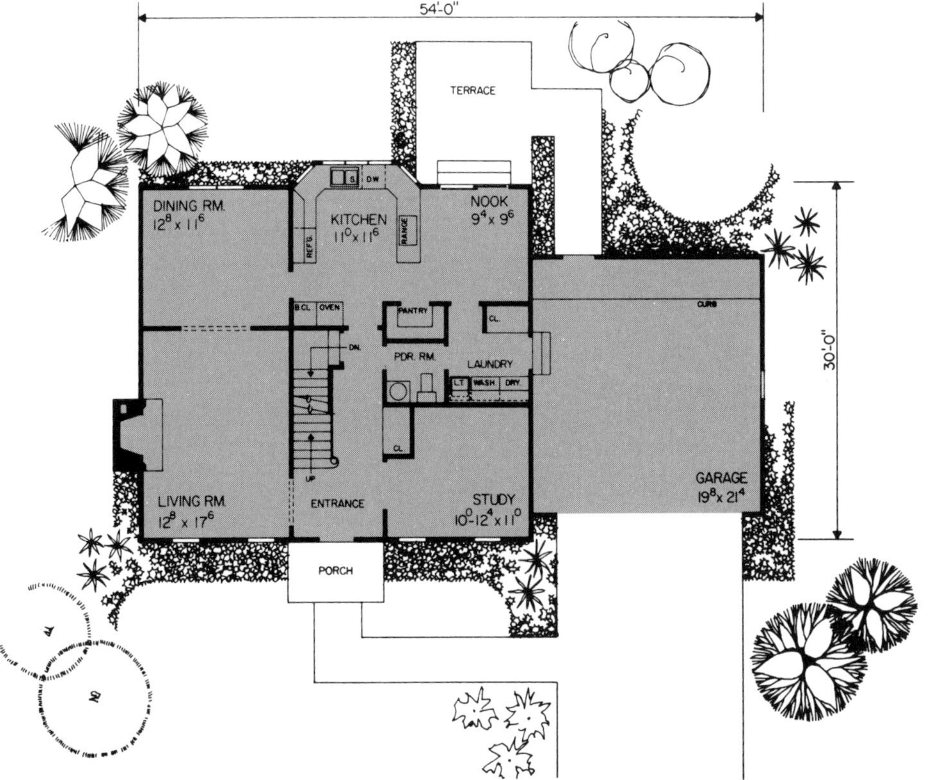

Design Q2731

First Floor: 1,039 square feet
Second Floor: 973 square feet
Total: 2,012 square feet

● Affordable style is the hallmark of this Colonial design. The U-shaped kitchen with large pantry and adjacent breakfast nook is a big center of attention. Next to it is a formal dining room. Living room with fireplace, first-floor study, and efficient service area round out a hard-working downstairs plan. The second floor features a sizable master suite, complete with twin vanities and roomy walk-in closet.

Design Q2998

First Floor: 2,260 square feet
Second Floor: 1,611 square feet
Total: 3,871 square feet

● Symmetrical and simply lovely, this gambrel-roofed two-story is a fine example of historical homes. Its details will enchant the most particular enthusiast of early architecture. The floor plan is a classic as well. Note the formal dining and living rooms flanking the entry hall. The living room has a fireplace and the dining room a bay window. A media room/study also sports a fireplace and has access to a rear terrace. The family room connects to the kitchen via a through snack bar. There's also another fireplace here. On the second floor are three bedrooms and two full baths. The third floor contains unfinished space which acts as superb storage and can be developed later into more bedrooms if needed.

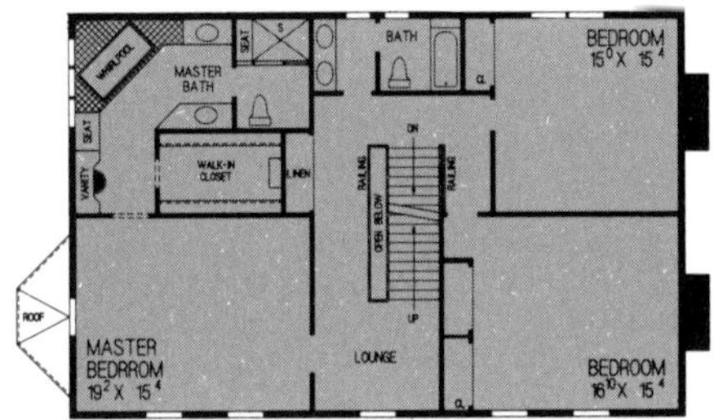

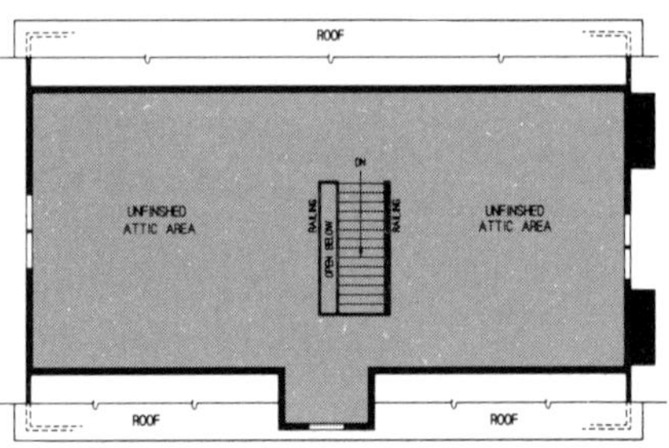

Design by
Home Planners, Inc.

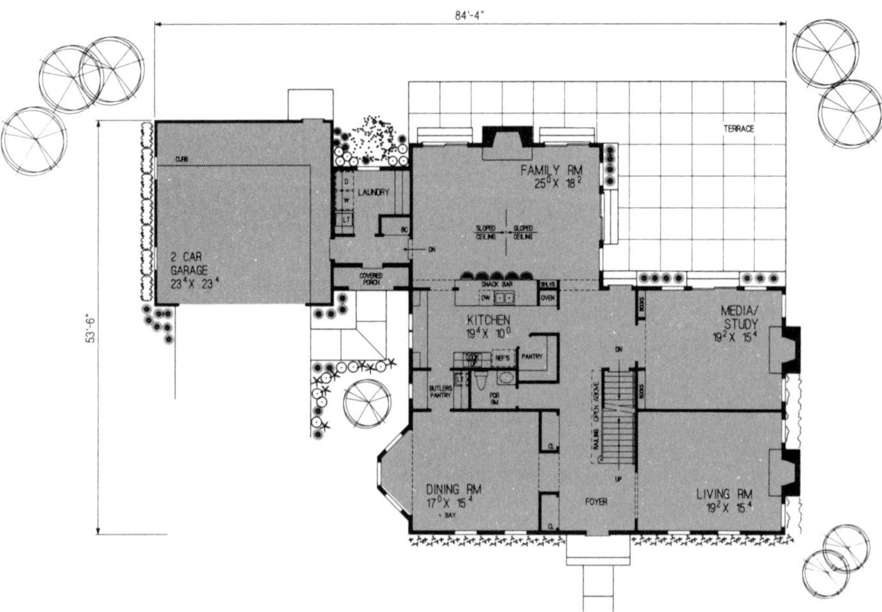

Design Q2538

First Floor: 1,503 square feet
Second Floor: 1,095 square feet
Total: 2,598 square feet

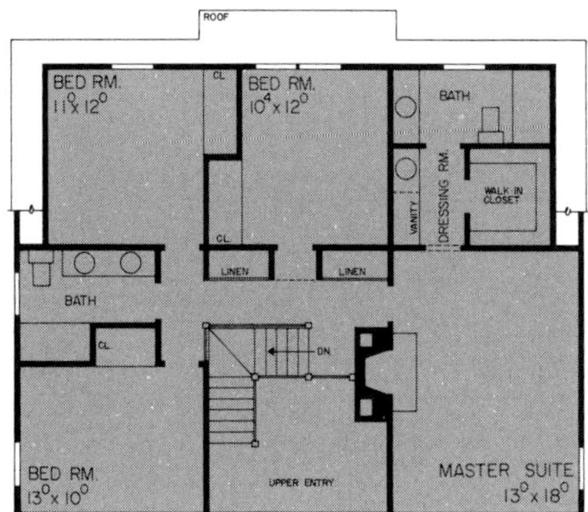

● This SaltBox is charming, indeed. The livability it has to offer to the large and growing family is great. The entry is spacious and is open to the second floor balcony. For living areas, there is the study in addition to the living and family rooms. The large kitchen has an island range and attached nook with sliding glass doors to the terrace. The master suite, on the second floor, has its own fireplace and a large walk-in closet in the dressing area. Three more bedrooms share a full bath.

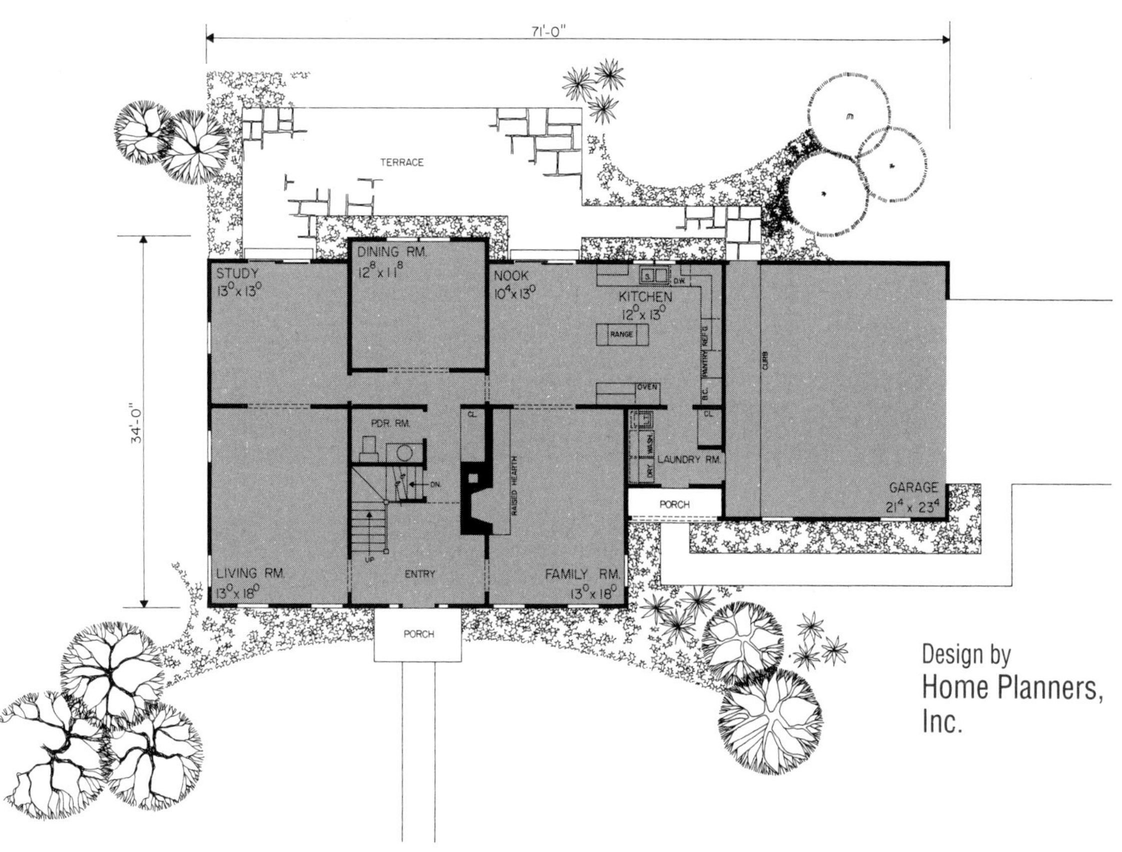

Design by
Home Planners, Inc.

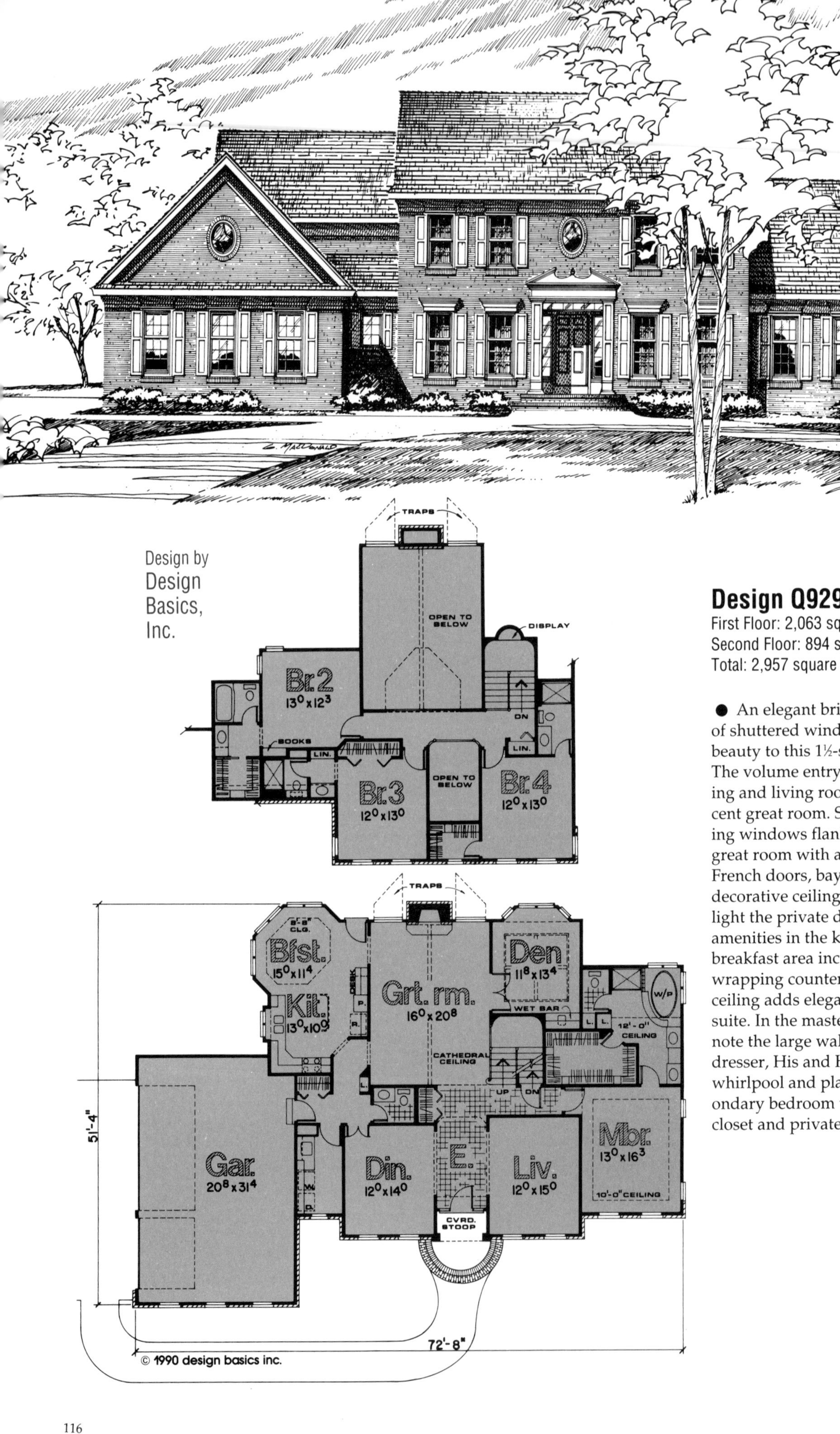

Design by
Design
Basics,
Inc.

Design Q9299

First Floor: 2,063 square feet
Second Floor: 894 square feet
Total: 2,957 square feet

● An elegant brick elevation and rows of shuttered windows lend timeless beauty to this 1½-story Colonial design. The volume entry surveys formal dining and living rooms and the magnificent great room. Sparkling floor-to-ceiling windows flank the fireplace in the great room with a cathedral ceiling. French doors, bayed windows and a decorative ceiling, plus a wet bar highlight the private den. Special lifestyle amenities in the kitchen and bayed breakfast area include a built-in desk, wrapping counters and island. A boxed ceiling adds elegance to the master suite. In the master bath/dressing area, note the large walk-in closet, built-in dresser, His and Hers vanities, oval whirlpool and plant shelves. Each secondary bedroom upstairs has a roomy closet and private bath.

EUROPEAN-INSPIRED FARMHOUSES

Centuries before coming to the New World, Europeans enjoyed farmhouse styles that were uniquely their own. Built originally of simple materials, these dwellings were functional, cozy and sturdy. They also reflected the distinct design bent of the country in which they were found, particularly with regard to rooflines. French country houses had the classic hipped roof so favored in that region; the Dutch maintained gambrel roofs; and the English added gabled roofs (often thatched) to their cottages. Each group incorporated design details that blended to charming result in the European-Inspired Farmhouse.

These homes are a development of European styles and influences imposed on basic American farmhouse structure. They represent an adaptation of those homes found in the countrysides of France, Germany, Holland and other Western European nations.

In general, the European Farmhouse has a classic, upright two-story stature. Like their historic equivalents, these homes may be characterized most easily by their roof types. While most are straight and gabled, they may vary to hipped versions in the French style or gambreled (or double-pitched) in the Flemish and Dutch tradition.

The windows, as well, echo European styling. Special details include metal-clad French bows and dormers, Dutch dormers protruding from the roof, Greek stone or brick arches over windows and doors, and the classic Palladian-style window grouping.

Siding on these homes is almost exclusively wood but may be accented with brick, stone or even stucco.

Among the European-Inspired Farmhouses in this section are some outstanding examples of the influences of various countries on the architectural details of the homes. Design Q9857, for instance, has many of the features of Country French homes: French bows with metal-clad roofs, a Palladian window and additional shuttered windows. Design Q9306 exudes more of a Modern French style with a strongly hipped roof and narrow, transommed windows. Dutch and Flemish design is apparent in Design Q2697 and Design Q9860. Both have gambrel roofs and twin chimney stacks, but Q9860 is sided almost entirely in stone while Q2697 sports only a stone fireplace.

All of the representative homes are alive with European country charm in conjunction with the best in up-to-date floor planning.

Design Q9870

First Floor: 2,155 square feet
Second Floor: 1,020 square feet
Total: 3,175 square feet

● To highlight the exterior of this home, wood siding and paneled shutters have been artfully combined with arched transoms, gables and a sweeping roof line to define the beautiful glass entry. The open foyer at once reveals the large living and dining rooms and a classic great room with coffered ceiling and hearth. Double doors open to the master bedroom with unique tray ceiling and fireplace. The master bath includes knee space with double vanities and shower, corner garden tub and His and Hers closets. The exercise room can be accessed from either the master bedroom or great room and opens onto the porch at the rear of the home. The generous corner breakfast area also opens to the porch. The large kitchen with a cook-top island, pantry and laundry room complete the main level. The gallery features built-in bookshelves and computer/study nook with easy access from all three bedrooms on the upper level. An unfinished bonus room with attic access offers room for expansion.

Design by
Design Traditions
Atlanta

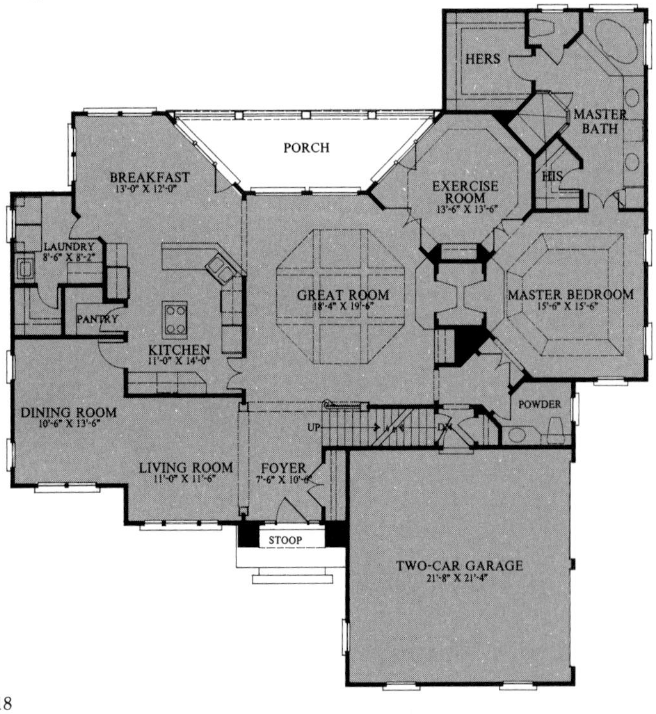

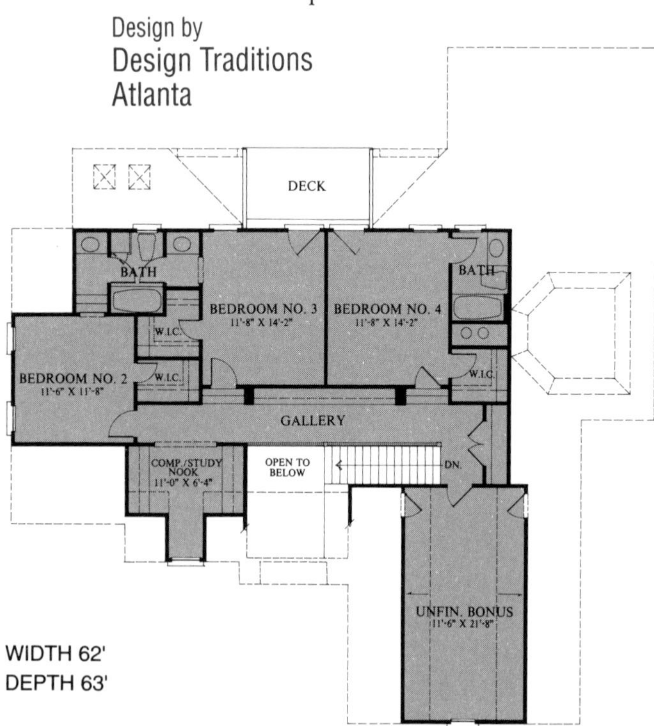

Design Q9869

First Floor: 1,475 square feet
Second Floor: 1,460 square feet
Total: 2,935 square feet

● This English country home of stucco and stone features elliptical keystone detailing and a covered entranceway. Through the columned entry, the two-story foyer opens to the living room with wet bar. The media room features a fireplace and is accessed from both the main hall and great room. A hall powder room and coat closet are located to the rear of the foyer. The two-story great room with fireplace is open to the breakfast area, kitchen and rear staircase, making entertaining a pleasure. The kitchen design is ideal with breakfast bar and preparation island and is conveniently located near the laundry room. The dining room with its elliptical window is ideal for formal entertaining. The upper level begins with the balcony landing overlooking the great room. The master bedroom features a bay-windowed sitting area and a tray ceiling. The master bath has dual vanities, a corner garden tub, separate shower, a large walk-in closet and an optional secret room. Across the balcony, Bedrooms 2 and 3 share a bath. Bedroom 4 in the front of the home has a private bath.

Design by
Design Traditions
Atlanta

DECK
BREAKFAST 9'-4" X 10'-6"
TWO STORY GREAT ROOM 16'-8" X 15'-4"
MEDIA ROOM 12'-0" X 12'-0"
KITCHEN 15'-8" X 14'-0"
UP
DN.
POWDER
WET BAR
STORAGE
LAUNDRY 6'-2" X 7'-6"
LIVING ROOM 12'-0" X 12'-2"
TWO-CAR GARAGE 21'-4" X 21'-4"
DINING ROOM 12'-0" X 13'-0"
TWO STORY FOYER 10'-6" X 13'-0"
PORCH

WIDTH 59'
DEPTH 46'-6"

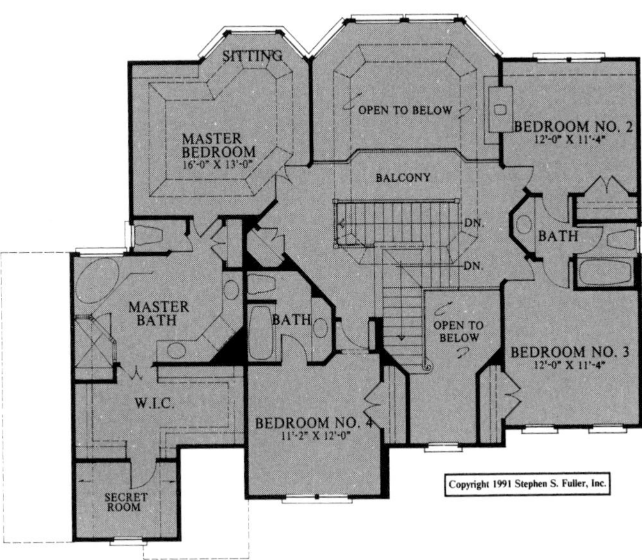

Design Q9855

Square footage: 2,902

● A one-story plan for even a large family, this home provides all the necessities and many luxuries as well. For formal occasions, there's a grand dining room just off the entry foyer. It has a vaulted ceiling and is just across the hall from the gourmet kitchen. The great room has beautiful ceiling treatment and access to the rear deck. For more casual times, the breakfast nook and adjoining keeping room with fireplace fill the bill. The master suite is huge and contains every amenity. Its sitting room allows access to the rear deck. Note the gigantic walk-in closet here. Two family bedrooms share a full bath. Each of these bedrooms has its own lavatory.

Design by
Design Traditions
Atlanta

Design Q9856

First Floor: 1,410 square feet
Second Floor: 1,490 square feet
Total: 2,900 square feet

● A gambrel roof, stone and wood frame exterior, flower boxes and accent shutters create this Dutch country cottage. Round accent windows frame the arched entrance with keystone details and double entrance doors. The spacious two-story foyer and staircase are interestingly designed with a landing to the right of the foyer and powder room to the left. The family room with wet bar, bay-windowed breakfast area and kitchen are open to one another, creating a practical living space that converts easily for entertaining. The laundry room is located between the kitchen and the two-car garage, with an additional door to the back yard. The dining room has an attractive bay window at one end and an opening to the living room on the other. The upper level begins with a landing overlooking the open foyer. Passing through double doors to the master bedroom, a tray ceiling and a luxurious sitting room with deep bay window are showcased. Diagonally set double doors lead to the master bath with a corner garden tub, two vanities and separate shower. Three bedrooms and two full baths complete the upper level.

Design by
Design Traditions
Atlanta

WIDTH 57'-10"
DEPTH 42'-10"

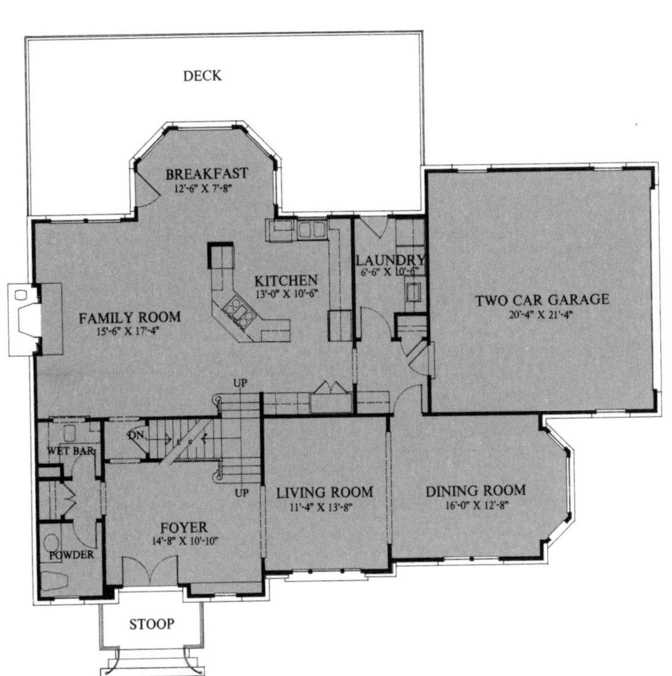

Design Q9857

First Floor: 1,105 square feet
Second Floor: 1,245 square feet
Total: 2,350 square feet

● This Traditional home combines an attractive classic exterior with an open and sophisticated interior design. On approach, notice the use of brick and siding, Palladian and box bay windows, flower boxes and a covered entrance flanked by columns. The two-story foyer has a staircase to the left and a coat closet and powder room straight ahead. Proceeding right from the foyer are both the living and dining rooms with their individual window treatments. Entering the kitchen from the dining room is a corner butler pantry for added convenience while entertaining. The open design flows from the breakfast area to the family room with two large bay windows. The open foyer staircase leads to the upper level, beginning with the master suite. The bay window extends the eye beyond the attractive master bedroom. The master bath contains a luxurious tub, separate shower and dual vanities, as well as a large linen closet. A large walk-in master closet completes the suite. Bedroom 2 is inviting with its bay window and large closet. All three secondary bedrooms share a hall bath with separate vanity and bathing areas.

Design by
Design Traditions
Atlanta

WIDTH 54'
DEPTH 39'

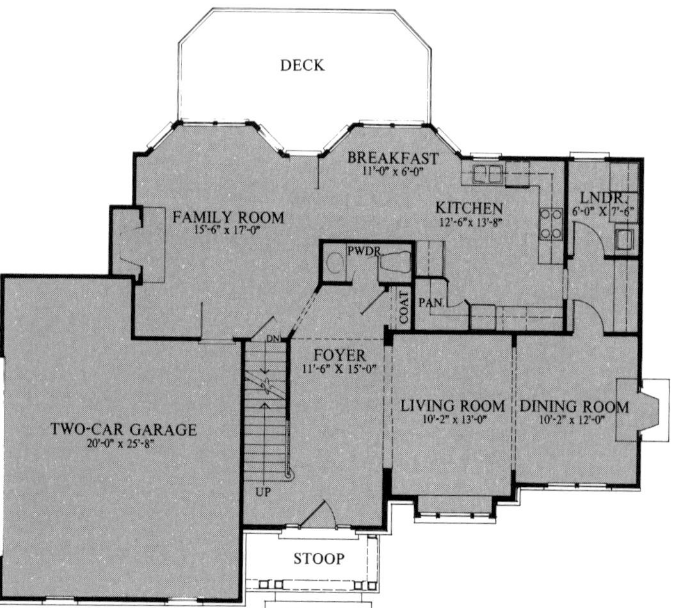

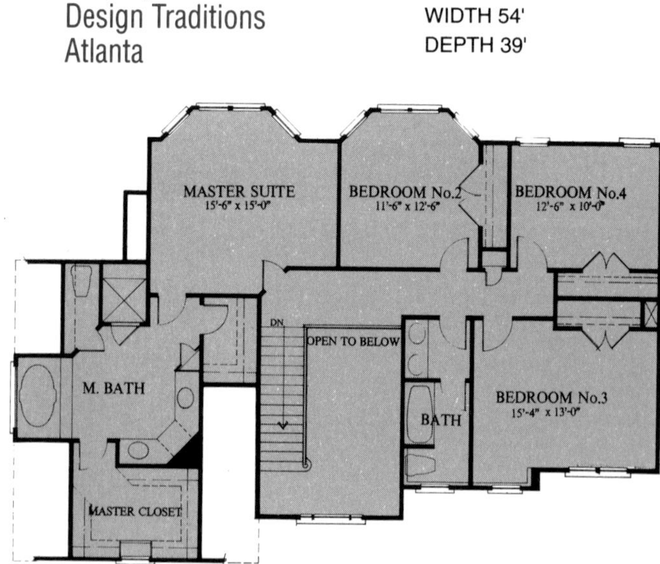

Design Q9858

First Floor: 1,554 square feet
Second Floor: 1,648 square feet
Total: 3,202 square feet

● This classic Americana design employs wood siding, a variety of window styles, and a detailed front porch. Upon entry, the large two-story foyer flows into the formal dining room with arched window accents and the combination study and living room with a large bay window. A short passage with wet bar accesses the family room with a wall of windows, French doors and a fireplace. The large breakfast area and open kitchen with cooking island are spacious and airy as well as efficient. The walk-in pantry, laundry, and entry to the two-car garage complete this level. Upstairs, the master suite's sleeping and sitting room feature architectural details including columns, tray ceilings and a fireplace. The elegant master bath contains a raised oval tub, dual vanities and separate shower. Generous His and Hers closets are located beyond the bath. Additional bedrooms are complete with closets and a variety of bath combinations.

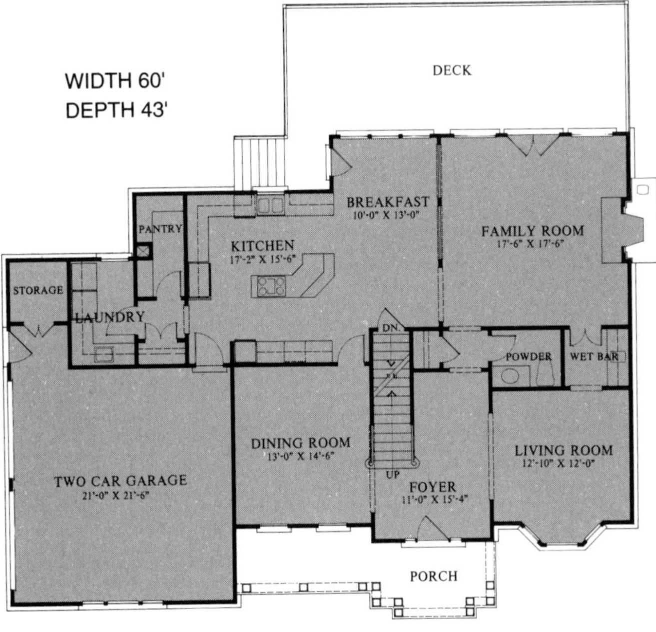

Design by
Design Traditions
Atlanta

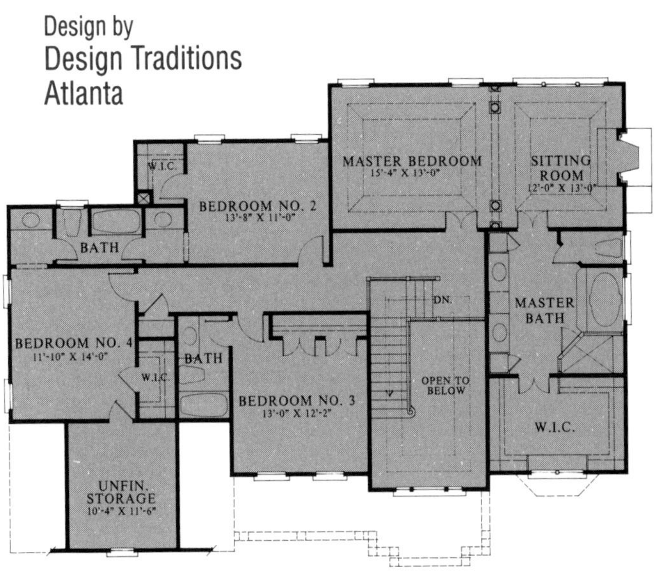

Design Q1986

First Floor: 896 square feet
Second Floor: 1,148 square feet
Total: 2,044 square feet

● This design with its gambrel roof is the essence of charm. There's lots of room to entertain or relax with the family in a front living room with raised-hearth fireplace and built-in wood box. The dining room attaches to the living room and has a sliding glass door to the rear terrace. The U-shaped kitchen features a pass-through to the breakfast room and overlooks the rear yard. Upstairs there are three bedrooms including a master suite with dressing room and dormer windows. The two family bedrooms share a full compartmented bath. The family room is located upstairs over the garage and is sunken down a few steps from the main body of this floor. It holds built-in bookcases for the family library.

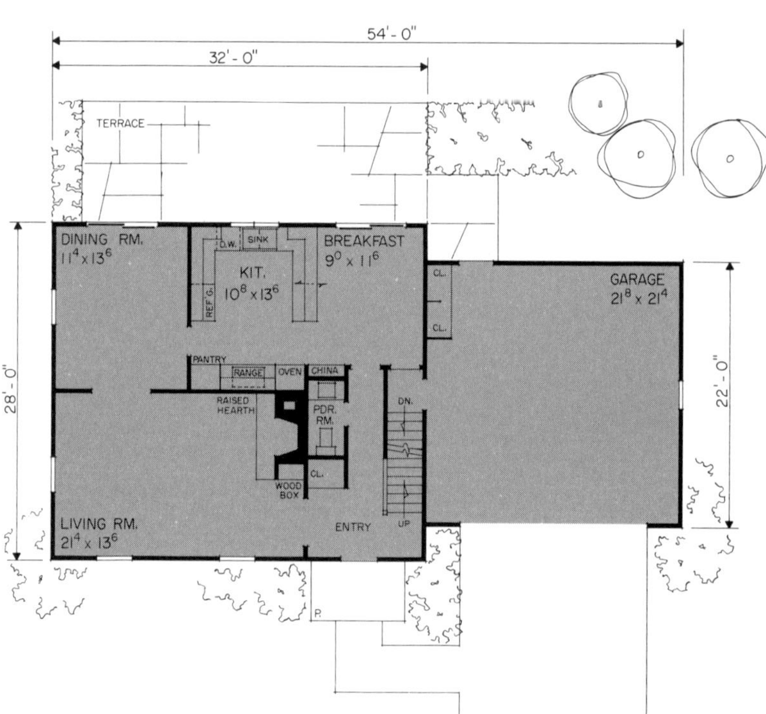

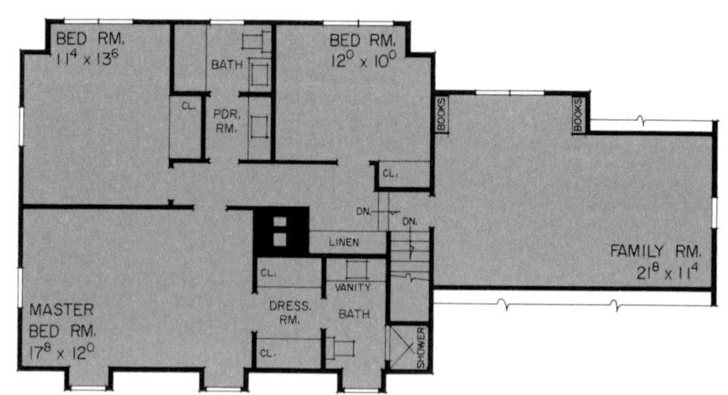

Design by
Home Planners, Inc.

Design Q2655

First Floor: 893 square feet
Second Floor: 652 square feet
Total: 1,545 square feet

TERRACE
SCREENED PORCH
BREAKFAST RM. 10⁰x 10⁰
KITCHEN 10⁰x 10⁰
DINING RM. 11⁰x 10⁰
STORAGE
LAUNDRY
WASH RM.
BOOKS
STUDY 10⁰x 10⁰
FOYER
LIVING RM. 12⁰x 15⁰
PORCH
CURB
STORAGE
GARAGE 13⁸x 23⁰
41'-0"
50'-0"

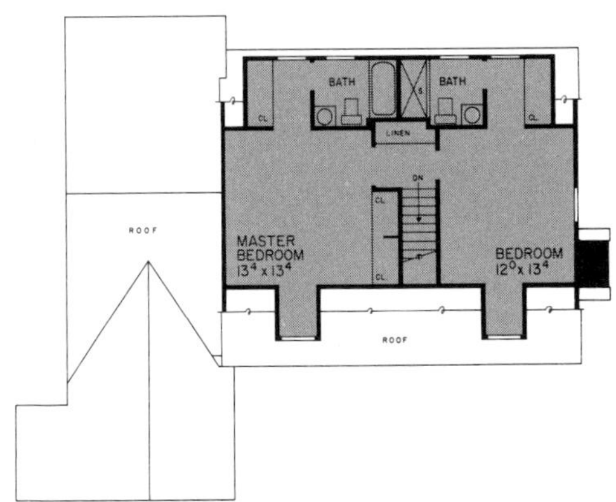

Design by
Home Planners, Inc.

● Wonderful things can be enclosed in small packages. This is the case for this two-story design. The total square footage is a mere 1,545 square feet yet its features are many, indeed. Its exterior appeal is very eye-pleasing with horizontal lines and two second story dormers. Livability will be enjoyed in this plan. The front study is ideal for a quiet escape. Nearby is a powder room also convenient to the kitchen and breakfast room. Two bedrooms and two full baths are located on the second floor.

Design Q2539

First Floor: 1,450 square feet
Second Floor: 1,167 square feet
Total: 2,617 square feet

● This appealingly proportional gambrel exudes an aura of coziness. The beauty of the main part of the house is delightfully symmetrical and is enhanced by the attached garage and laundry room. The center entrance routes traffic directly to all major zones of the house. Note the bay window in the nook and the raised-hearth fireplace in the family room. Upstairs there are four bedrooms including a master with walk-in closet and dormered bath. One of the family bedrooms also has a walk-in closet.

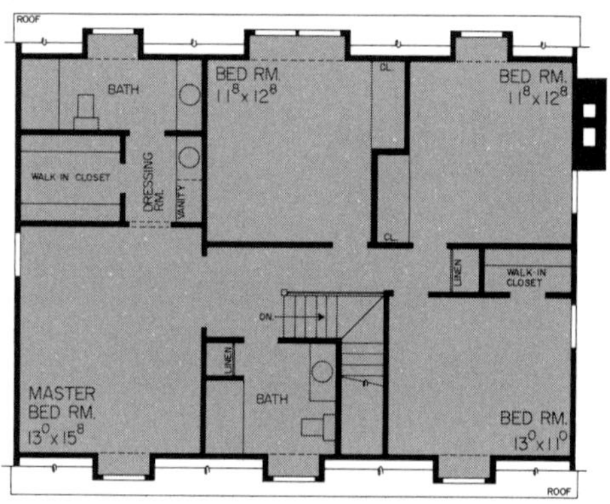

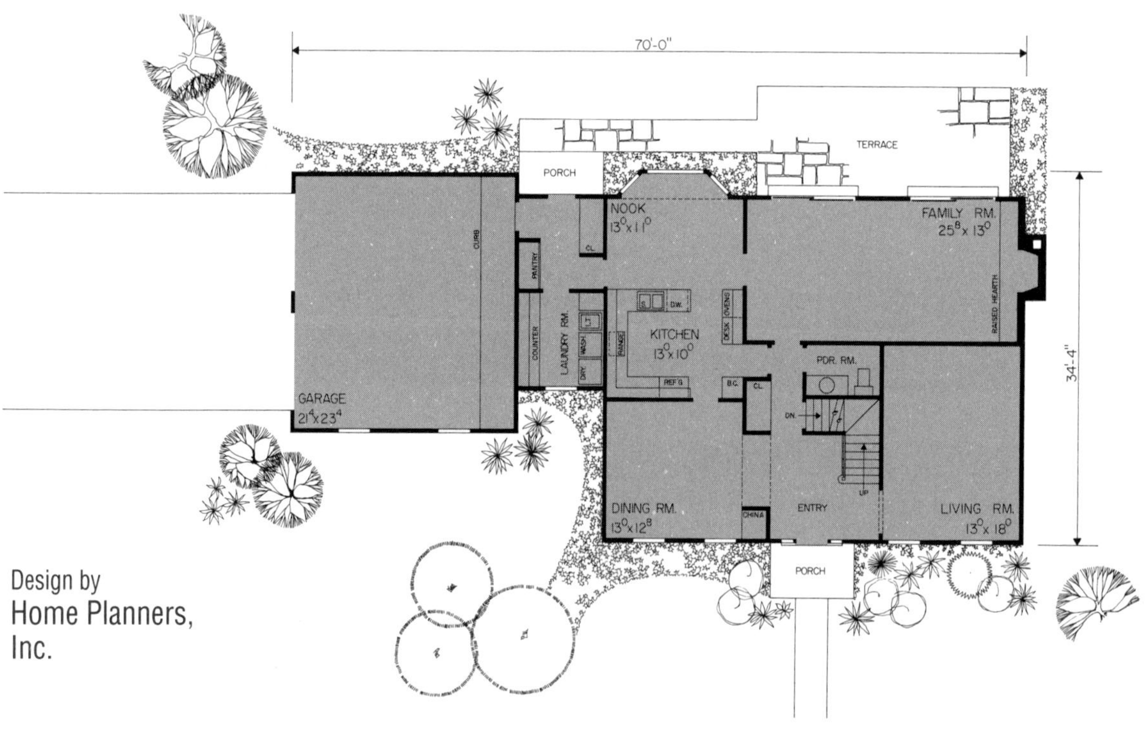

Design by
Home Planners,
Inc.

Design Q2131

First Floor: 1,214 square feet
Second Floor: 1,097 square feet
Total: 2,311 square feet

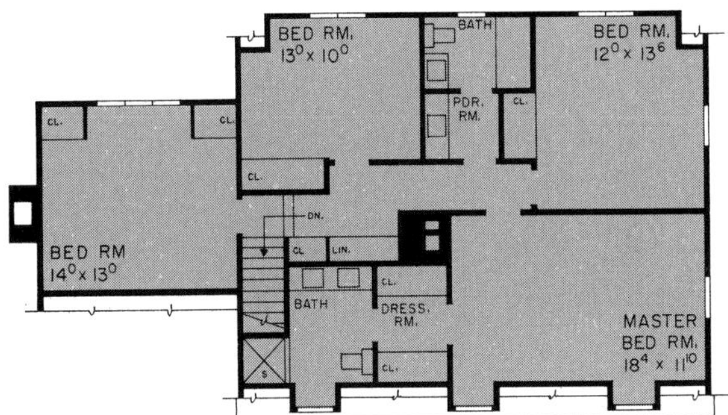

● The gambrel roof is the very embodiment of charm from the Early Colonial Period. Fine proportion and detailing were hallmarks of the era. The floor plan serves family needs well. A formal living room with fireplace and built-in wood box adjoins a dining room with corner built-in china cabinets. The kitchen/breakfast area is near the beamed-ceilinged family room (another fireplace!) which leads to the two-car garage. Upstairs are three generous bedrooms with ample closet space. The master has a dressing room and double sinks in the bath. Note the wide terrace to the rear of the plan.

Design by
Home Planners, Inc.

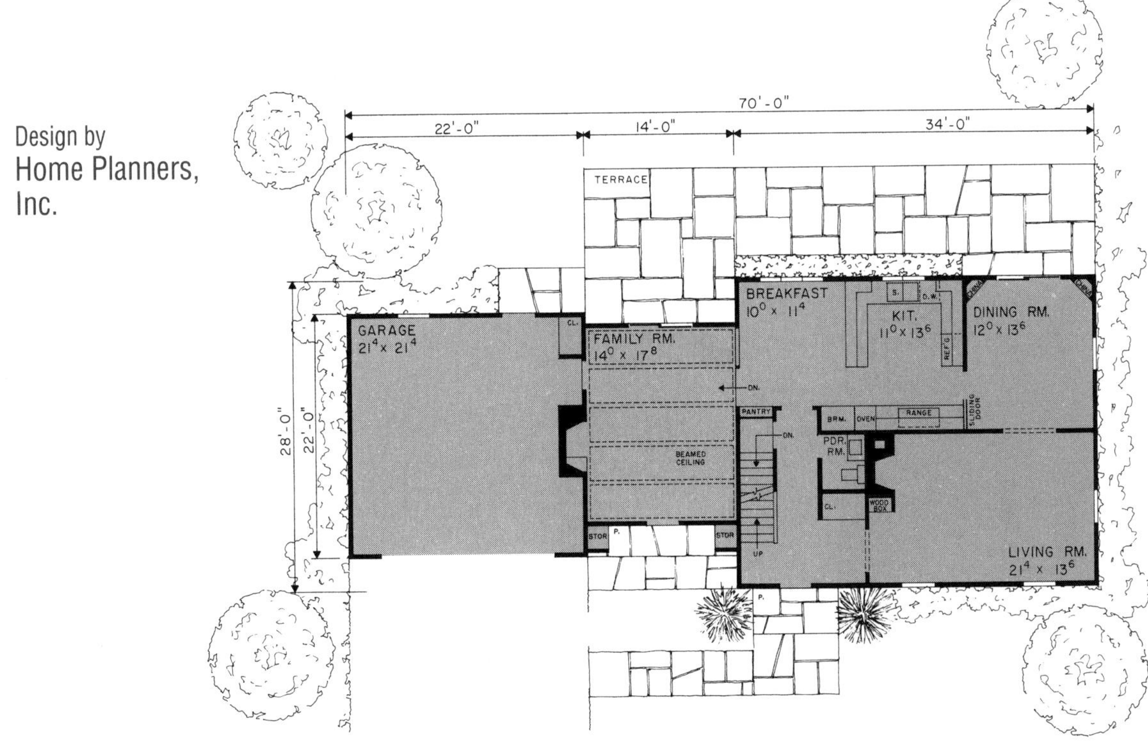

Design Q2713

First Floor: 1,830 square feet
Second Floor: 1,056 square feet
Total: 2,886 square feet

● A country charmer—this gambrel-roofed home has detailing that delights from the first glance. A covered porch at the service entrance connects the main part of the home to the two-car garage. Behind the garage is the beamed-ceilinged family room with raised-hearth fireplace and built-in wood box. Formal entertaining is accomplished in the living and dining rooms flanking the entry. Upstairs are three bedrooms and two full baths. Note the double walk-in closets and double lavs in the master suite.

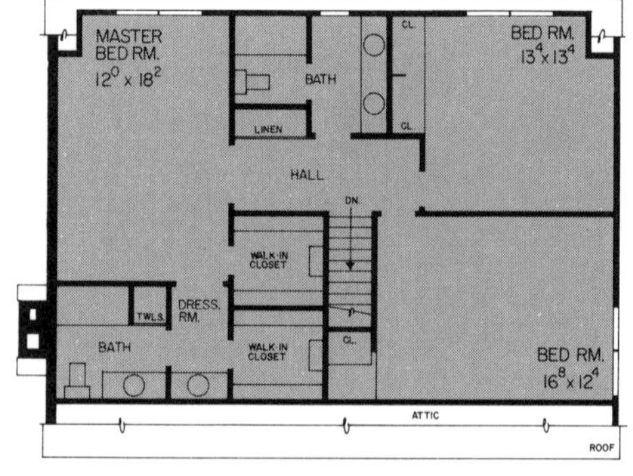

Design by
Home Planners, Inc.

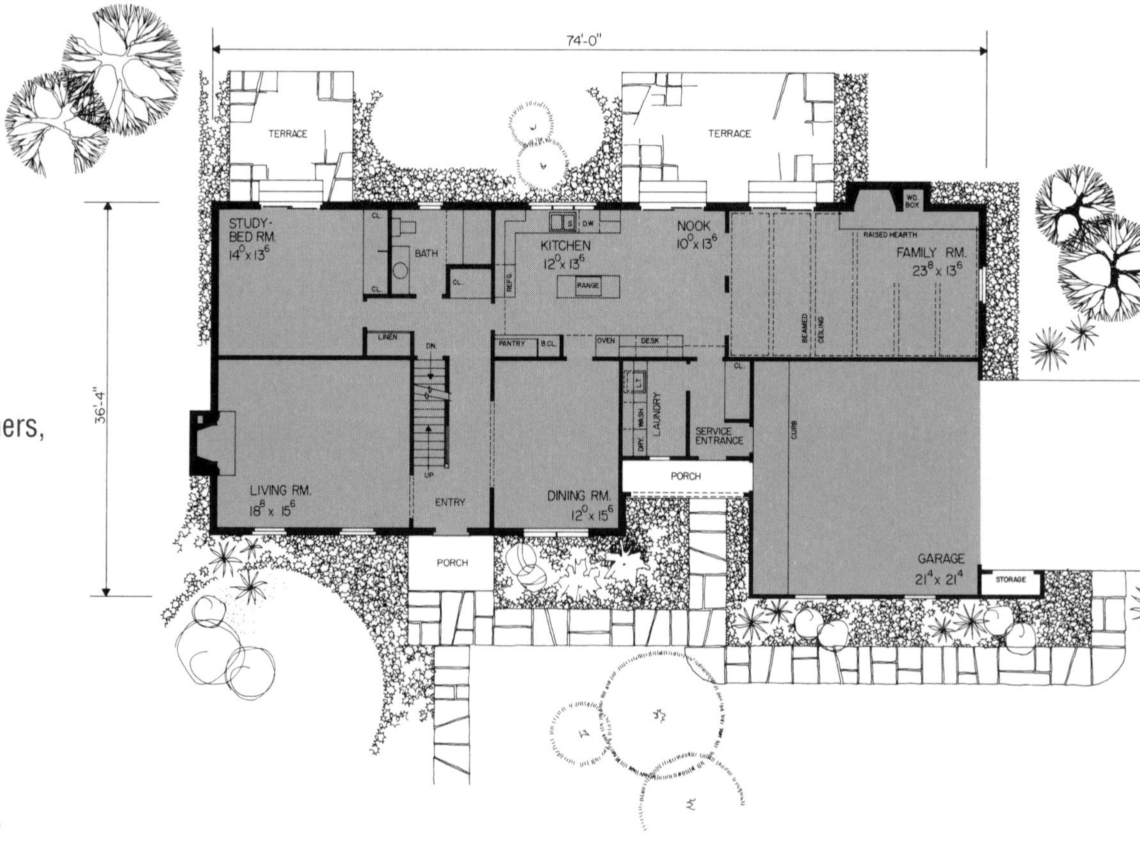

Design Q2689 First Floor: 1,385 square feet
Second Floor: 982 square feet; Total: 2,367 square feet

● This cozy three-bedroom Gambrel offers charming elegance with country comfort. A large country kitchen with bay overlooks a rear terrace. There's also a separate dining room downstairs, plus a living room and screened porch. All three bedrooms are upstairs, away from the distractions of rest of the house.

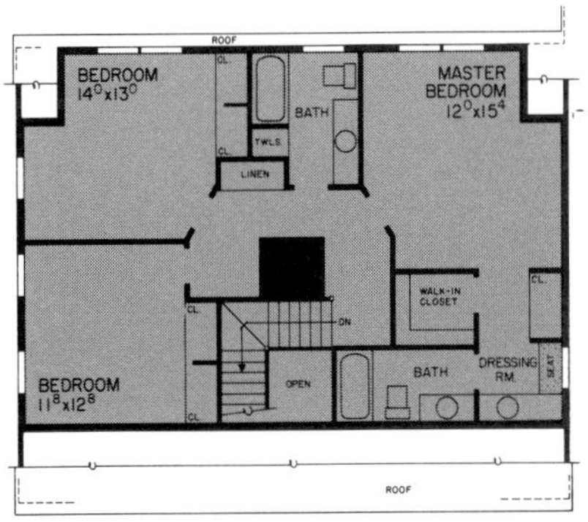

Design by Home Planners, Inc.

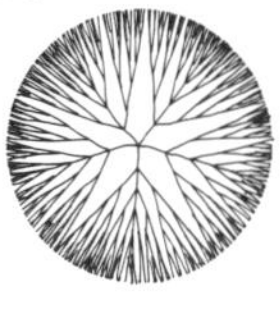

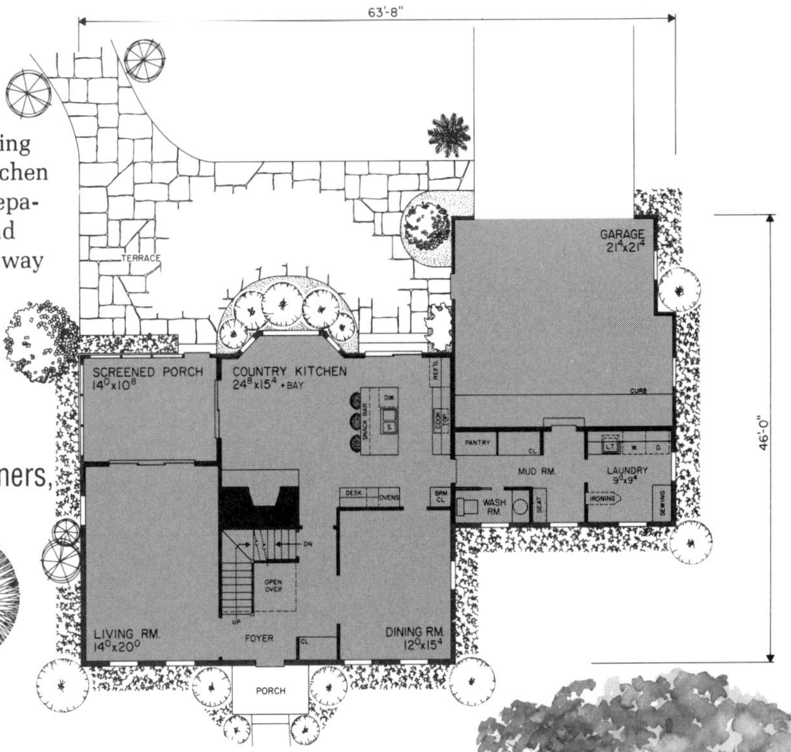

Design Q9305

Square Footage: 2,015

● Romantic appeal radiates from the elegant covered porch and gracious features of this ranch home. A formal dining room with bright windows is viewed from the entry. In the great room, featuring an entertainment center and bookcases, warmth emanates from the three-sided through-fireplace. Homeowners will enjoy the cozy retreat of the bay-windowed hearth room with 10-foot ceiling. Near the hearth is an open breakfast area and kitchen with snack bar, pantry and ample counter space. A window seat framed by closets highlights secondary Bedroom 2. The third bedroom easily converts to an optional den for quiet study. Designed for privacy, the master suite enjoys a boxed ceiling, skylit dressing area with His and Hers lavs, corner whirlpool and large walk-in closet. With many dramatic elements, this will be the home of your dreams!

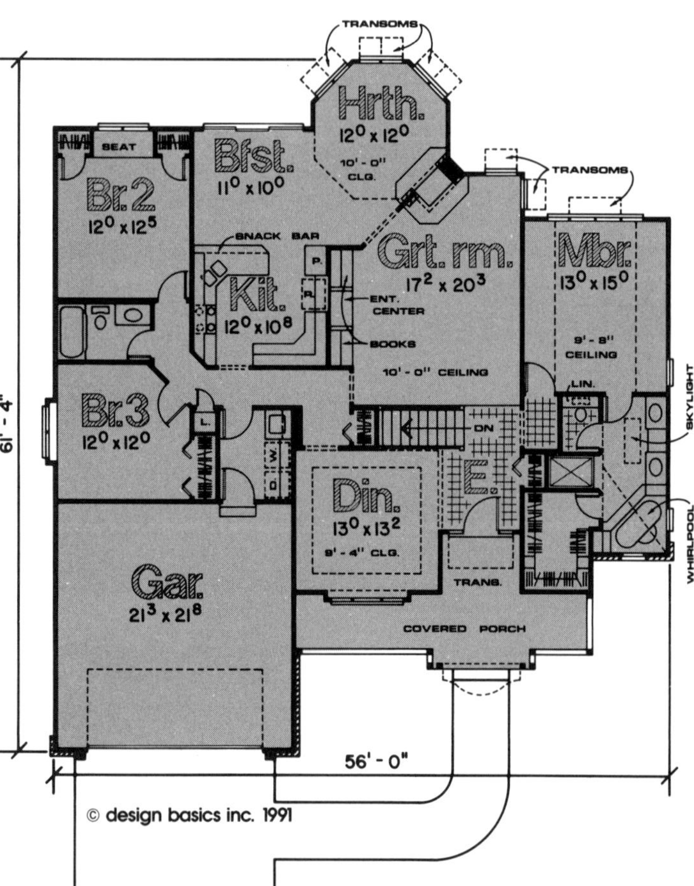

Design by
Design
Basics,
Inc.

TRANSOMS
TRANSOMS
Kit. 8^4 x 13^7
Bfst. 10^8 x 13^7
Grt. rm. 15^0 x 20^0
10'-0" CEILING
Mbr. 13^0 x 15^0
9'-0" CLG.
SKYLIGHT
DESK
R. P.
W. D.
WET BAR SERVERY
WHIRL-POOL
SEAT
LIN.
ON
LIN
Gar. 20^8 x 23^0
HUTCH
Din. 12^0 x 14^0
10'-0" CLG.
E.
Br. 2 11^0 x 11^0
10'-0" CLG.
OPTIONAL DEN
Br. 3 11^0 x 11^0
TRANSOMS
COVERED PORCH
TRANSOMS
48'-0"
62'-0"

Design Q9304

Square Footage: 1,850

● European style influences the elevation of this distinctive ranch home. Appealing rooflines and a covered porch with repeating arches provide stunning curb appeal. Inside, an impressive 10-foot high entry greets family and friends. An open concept pervades the kitchen/dinette area. Picture your family enjoying the bayed eating area, wrapping counters, desk, island and wet/bar servery ideal for entertaining. The decorative hutch space adds appeal to a formal dining room. Bright windows frame a fireplace in the great room. Sure to please is the service entry to the laundry/mud room with soaking sink and counter space. Bedroom 2 can easily be converted into a private den. A boxed ceiling decorates the master suite while three windows provide natural lighting. Dual lavs, a walk-in closet, whirlpool and cedar-lined window seat enhance the master bath.

Design by
Design
Basics,
Inc.

Design Q9306

First Floor: 1,268 square feet
Second Floor: 1,075 square feet
Total: 2,343 square feet

● Captivating! A covered front porch hints at the comfort within. An added perk is the large 3-car garage. Formal rooms are surveyed by the entry. To the right, a volume ceiling, elegant windows and through-fireplace lend atmosphere to the living room. A volume family room includes repeating arched windows, an entertainment center and bookcases. The sunny dinette area is served by a roomy kitchen with wrapping counters, snack bar and planning desk. Convenience was designed into the main floor utility/laundry room and large closet. Upstairs, comfortable secondary bedrooms are served by a walk-in linen closet and bath with dual lavs. French doors lead into the master suite with vaulted ceiling, whirlpool, dual vanities and a huge walk-in closet.

Br. 2
11³ x 12²
Mbr.
16⁴ x 13³
9'-4" CEILING
WHIRLPOOL
DN
LIN.
LINEN
Br. 3
11⁰ x 11⁰
Br. 4
11⁰ x 11⁰

Design by
Design Basics, Inc.

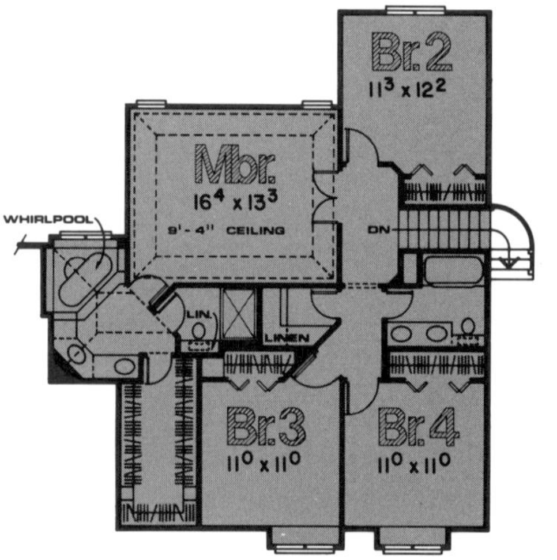

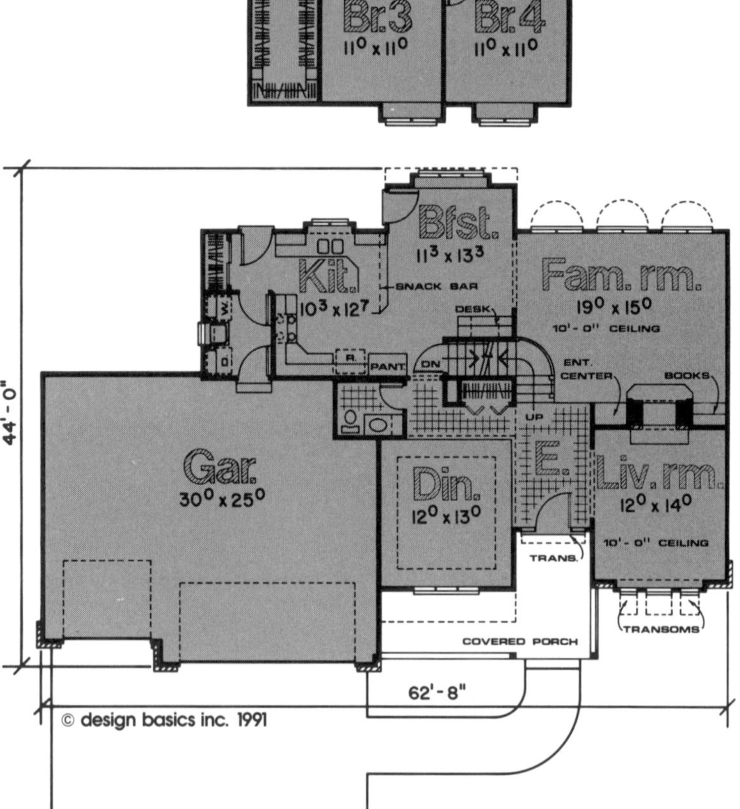

Design Q9267

Square Footage: 2,068

● Walk through an elegant covered veranda to enter this spacious ranch home. A spectacular window provides a view out the back from the expansive great room. Gathering areas are warmed by a three-sided fireplace and served by a well-planned kitchen with a pantry, desk and island counter with snack bar. An irresistible master suite features a private covered deck and a pampering dressing area with a whirlpool and large walk-in closet. The den could be used as a third bedroom with an alternate door location. An abundance of windows throughout the plan brightens this home.

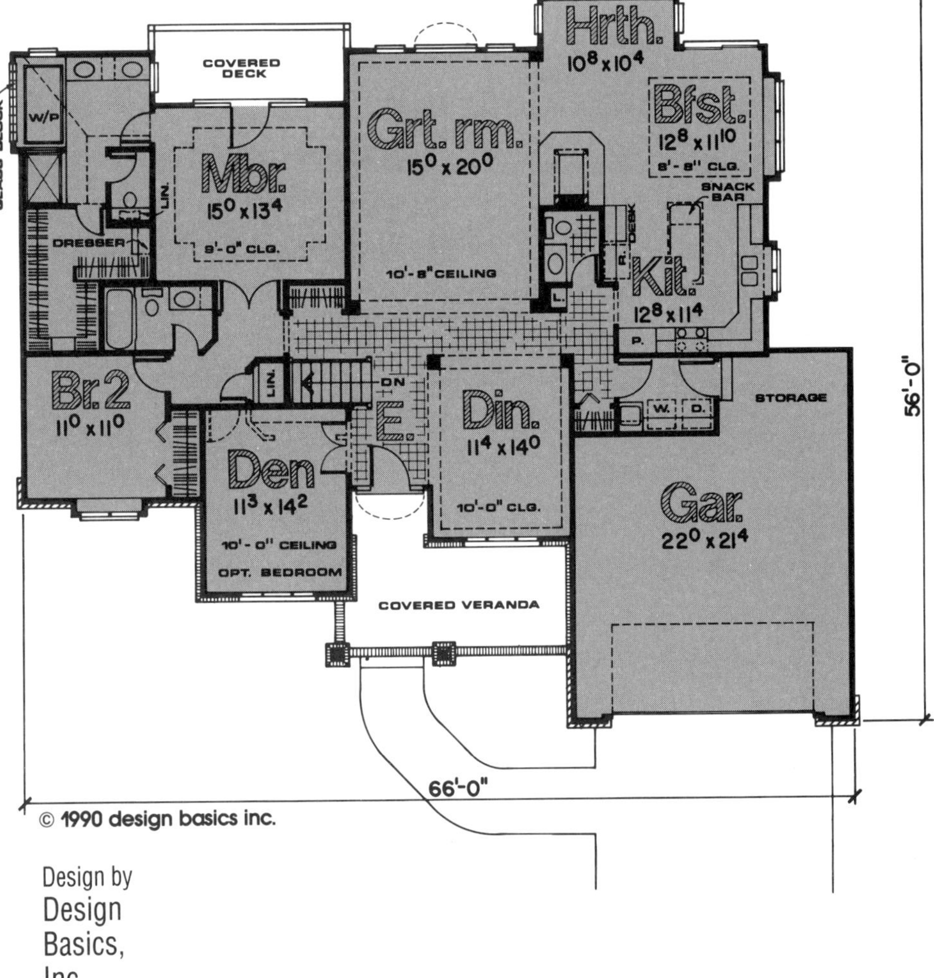

Design by Design Basics, Inc.

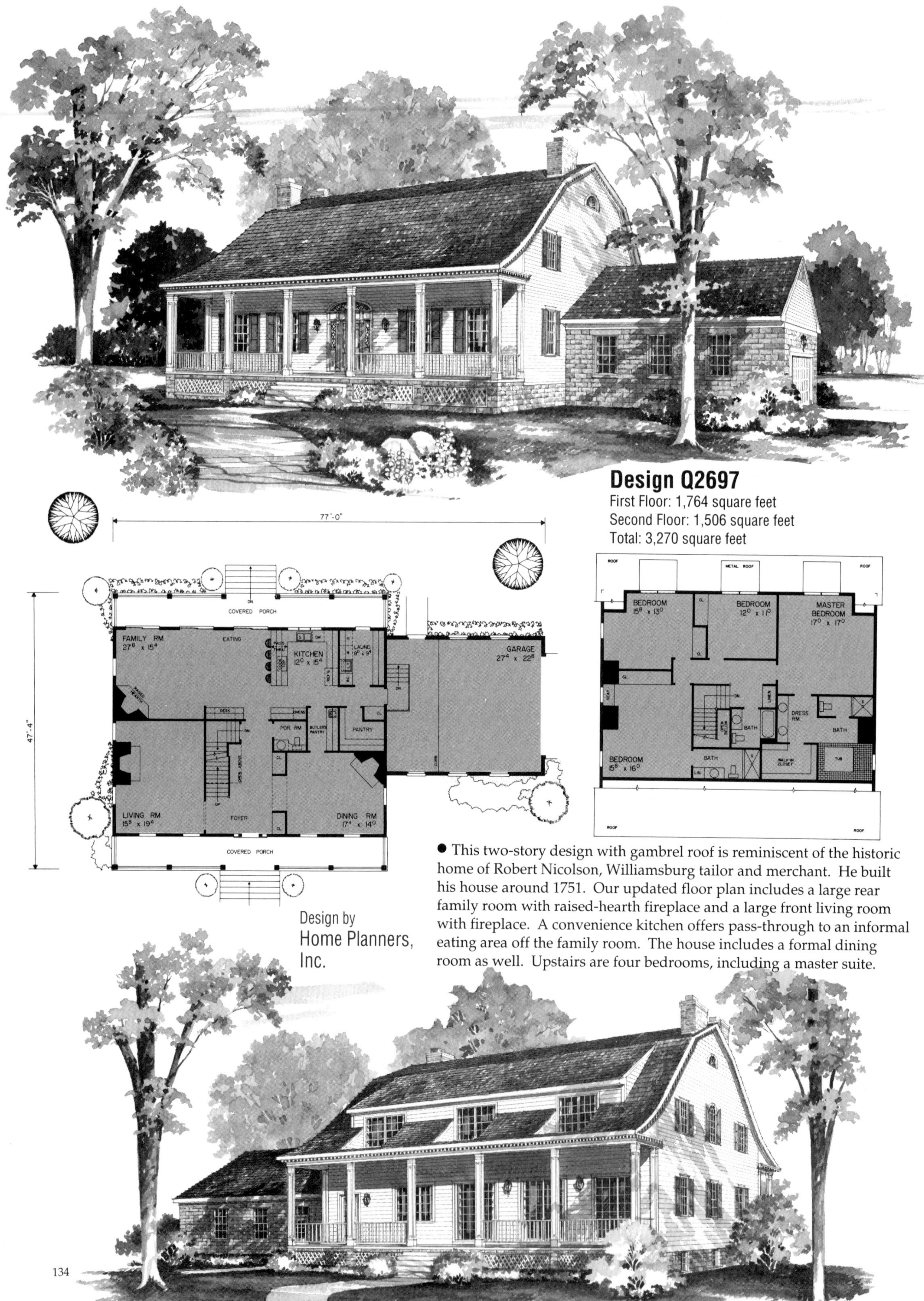

Design Q2697

First Floor: 1,764 square feet
Second Floor: 1,506 square feet
Total: 3,270 square feet

● This two-story design with gambrel roof is reminiscent of the historic home of Robert Nicolson, Williamsburg tailor and merchant. He built his house around 1751. Our updated floor plan includes a large rear family room with raised-hearth fireplace and a large front living room with fireplace. A convenience kitchen offers pass-through to an informal eating area off the family room. The house includes a formal dining room as well. Upstairs are four bedrooms, including a master suite.

Design by
Home Planners, Inc.

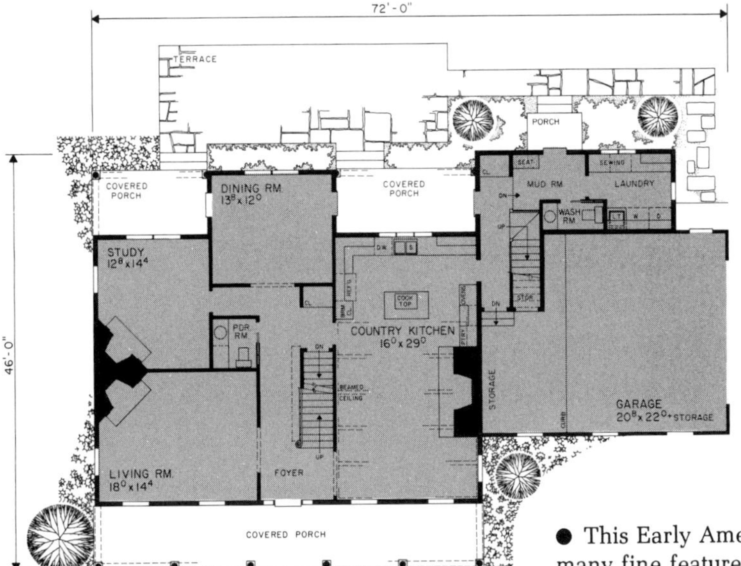

Design Q2680 First Floor: 1,707 square feet

Second Floor: 1,439 square feet; Total: 3,146 square feet

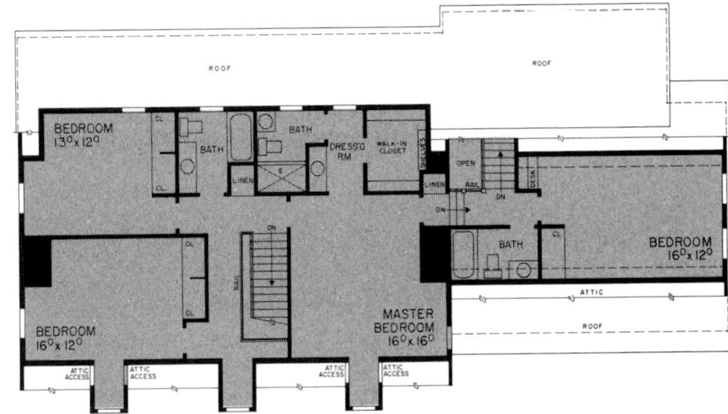

- This Early American, Dutch Colonial not only has charm, but offers many fine features. The foyer allows easy access to all rooms on the first floor - excellent livability. Note the large country kitchen with beamed ceiling, fireplace and island cook top. A large, formal dining room and powder room are only a few steps away. A fireplace also will be found in the study and living room. The service area, mud room, wash room and laundry are tucked near the garage. Two bedrooms, full bath and master bedroom suite will be found on the second floor. A fourth bedroom and bath are accessible through the master bedroom or stairs in the service entrance.

Design by
Home Planners, Inc.

Design Q9859

First Floor: 1,370 square feet
Second Floor: 1,334 square feet
Total: 2,704 square feet

● This Early American design possesses a rare charm, largely due to its proportions and breezeway. True to tradition are the gambrel roof, brick and siding combination, covered entrance and detailed columns and balustrade. The main level begins with equally proportioned dining and living rooms framed by columns. A powder room is located on the right before the great room complete with fireplace and a wall of windows. The kitchen is large and opens directly onto the breezeway porch, which leads to the two-car garage. The upper level begins with a children's den at the top of the staircase. Just beyond, the private guest bedroom awaits visitors with a complete bath and walk-in closet. Additional bedrooms feature a shared bath, generous closets and dormer windows. The master suite consists of a very large sleeping area with fireplace, a master bath with bay window, separate shower and two walk-in closets.

WIDTH 68'-6"
DEPTH 46'-6"

LAUNDRY 6'-8" X 8'-0"
BREAKFAST 10'-4" X 10'-6"
KITCHEN 11'-6" X 16'-4"
GREAT ROOM 19'-0" X 17'-6"
PORCH 15'-0" X 14'-0"
TWO-CAR GARAGE 21'-4" X 21'-4"
DN
UP
POWDER
WET BAR
DINING ROOM 11'-0" X 14'-4"
FOYER 7'-4" X 14'-4"
LIVING ROOM 11'-0" X 14'-4"
STOOP

MASTER BATH
HIS
HERS
MASTER BEDROOM 15'-10" X 17'-6"
GUEST BEDROOM 15'-4" X 10'-0"
DEN 18'-0" X 7'-6"
DN.
BATH
BEDROOM NO. 3 11'-4" X 11'-8"
BEDROOM NO. 2 14'-4" X 11'-4"
BATH

Design by
Design Traditions
Atlanta

Design Q9860

First Floor: 1,530 square feet
Second Floor: 1,515 square feet
Total: 3,045 square feet

Design by
Design Traditions
Atlanta

● The Country French charm of this home is irresistible; with gambrel roof, combined use of stone and wood, and segmented stone arch window detailing. The two-story foyer with staircase and tray ceiling gives a first impression of space and style. The large living and dining rooms are complemented by large window areas, a fireplace and detailed columns. The art of cooking is emphasized in the kitchen, with a work island and charming breakfast room that opens into a large family room with fireplace and wet bar. A second staircase from the family room allows easy access to the upper level. Touring the upper level, the hallway leads to additional bedrooms, both with large closets and a shared bath. A fourth bedroom has a walk-in closet and private bath. The master suite includes a large bay-windowed sitting area, a luxurious master bath and an extensive walk-in closet, as well as a perfectly located exercise room or hideaway.

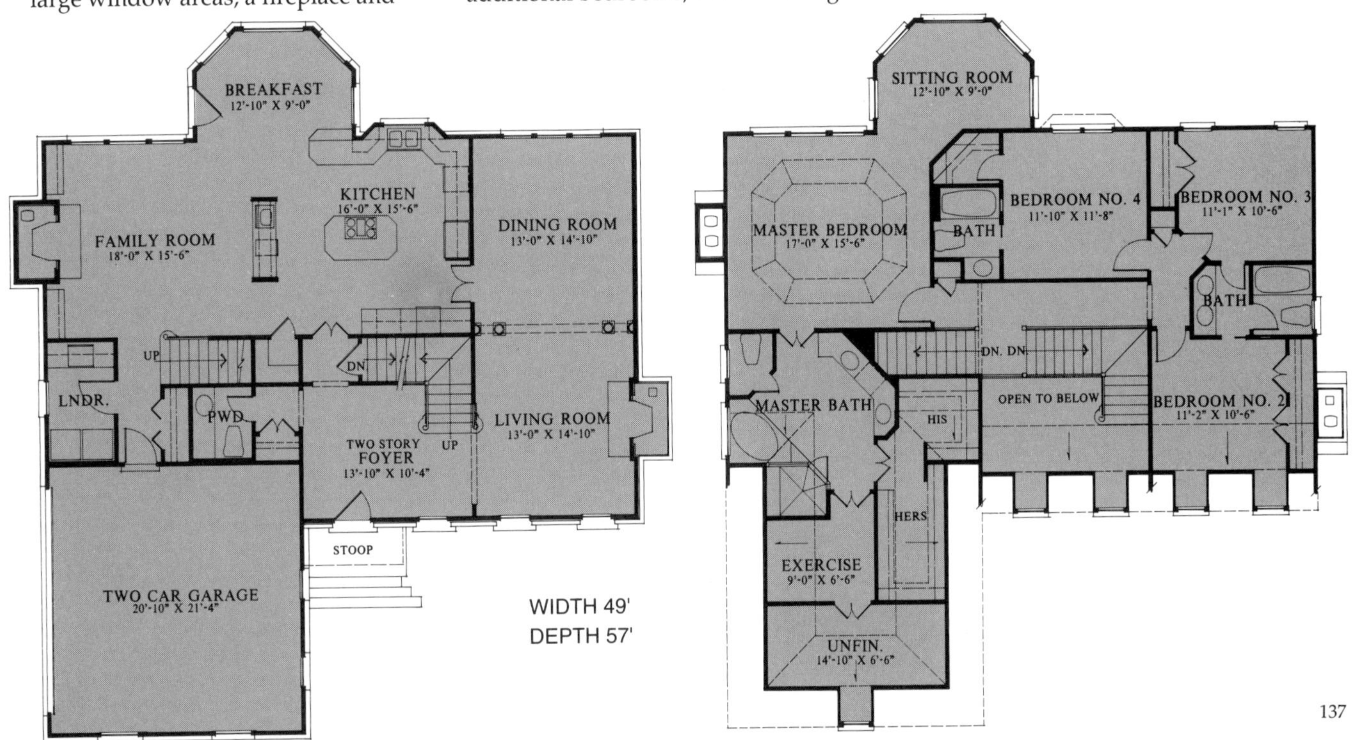

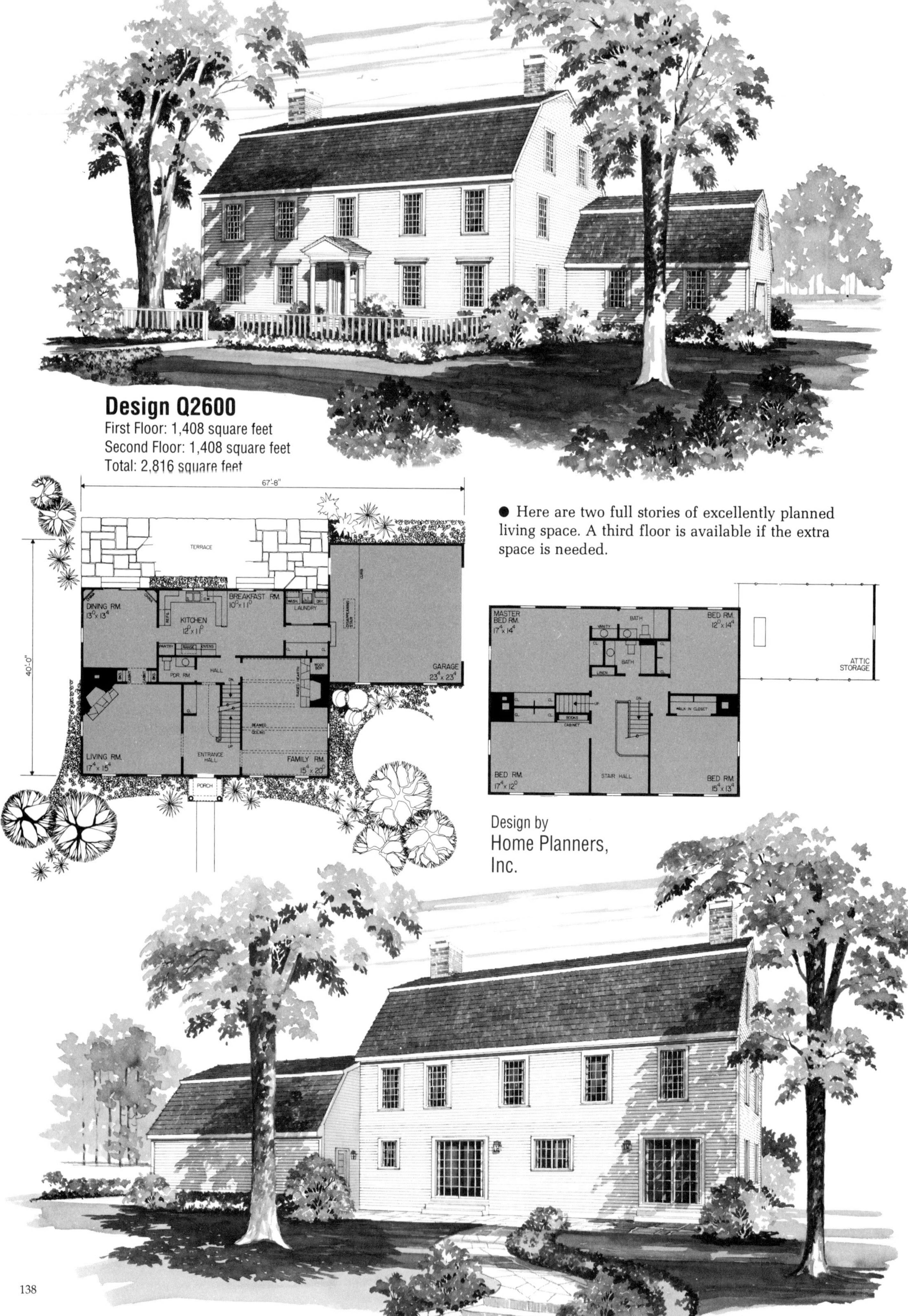

Design Q2600

First Floor: 1,408 square feet
Second Floor: 1,408 square feet
Total: 2,816 square feet

● Here are two full stories of excellently planned living space. A third floor is available if the extra space is needed.

Design by
Home Planners, Inc.

COUNTRY-STYLE CAPES & COTTAGES

Country Capes and Cottages are simple, economical homes with a New England Colonial heritage. They have roots in the down-to-earth shelters constructed by the early settlers which featured a basic, boxy design. These early models were small, square and simple, and, consequently, were easy to construct. They provided practical housing that could be expanded as needed. Today's Country Cape fits comfortably almost anywhere but works especially well situated on the smaller lots in lakeside and seaside settings.

The modern versions of this style are constructed in simple box-like fashion usually with classic horizontal siding and a steeply pitched gabled roof. They may be a full Cape with a center-hall floor plan or the entry may be off-center as in the half-Cape or the three-quarter Cape. Many are designed to "grow" by the addition of winged appendages that give these great starter houses an expandable nature.

Following classic traditional architecture for a facade, the Country Cape may be updated nicely with projecting dormers and sun rooms to the rear. They almost always feature symmetric, multi-paned shuttered windows and may include dormers on the second floor.

Decorative detailing may be very sparse or can include dove-cotes, cupolas, and arched garage doors or service entries. Some versions even have Victorian-style gingerbread details. Western examples of the Country Cape are more rustic and cabin-like and often include a front porch. It is common to see this style used for second homes or leisure living because of their time-honored design and low building costs.

Country Capes seem almost to be defined by their expandable nature. Consider, for example, Design Q2682 in this section which begins as a simple "half house" then adds double wings for a study and a garage. A large plan, Design Q2699, is a Full Telescoping Cape with multiple wings and true Cape Cod, 1½-story style.

Adapted versions include Design Q2615, a Modified Country Cape, and Design Q9007, a Victorian-Style Cape. Though both of these designs have elements of Cape Cod design, they have been altered with details borrowed from other styles to create a new look. Likewise, Designs Q2661 and Q9666 have taken on more dramatic country elements: shake roof, covered front porch, stone chimney stack.

Always a favorite, Cape Cods gain even more popularity when done in country accents. This section of Country-Style Capes and Cottages shows off the best components of this adapted design.

Design Q2682

First Floor (Basic Plan): 976 square feet
First Floor (Expanded Plan): 1,230 square feet
Second Floor (Both Plans): 744 square feet
Total (Basic Plan): 1,720 square feet
Total (Expanded Plan): 1,974 square feet

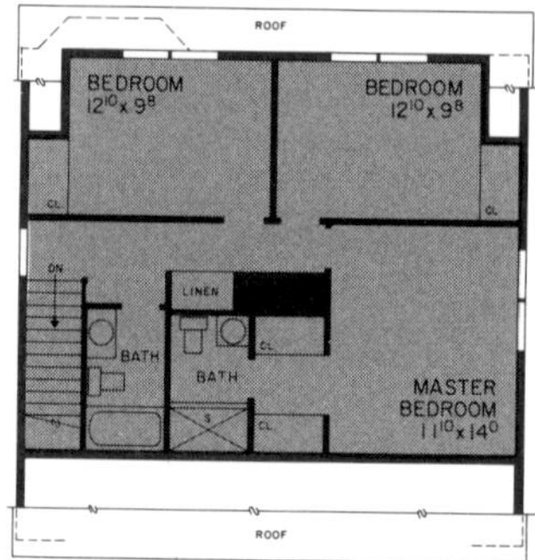

● Here is an expandable Colonial with a full measure of Cape Cod Charm. For those who wish to build the basic house, there is an abundance of low-budget livability. Twin fireplaces serve the formal living room and the informal country kitchen. Note the spaciousness of both areas. A dining room and powder room are also on the first floor of this basic plan. Upstairs three bedrooms and two full baths.

Design by
Home Planners, Inc.

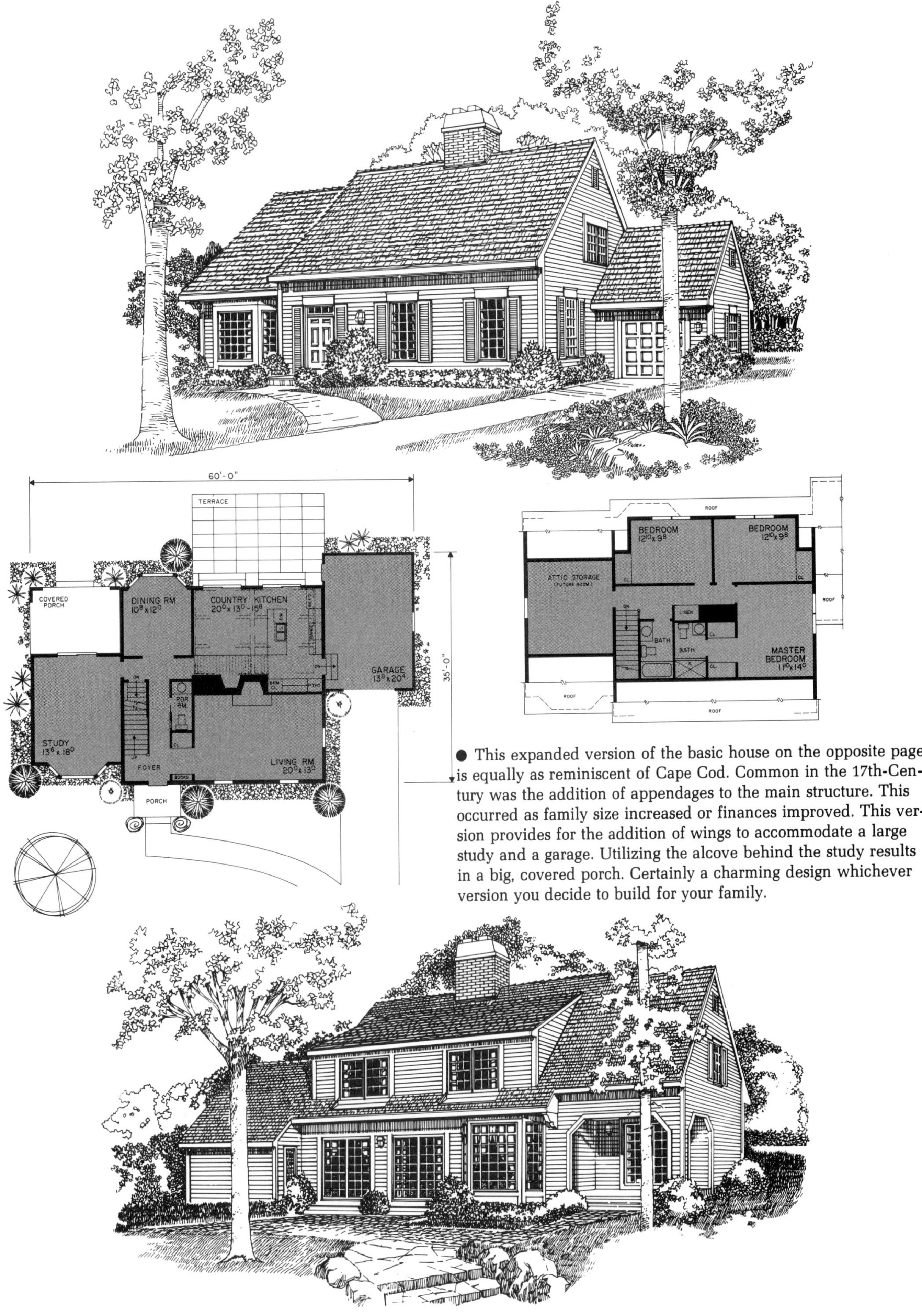

● This expanded version of the basic house on the opposite page is equally as reminiscent of Cape Cod. Common in the 17th-Century was the addition of appendages to the main structure. This occurred as family size increased or finances improved. This version provides for the addition of wings to accommodate a large study and a garage. Utilizing the alcove behind the study results in a big, covered porch. Certainly a charming design whichever version you decide to build for your family.

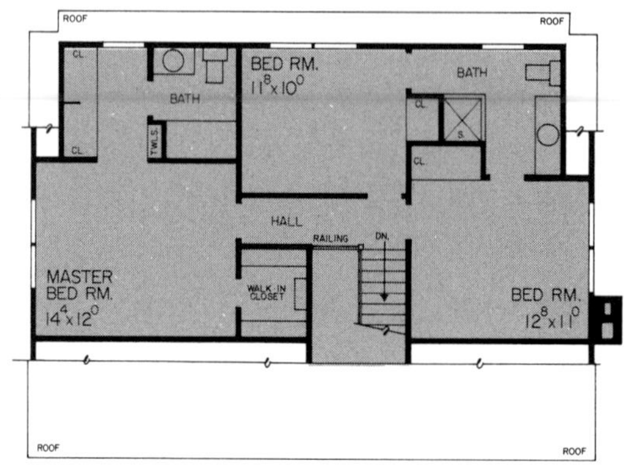

Design Q2571

First Floor: 1,137 square feet
Second Floor: 795 square feet
Total: 1,932 square feet

● This cozy Cape has an efficient plan that's long on affordable livability. Note the comfortable family room, which has both a fireplace and snack bar; separate dining room with gorgeous bay window; formal living room; and full bath down next to a study that could also be a fourth bedroom. Upstairs are three bedrooms, including a master suite, and two more full bathrooms.

Design by
Home Planners,
Inc.

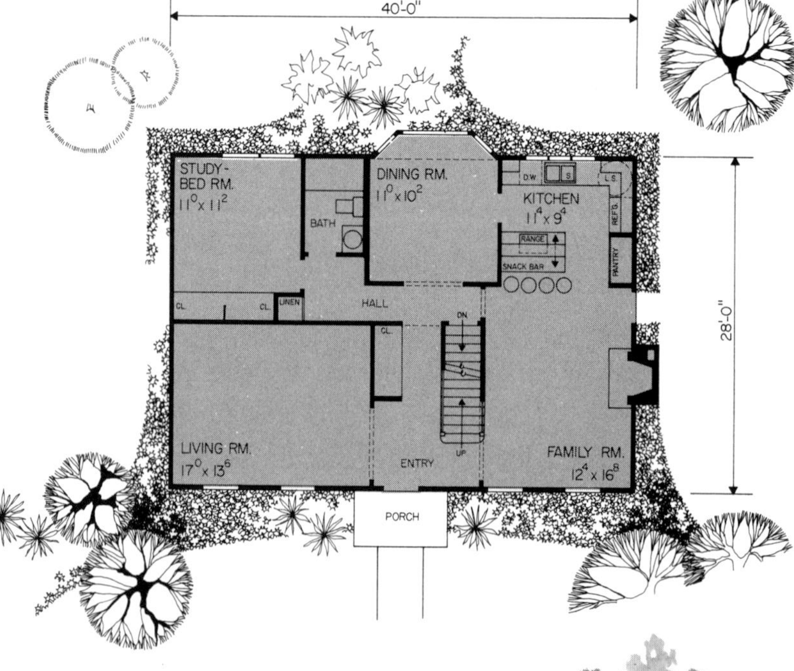

Design Q2852 First Floor: 919 square feet
Second Floor: 535 square feet; Total: 1,454 square feet

● Compact enough for even the smallest lot, this cozy design provides comfortable living space for a small family. At the heart of the plan is a spacious country kitchen. It features a cooking island, snack bar, and a dining area that opens to a house-wide rear terrace. The nearby dining room also opens to the terrace. At the front of the plan is a living room, warmed by a fireplace. Across the central foyer is a cozy study. Two second-floor bedrooms are serviced by two baths. Note the first-floor powder room and storage closet located next to the side entrance. The charm and warmth of this Cape Cod cottage design will be a delight to the family and a practical investment.

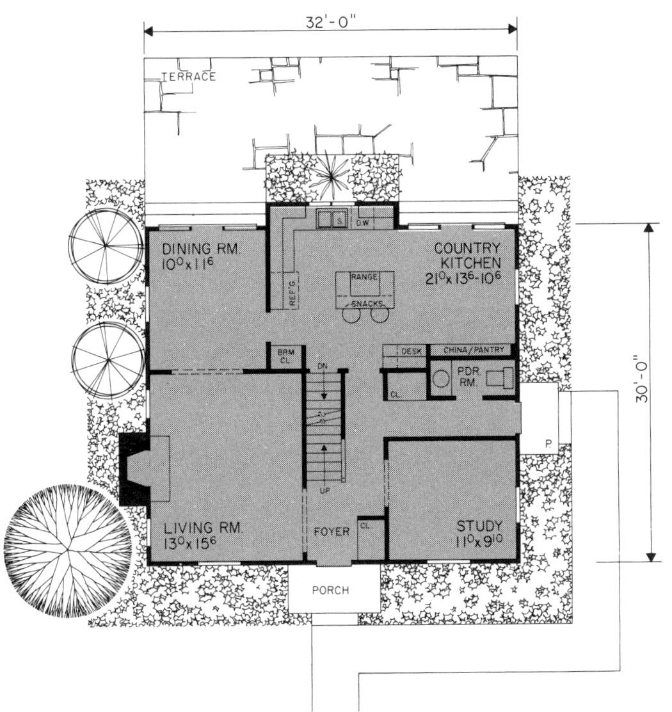

Design by
Home Planners, Inc.

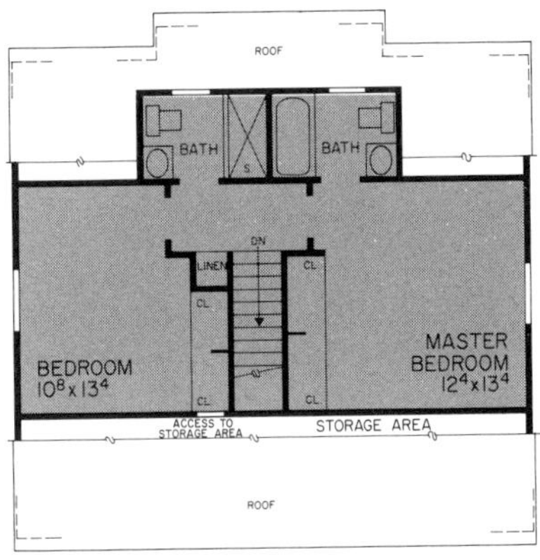

Design Q3372

First Floor: 1,259 square feet
Second Floor: 942 square feet
Total: 2,201 square feet

● Charm is the key word for this delightful plan's exterior, but don't miss the great floor plan inside. Formal living and dining rooms flank the entry foyer to the front; a family room and breakfast room with beamed ceilings are to the rear. The kitchen and service areas function well together and are near the garage and service entrance for convenience. Upstairs are the sleeping accommodations: two family bedrooms and a master suite of nice proportion.

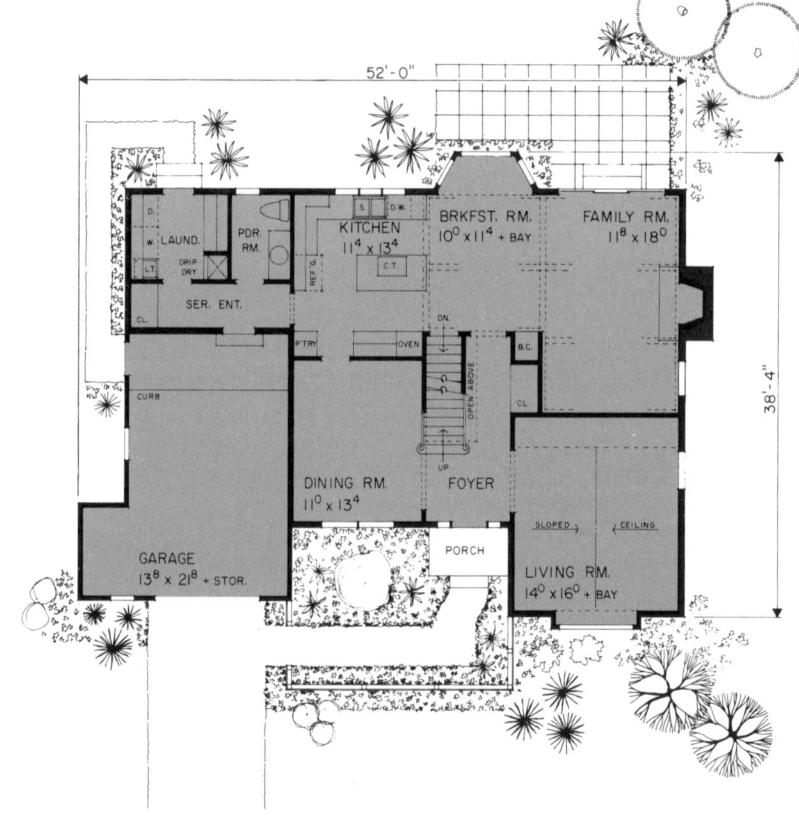

Design by
Home Planners, Inc.

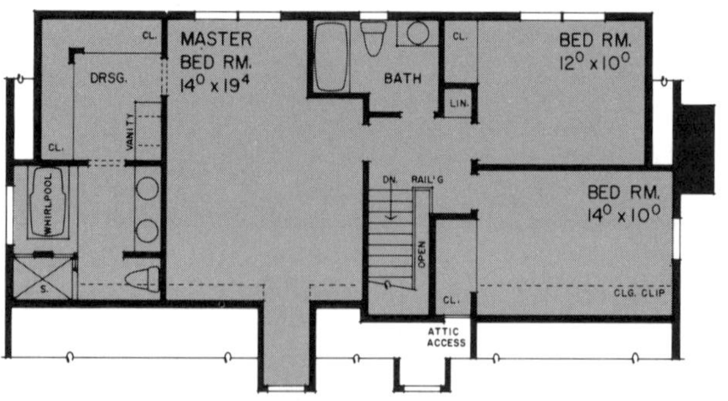

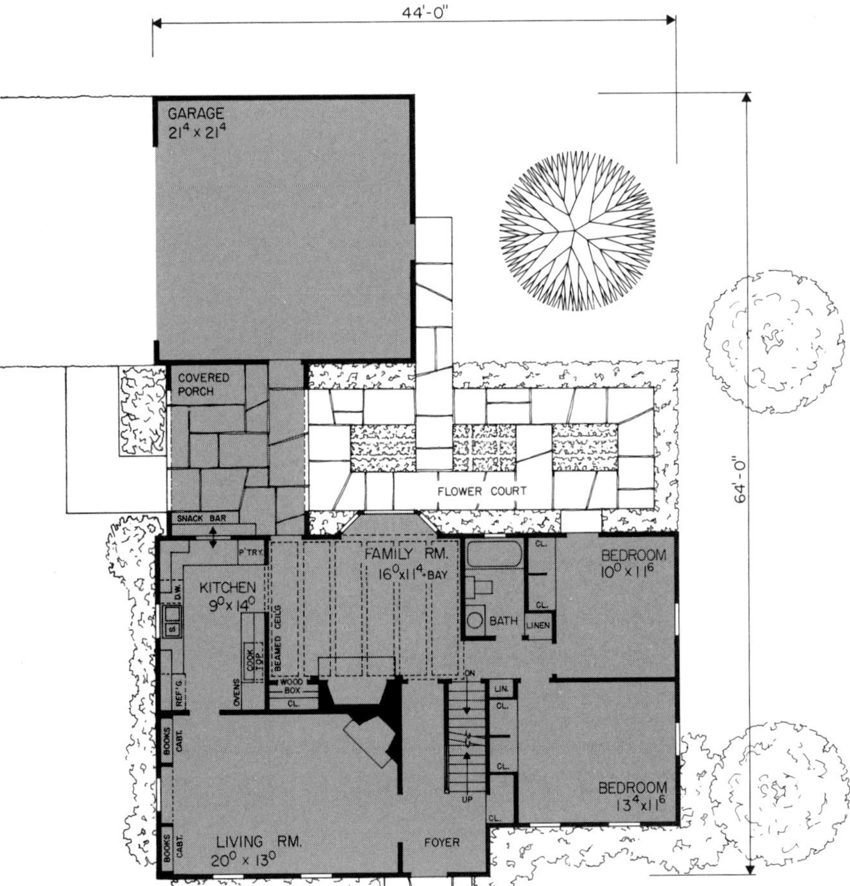

Design Q2145

First Floor: 1,182 square feet
Second Floor: 708 square feet
Total: 1,890 square feet

● Historically referred to as a "half house", this authentic adaptation has its roots in the heritage of New England. With completion of the second floor, the growing family doubles their sleeping capacity. Notice that the overall width of the house is only 44 feet. Take note of the covered porch leading to the garage and the flower court.

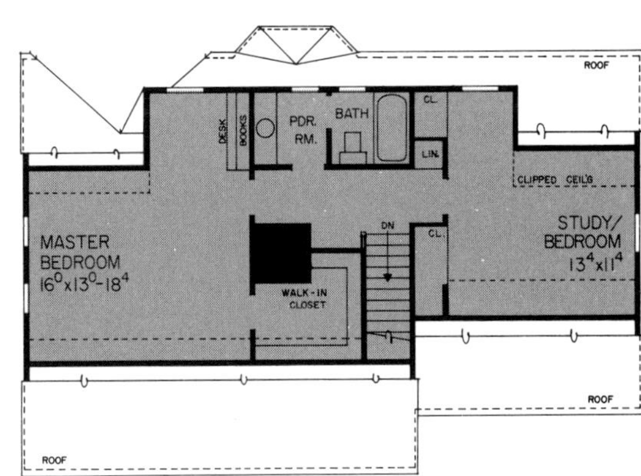

Design by
Home Planners, Inc.

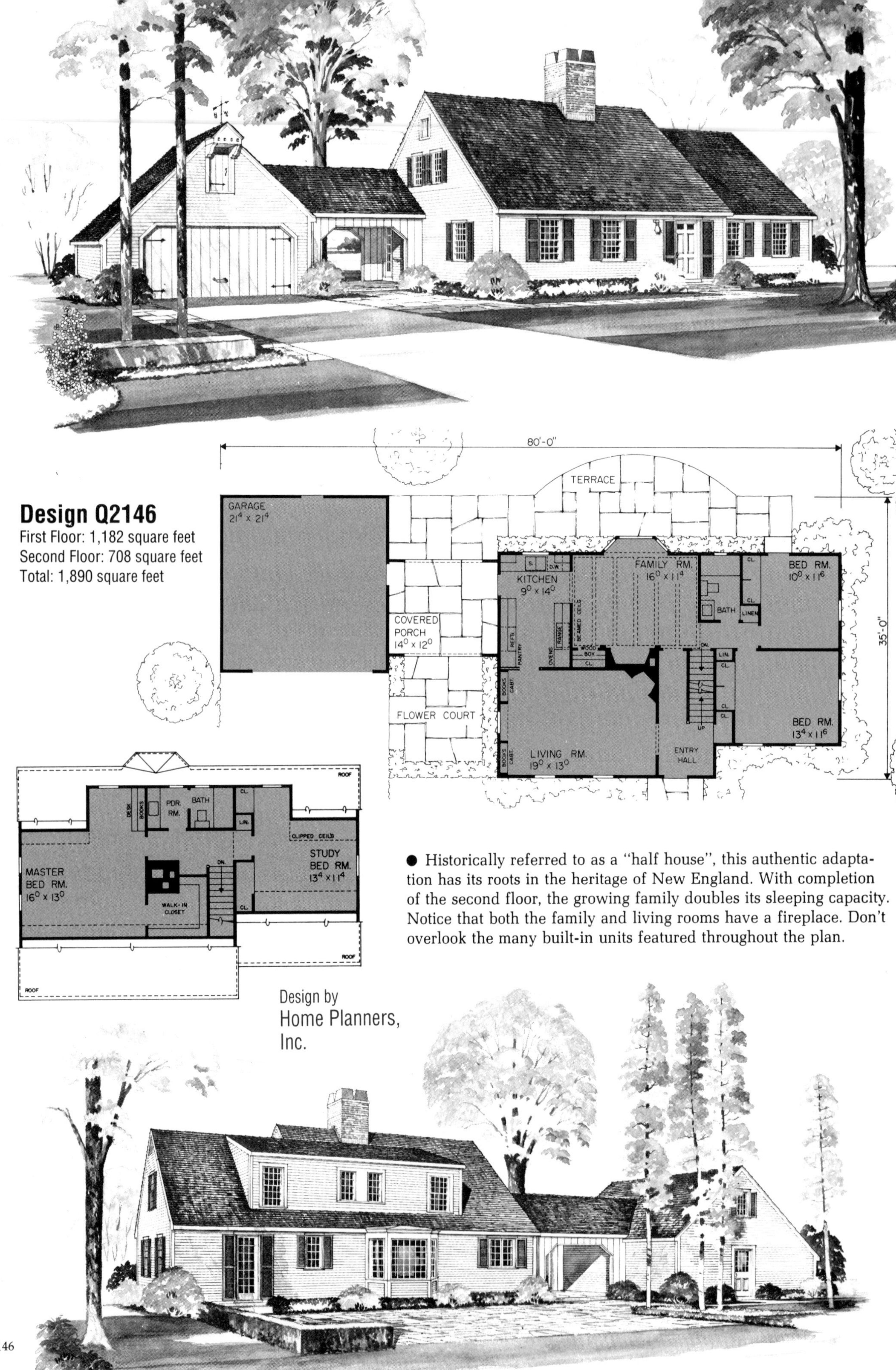

Design Q2146

First Floor: 1,182 square feet
Second Floor: 708 square feet
Total: 1,890 square feet

● Historically referred to as a "half house", this authentic adaptation has its roots in the heritage of New England. With completion of the second floor, the growing family doubles its sleeping capacity. Notice that both the family and living rooms have a fireplace. Don't overlook the many built-in units featured throughout the plan.

Design by
Home Planners, Inc.

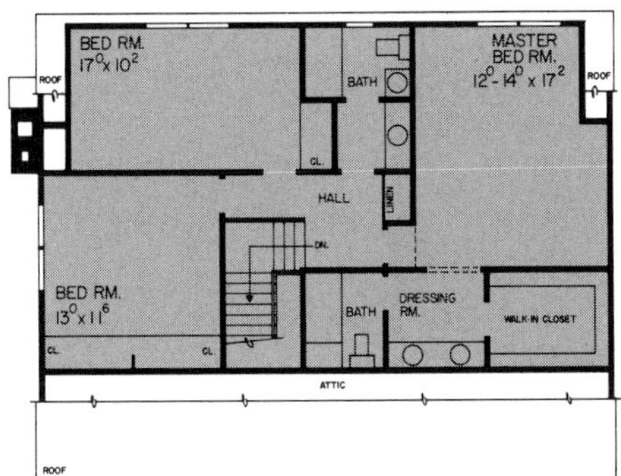

Design Q2596

First Floor: 1,489 square feet
Second Floor: 982 square feet
Total: 2,471 square feet

Design by
Home Planners, Inc.

● A splendid rendition of Cape Cod styling, this plan is a cozy space to come home to. An L-shaped kitchen with island range, adjacent eating area, and family room that features a raised-hearth fireplace and access to a rear terrace are first-floor highlights. Note, too, the formal dining room, comfy living room, spacious entry, and sheltered service entrance that leads to an extra-large laundry room with additional counter space. Upstairs are big bedrooms, including a master suite with a

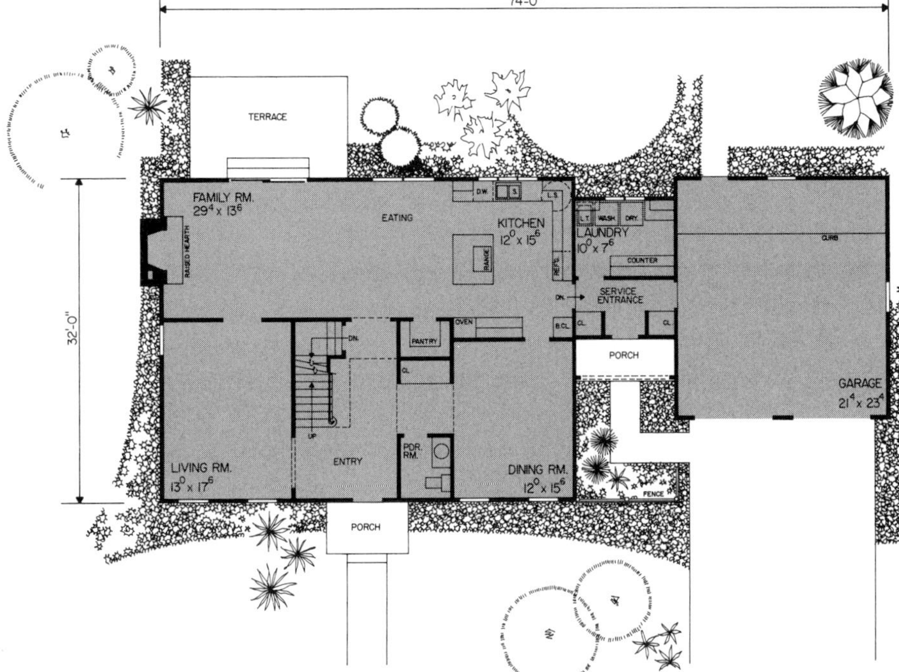

Design Q2500

First Floor: 1,851 square feet
Second Floor: 762 square feet
Total: 2,613 square feet

● The large family will enjoy the wonderful living patterns of this charming home. Don't miss the covered rear porch and the many features of the family room. The master suite, conveniently separated from the family bedrooms on the second floor, has its own bath and a huge walk-in closet. Two more giant-sized storage areas—one a linen closet—are found upstairs.

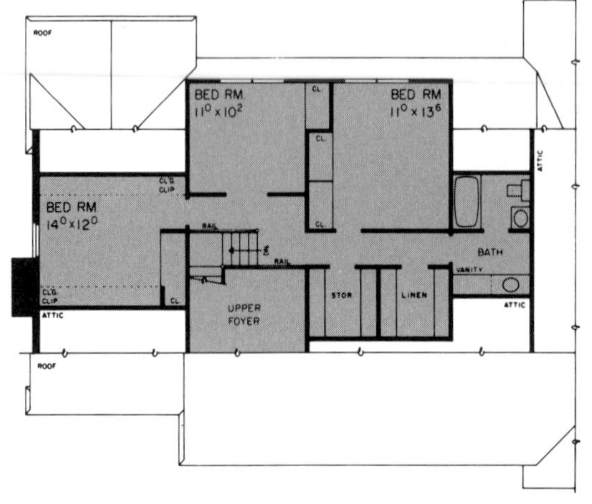

Design by
Home Planners, Inc.

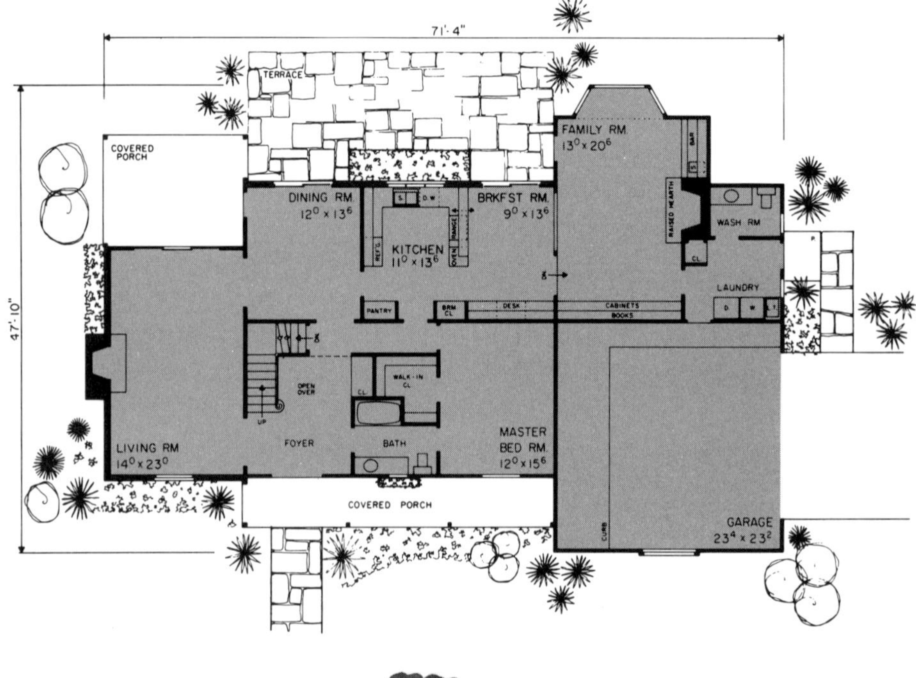

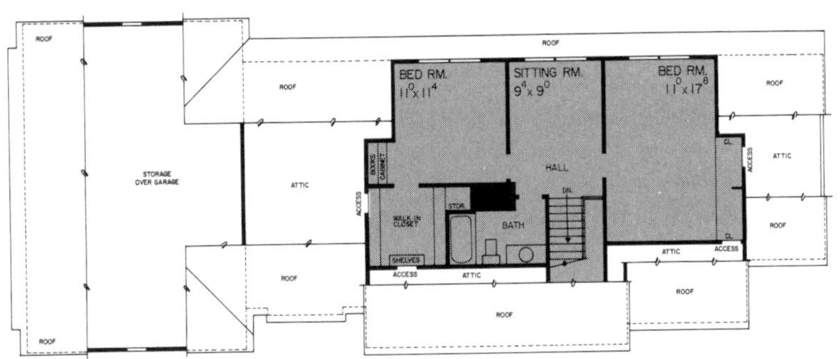

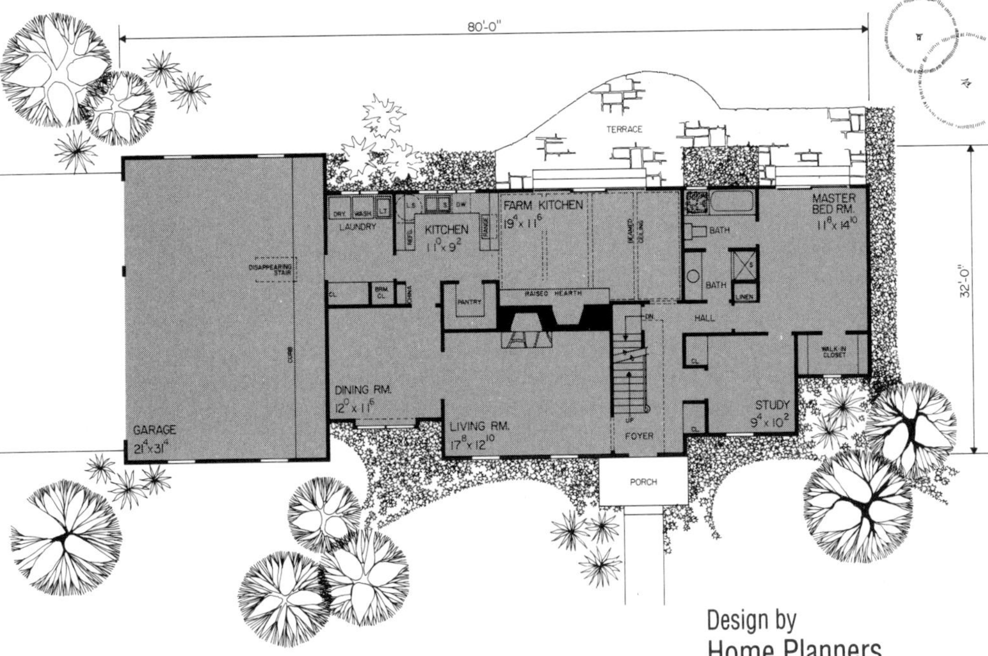

Design Q2563

First Floor: 1,500 square feet
Second Floor: 690 square feet
Total: 2,190 square feet

● This charming Cape Cod definitely will capture your heart with its warm appeal. This home offers you and your family a lot of livability. Upon entering this home, to your left, is a nice-sized living room with fireplace. Adjacent is a dining room. An efficient kitchen and a large, farm kitchen eating area with fireplace will be enjoyed by all. A unique feature on this floor is the master bedroom with a full bath and walk-in closet. Also take notice of the first floor laundry, the pantry and a study for all of your favorite books. Note the sliding glass doors in the farm kitchen and master bedroom. Upstairs you'll find two bedrooms, one with a walk-in closet. Also here, a sitting room and a full bath are available. Lastly, this design accommodates a three car garage.

Design by
Home Planners, Inc.

Design Q9639

Square Footage: 1,541

● This traditional three-bedroom home projects the appearance of a much larger home. The great room features a cathedral ceiling, fireplace and an arched window above the sliding glass door to the expansive rear deck. The master suite contains a pampering master bath and walk-in closet. Two other bedrooms share a full bath with double bowl vanity.

Design by
Donald A.
Gardner,
Architect, Inc.

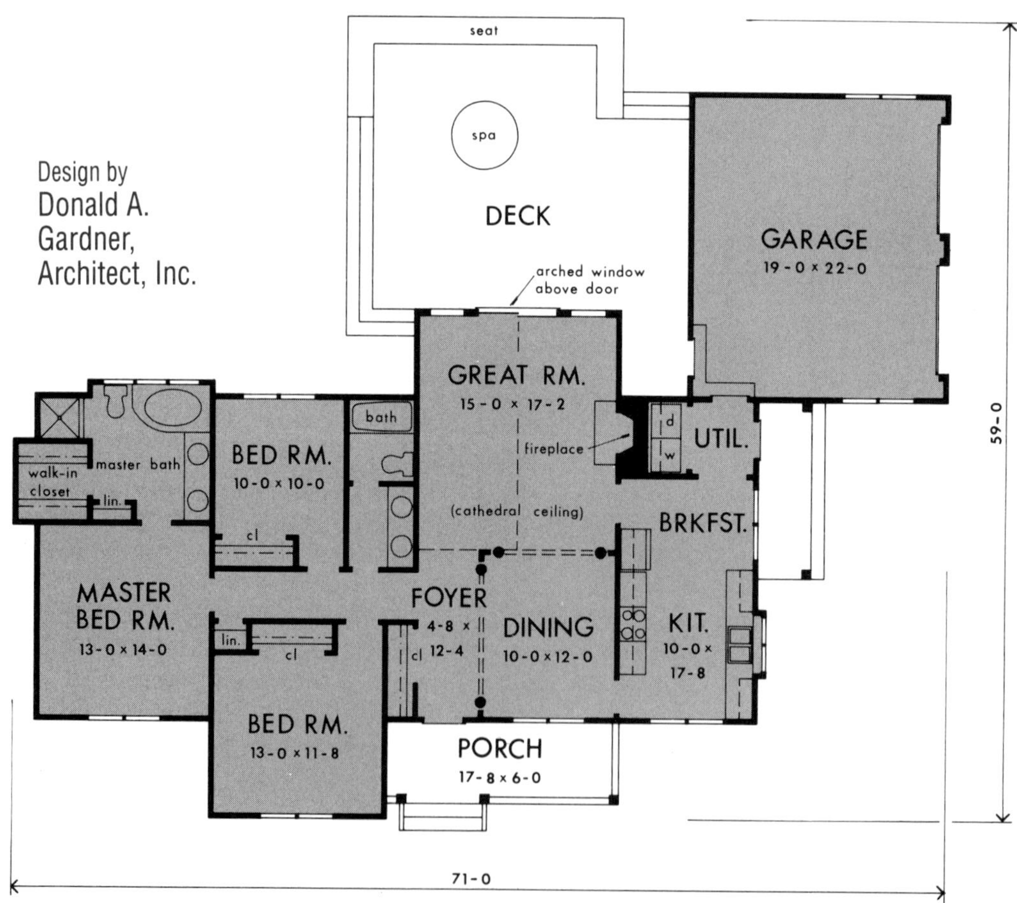

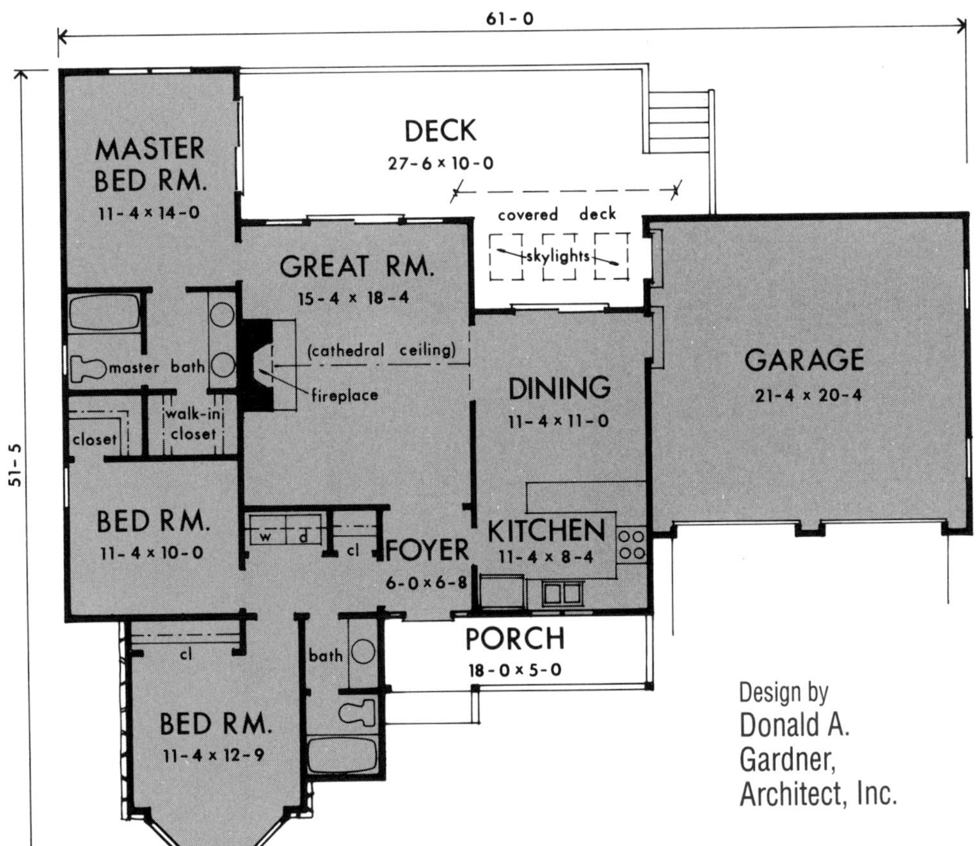

Design by
Donald A.
Gardner,
Architect, Inc.

Design Q9620

Square Footage: 1,310

● A multi-paned bay window, dormers, a cupola, a covered porch and a variety of building materials dress up this one-story cottage. The entrance foyer leads to an impressive great room with cathedral ceiling and fireplace. The U-shaped kitchen, adjacent to the dining room, provides an ideal layout for food preparation. An expansive deck offers shelter while admitting cheery sunlight through skylights. A luxurious master bedroom located to the rear of the house takes advantage of the deck area and is assured privacy from two other bedrooms at the front of the house. These family bedrooms share a full bath.

Design Q2631

First Floor: 1,634 square feet
Second Floor: 1,011 square feet
Total: 2,645 square feet

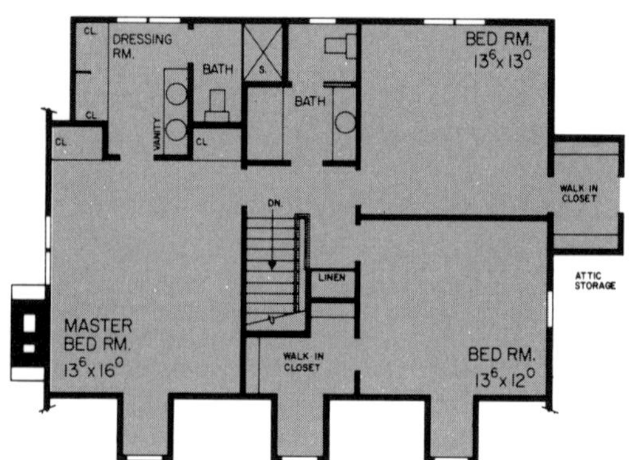

● Two fireplaces and much more! Notice how all the rooms are accessible from the main hall. That keeps traffic in each room to a minimum, saving you work by preserving your furnishings. There's more. A large family room featuring a beamed ceiling, a fireplace with built-in wood box and double doors onto the terrace. An exceptional U-shaped kitchen is ready to serve you. It has an adjacent breakfast nook. Built-ins, too . . a desk, storage pantry, oven and range. Plus a first floor laundry close at hand.

Design by
Home Planners, Inc.

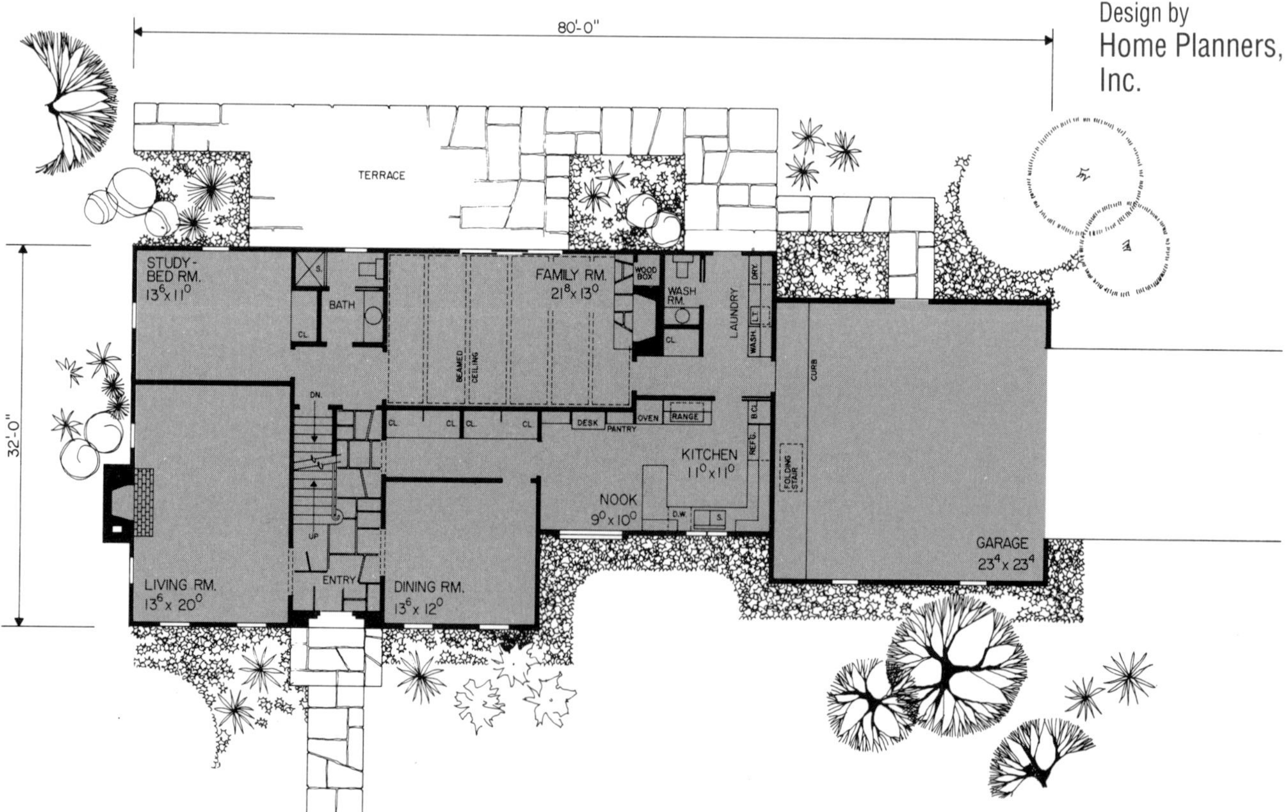

Design Q2395

First Floor: 1,481 square feet
Second Floor: 861 square feet
Total: 2,342 square feet

● New England revisited—the appeal of this type of home is ageless. As for its livability, it will serve its occupants admirably for generations to come. Besides a giant-sized formal living room, there is an equally large family room and a U-shaped kitchen with attached eating area. With two bedrooms downstairs, you may want to finish off the second floor at a later date.

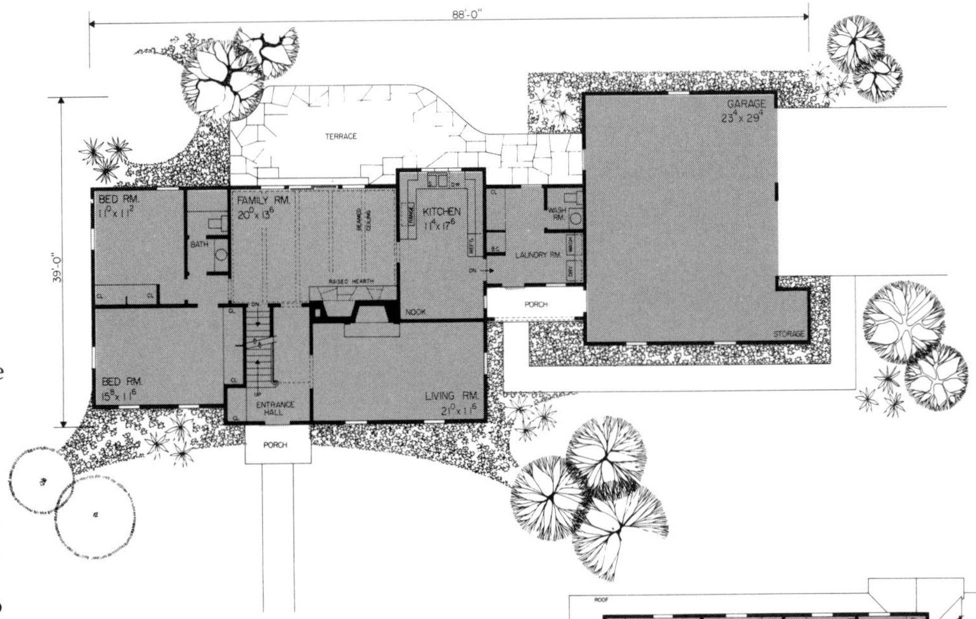

Design by
Home Planners, Inc.

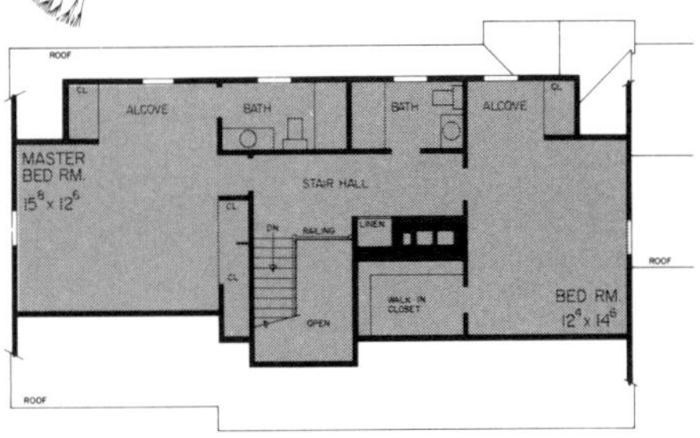

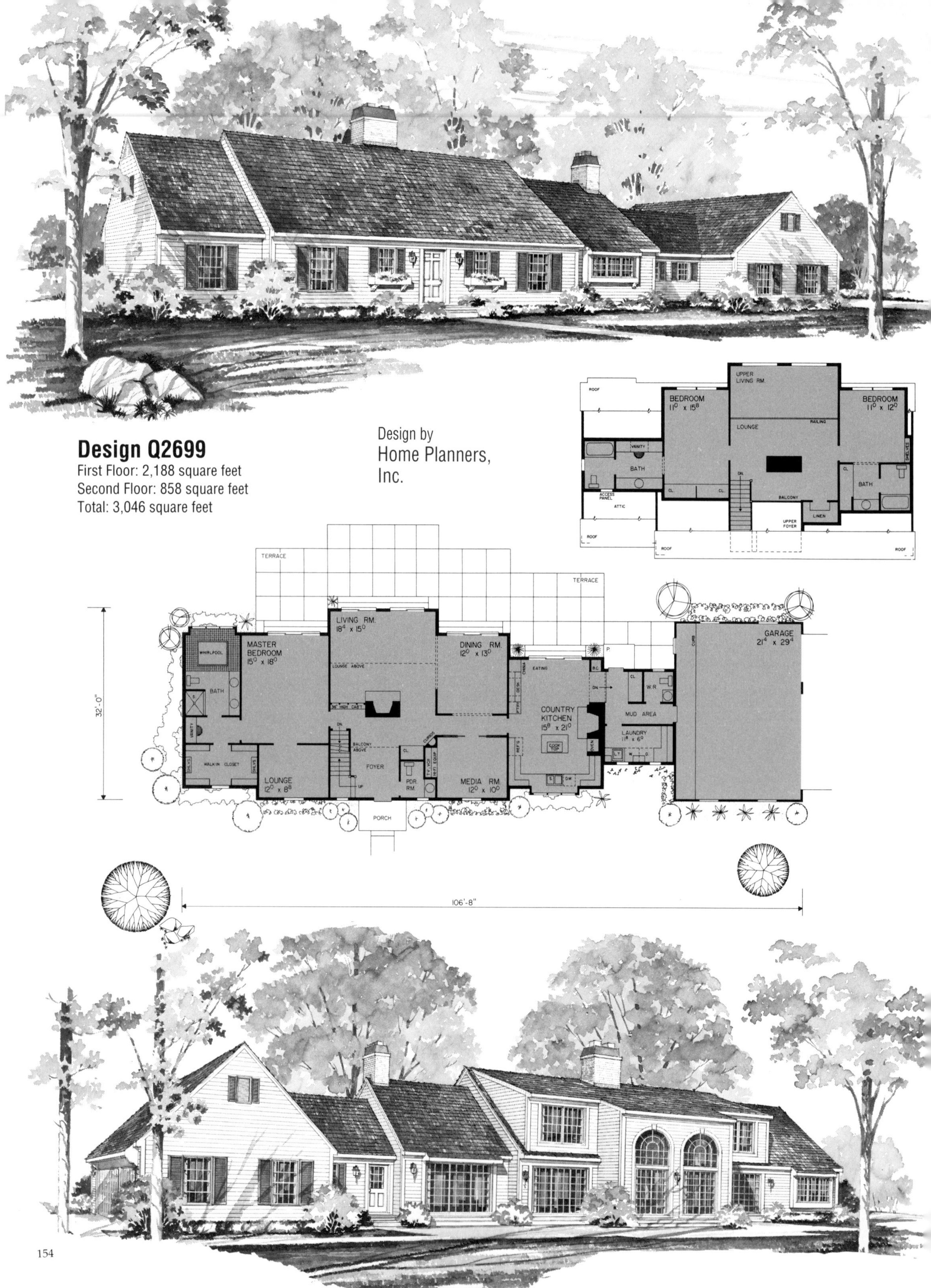

Design Q2699

First Floor: 2,188 square feet
Second Floor: 858 square feet
Total: 3,046 square feet

Design by
Home Planners, Inc.

Design Q1718

First Floor: 2,012 square feet
Second Floor: 589 square feet
Total: 2,601 square feet

● This house has everything—an extremely attractive exterior and a fine, working floor plan. Its varying roof lines and arched details at the service entrance and garage doors are fine complements to the shuttered windows and giant chimney stack. The entry leads directly to formal living and dining rooms. The rear of the plan is dominated by casual living in the family room with fireplace and beamed ceiling. The U-shaped kitchen is nearby for convenience. Three bedrooms (or two and a study) are located on this floor and share a full bath. Upstairs is the magnificent master suite. It has its own lounge area, built-in bookcases, walk-in closet and fine bath. Two large storage areas are also found on this floor: one accessed through the master closet and one over the two-car garage.

Design by
Home Planners, Inc.

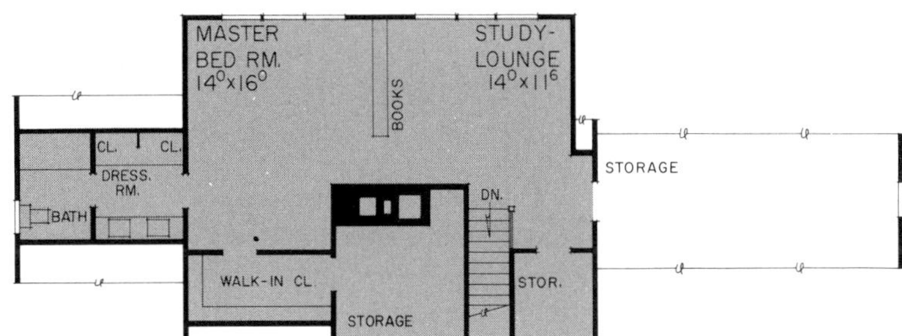

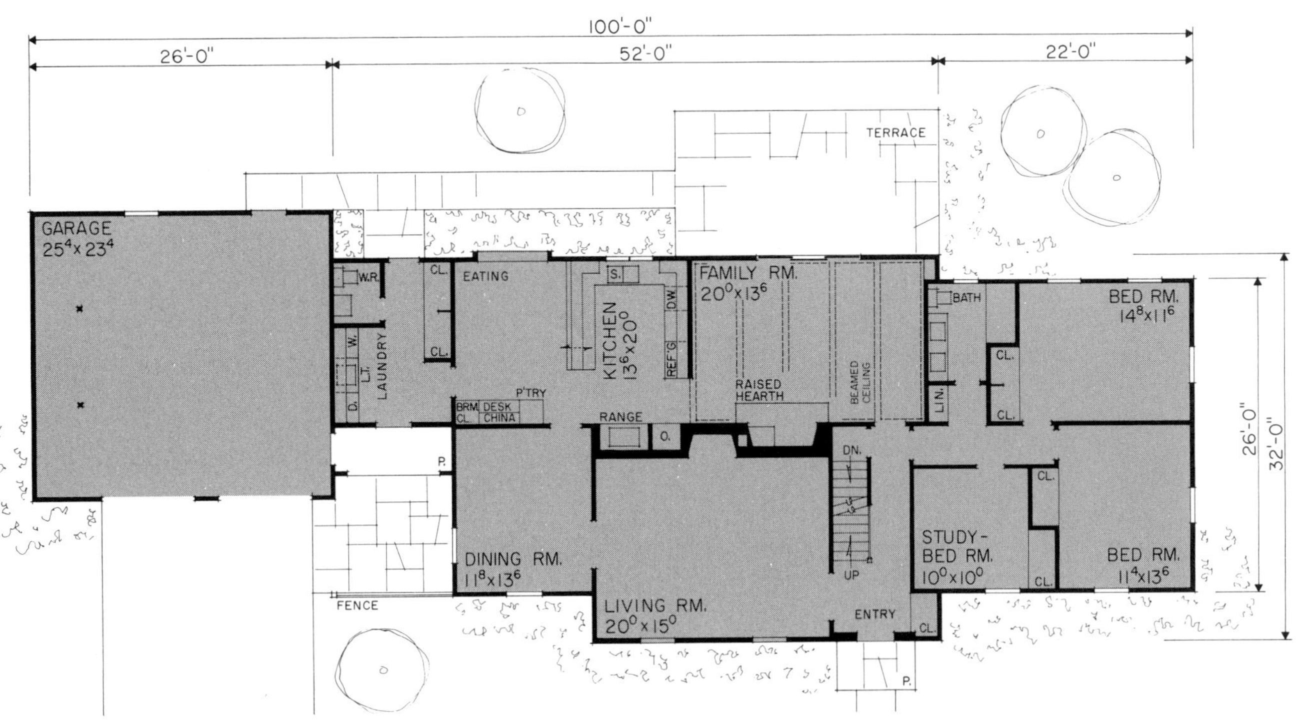

Design Q2995

First Floor: 2,465 square feet
Second Floor: 617 square feet
Total: 3,082 square feet

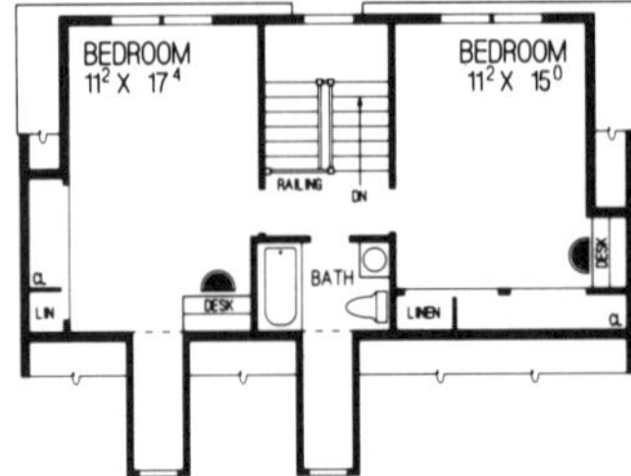

● This New England Colonial delivers beautiful proportions and great livability on 1½ levels. The main area of the house, the first floor, holds a living room, library, family room, dining room and gourmet kitchen. The master bedroom, also on this floor, features a whirlpool tub and sloped ceiling. A long rear terrace stretches the full width of the house. Two bedrooms on the second floor share a full bath; each has a built-in desk.

Design by
Home Planners, Inc.

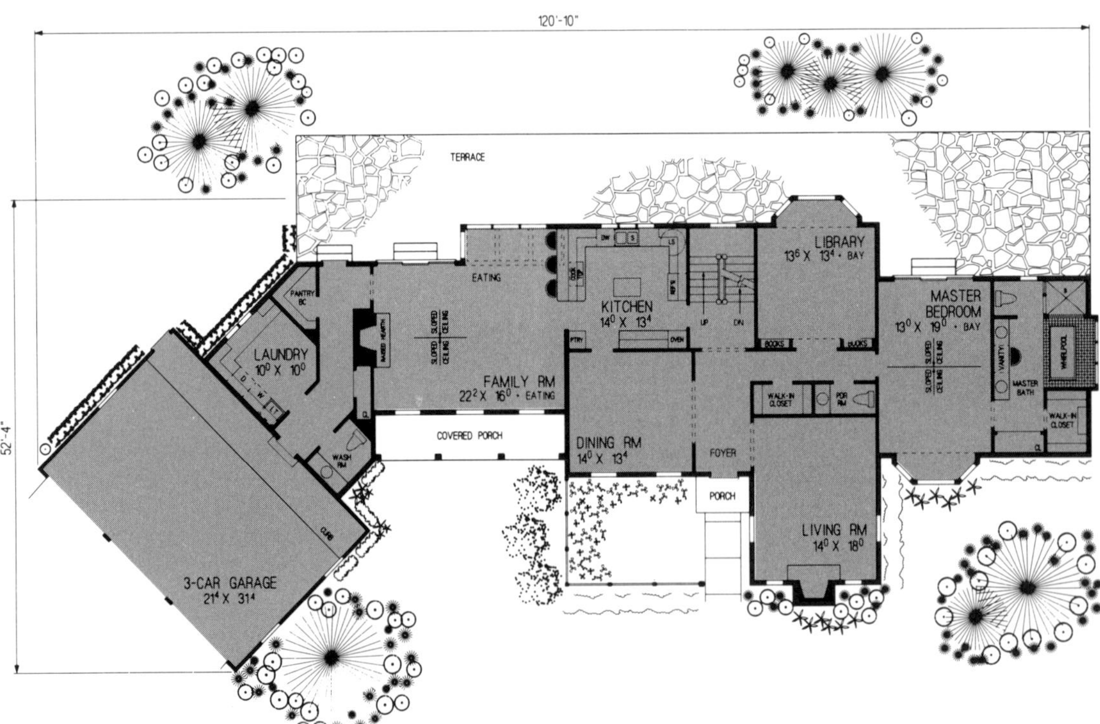

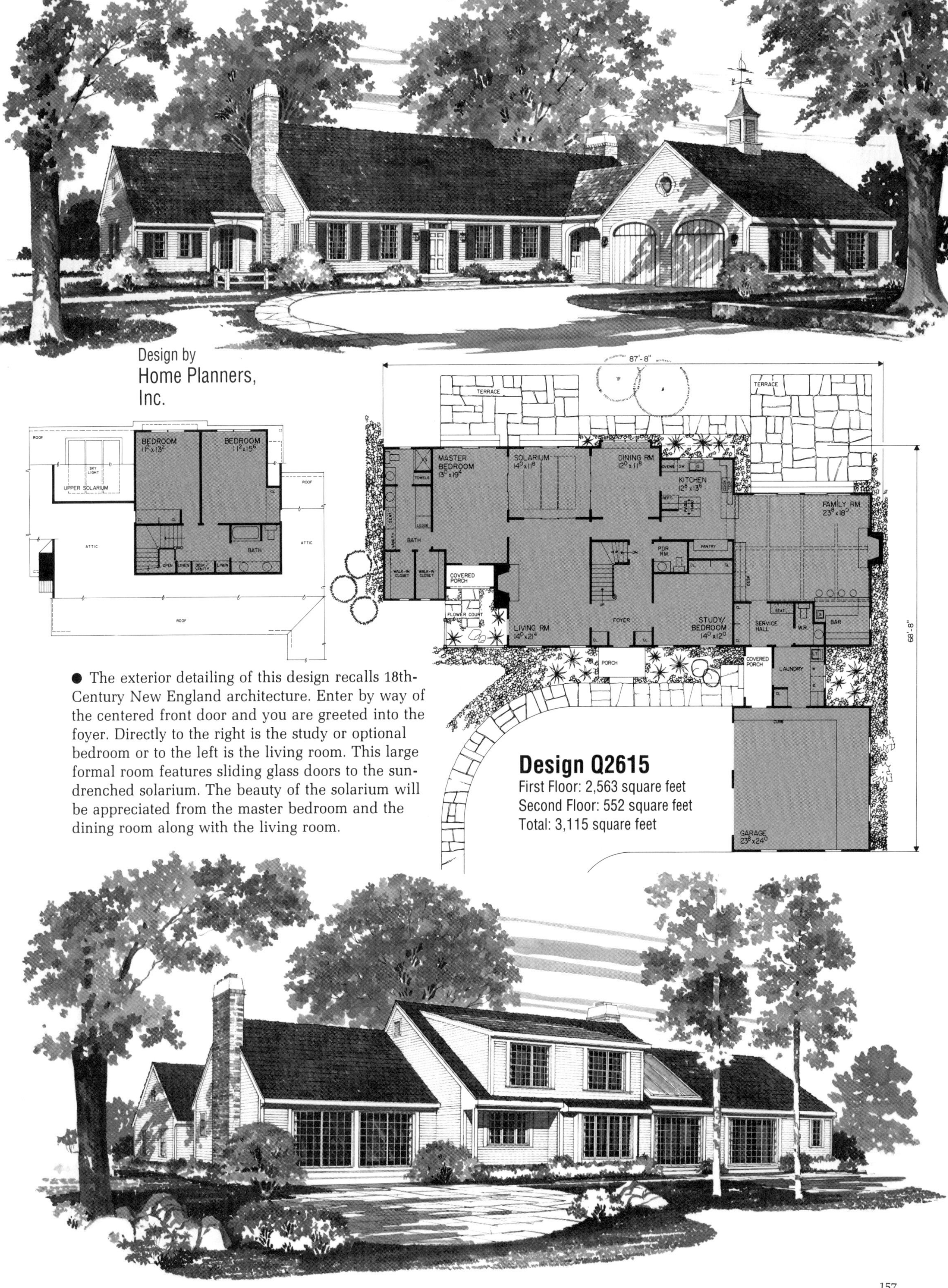

Design by
Home Planners, Inc.

● The exterior detailing of this design recalls 18th-Century New England architecture. Enter by way of the centered front door and you are greeted into the foyer. Directly to the right is the study or optional bedroom or to the left is the living room. This large formal room features sliding glass doors to the sun-drenched solarium. The beauty of the solarium will be appreciated from the master bedroom and the dining room along with the living room.

Design Q2615

First Floor: 2,563 square feet
Second Floor: 552 square feet
Total: 3,115 square feet

Design Q9307

Square Footage: 1,948

● Wood and brick details along with an elegant porch highlight the elevation of this special design. A 10-foot-high entry views the open dining room with tapered columns. Gourmet cooks will delight in the island kitchen with pantry and wrapping wet bar/servery. Outdoor access is available from the sunny bayed dinette. In the great room, a cozy fireplace is flanked by large windows with arched transoms above. Two secondary bedrooms share a Hollywood bath with a linen cabinet. At night, the lucky homeowners can retreat to the elegant master suite complete with vaulted ceilings and a pampering master bath. Special amenities include His and Hers vanities, linen closet, corner whirlpool, special shower and roomy walk-in closet. Truly, this home is delightful inside and out.

WHIRLPOOL
Mbr. $13^0 \times 16^1$
9'-0" CLG.
LIN.
Grt. rm. $16^0 \times 20^0$
10'-0" CEILING
Bfst. $16^0 \times 11^0$
WET BAR
P.
R.
DN
Kit. $12^8 \times 10^7$
Br.3 $11^0 \times 11^0$
Br.2 $11^3 \times 12^0$
E.
Din. $13^0 \times 13^0$
9'-6" CEILING
COVERED PORCH
TRANSOMS
STORAGE
Gar. $20^7 \times 20^8$
52'-0"
64'-0"

Design by
Design Basics, Inc.

Design Q9308

First Floor: 1,309 square feet
Second Floor: 1,157 square feet
Total: 2,466 square feet

● Sleek lines, Palladian windows and brick and wood detailing create tremendous curb appeal for this four-bedroom, two-story home. Bright windows throughout provide natural warmth and light. A volume entry views three rooms and a dramatic curved stairway. French doors access the family room from the living room with its bright wall of windows and cozy fireplace. The gourmet island kitchen has a pantry, ample counter space and sunny dinette with planning desk in the comfortable breakfast area. Three secondary bedrooms upstairs were designed for family livability. Each has easy access to a roomy bath with dual lavs and a large hall linen closet. A pampering master bedroom includes a cathedral ceiling and breathtaking arched window. In the master bath, who could overlook the walk-in closet, iron-a-way, His and Hers vanities and whirlpool, plus, exquisite window treatments?

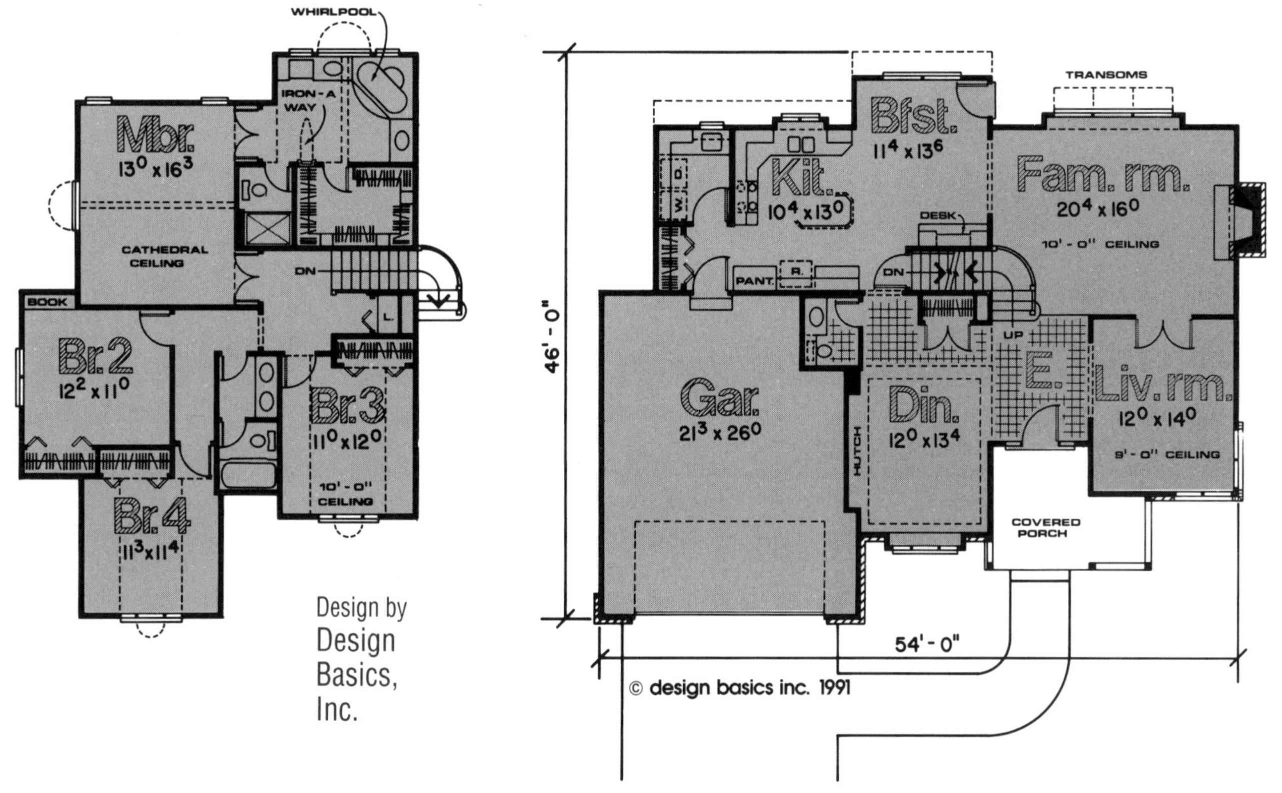

Design by Design Basics, Inc.

Design Q9035

Square Footage: 1,341

● Great for narrow lots, this home delivers amazing livability within modest square footage. Notice the efficient U-shaped kitchen with attached dining room. Counter space is abundant for serving and eating. The large family room with fireplace and gambrel ceiling offers an open area that easily accommodates family gatherings and formal entertaining. The three-bedroom sleeping area includes a master suite with full bath and walk-in closet. Bedroom number 3 overlooks the welcoming covered front porch.

Design by
Larry W. Garnett & Associates, Inc.

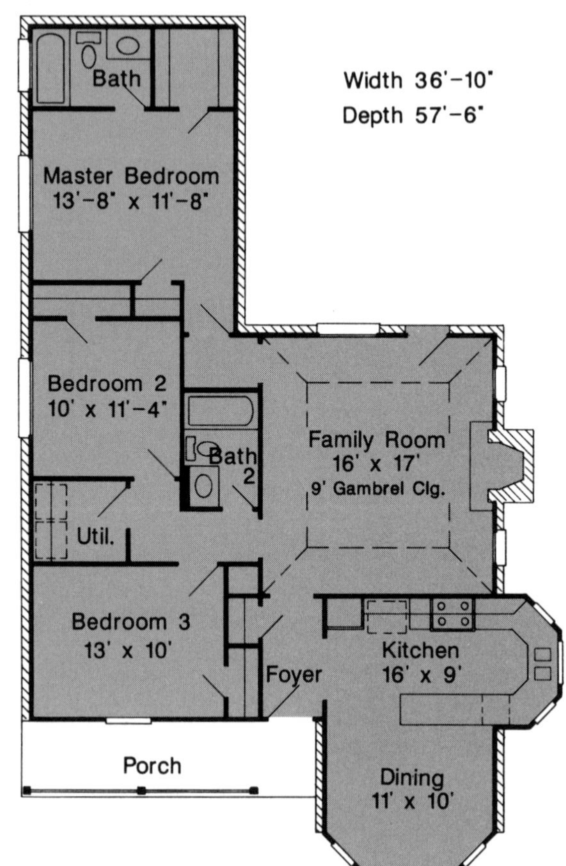

Design by
Larry W.
Garnett &
Associates, Inc.

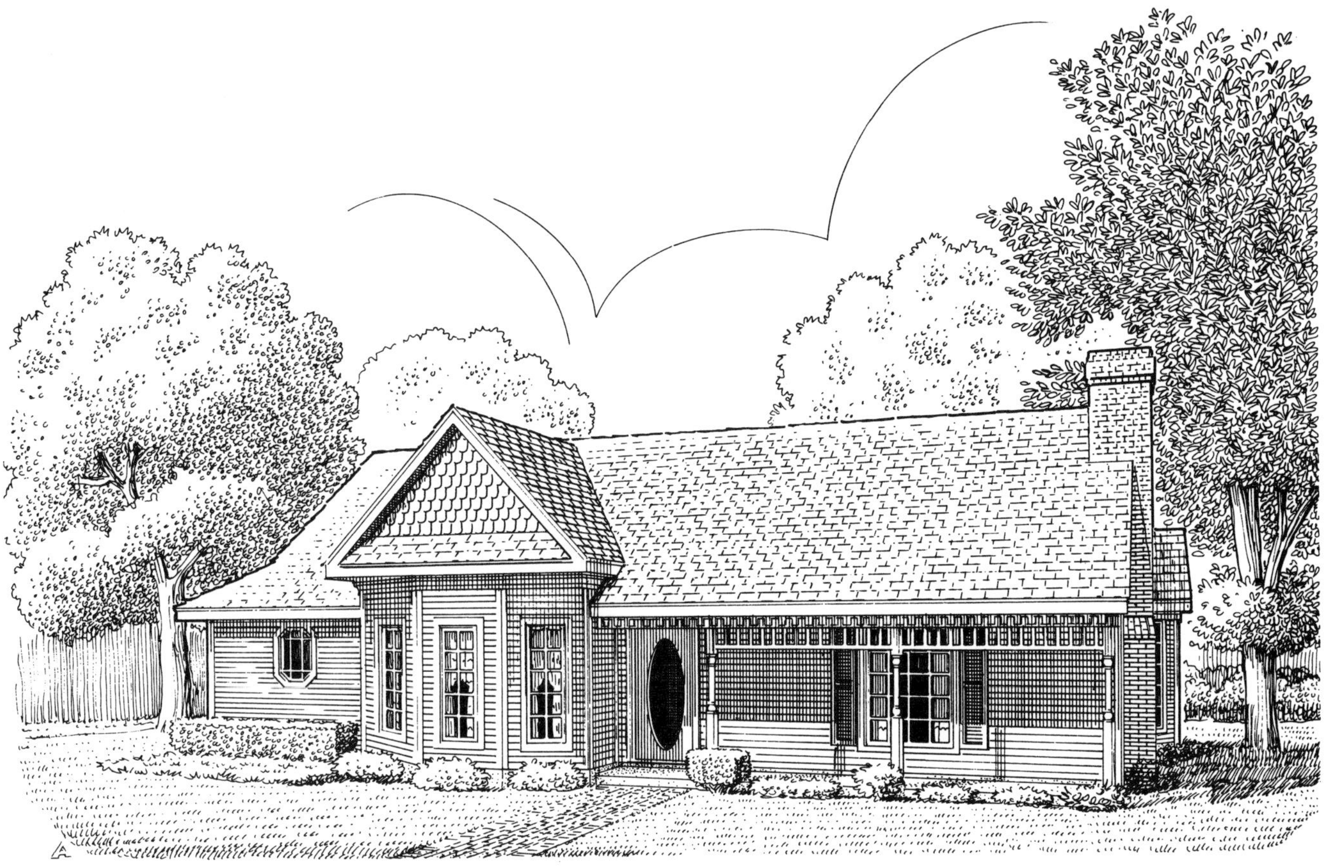

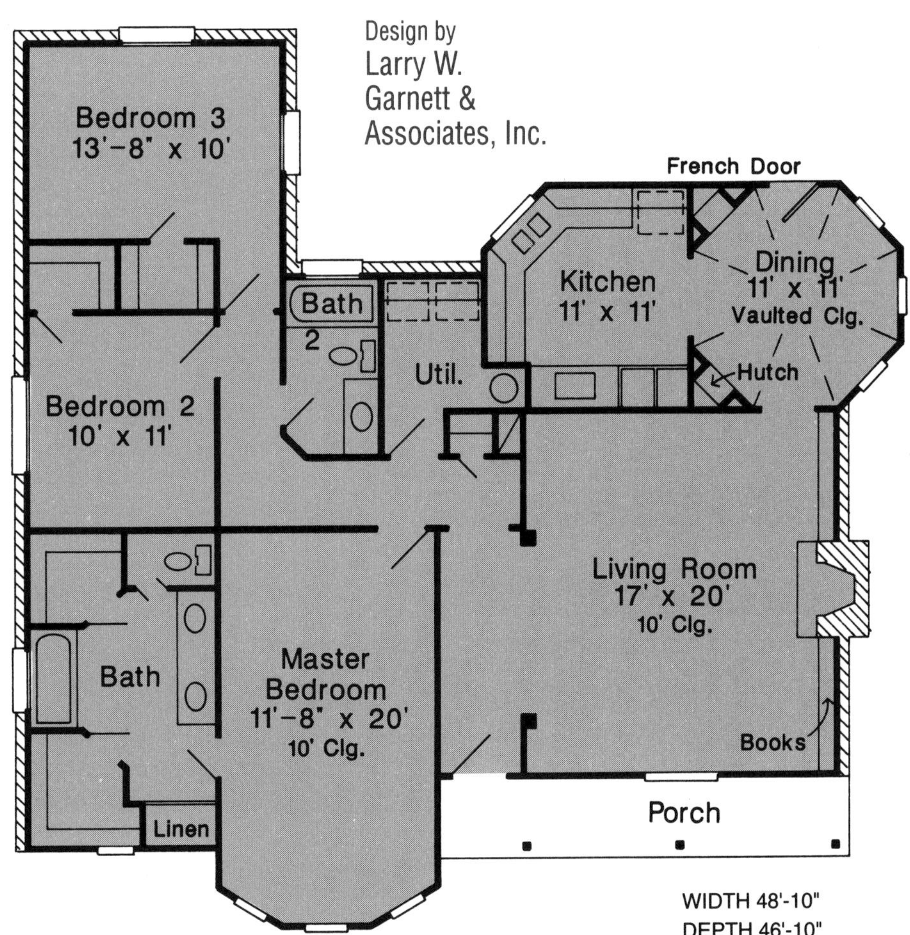

Design Q9007

Square Footage: 1,669

● With an efficient floor plan and plenty of closet space, this farmhouse is rather economical to build. The simple roof design and well-proportioned bay window and front porch, which are far less costly than many farmhouse designs, allow extras: ten-foot ceilings in the master bedroom and the living room and a unique "gazebo" vaulted ceiling in the dining area. Optional bookcases are located on each side of the fireplace. The laundry room is conveniently located near the bedrooms. The sides and part of the rear of the home are brick veneer, providing for much less maintenance and painting. Plans for a two-car detached garage are included with this design.

Design by
Larry W.
Garnett &
Associates, Inc.

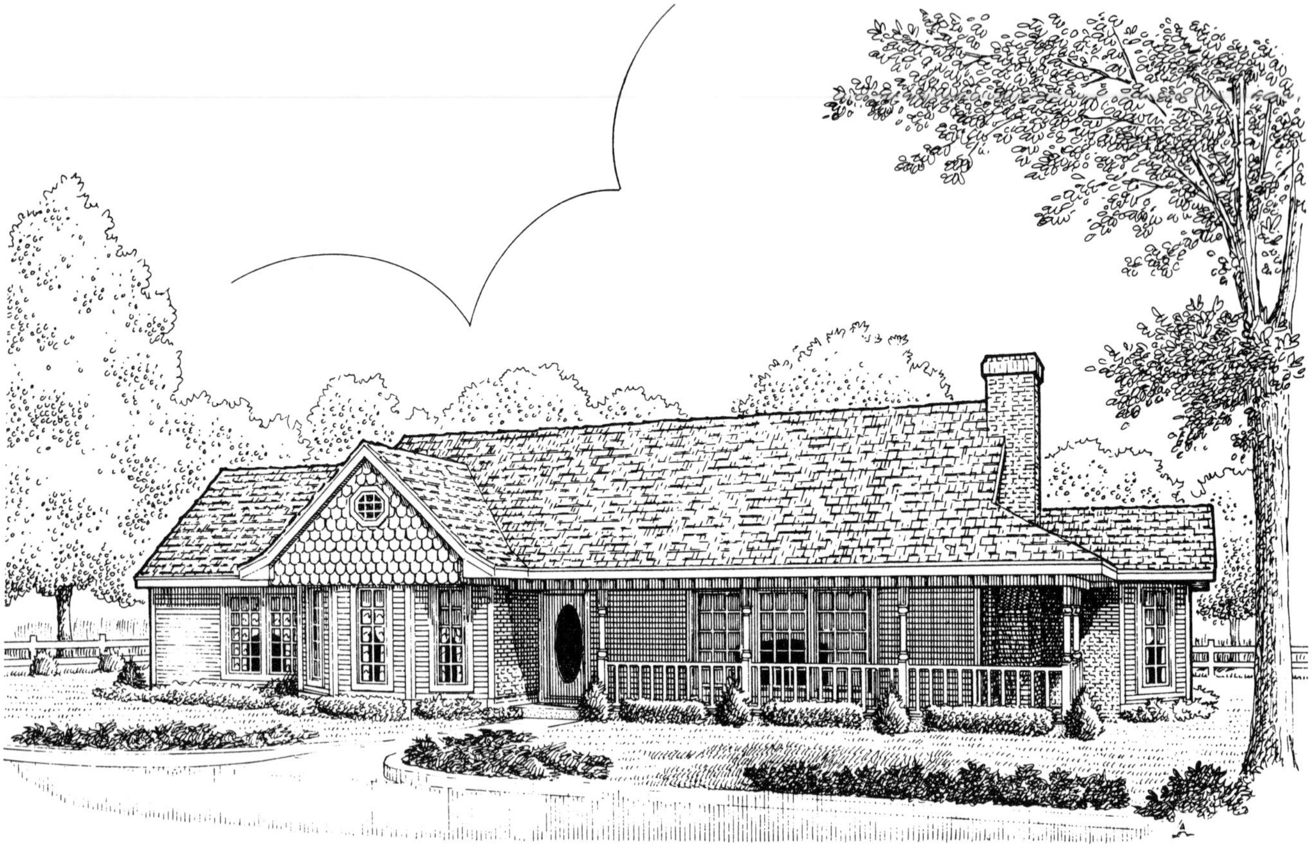

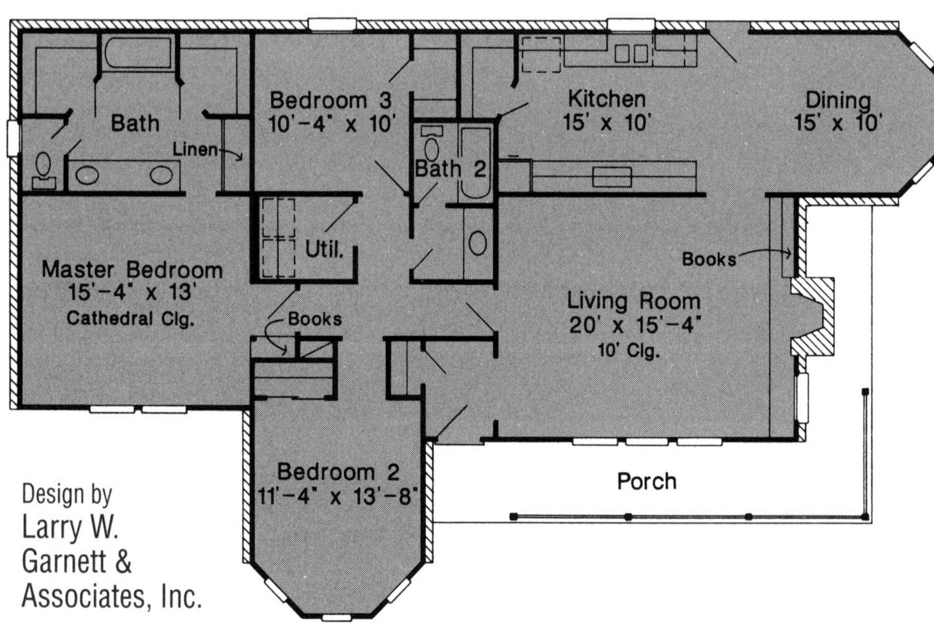

Width 63'-4"
Depth 37'-10"

Design Q9038

Square Footage: 1,659

● Here's a three-bedroom home with style and comfort that meets family living requirements with less than 2,000 square feet! Gathering areas are accommodated in the living room with built-in bookshelves and fireplace, and the well-planned kitchen/dining area combination. Besides two family bedrooms, there is a lovely master with cathedral ceiling and bath with double vanity. The bay windows, covered front porch and other special design details make this a house to remember.

Design Q9039

Square Footage: 1,978

● In addition to the wrapping covered front porch of this farmhouse design, there is a second porch to the rear with French-door access to the eating area. Between the two, lies a great floor plan with features often found only in much larger homes: a ten-foot gambrel ceiling in the family room, a large dining room connecting directly to an efficiently planned kitchen, an octagonal breakfast room, and three bedrooms with walk-in closets. Little extras like the bay window in the master bedroom and the double vanity in the master bath make this home a true stand-out.

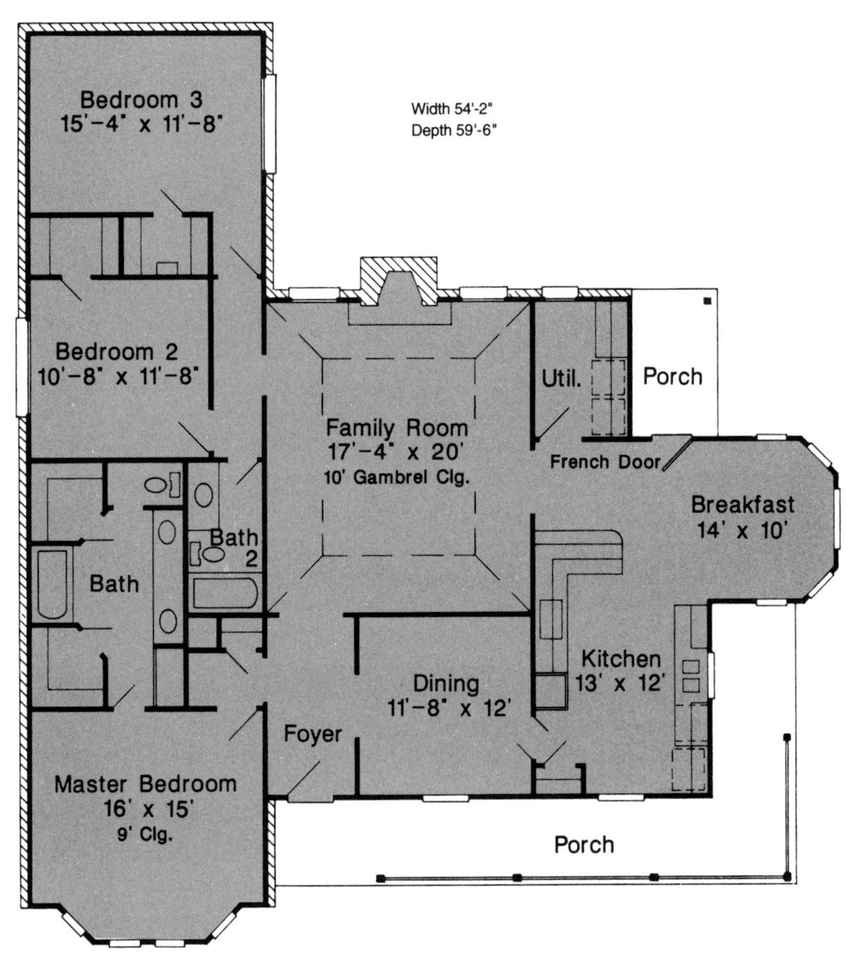

Design by
Larry W. Garnett & Associates, Inc.

Design Q9430

First Floor: 1,150 square feet
Second Floor: 543 square feet
Total: 1,693 square feet

● While fitting on some of the smallest lots imaginable, this great 1½-story still encompasses some dynamic features. Check out the dramatic, two-story hearth room that serves as the main living area in the home. Tall windows flank the fireplace and a glass door leads to the outdoor living area. A section of the upper hallway overlooks the hearth room integrating the upper floor with the lower floor. The master bedroom is conveniently located on the main floor overlooking the back yard, with direct access to the full bath serving the lower floor. Two large bedrooms and a bath round out the upper floor.

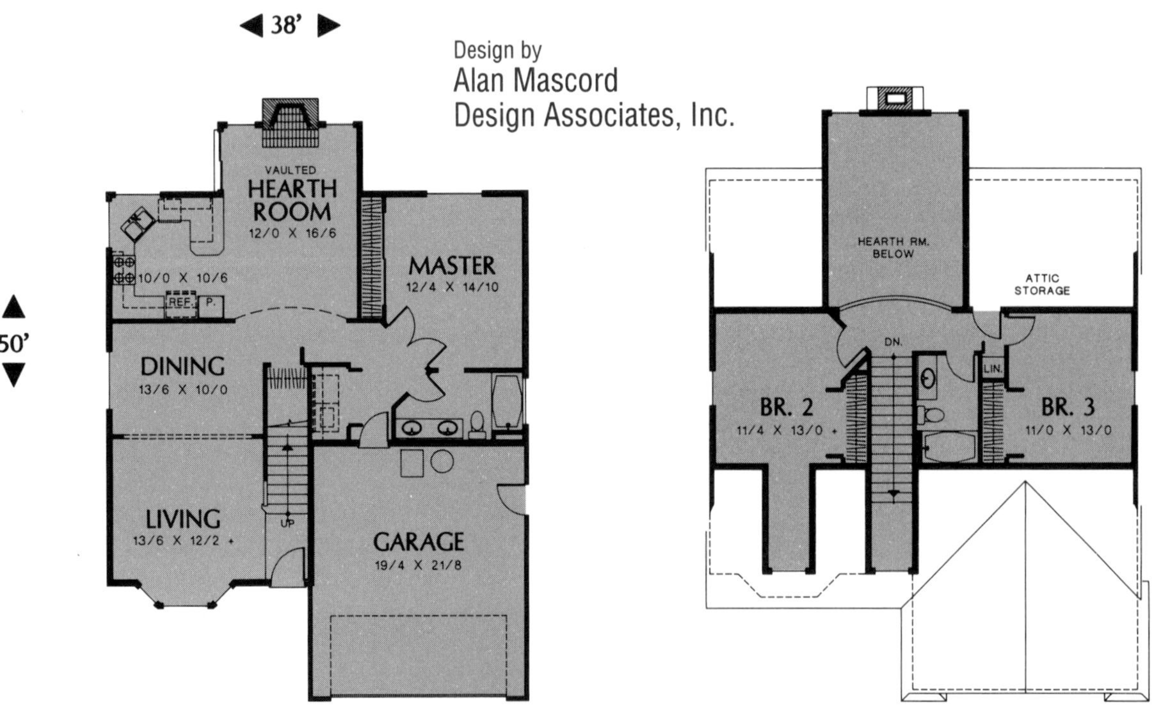

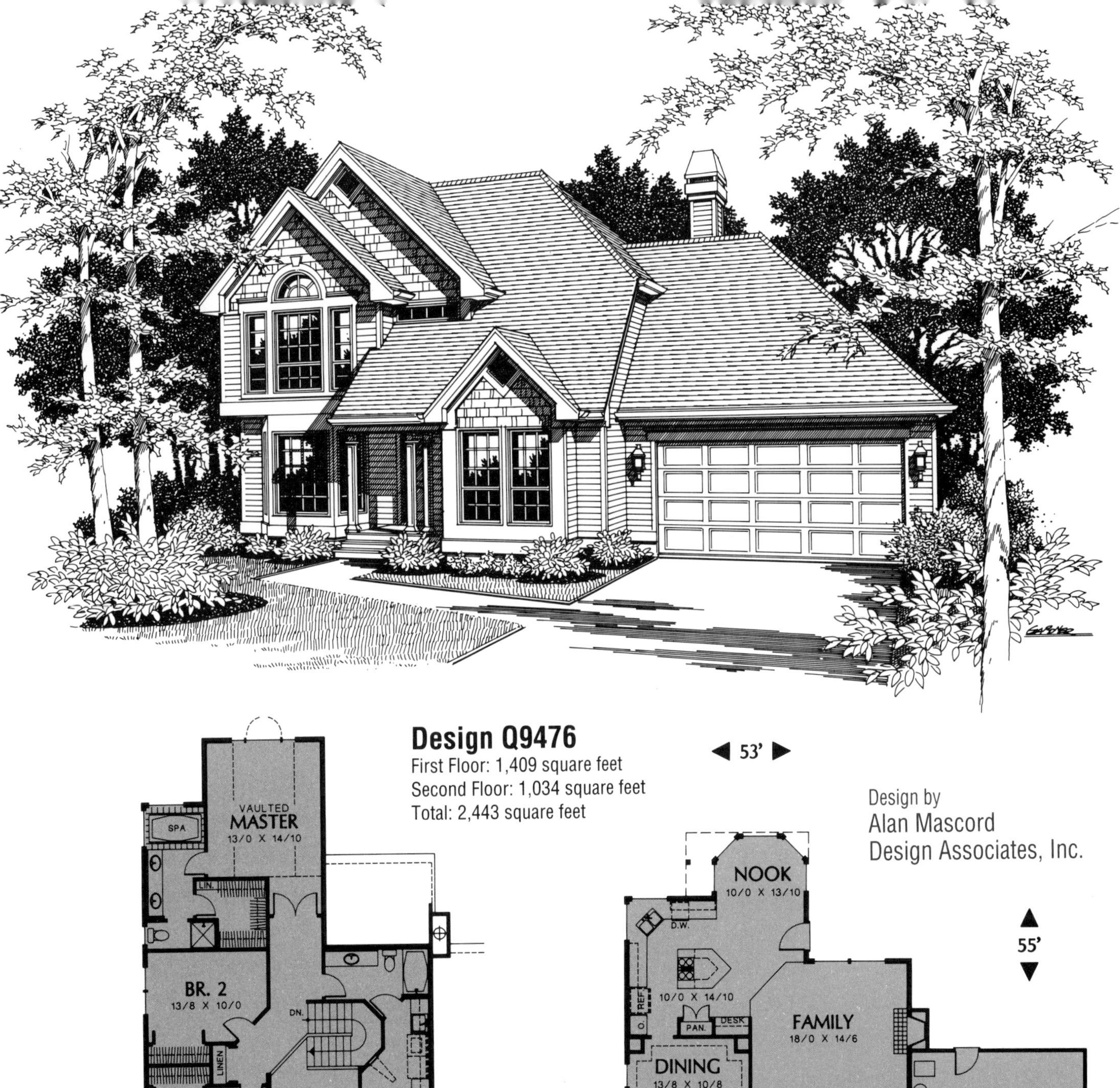

Design Q9476

First Floor: 1,409 square feet
Second Floor: 1,034 square feet
Total: 2,443 square feet

Design by
Alan Mascord
Design Associates, Inc.

● A pleasant mix of materials and a columned front porch add visual appeal to a livable floor plan in this exciting two-story design. Living and dining areas on the first floor include a family room with fireplace, living room with bay window, formal dining room and cozy breakfast nook. The den is located just off the entry foyer, away from living areas and noise. Upstairs are three bedrooms including a master suite with full bath. Attic storage over the garage is reached through the second bathroom.

Design by
Larry W.
Garnett &
Associates, Inc.

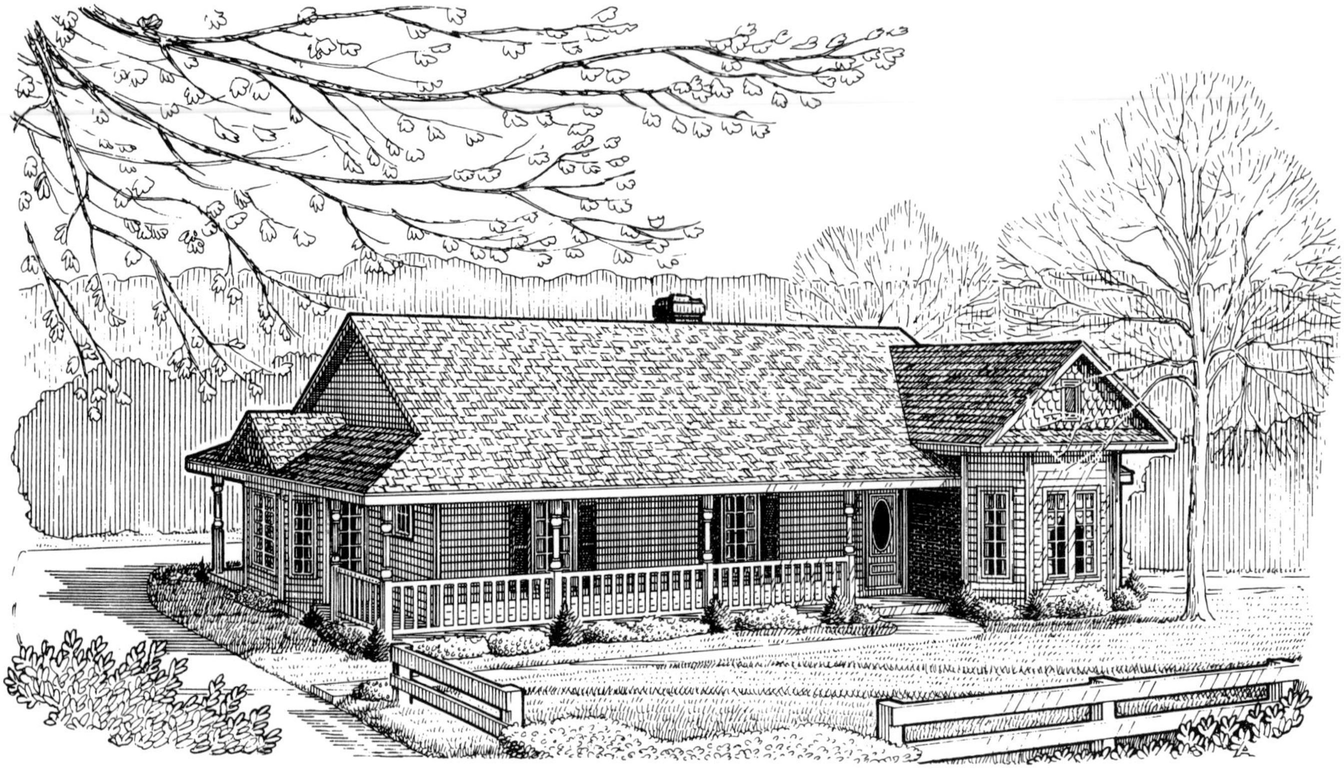

Design Q9006

Square Footage: 1,772

● Designed for casual living inside and out, this one-story farmhouse is an ideal family home. The family room features a ten-foot ceiling and a corner fireplace. An enormous dining area can handle even the largest family dinners. The large rear porch is perfect for outdoor entertaining. The laundry room is conveniently located near the three bedrooms. His and Hers walk-in closets and twin lavatories are part of the luxurious master bath. Plans for a 24′ x 24′ detached garage are included with this design.

WIDTH 51'-2"
DEPTH 52'-10"

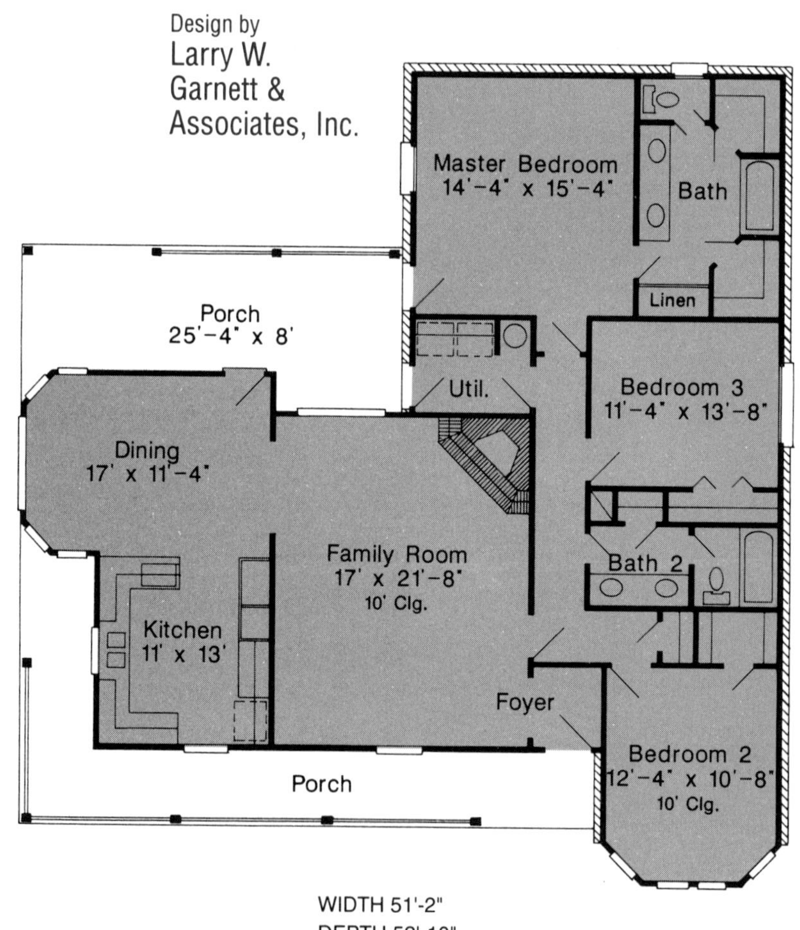

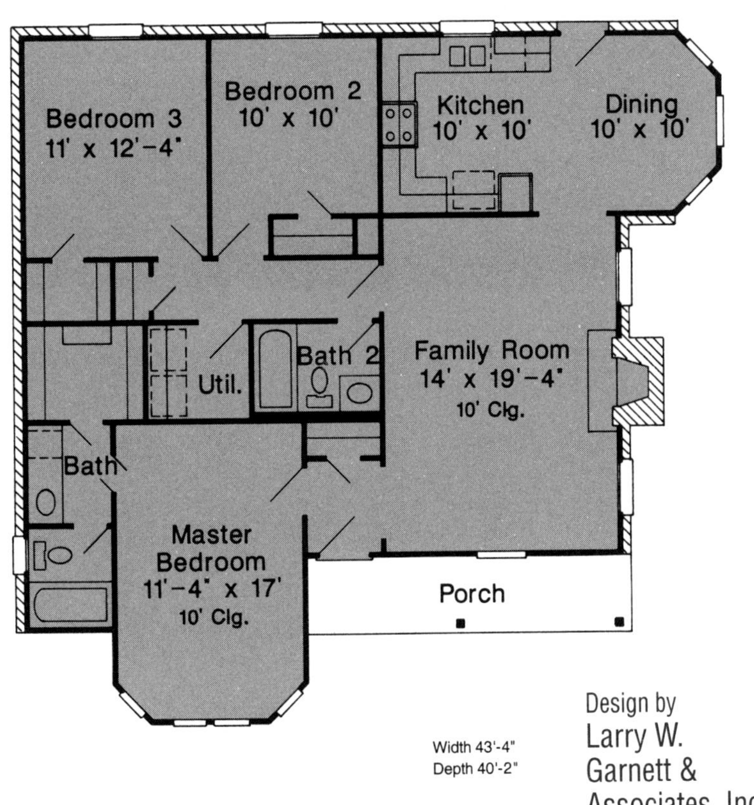

Design Q9032

Square Footage: 1,358

● This cozy little farmhouse presents all those special traits that makes it the perfect place to call home. From the covered front porch to the efficient floor plan, this is one that is sure to catch your eye. Living areas to the right of the front entry include a large family room with fireplace, octagonal dining area and U-shaped kitchen with rear yard access. The master bedroom is cleverly separated from two family bedrooms and has its own full bath and a walk-in closet. Note the location of the laundry room—near the bedrooms, the source of dirty clothes.

Design by
Larry W.
Garnett &
Associates, Inc.

Design Q9608

First Floor: 1,228 square feet
Second Floor: 492 square feet
Total:.1,720 square feet

● An open and spacious interior with the best in up-to-date floor planning offers new excitement in this delightful compact country-style home. Besides the oversized great room with fireplace, there is a wonderful country kitchen incorporating dining space and having access to the sun room for alternate dining and entertaining. The generous master bedroom has its own fireplace and also access to the sun room. A walk-in closet assures plenty of storage space. Upstairs, in addition to two bedrooms sharing a full bath, there is a charming balcony and ample attic storage. A covered porch and a deck — front and rear — add to outdoor lifestyles.

Design by
Donald A.
Gardner,
Architect, Inc.

Design Q9666

First Floor: 1,027 square feet
Second Floor: 580 square feet
Total: 1,607 square feet

● This economical, rustic three-bedroom plan sports a relaxing country image with both front and back covered porches. The openness of the expansive great room to kitchen/dining areas and loft/study areas is reinforced with a shared cathedral ceiling for impressive space. The first level allows for two bedrooms, a full bath and a utility area. The master suite on the second level has a walk-in closet and a master bath with whirlpool tub, shower and double-bowl vanity. The plan is available with a crawl-space foundation.

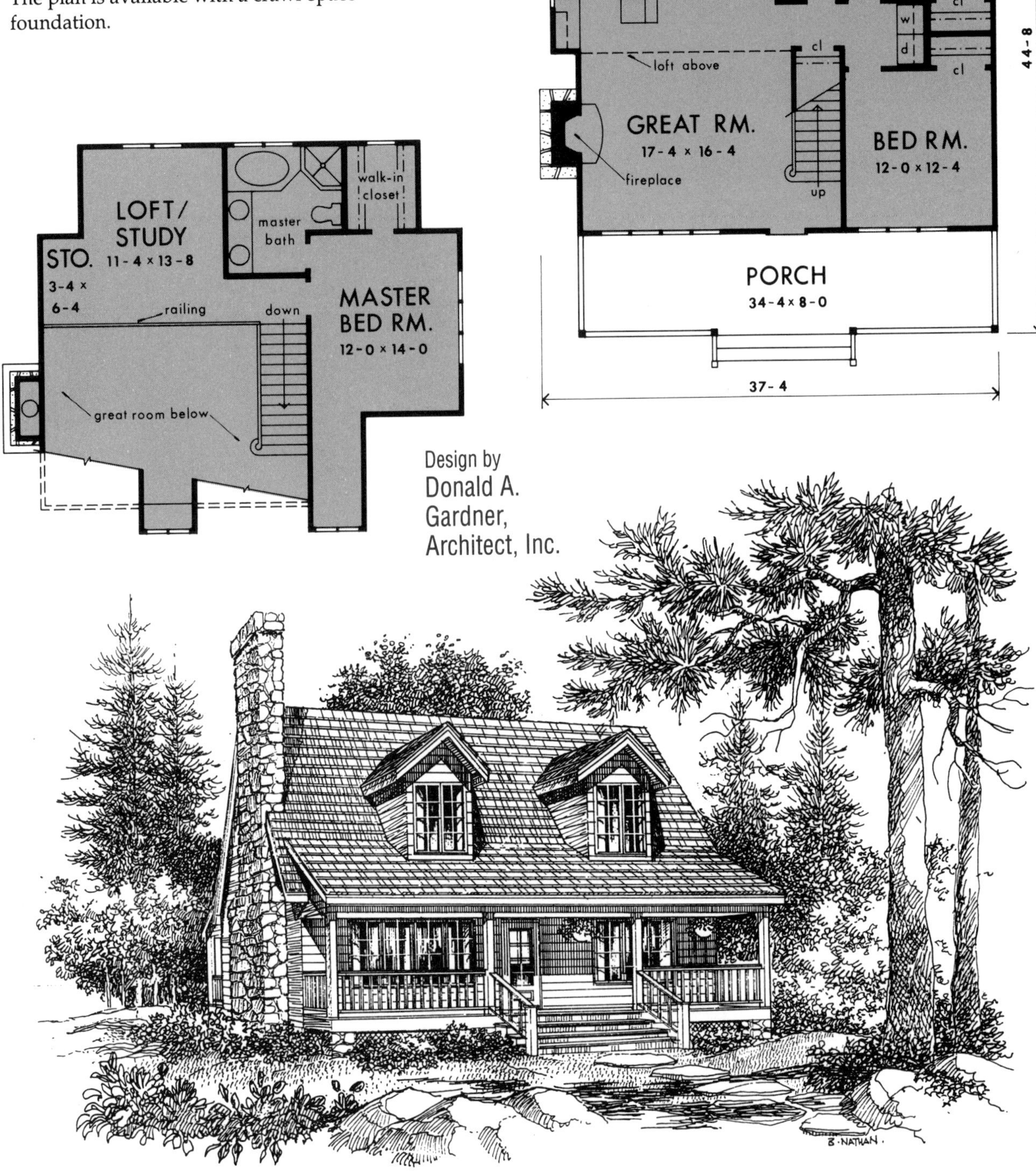

Design by
Donald A.
Gardner,
Architect, Inc.

Design Q2661

First Floor: 1,020 square feet
Second Floor: 777 square feet
Total: 1,797 square feet

● Any other starter house or retirement home couldn't have more charm than this design. Its compact frame houses a very livable plan. An outstanding feature of the first floor is the large country kitchen. Its fine attractions include a beamed ceiling, raised-hearth fireplace, built-in window seat and a door leading to the outdoors. A living room is in the front of the plan and has another fireplace which shares the single chimney. The rear dormered second floor houses the sleeping and bath facilities.

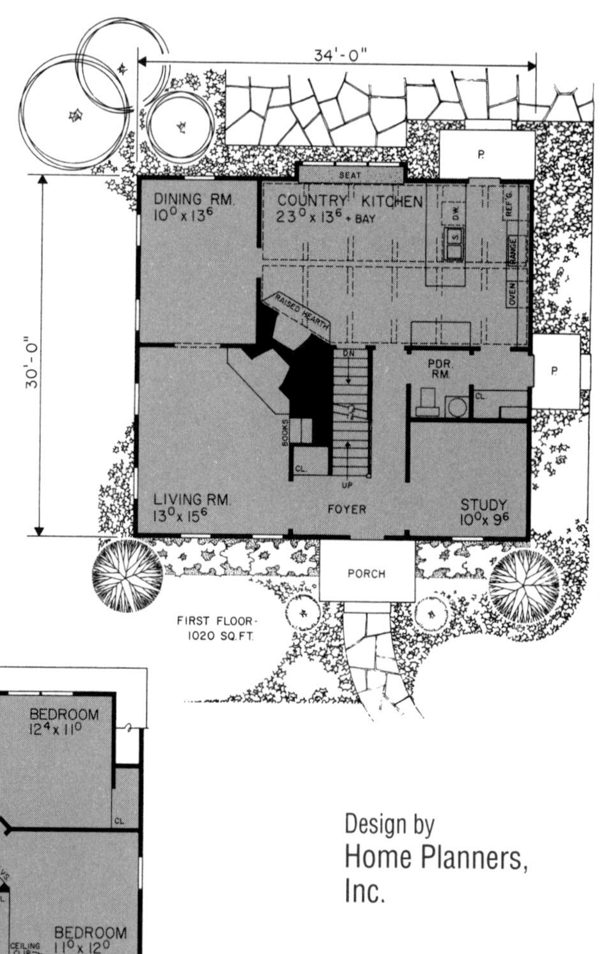

Design by
Home Planners, Inc.

BRICK OR STONE FARMHOUSES

Though not formally a *style* of Farmhouse, the brick or stone exterior is a popular choice for just about any variation. Because of their solid-looking appearance, brick and stone are used as a statement of permanence, antiquity and heritage. Either may be found as an exterior ingredient; one or both may serve as an accent or embellishment to other exterior sidings. These materials are easy to care for and retain their good looks and durability for many years.

Effective use of brick is accomplished in the Prairie Farmhouse, Design Q9074, where it is used as the primary exterior material. It is complemented by wood railings and wooden shutters at each of the first-floor windows. Also employing brick almost completely throughout the exterior is Design Q2963, a Traditional Farmhouse, borrowing design elements from winged Colonials and Center-Hall designs. Design Q9206, a Modern French-Style Brick, uses brick extensively but heightens the appeal with horizontal wood trim, wooden window trim and wooden trim at the pediment over the garage.

Stone takes on rustically defined proportions in Design Q2527, a Simple Ranch House, and Design Q3351, a Cape Cod Farmhouse, where it is employed in combination with wood siding and other wood design details. A Classic Pennsylvania Stone Farmhouse, Design Q2542, uses stone almost to the exclusion of any other material. Even the chimney stacks are constructed in stone. A French Country House, Design Q9862, presents a unique stone facade with horizontal wood accent at the wing extension. This home is further enhanced by stone chimney stacks and metal-clad roofs over the box window and dining porch.

All of the Farmhouse versions presented, from the basic one-story version to the elaborate two-story country estate, are representative of the sturdiness and long-lasting appeal of brick and stone.

Design Q9033

Square Footage: 1,528

● Fine farmhouse living takes to one story. In this quaint design, the front porch introduces a fine floor plan. The family room is large and open and acts as a hub for the rest of the home. Nearby is the galley kitchen and a dining area with rear porch access. A fireplace keeps it cozy. Three bedrooms all feature walk-in closets. The master has double sinks in its private bath. Note the utility room with laundry space.

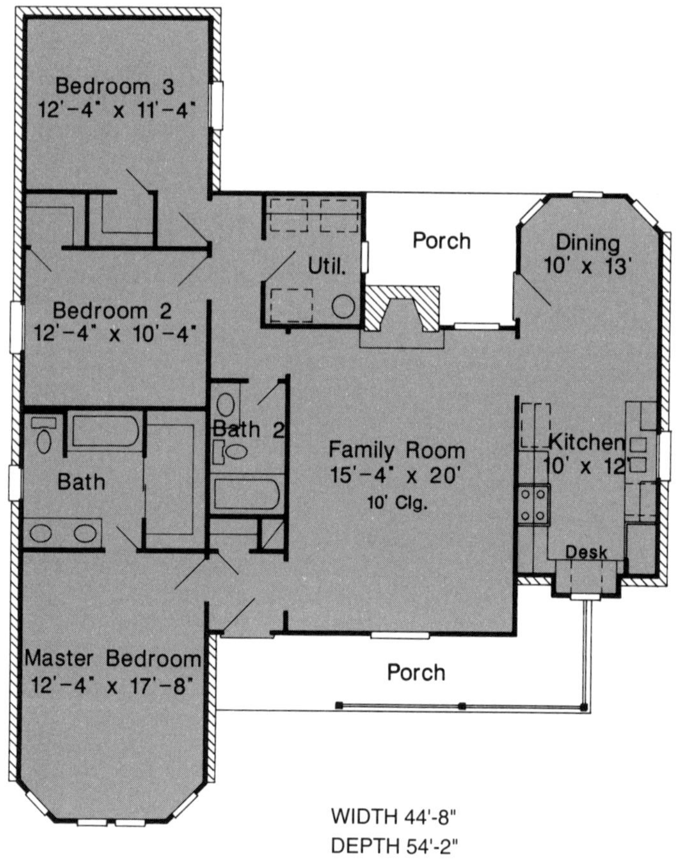

WIDTH 44'-8"
DEPTH 54'-2"

Design by
Larry W.
Garnett &
Associates, Inc.

Design Q9074 First Floor: 1,288 square feet Second Floor: 495 square feet; Total: 1,783 square feet

● With its brick-veneer exterior, dormer windows and wraparound porch, this home is a blend of the early 1900s farmhouse and the prairie style. Corner box windows provide a cozy sitting area next to the fireplace in the family room. The efficient kitchen overlooks the breakfast area with its full-length windows. A French door opens to a large covered porch. Double doors open to the master bedroom with a ten-foot gambrel ceiling. The bath features mirrored closet doors and double lavatories. Upstairs, there are two bedrooms, each with dormer window alcoves and sloping ceilings. Plans for a two-car detached garage are included.

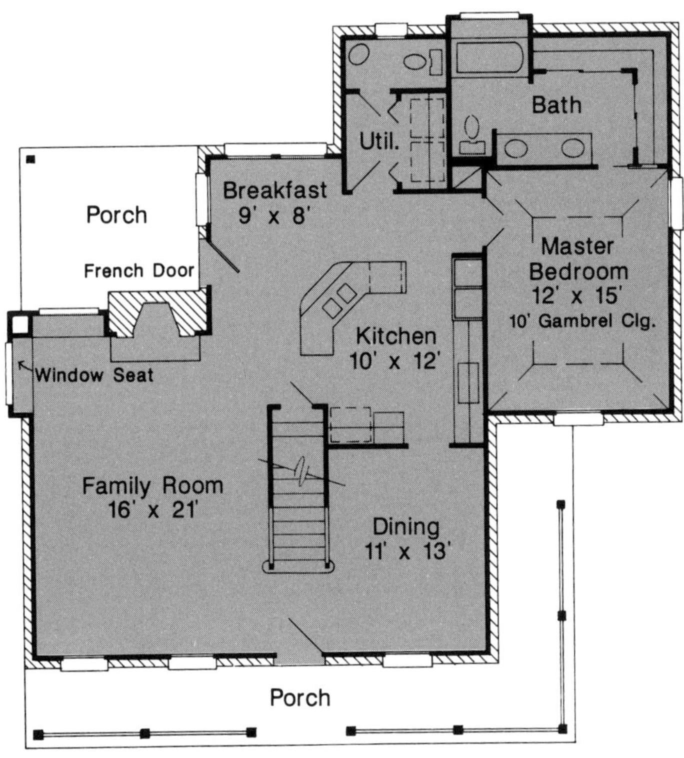

Width 44'
Depth 45'

Design by
Larry W.
Garnett &
Associates, Inc.

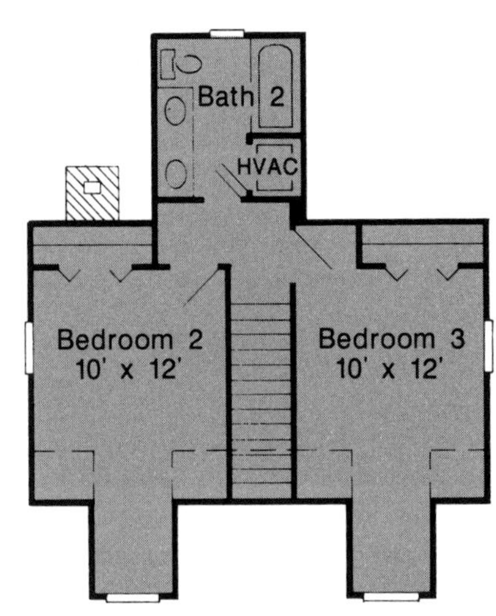

Design Q2805

Square Footage: 1,547

● Compact but completely livable, this one-story home offers the best in country living. From its delightful stone exterior to rear covered porch the look is definitely distinctive. Inside, there's a large living room/dining room area with fireplace and sloped ceiling. It adjoins a breakfast room and U-shaped kitchen for convenient cooking and serving. The bedrooms are located to the front of the plan and include a master bedroom and two family bedrooms (or make one a study or TV room). The main part of the home connects to the two-car garage with a mud room. A huge storage area is found in the garage.

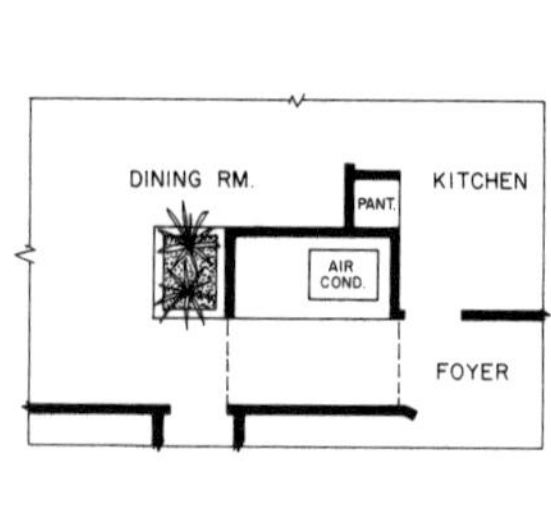

OPTIONAL NON-BASEMENT

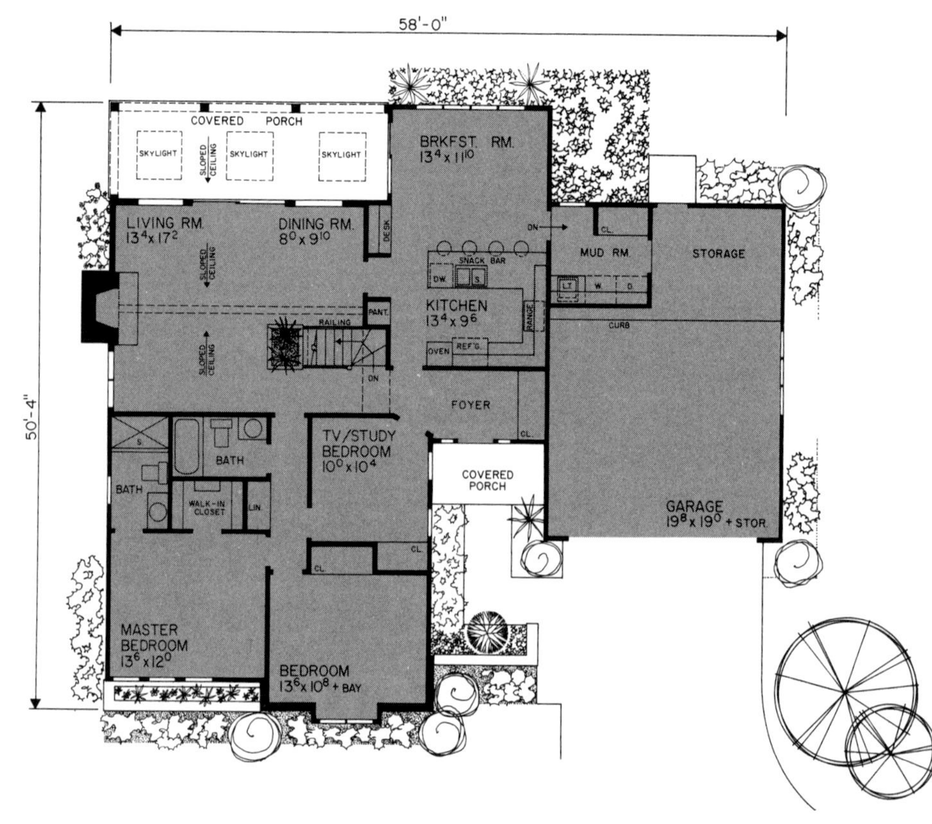

Design by
Home Planners, Inc.

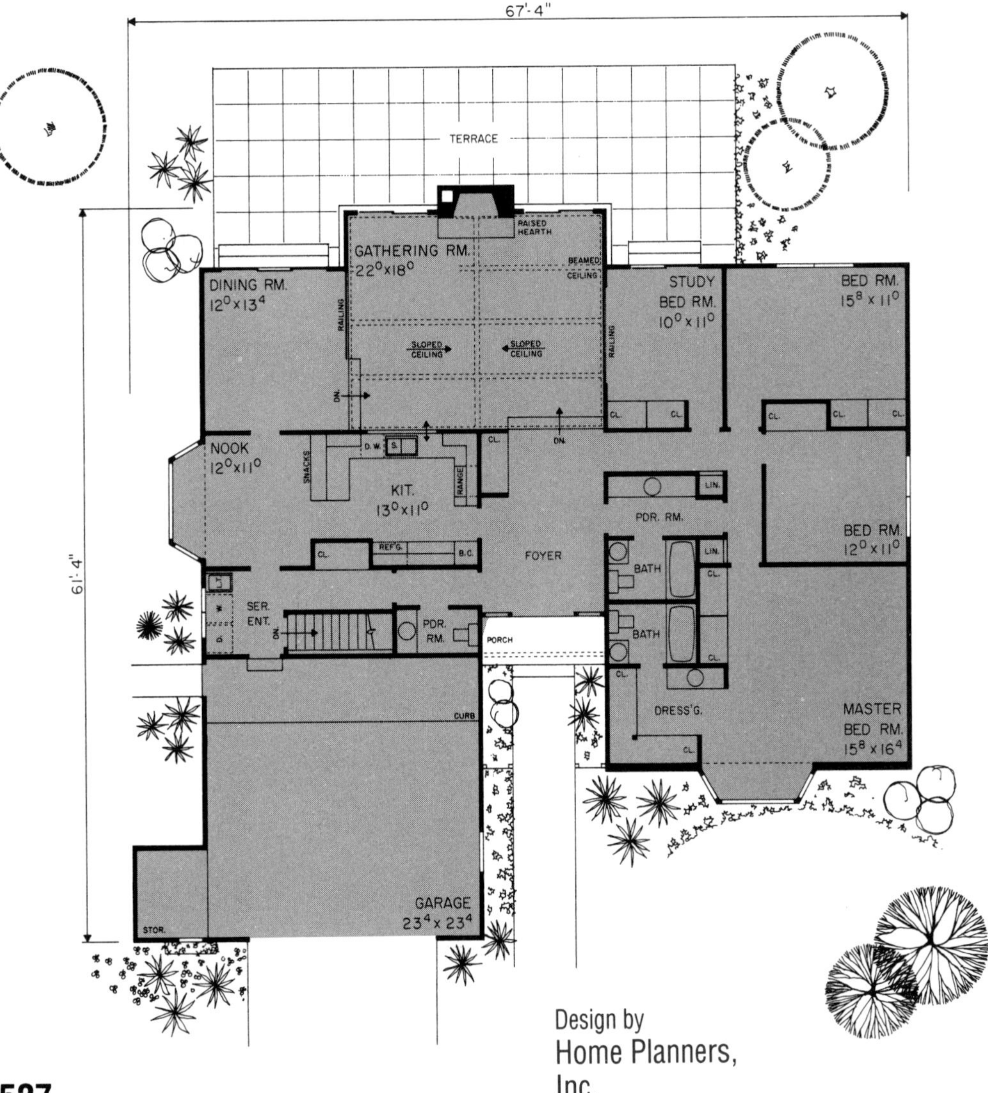

Design by
Home Planners,
Inc.

Design Q2527

Square Footage: 2,392

● Vertical boards and battens, fieldstone, bay window, a dovecote, a gas lamp and a recessed front entrance are among the appealing exterior features of this U-shaped design. Through the double front doors, flanked by glass side lites, one enters the spacious foyer. Straight ahead is the cozy sunken gathering room with its sloping, beamed ceiling, raised hearth fireplace and two sets of sliding glass doors to the rear terrace. To the right of the foyer is the sleeping wing with its three bedrooms, study (make it the fourth bedroom if you wish) and two baths. To the left is the strategically located powder room and large kitchen with its delightful nook and bay window.

Design Q2174

First Floor: 1,506 square feet
Second Floor: 1,156 square feet
Total: 2,662 square feet

● Your building budget could hardly buy more charm, or greater livability. The appeal of the exterior is wrapped up in a myriad of design features. They include: the interesting roof lines; the effective use of brick and horizontal siding; the delightful window treatment; the covered front porch; the chimney and dove-cote detailing. The livability of the interior is represented by a long list of convenient living features. There is a formal area consisting of a living room with fireplace and dining room. The family room has a raised hearth fireplace, wood box and beamed ceiling. Also on the first floor is a kitchen, laundry and bedroom with adjacent bath. Three bedrooms, lounge and two baths upstairs plus plenty of closets and bulk storage over garage. Don't overlook the sliding glass doors, the breakfast area and the basement. An excellent plan.

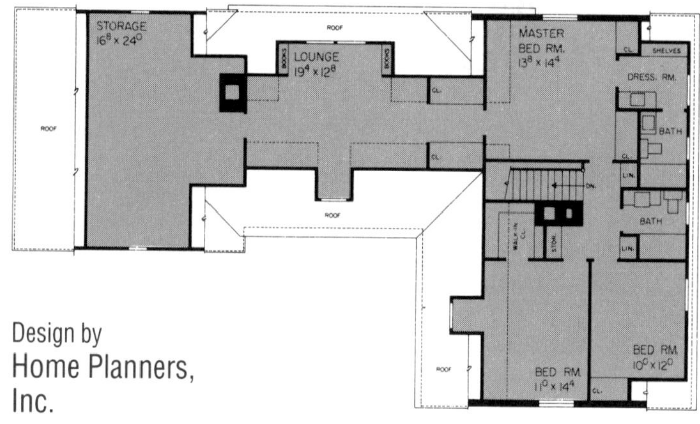

Design by
Home Planners,
Inc.

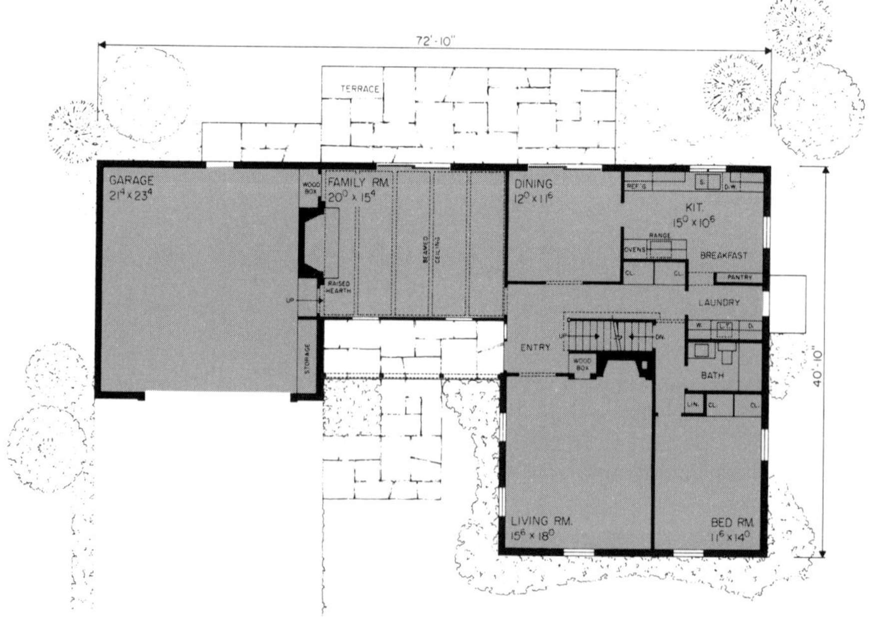

Design Q2614

First Floor: 1,701 square feet
Second Floor: 1,340 square feet
Total: 3,041 square feet

● Pleasing appearance, with an excellent floor plan. Notice how all the rooms are accessible from a hall. That's a plus for easy housekeeping. Some other extras: an exceptionally large family room which is more than 20' x 15', a gracious living room, formal dining room adjacent to the kitchen/nook area, four large bedrooms, a secluded guest suite plus a huge storage area.

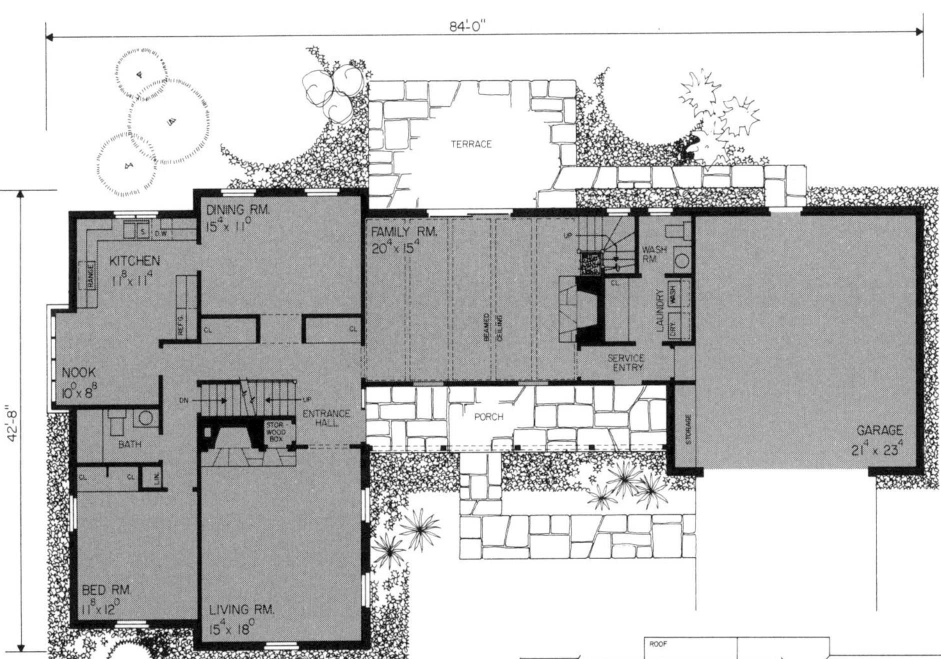

Note that the large guest suite, featuring a full bath, is only accessible by the back stairs in the family room. You could use it as a spacious library, playroom, or a hobby area. Two fireplaces (one with a built-in wood box), walk-in closets, covered front porch and rear terrace also highlight this home.

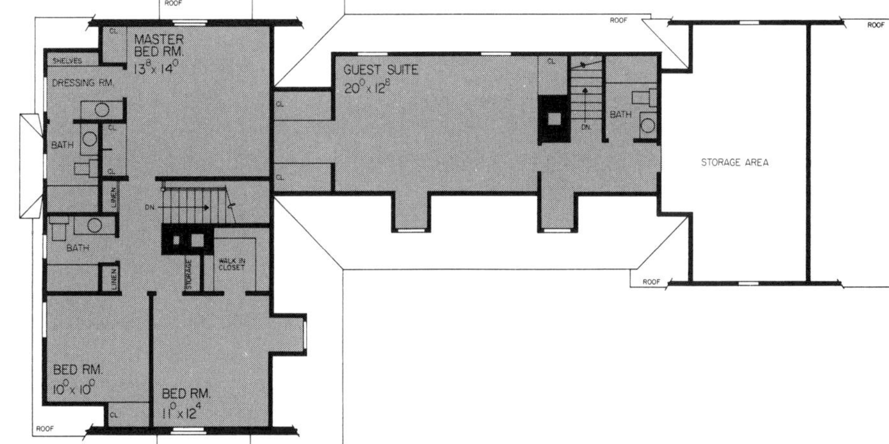

Design by
Home Planners, Inc.

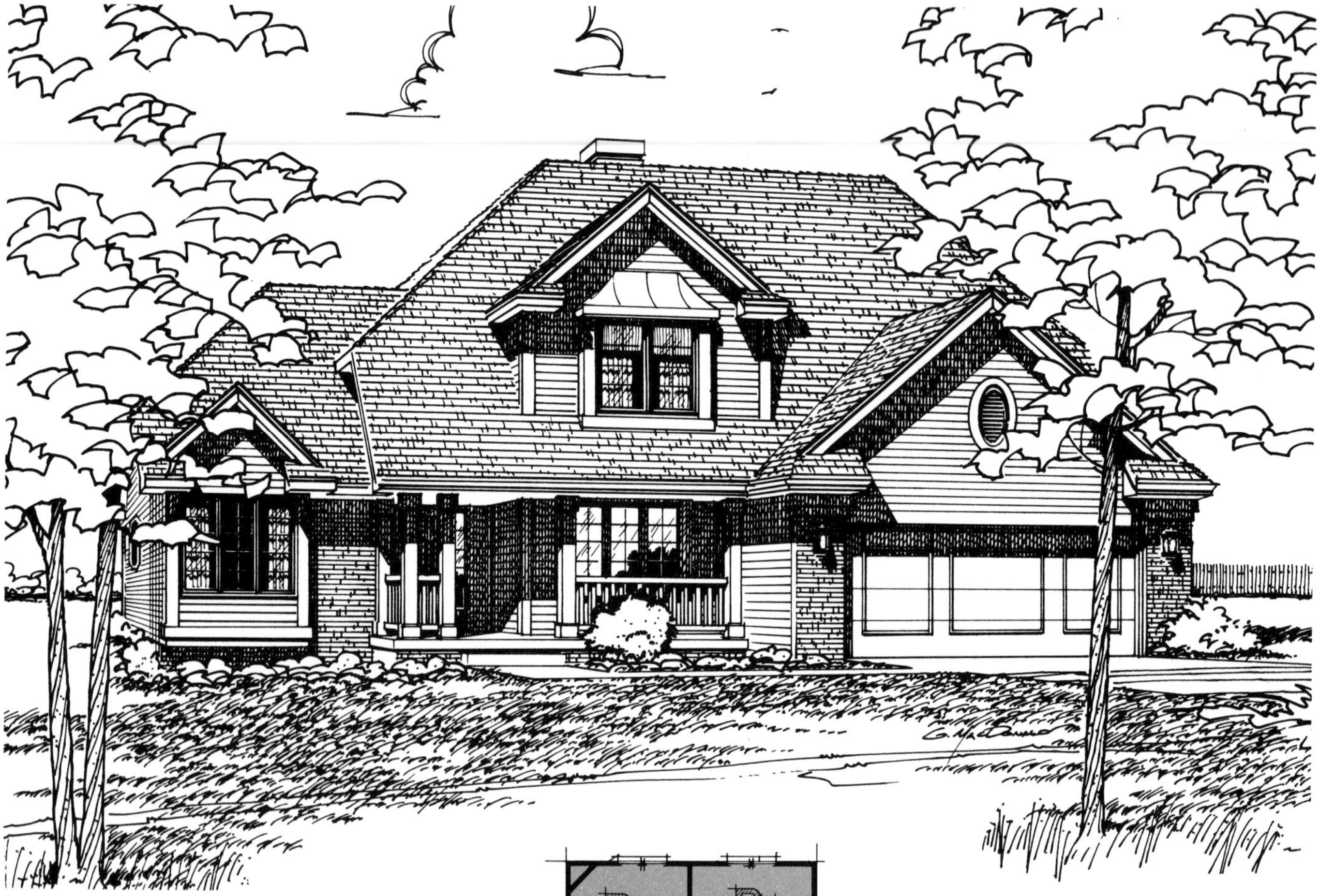

Design Q9206

First Floor: 1,421 square feet
Second Floor: 578 square feet
Total: 1,999 square feet

● Growing families will love this unique plan which combines all the essentials with an abundance of stylish touches. Start with the living areas — a spacious great room with high ceilings, windows overlooking the back yard, a through-fireplace to the kitchen and access to the rear yard. A dining room with hutch space accommodates formal occasions. The hearth kitchen features a well-planned work area and a bay-windowed breakfast area. The master suite with whirlpool and walk-in closet is found downstairs while three family bedrooms are upstairs.

© 1988 design basics inc.

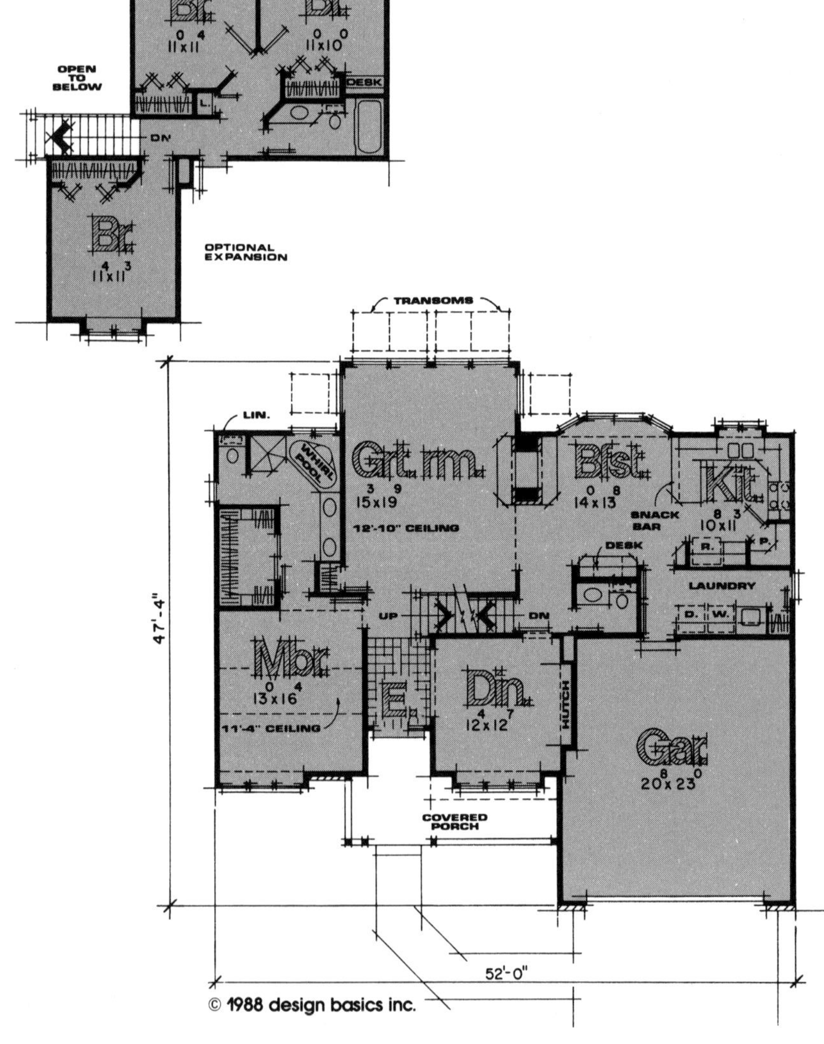

Design by
Design
Basics,
Inc.

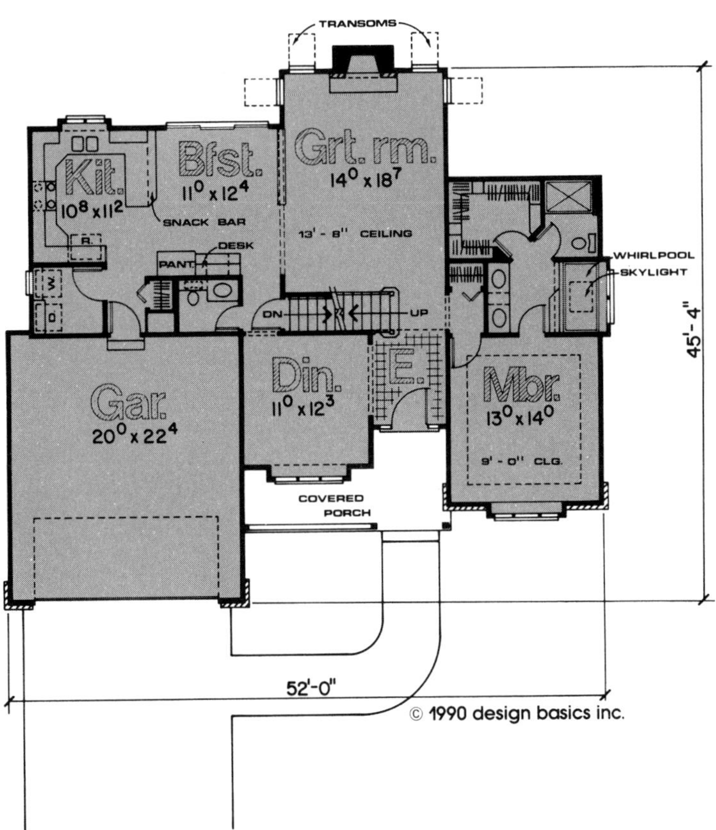

Design Q9247

First Floor: 1,297 square feet
Second Floor: 558 square feet
Total: 1,855 square feet

● Here's the perfect family plan with loads of livability. Go beyond the front covered porch and you'll find a thoughtful floor plan. A formal dining room with large boxed window is a complement to the great room with handsome fireplace and tall windows. A snack bar, pantry, two lazy Susans and planning desk grace the kitchen/breakfast room area. The master suite is conveniently located on the first floor and features a boxed window and well-appointed bath. Three family bedrooms upstairs share a full bath. Note the volume ceiling above the arched window in bedroom 4.

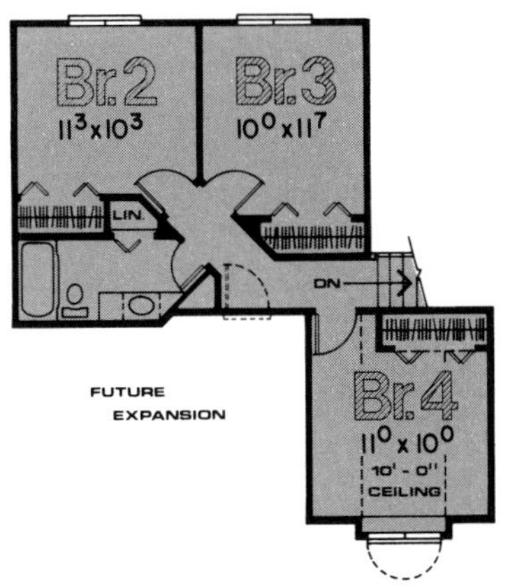

Design by
Design
Basics,
Inc.

Design Q9309

First Floor: 1,506 square feet
Second Floor: 633 square feet
Total: 2,139 square feet

● Graceful lines and arched windows create a delightful country flair for this 1½-story home. From the volume entry, there's a clear view of the stunning great room enhanced by the handsome fireplace and windows with a view. The adjacent dining room is perfect for entertaining. A dinette, open to the island kitchen, allows sunlight to brighten and warm this family-sized eating area. The covered patio is accessed from the dinette. In the gourmet kitchen, convenience is evident through features such as a snack bar, planning desk and walk-in pantry. The main-floor master suite sports a beautiful arched window, double doors and sloped ceiling. A two-person whirlpool, His and Hers vanities and a decorator plant ledge complement the master dressing area. Three secondary bedrooms upstairs share a hall bath.

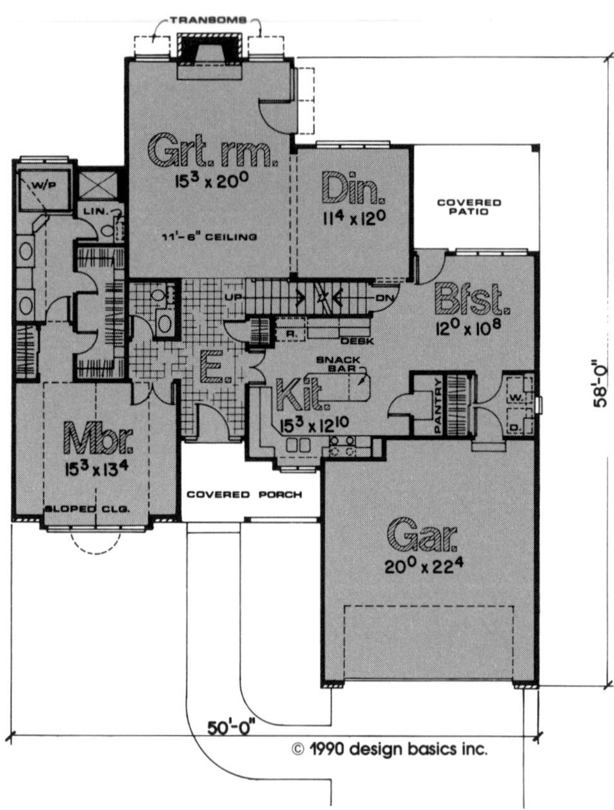

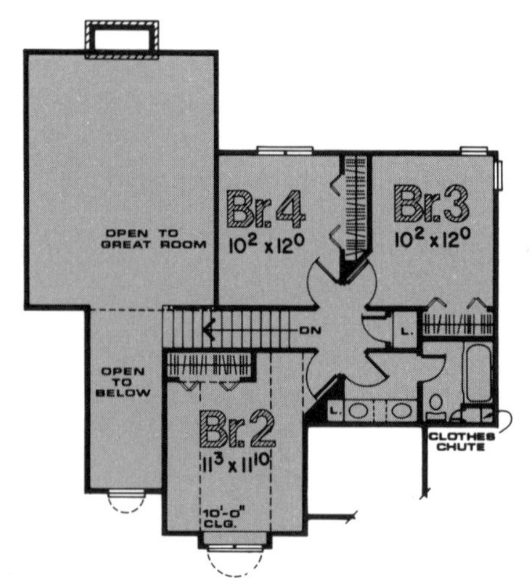

Design by
Design
Basics,
Inc.

Design Q9219

First Floor: 1,132 square feet
Second Floor: 1,087 square feet
Total: 2,219 square feet

● The detailed front porch, attractive chimney and overall pleasing exterior make this home a delight in any neighborhood. The interior features a floor plan for active families. The front dining room includes a formal, tiered ceiling and hutch space. The great room with fireplace and ten-foot ceiling provides multi-purpose living space. The ample kitchen includes a breakfast room with bay window. The highlight of the four-bedroom sleeping area is the master suite with elegant vaulted ceiling and skylit bath with whirlpool.

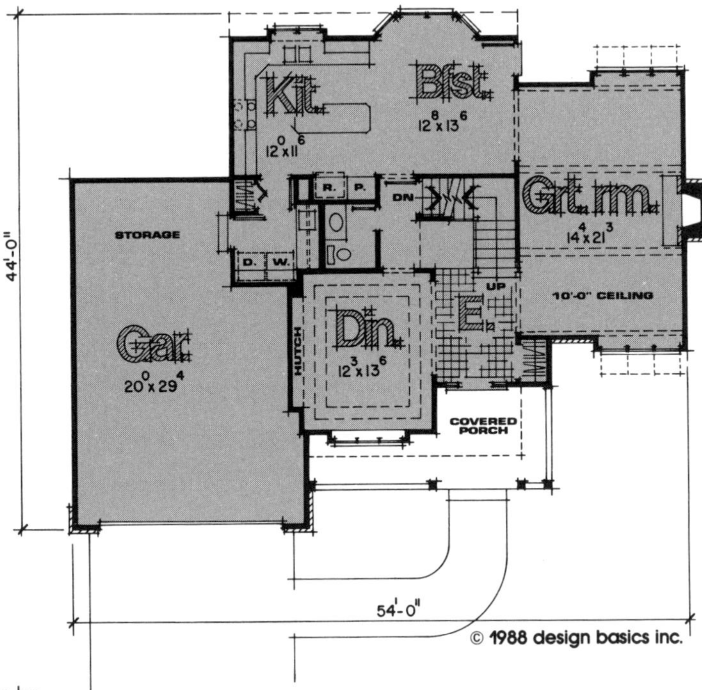

Design by
Design Basics, Inc.

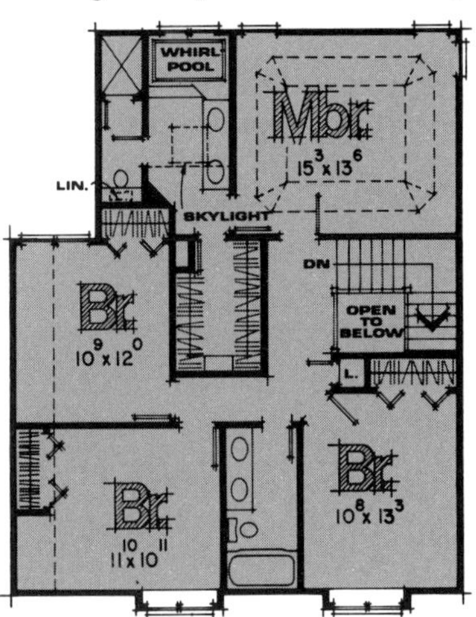

Design Q3356

First Floor: 1,610 square feet
Second Floor: 1,200 square feet
Total: 2,810 square feet

● Traditionally speaking, this home takes blue ribbons. Its family room has a raised-hearth fireplace and there's a covered porch reached through sliding glass doors for informal eating. The living room also has a fireplace and is near the boxed-windowed dining room. A large clutter room off the garage could be turned into a hobby or sewing room. Four bedrooms on the second floor include a master suite with His and Hers walk-in closets and three family bedrooms.

Design by
Home Planners, Inc.

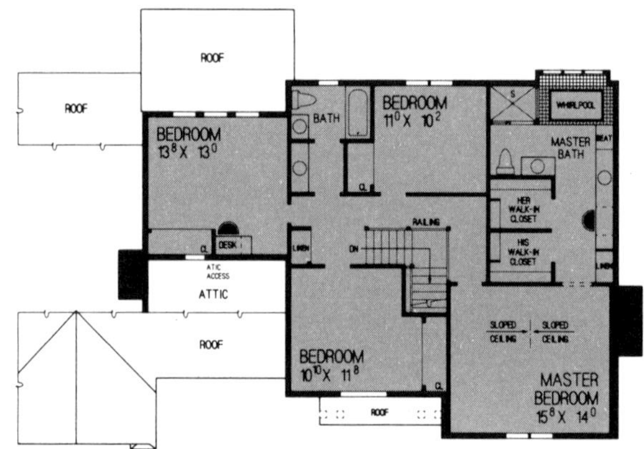

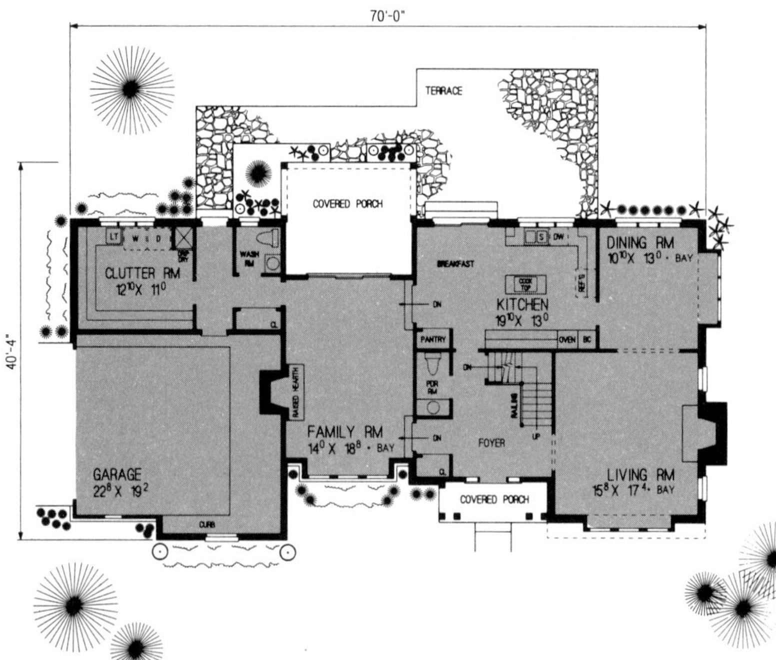

Design Q3351

First Floor: 1,794 square feet
Second Floor: 887 square feet
Total: 2,681 square feet

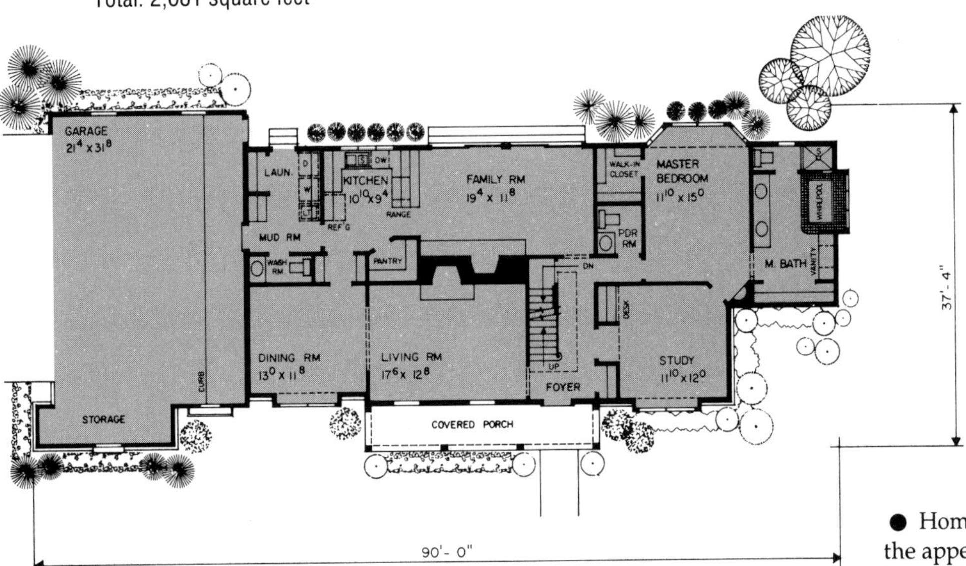

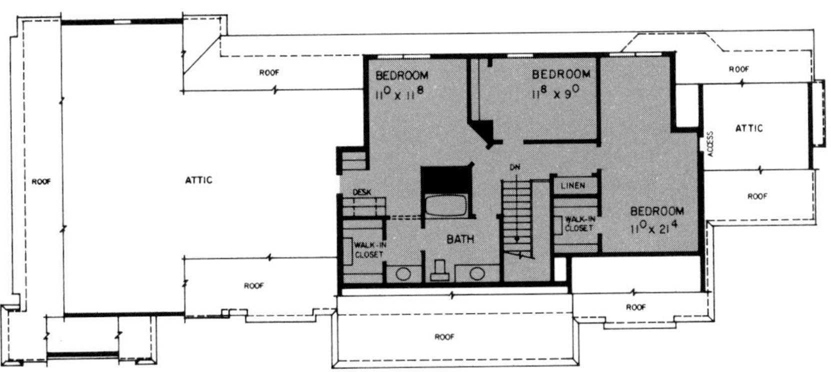

● Home-grown comfort is the key to the appeal of this traditionally styled home. From the kitchen with attached family room to the living room with fireplace and attached formal dining room, this plan has it all. Notice the first-floor master bedroom with whirlpool tub and adjacent study. A nearby powder room turns the study into a convenient guest room. On the second floor are three more bedrooms with ample closet space and a full bath. The two-car garage has a large storage area.

Design by
Home Planners, Inc.

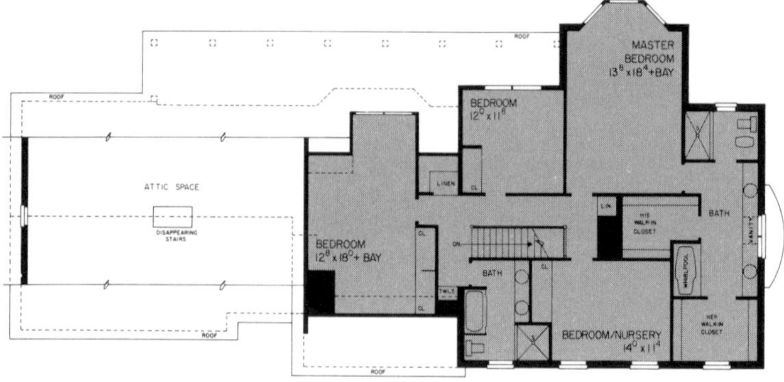

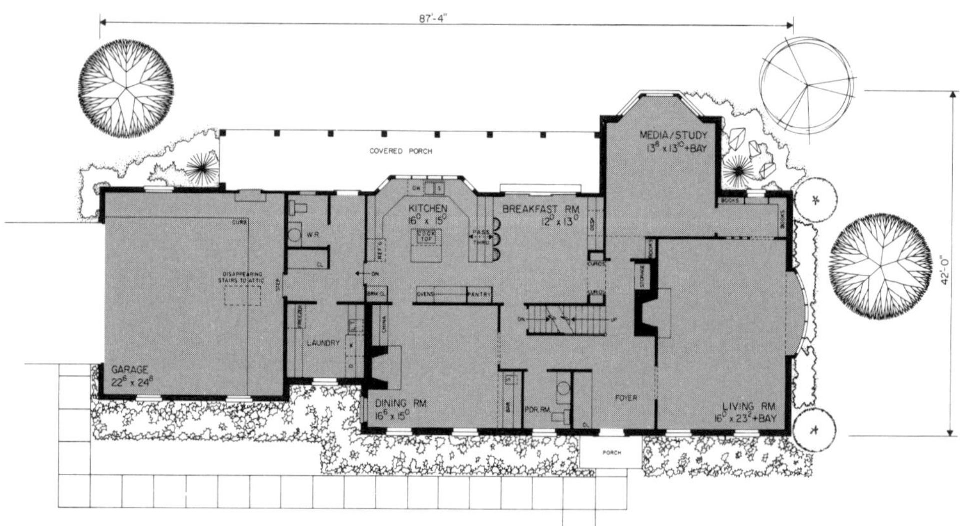

Design Q2963

First Floor: 2,046 square feet
Second Floor: 1,644 square feet
Total: 3,690 square feet

● Featuring a gracious foyer and stairway at the entry, this home in the Colonial tradition is actually a modified version of the center-hall classic. Unlike the classic standard, the entrance here is off-center in the facade, with three windows to the left and two to the right of the entry door. Yet the design offers the dignity and grace so readily associated with its center-hall cousin. In addition, the rambling proportions of the house reflect Colonial precedents–as families grew, so did their houses. Both the dining and living rooms boast large fireplaces. Family meals are likely to be served in the cozy nook attached to the kitchen. Ample cabinet, shelf, and pantry space is provided wherever storage space is most needed. To retreat from the clamor of an active household, family members can read a good book in the study tucked in behind the living room, where generous provision is made for an entire library. Upstairs, four bedrooms provide a comfortable arrangement for each family member.

Design by
Home Planners, Inc.

Design Q2542 First Floor: 2,025 square feet
Second Floor: 1,726 square feet; Total: 3,751 square feet

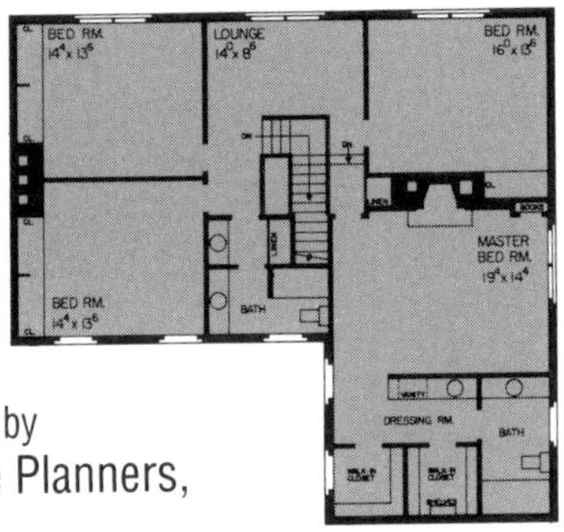

Design by
Home Planners,
Inc.

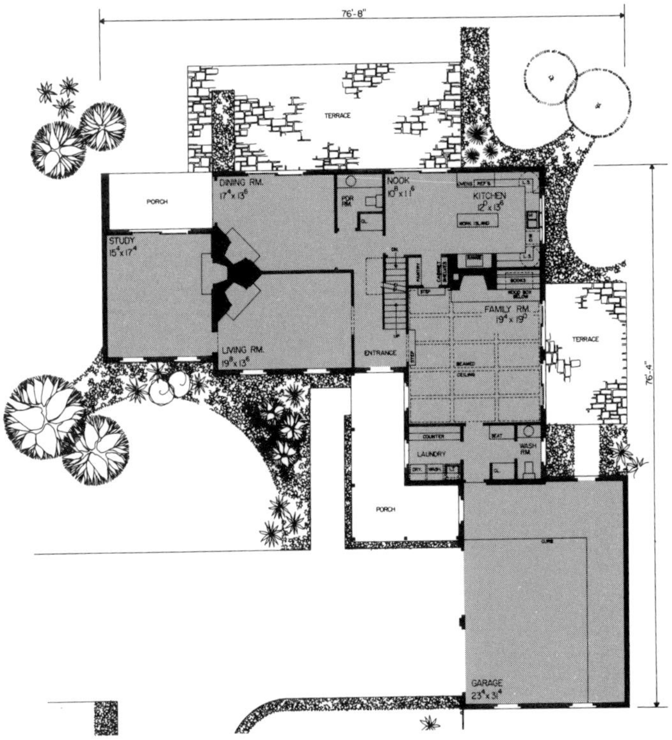

● Here is a fieldstone Farmhouse that has its roots in the rolling countryside of Pennsylvania. In addition to its stone exterior, the charm of such a house is characterized by the various appendages. These additions, of course, came into being as the size of the family fortune increased. The living potential offered by this Farmhouse adaptation can hardly be topped. Imagine, five fireplaces! Study the outstanding livability offered in this house from the past. Surely its floor plan has been up-dated to serve today's contemporary family.

Design Q9862

Square Footage: 2,120

● This classic cottage features a stone and wooden exterior with an arch-detailed porch and box bay window. From the foyer, double doors open to the den with built-in bookcases and a fireplace. A full bath is situated next to the den, allowing for an optional guest room. The family room is centrally located, just beyond the foyer. Its hearth is framed by windows overlooking the porch at the rear of the home. The master bedroom opens onto the rear porch. The master bath, with large walk-in closet, double vanities, corner tub and separate shower completes this relaxing retreat. Left of the family room awaits a sun room with access to the covered porch. A breakfast area complements the attractive and efficiently-designed kitchen. A short hallway from the sun room leads to two bedrooms with large closets and shared full bath featuring double vanities.

Design by
Design Traditions
Atlanta

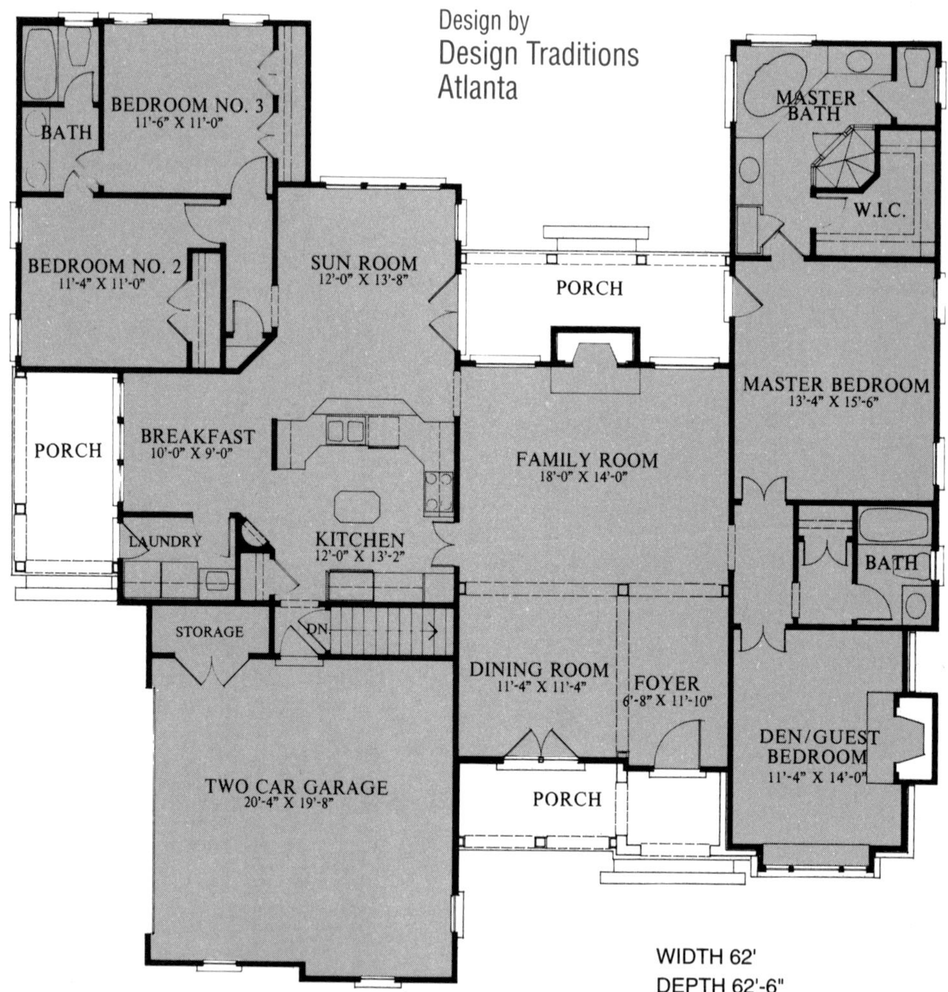

WIDTH 62'
DEPTH 62'-6"

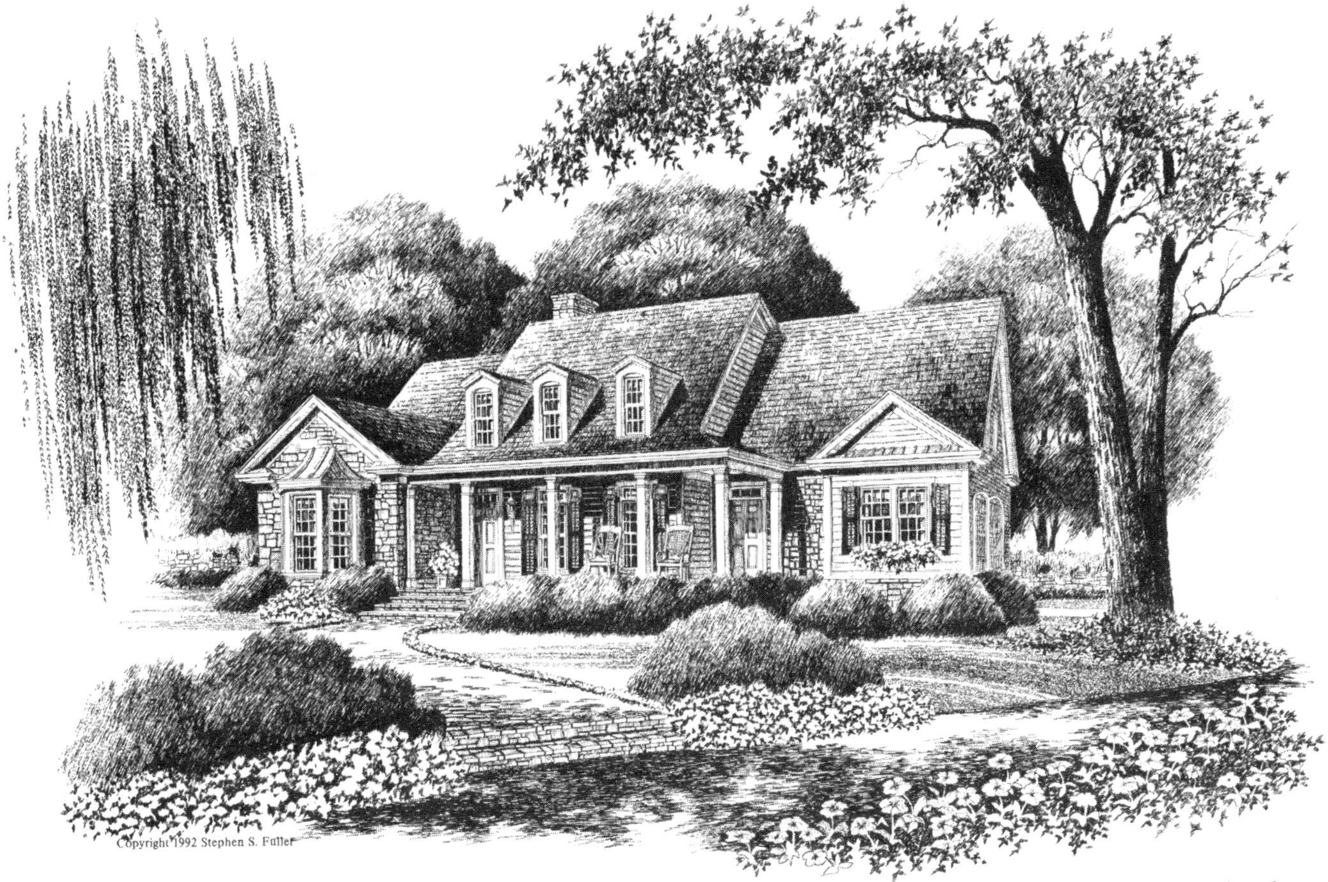

Design Q9861

First Floor: 1,945 square feet
Second Floor: 960 square feet
Total: 2,905 square feet

● The facade of this charming home is Americana at its best with a rocking-chair porch, bay window and dormers above, finished in stone and wood siding and faithfully detailed. A convenient outdoor entrance to the two-car garage is located to the right of the front porch. The main level features an easy flow, beginning with the dining room to the right of the foyer. A hallway between the foyer and main staircase helps to promote a sense of openness. The great room features a large hearth and French doors to the patio, and leads directly to the breakfast area and kitchen. Storage closets and a counter-top desk area highlight the kitchen which, along with the laundry room, is conveniently located to the rear of the home. Left of the foyer is an attractive study with a large bay window. The master suite, featuring a bay-windowed sitting area, large master bath with double vanities and shower and ample closet space, completes the main level. On the upper level, bedroom two features a full bath and has three dormer windows overlooking the front lawn. The third and fourth bedrooms share another full bath.

Design by
Design Traditions
Atlanta

WIDTH 64'-6"
DEPTH 50'

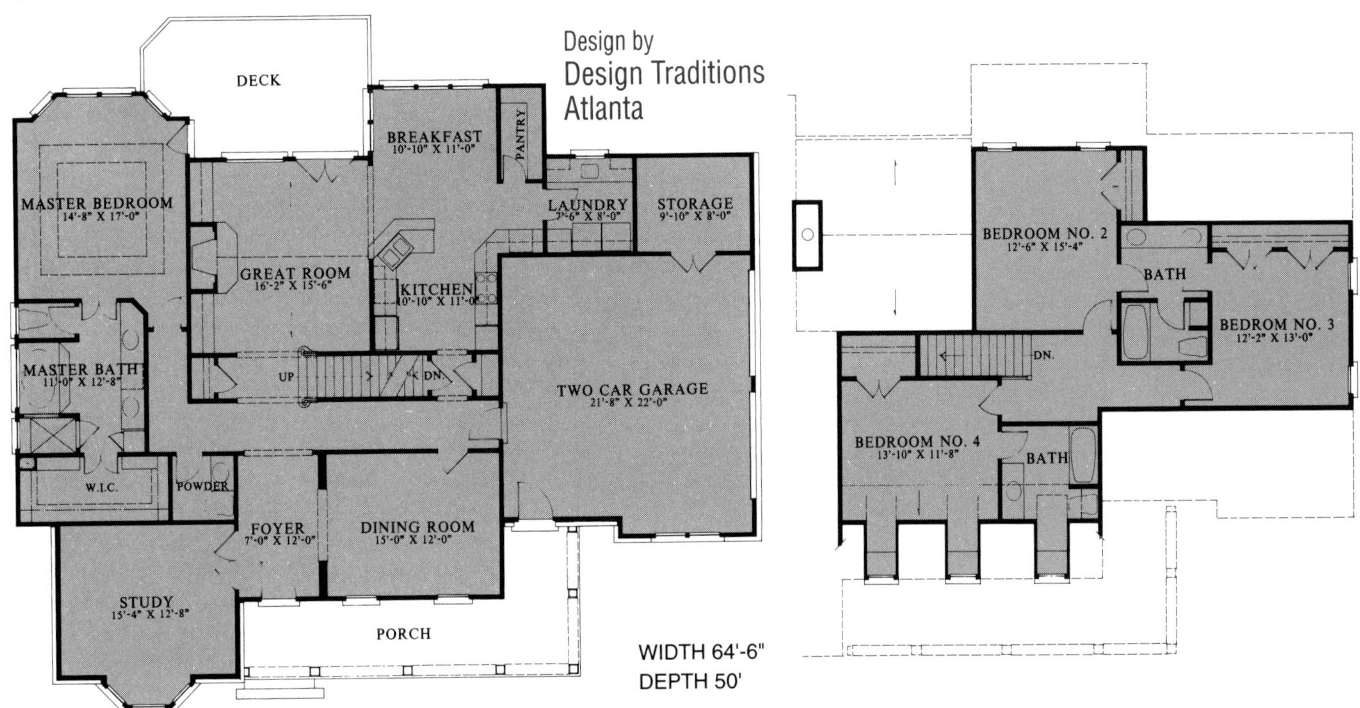

Design Q2633

First Floor: 1,338 square feet
Second Floor: 1,200 square feet
Third Floor: 506 square feet
Total: 3,044 square feet

● This is certainly a pleasing Georgian. Its facade features a front porch with a roof supported by 12" diameter wooden columns. The garage wing has a sheltered service entry and brick facing which complements the design. Sliding glass doors link the terrace and family room, providing an indoor/outdoor area for entertaining as pictured in the rear elevation. The floor plan has been designed to serve the family efficiently. The stairway in the foyer leads to four second-floor bedrooms. The third floor is windowed and can be used as a studio and study.

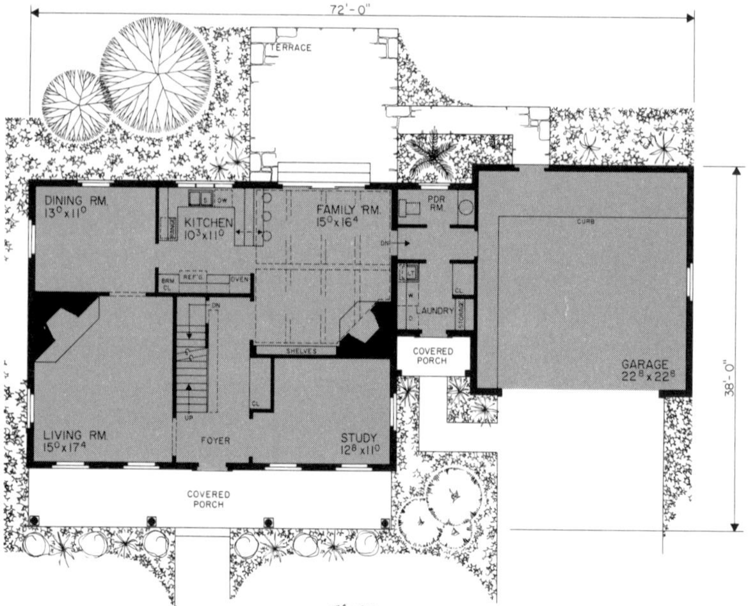

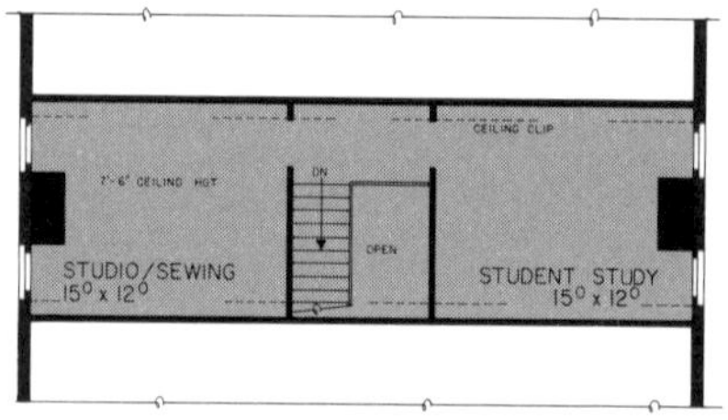

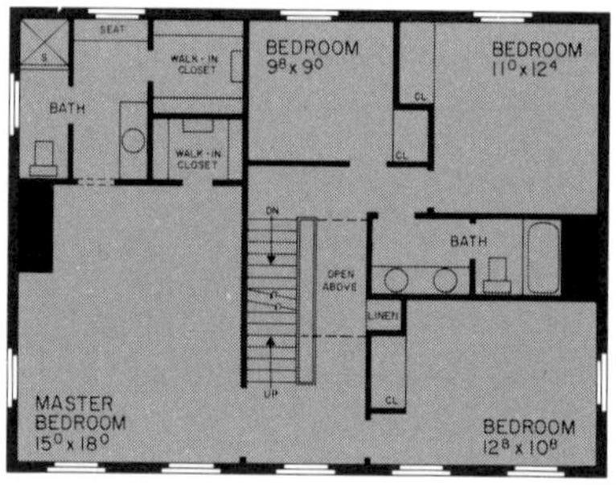

72'-0"
TERRACE
DINING RM. 13⁰x11⁰
KITCHEN 10³x11⁰
FAMILY RM. 15⁰x16⁴
PDR RM.
LAUNDRY
COVERED PORCH
GARAGE 22⁸x22⁸
38'-0"
LIVING RM. 15⁰x17⁴
FOYER
STUDY 12⁸x11⁰
COVERED PORCH

7'-6" CEILING HGT
CEILING CLIP
OPEN
STUDIO/SEWING 15⁰x12⁰
STUDENT STUDY 15⁰x12⁰

BATH
WALK-IN CLOSET
BEDROOM 9⁸x9⁰
BEDROOM 11⁰x12⁴
OPEN ABOVE
BATH
LINEN
MASTER BEDROOM 15⁰x18⁰
BEDROOM 12⁸x10⁸

Design by
Home Planners,
Inc.

● This two-story farmhouse brings to mind the stone houses of Bucks County, Pa. The recessed center entrance opens to the foyer. To the left is the living room with its adjacent music alcove. The sunken study offers a guest retreat. The efficient, U-shaped kitchen functions

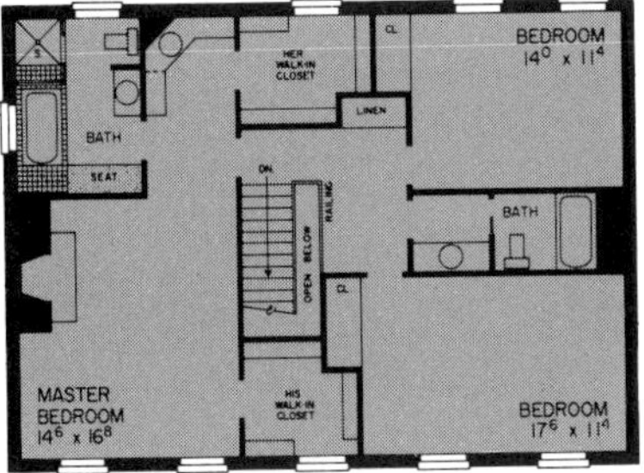

well with the large breakfast room and separate dining room with fireplace. The three bedroom upstairs features nice sized rooms and a fourth fireplace. Note the laundry.

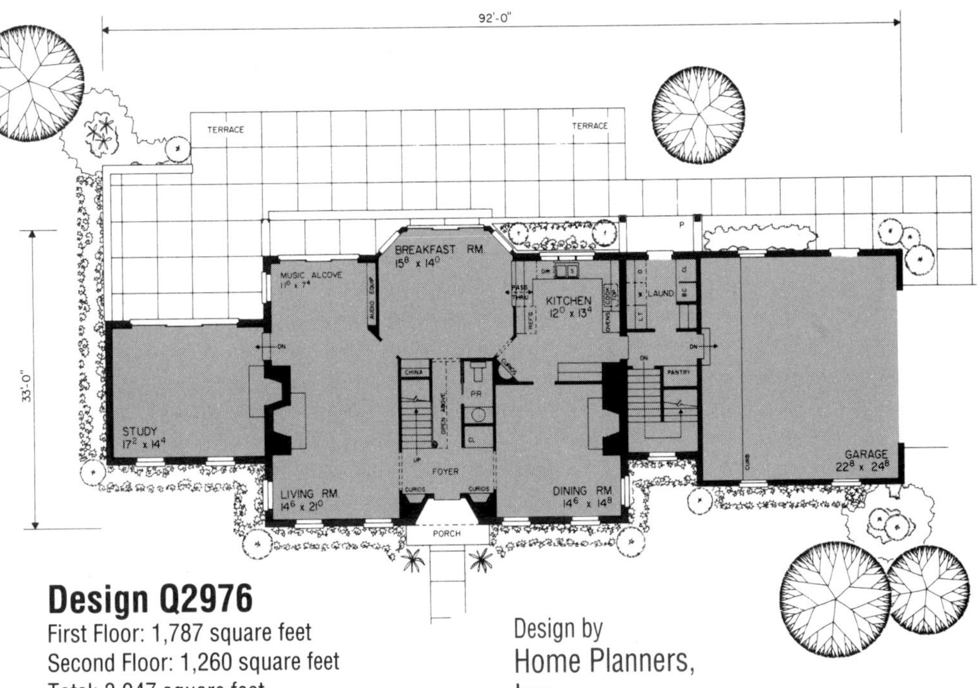

Design Q2976

First Floor: 1,787 square feet
Second Floor: 1,260 square feet
Total: 3,047 square feet

Design by
Home Planners, Inc.

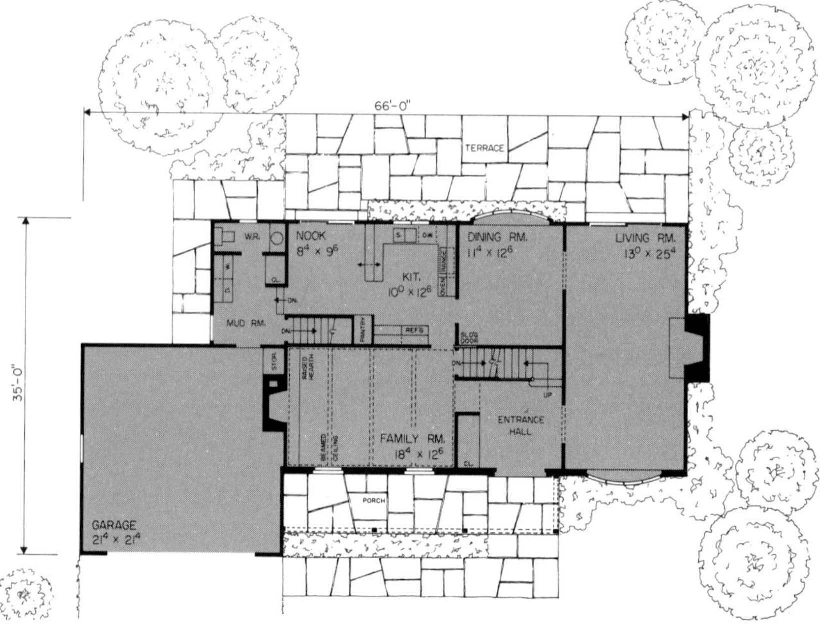

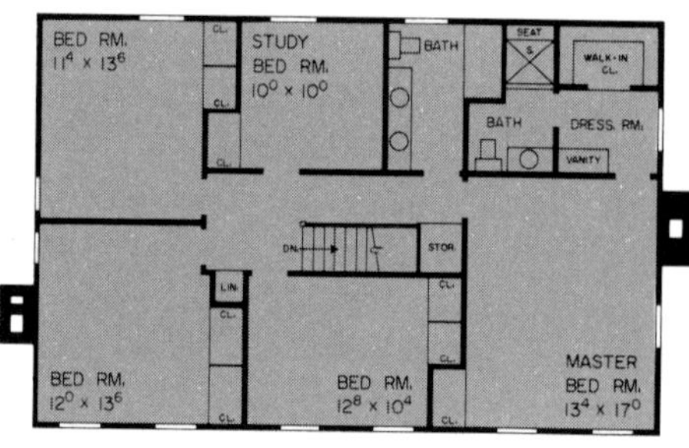

Design by
Home Planners,
Inc.

Design Q2223 First Floor: 1,266 square feet
Second Floor: 1,232 square feet; Total: 2,498 square feet

● The appealing double front doors of this home open wide to fine livability for the large, growing family. The spacious entrance hall is flanked by the formal, end living room and the all-purpose, beamed ceiling family room. Both rooms have a commanding fireplace. The U-shaped kitchen overlooks the rear yard and is but a step, or two, from the breakfast nook and the formal dining room. The mud room controls the flows of traffic during the inclement weather. Observe the laundry equipment and the washroom. Five bedrooms, two full baths, and plenty of closets are what make the second floor truly outstanding. There are a number of other convenient living features that make this design distinctive. How many of these can you list?

CONTEMPORARY FARMHOUSES

Seemingly diverse, the notions of *contemporary* and *farmhouse* blend surprisingly well. In the Contemporary Farmhouse, design takes a classic 1½- or two-story farmhouse structure and modifies it with more rounded, open or vaulted forms.

The style may have begun in the West, particularly California and the Pacific Coast, and spread eastward to the Midwest, South and East — in direct opposition to traditional farmhouse evolution.

Wood, stone and glass are the major components of the style and afford it a contemporary look and ambience. The contemporary use of glass gives the style its characteristic open-air, light-filled properties. The open floor plans that are usually contained in these homes allow for easy traffic patterns and great indoor/outdoor livability.

Many fine examples of this divergent style are presented. Designs Q9310 and Q9311 represent the Modern Midwest Wood style and take their forms and feeling from traditional dwellings popular in the Midwest. Adding a more contemporary feel, however, are the arched details, half-round windows and the clean, simple lines. More reminiscent of the Pacific Northwest are designs such as Q9480 which stands tall and upright and features French-styled rooflines. The arched window in the foyer is repeated in the bonus room over the garage. In the best Southern tradition are two designs, Q9600 and Q9619, which feature contemporary additions such as the skylit sun rooms and the lovely rear decks. Maintaining traditional appeal, however, is the chimney cap on Design Q9619. Designs Q3404 and Q3438 are exquisite echoes of the Tin-Roof or Shed-Roof style but are often referred to as the California Farmhouse or California Contemporary Farmhouse. Each has the bold statement of contemporary design, yet keeps a rustic sense. Both floor plans are open and spacious in the best contemporary style. Blending the best elements of traditional and contemporary details, Design Q2931 can be classified as a Transitional home. Resembling a Cape Cod, with winged extensions and multi-paned windows, it also incorporates large patio areas and vertical wood siding, giving it a contemporary accent.

The Contemporary Farmhouses in this section represent an entirely new and exciting form for the standard country residence. Though perhaps not for the farmhouse purist, these evolved designs provide a wonderful option for those who love the fluidity of contemporary form and the grace of traditional style.

Design Q9311 First Floor: 1,032 square feet
Second Floor: 865 square feet; Total: 1,897 square feet

● Today's home buyer will enjoy the comfort of country living in this two-story home with a covered front porch. Combining lap siding, distinctive trim detail and brick accents, this elevation will surely capture your imagination! Just off the tiled entry, the volume living room shares an open arrangement with the formal dining room. Meals prepared in the generous kitchen will be enjoyed in the adjoining bayed dinette which features a large pantry. After dinner, homeowners may relax in the spacious family room with raised-hearth fireplace. Upstairs, the master bedroom suite contains His and Hers closets which separate the master bedroom from the master bath with double vanity. The whirlpool tub is brightened by an arch-top window. Three secondary bedrooms are served by their own convenient bath and linen closet.

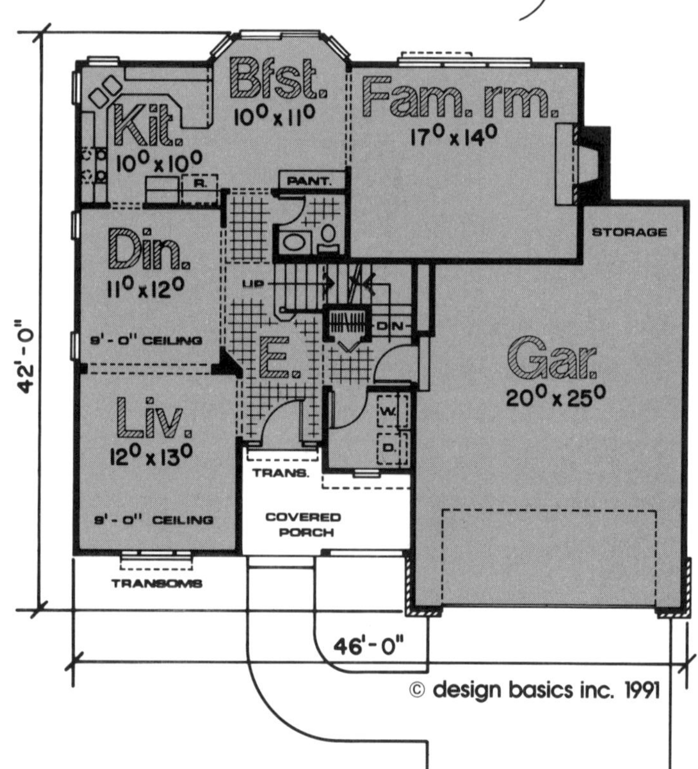

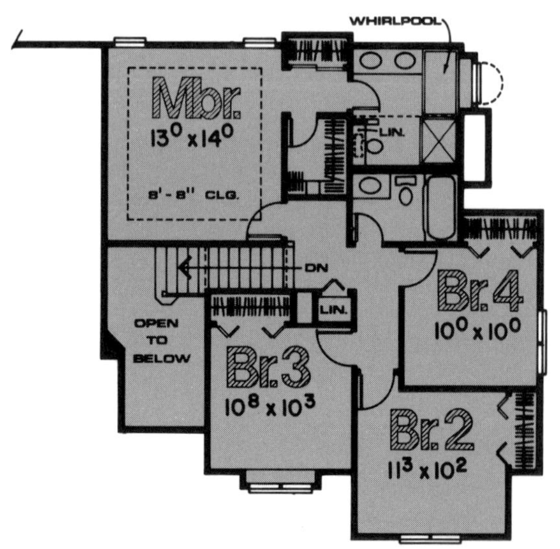

Design by
Design Basics, Inc.

Design Q9310

First Floor: 1,505 square feet
Second Floor: 610 square feet
Total: 2,115 square feet

● Many windows, lap siding and a covered porch give this elevation a welcoming country flair. The formal dining room with hutch space is conveniently located near the island kitchen. A main floor laundry room with sink is discreetly located next to the bright dinette with desk and pantry. Highlighting the spacious great room are a raised hearth fireplace, cathedral ceiling and trapezoid windows. Special features in the master suite include a large dressing area with double vanity, skylight, step-up corner whirlpool and a generous walk-in closet. Upstairs, the three secondary bedrooms are well separated from the master bedroom and share a hall bath.

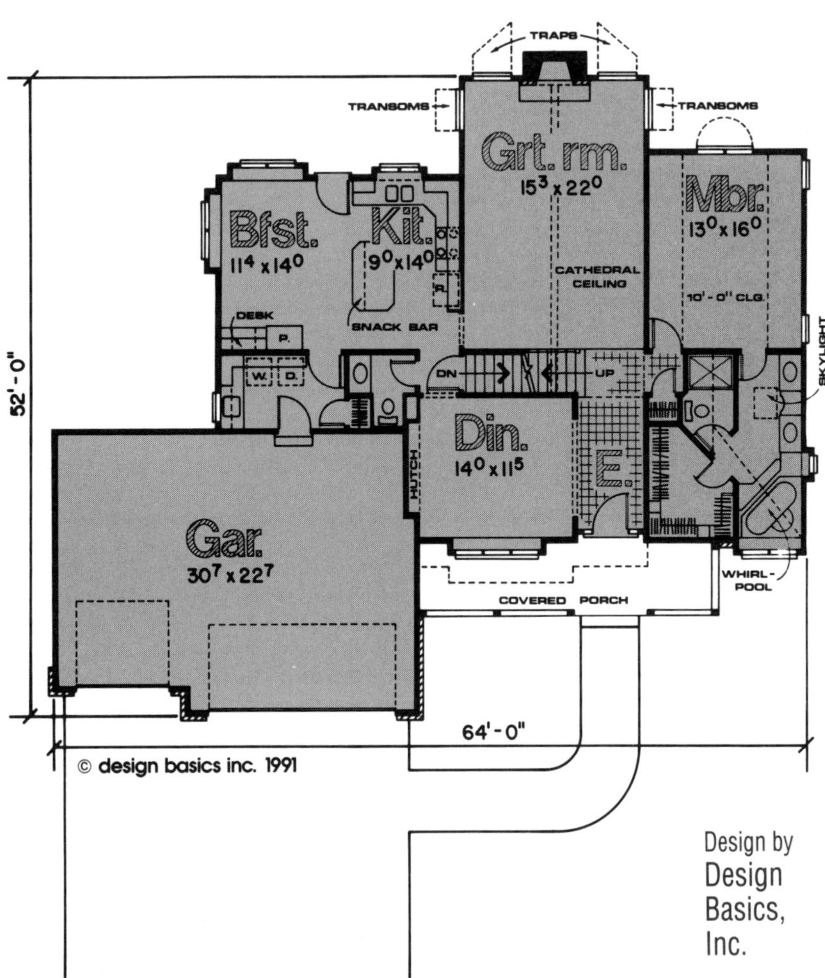

Design by Design Basics, Inc.

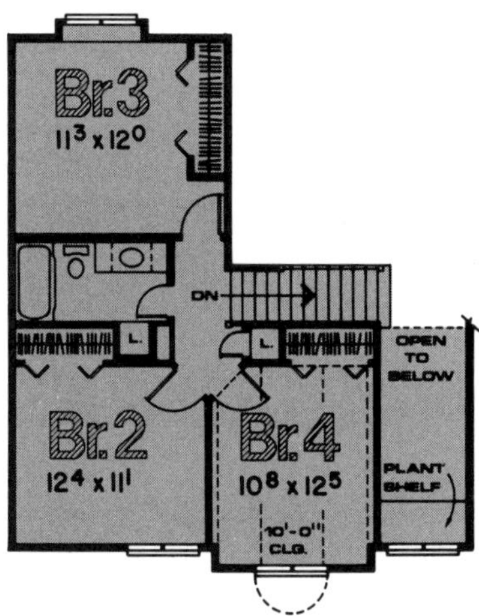

Design Q9312

First Floor: 1,150 square feet
Second Floor: 1,120 square feet
Total: 2,270 square feet

● Lap siding, special windows and a covered porch enhance the elevation of this popular style. The spacious two-story entry surveys the formal dining room with hutch space. An entertainment center, through-fireplace and bayed windows add appeal to the great room. Families will love the spacious kitchen, breakfast and hearth room. Enhancements to this casual living area include a through-fireplace, gazebo dinette, wrapping counters, an island kitchen and planning desk. An efficient U-shaped staircase routes traffic throughout. Comfortable secondary bedrooms and a sumptuous master suite feature privacy by design. Bedroom 3 is highlighted by a half round window, volume ceiling and double closets while Bedroom 4 features a built-in desk. The master suite has a vaulted ceiling, large walk-in closet, His and Hers vanities, compartmented stool/shower area and an oval whirlpool tub.

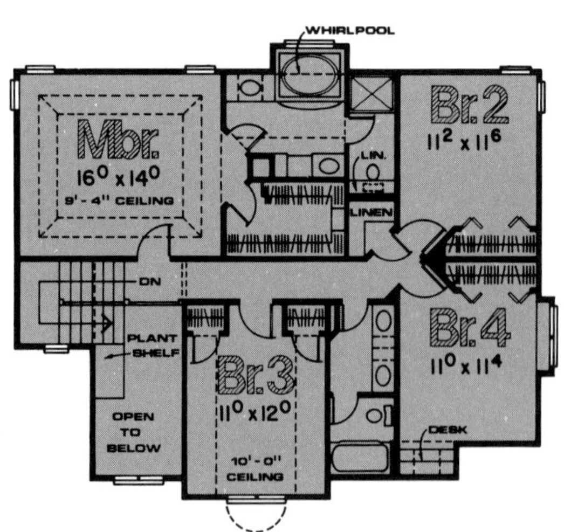

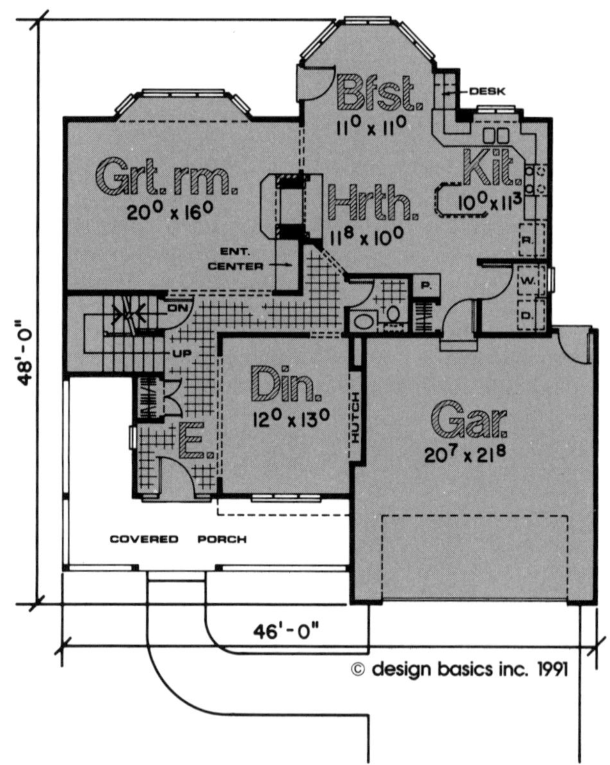

Design by
Design
Basics,
Inc.

Design Q9313

First Floor: 1,426 square feet
Second Floor: 1,294 square feet
Total: 2,720 square feet

● Country living is evident from the covered porch and charming window boxes on this elevation. A private den with French doors and spider-beamed ceiling, is viewed from the entry, as well as the dining room with hutch space. An open kitchen/dinette is complete with a planning desk, pantry and snack bar. The hearth room is accented by a bayed window, entertainment center and through-fireplace. Home buyers will consider the volume great room a dynamic living space due to its comfort, bright windows and French door access to the hearth room. An open stairway accesses the second floor. Secondary bedrooms 2 and 3 include built-in desks. Sunny windows, a boxed ceiling, two closets, whirlpool and His and Hers vanities exude luxury in the master suite.

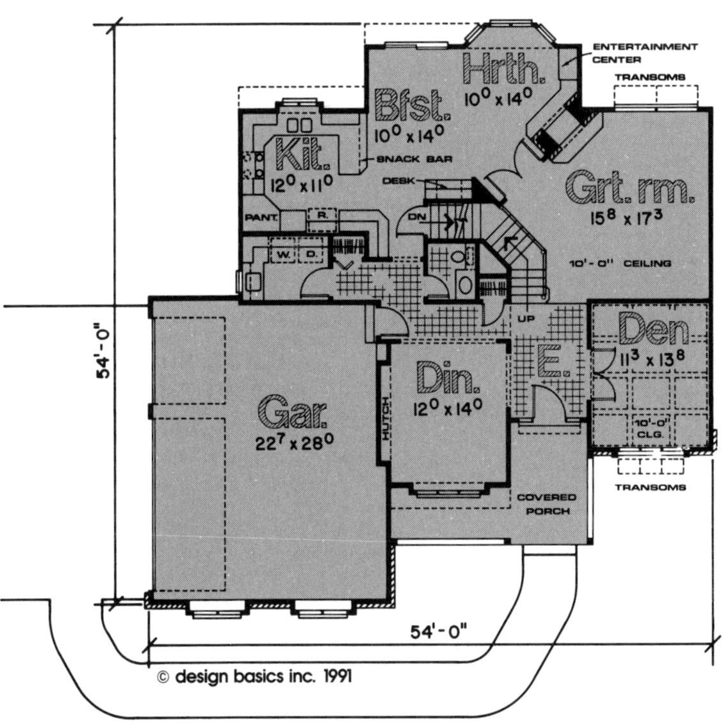

Design by
Design Basics, Inc.

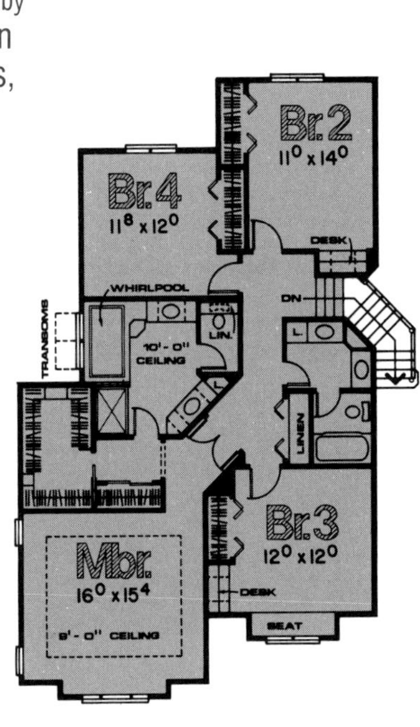

Design Q9481

First Floor: 1,157 square feet
Second Floor: 980 square feet
Total: 2,137 square feet

● This charming farmhouse plan holds a wealth of living potential in a relatively small square footage. Beyond the covered front porch is an entry flanked by a formal parlor and dining room. The angled stairway to the second floor is both beautiful and functional. To the rear of the plan is a family room with fireplace which adjoins the nook and kitchen. A handy laundry area connects the main house to the two-car garage. Upstairs are four bedrooms and two full baths. Note the abundant closet space in each bedroom.

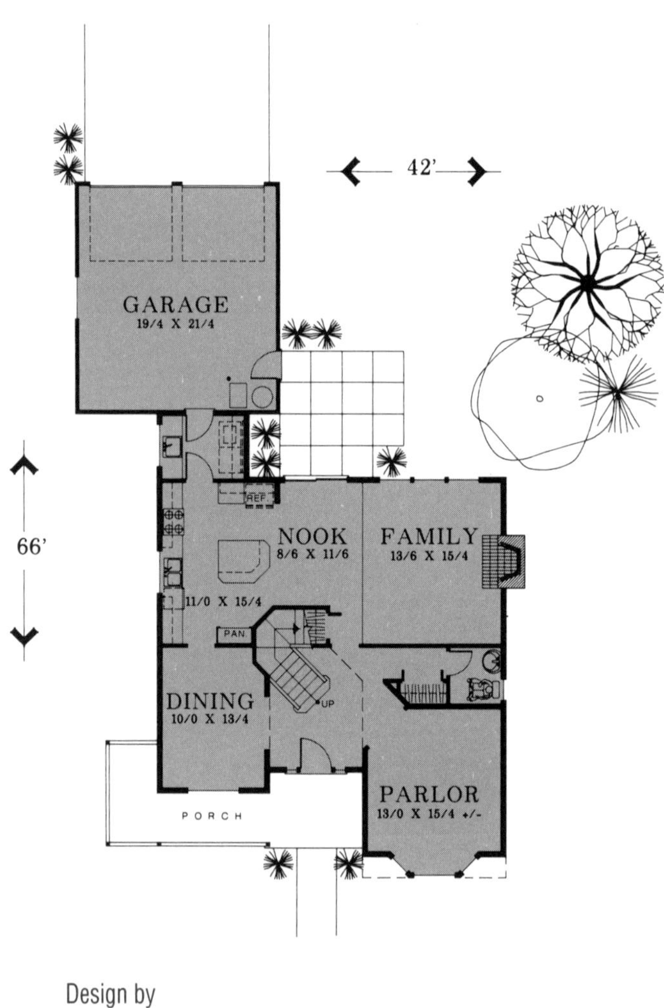

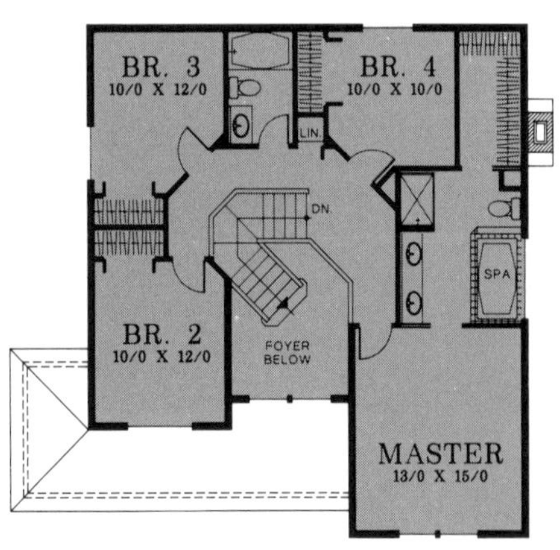

Design by
Alan Mascord
Design Associates, Inc.

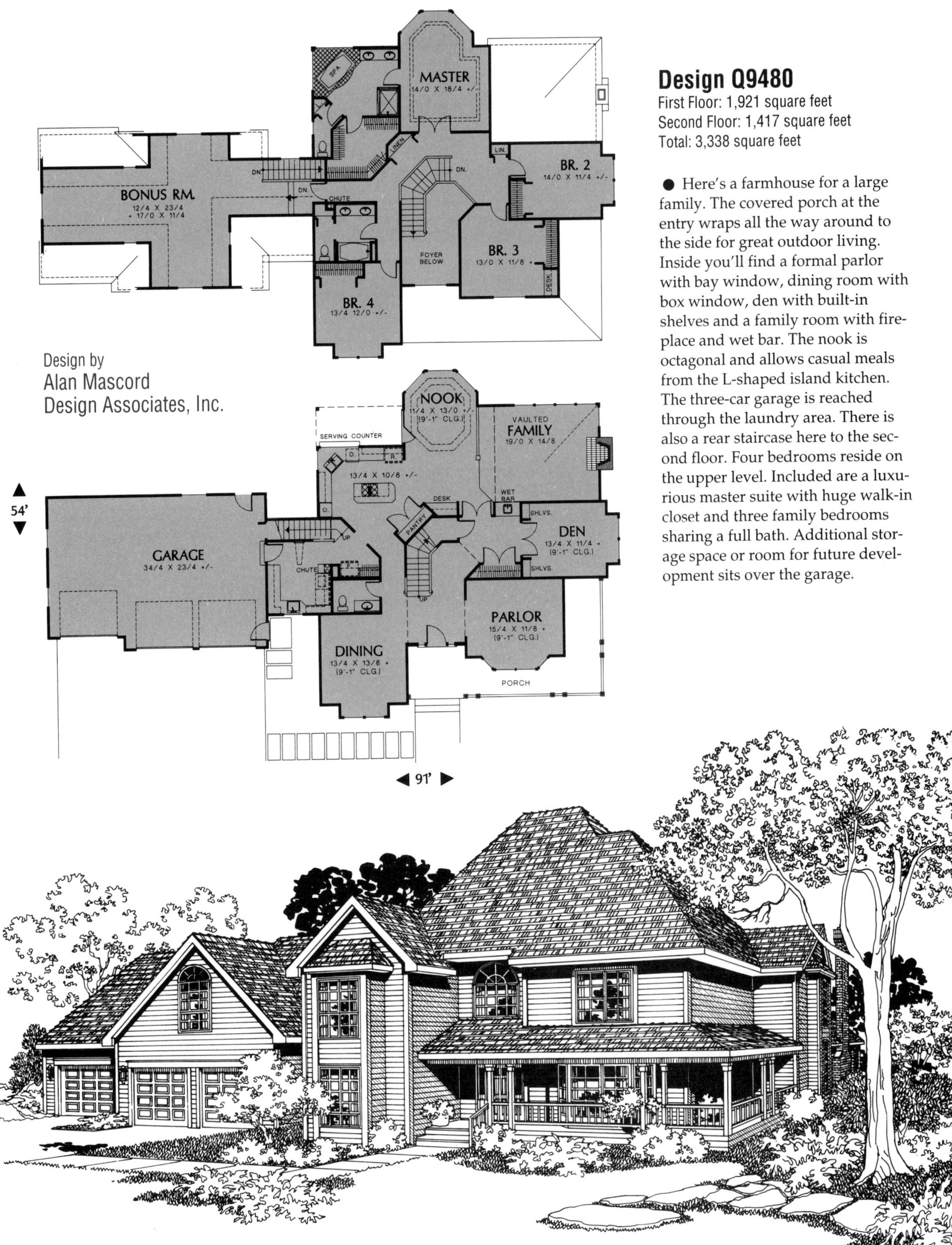

Design by
Alan Mascord
Design Associates, Inc.

Design Q9480

First Floor: 1,921 square feet
Second Floor: 1,417 square feet
Total: 3,338 square feet

● Here's a farmhouse for a large family. The covered porch at the entry wraps all the way around to the side for great outdoor living. Inside you'll find a formal parlor with bay window, dining room with box window, den with built-in shelves and a family room with fireplace and wet bar. The nook is octagonal and allows casual meals from the L-shaped island kitchen. The three-car garage is reached through the laundry area. There is also a rear staircase here to the second floor. Four bedrooms reside on the upper level. Included are a luxurious master suite with huge walk-in closet and three family bedrooms sharing a full bath. Additional storage space or room for future development sits over the garage.

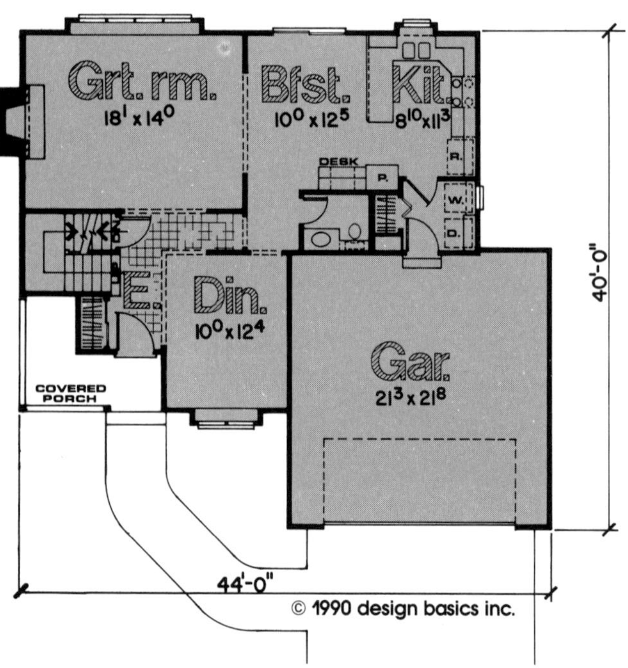

Design Q9260

First Floor: 891 square feet
Second Floor: 759 square feet
Total: 1,650 square feet

● A quaint covered porch leads to a volume entry with decorator plant ledge above the closet in this home. The formal dining room has a boxed window that can be seen from the entry. A fireplace in the large great room adds warmth and coziness to the attached breakfast room and well-planned kitchen. Notice the nearby powder room for guests. Upstairs are three bedrooms. Bedroom 3 has a beautiful arched window under a volume ceiling. The master bedroom has a walk-in closet and pampering dressing area with double vanity and a whirlpool under a window. The upstairs landing overlooks the entry below.

Design by
Design
Basics,
Inc.

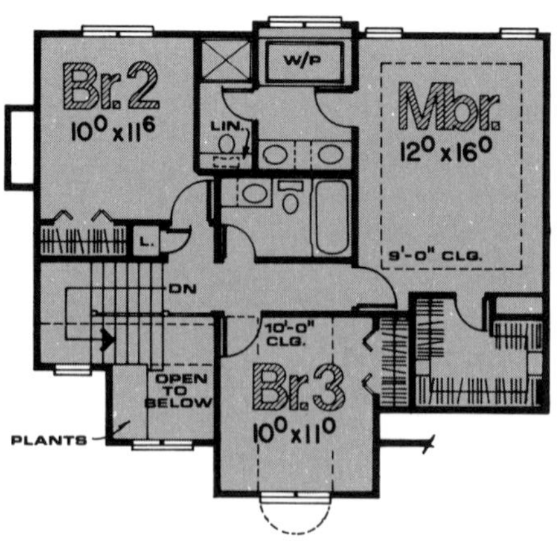

Design Q9235

First Floor: 919 square feet
Second Floor: 927 square feet
Total: 1,846 square feet

● Wonderful country design begins with the wraparound porch of this plan. Explore further and find a two-story entry with a coat closet and plant shelf above and a strategically placed staircase alongside. The island kitchen with a boxed window over the sink is adjacent to a large bay-windowed dinette. The great room includes many windows and a fireplace. A powder bath and laundry room are both conveniently placed on the first floor. Upstairs, the large master suite contains His and Hers walk-in closets, corner windows and a bath area featuring a double vanity and whirlpool tub. Two pleasant secondary bedrooms have interesting angles and a third bedroom in the front features a volume ceiling and arched window.

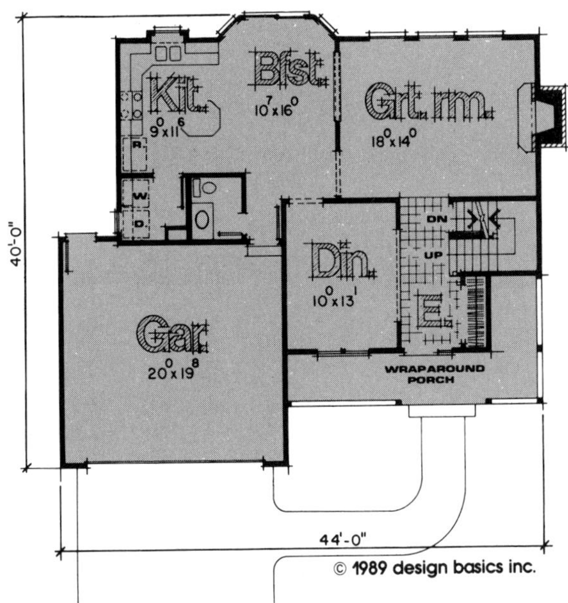

Design by Design Basics, Inc.

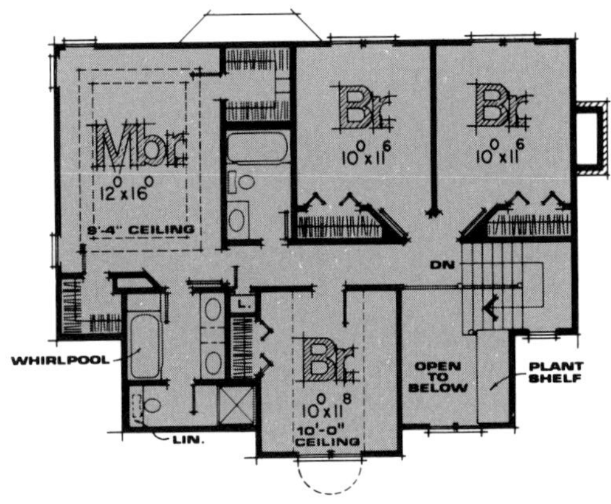

Design Q9457

First Floor: 1,105 square feet
Second Floor: 950 square feet
Total: 2,055 square feet
(5th bedroom option adds 190 square feet)

● There's space here for even the largest of families—four or even five bedrooms on the second floor allow everyone to have a room of their own. First-floor living space includes a living room/dining room combination, family room with attached nook and galley-style kitchen. The nook and living room both have bay windows; the family room looks out onto a rear terrace.

Design by
Alan Mascord
Design Associates, Inc.

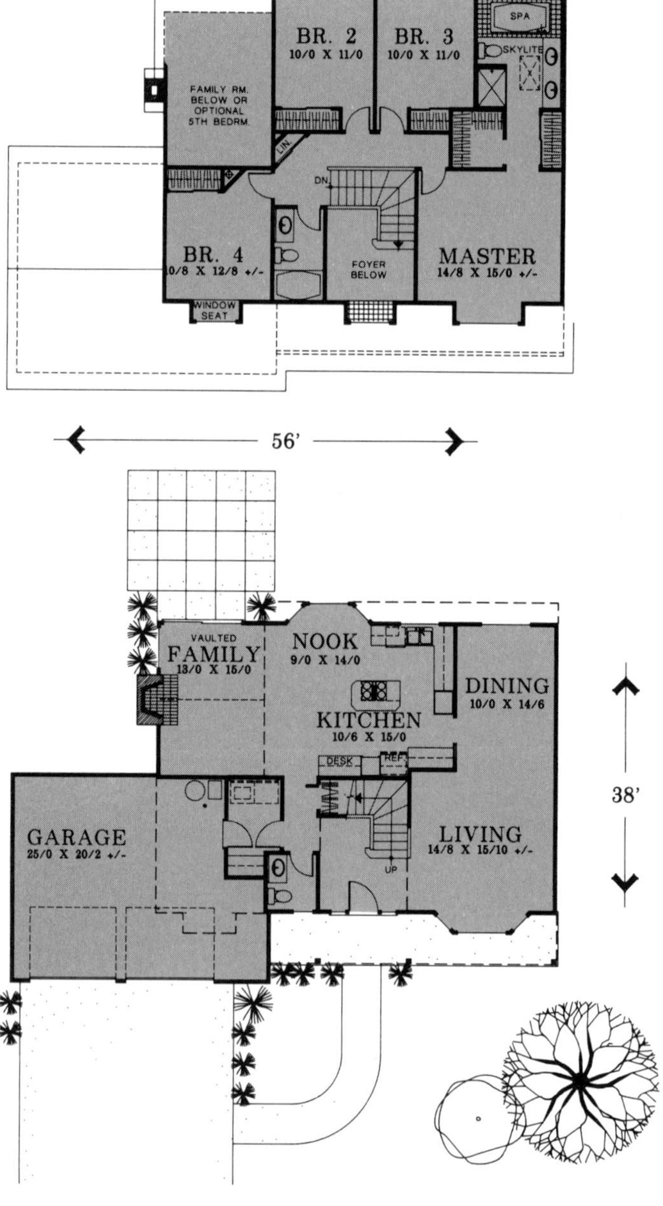

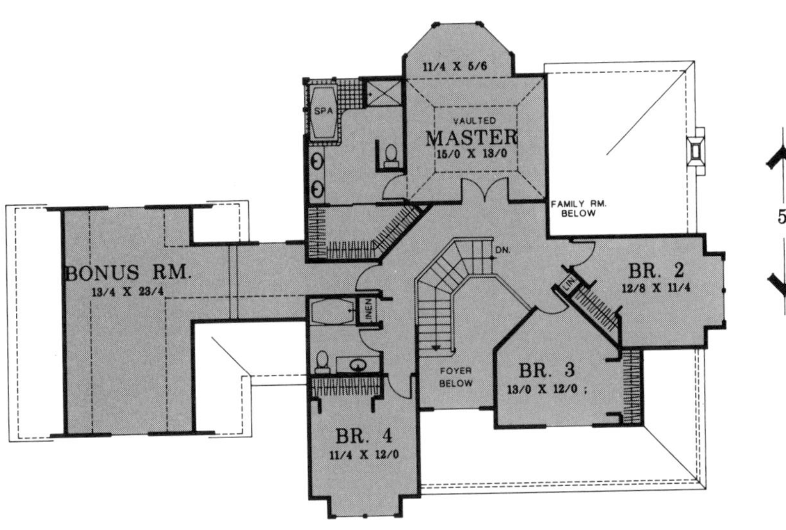

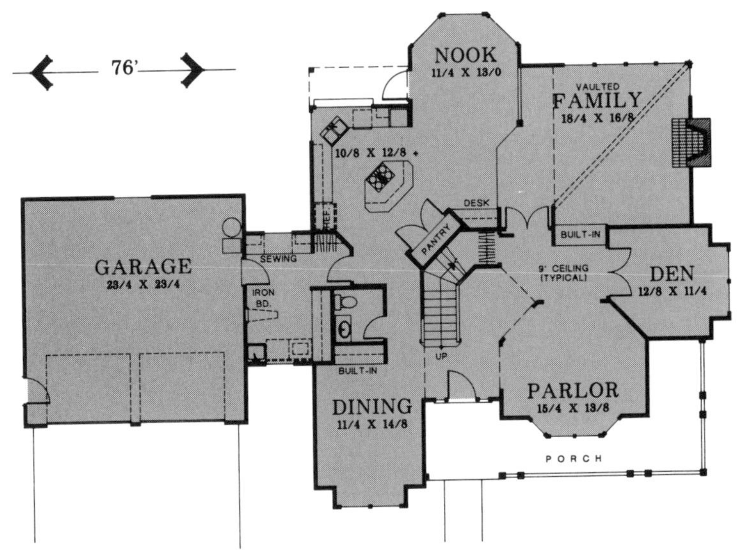

Design Q9458

First Floor: 1,730 square feet
Second Floor: 1,215 square feet
Total: 2,945 square feet
Bonus Room: 462 square feet

● Though its facade says country casual, this home has a floor plan that is as elegant and modern as any. The front porch wraps around a formal farmhouse parlor with bay window. This room is almost completely open to the foyer and sits right next to the more private den. The large family room features a vaulted ceiling and fireplace. It blends into the bay-windowed nook adjacent to the L-shaped island kitchen. A powder room separates the space between the kitchen and formal dining room with boxed window. Up an open staircase is the four-bedroom second floor. Three family bedrooms share a full bath. The master suite has a vaulted ceiling, large walk-in closet and bath with spa.

Design by
Alan Mascord
Design Associates, Inc.

REAR

Design Q9600

Square Footage: 2,053

● This three-bedroom country cottage with sun room at the front takes advantage of south-facing lots. The generous entry foyer allows direct access to the great room, dining room and sun room. A country kitchen with breakfast bar and cooking island provides an abundance of cabinet space. Split away from two family bedrooms is a private master suite with walk-in closets and master bath with whirlpool tub, shower and double-bowl vanity. The great room has direct access to a deck and the sun room. Both the great room and sun room have cathedral ceilings (note skylights in the sun room). A covered breezeway connects the house to the garage. The house is built on a crawlspace foundation.

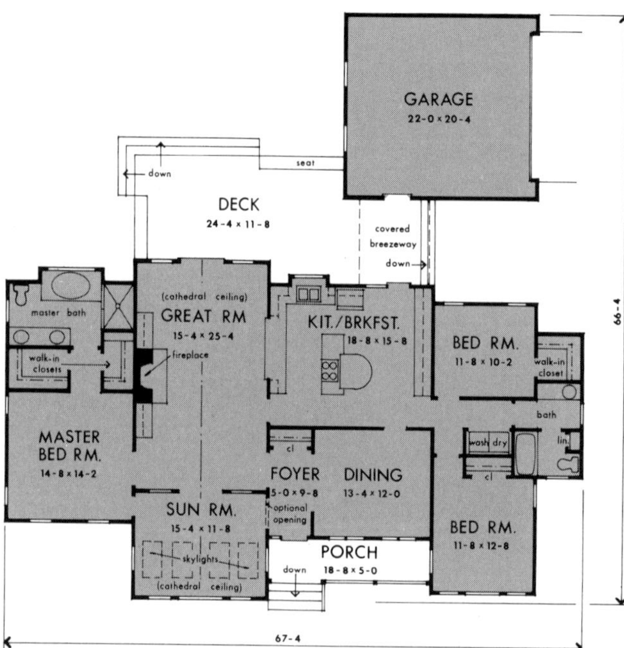

Design by Donald A. Gardner, Architect, Inc.

FRONT

REAR

Design Q9619

Square Footage: 2,021

Design by
Donald A. Gardner, Architect, Inc.

● Multi-paned windows, shutters, dormers, bay windows and a delightful covered porch grace the facade of this country cottage. Inside, the floor plan is no less appealing. Note that the great room has a fireplace, cathedral ceiling and sliding glass doors with an arched window above to allow for natural illumination of the room. A sun room with hot tub leads to an adjacent deck. This space can also be reached from the master bath. The generous master bedroom has a walk-in closet and spacious bath with double bowl vanity, shower and garden tub. Two additional bedrooms are located at the other end of the house for privacy. The garage is connected to the house by a breezeway.

GARAGE 20-4 × 20-4
DECK 36-8 × 10-0
covered breezeway
SUN RM. 15-8 × 7-10
hot tub
GREAT RM. 20-0 × 15-6 (cathedral ceiling)
fireplace
UTILITY 9-0 × 5-4
wash
dry
powder rm.
bath
cl
lin
BED RM. 11-4 × 13-8
master bath
walk-in closet
rail
FOYER 4-6 × 12-4
DINING 12-0 × 12-0
KITCHEN 14-4 × 12-0
BED RM. 14-8 × 11-0
MASTER BED RM. 13-4 × 16-8
PORCH 19-2 × 5-0
BRKFST. 13-4 × 7-8
67-4
67-6

FRONT

Design Q3438

First Floor: 1,489 square feet
Second Floor: 741 square feet
Total: 2,230 square feet

● A unique farmhouse plan which provides a grand floor plan, this home is comfortable in country or suburban settings. Formal entertaining areas share first-floor space with family gathering rooms and work and service areas. The master suite is also on this floor for convenience and privacy. Upstairs is a guest bedroom, private bath and loft area that makes a perfect studio. Special features make this a great place to come home to.

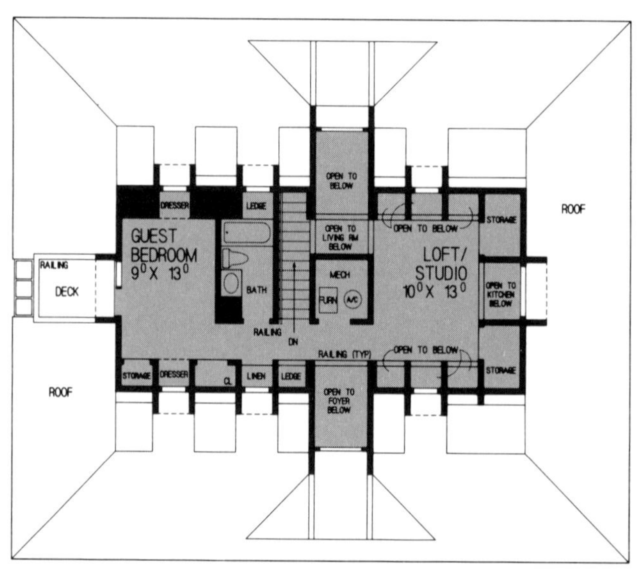

Design by
Home Planners, Inc.

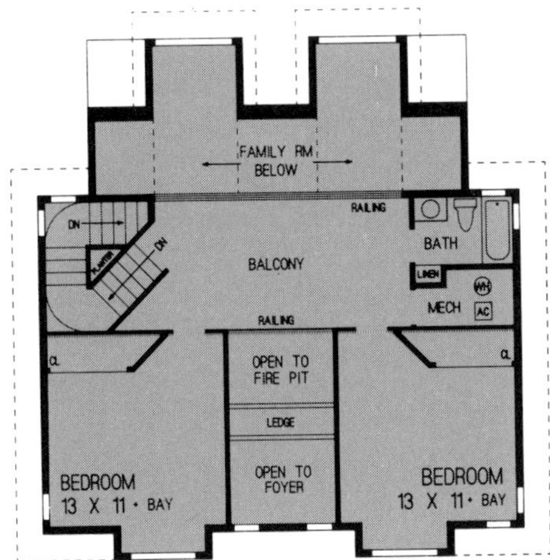

Design Q3404

First Floor: 3,358 square feet
Second Floor: 868 square feet
Total: 4,226 square feet

● Farmhouse design does a double take in this unusual and elegant rendition. Notice that most of the living takes place on the first floor: formal living room and dining room, gigantic family room with enormous firepit and porch access, guest bedroom or den and master bedroom suite. Upstairs there are two smaller bedrooms and a dramatic balcony overlook to the family room below.

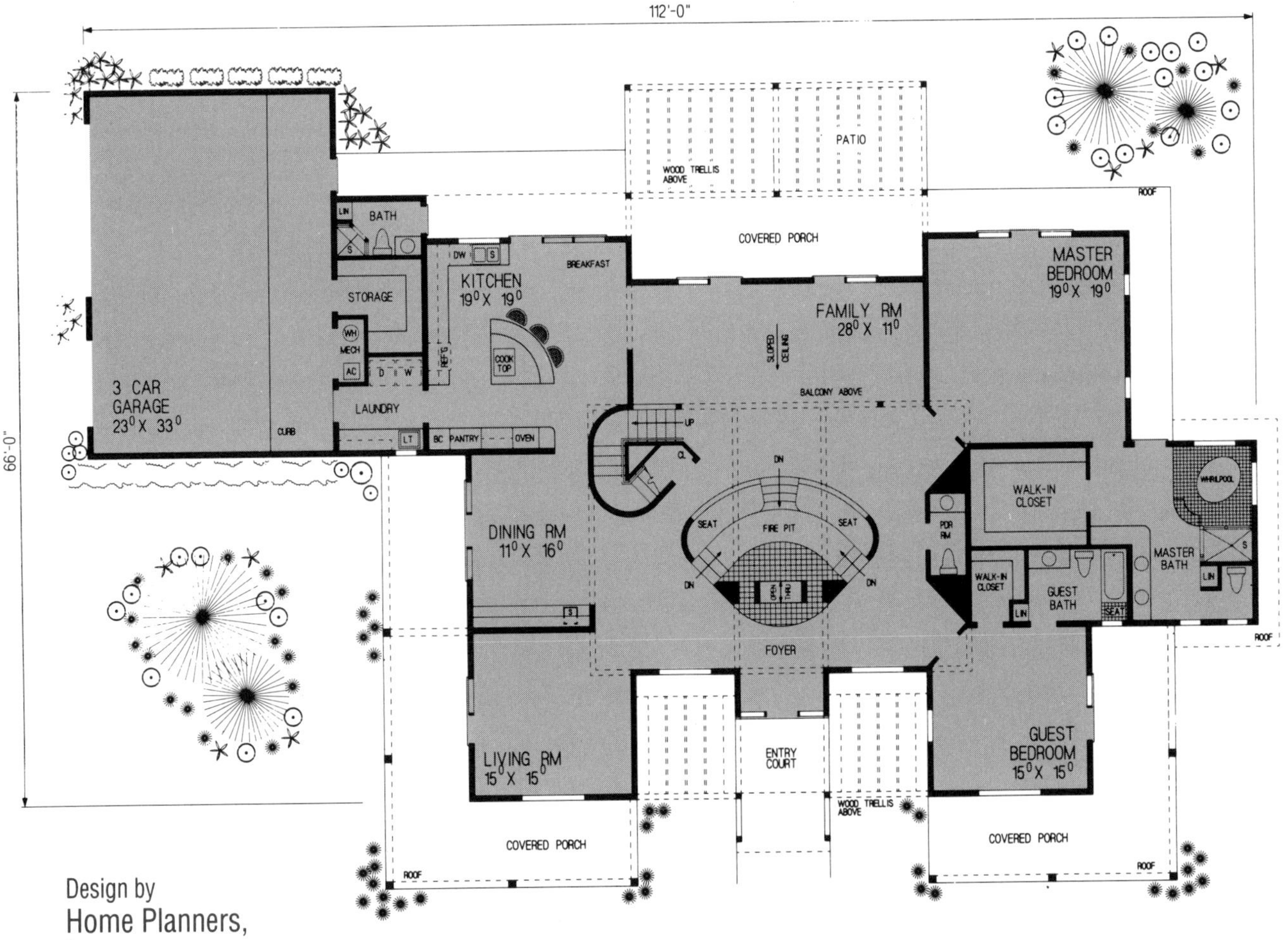

Design by
Home Planners, Inc.

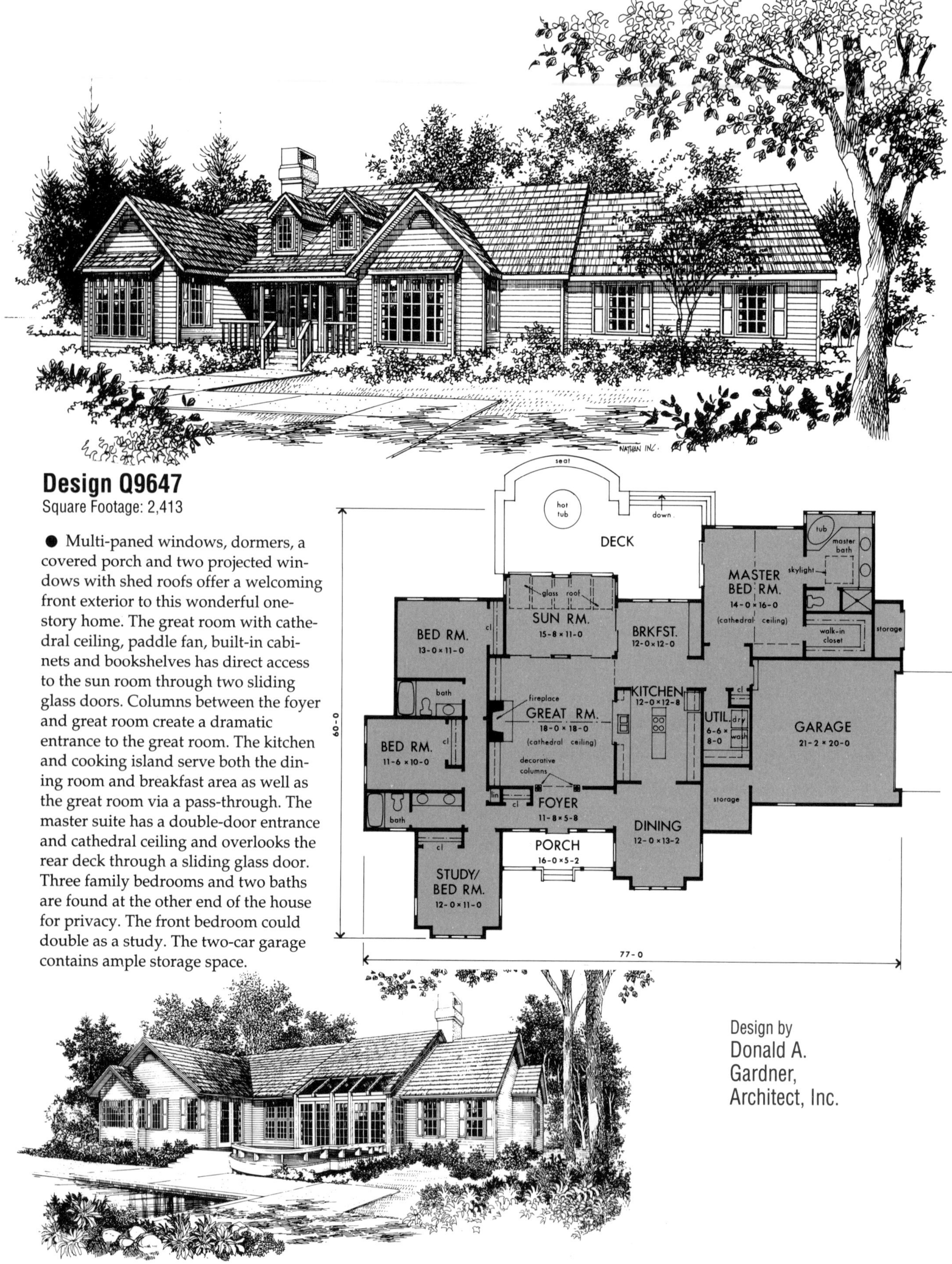

Design Q9647

Square Footage: 2,413

● Multi-paned windows, dormers, a covered porch and two projected windows with shed roofs offer a welcoming front exterior to this wonderful one-story home. The great room with cathedral ceiling, paddle fan, built-in cabinets and bookshelves has direct access to the sun room through two sliding glass doors. Columns between the foyer and great room create a dramatic entrance to the great room. The kitchen and cooking island serve both the dining room and breakfast area as well as the great room via a pass-through. The master suite has a double-door entrance and cathedral ceiling and overlooks the rear deck through a sliding glass door. Three family bedrooms and two baths are found at the other end of the house for privacy. The front bedroom could double as a study. The two-car garage contains ample storage space.

Design by
Donald A. Gardner, Architect, Inc.

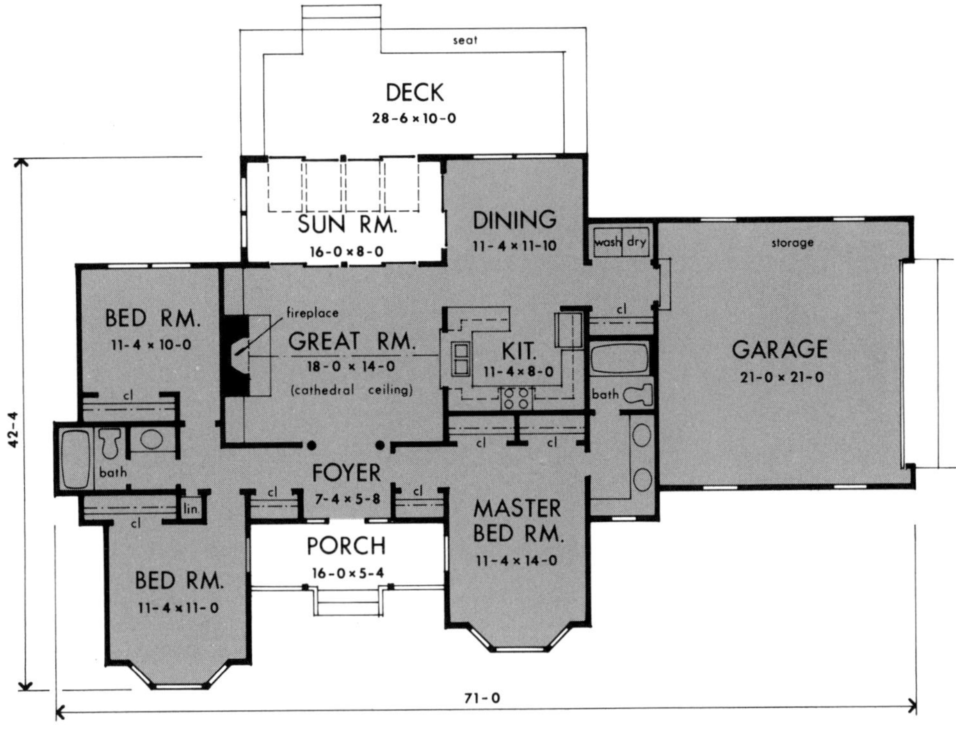

Design by
Donald A.
Gardner,
Architect, Inc.

Design Q9604

Square Footage: 1,506

● This unusual compact house maximizes its use of living areas and offers features found mostly only in larger house plans. A lovely facade, adorned with multi-paned windows, shutters, dormers, bay windows and a covered porch, gives way to a truly livable floor plan. The great room with cathedral ceiling, fireplace, paddle fan, built-in cabinets and bookshelves has direct access to the sun room through two sliding glass doors. Decorative columns between the foyer and great room create a dramatic entrance. Sleeping accommodations include a master with ample closet space and two family bedrooms. Note the split-bedroom plan configuration —providing utmost privacy.

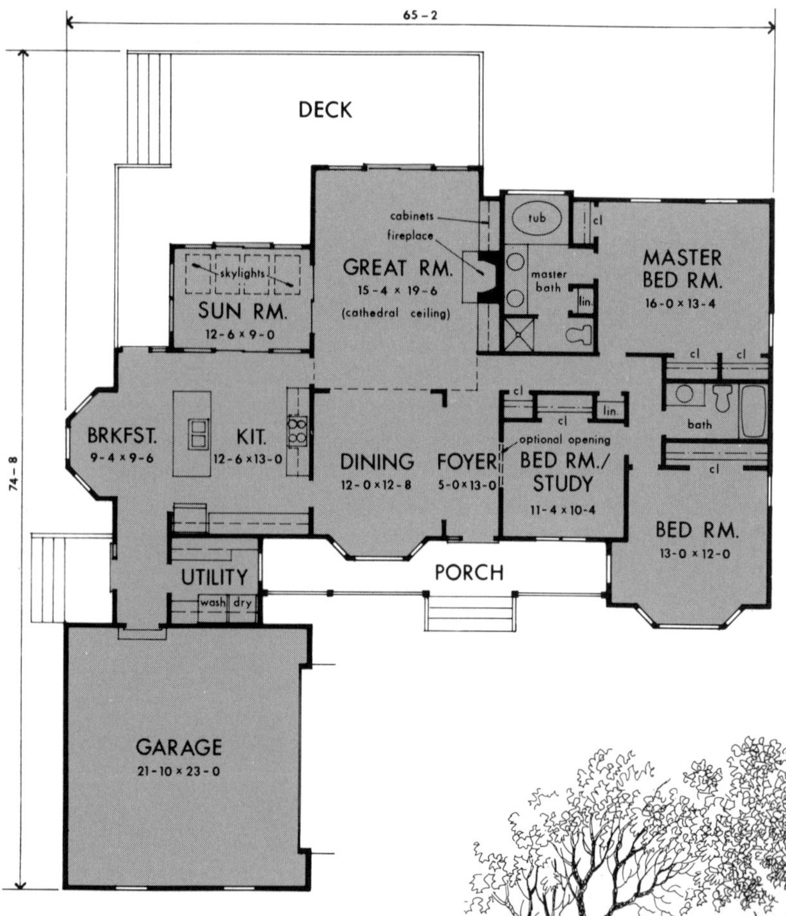

Design Q9670

Square Footage: 2,046

● This three-bedroom country cottage projects an intriguing appearance with its bay windows, dormers and L-shaped layout. The great room has a cathedral ceiling along with an arched window above the exterior door leading to the deck. The sun room with operable skylights is accessible from the great room, kitchen and deck for maximum exposure. The centrally located kitchen allows direct access to eating and living areas. Three bedrooms include a master suite and a bedroom that might also be useful as a study.

Design by
Donald A.
Gardner,
Architect, Inc.

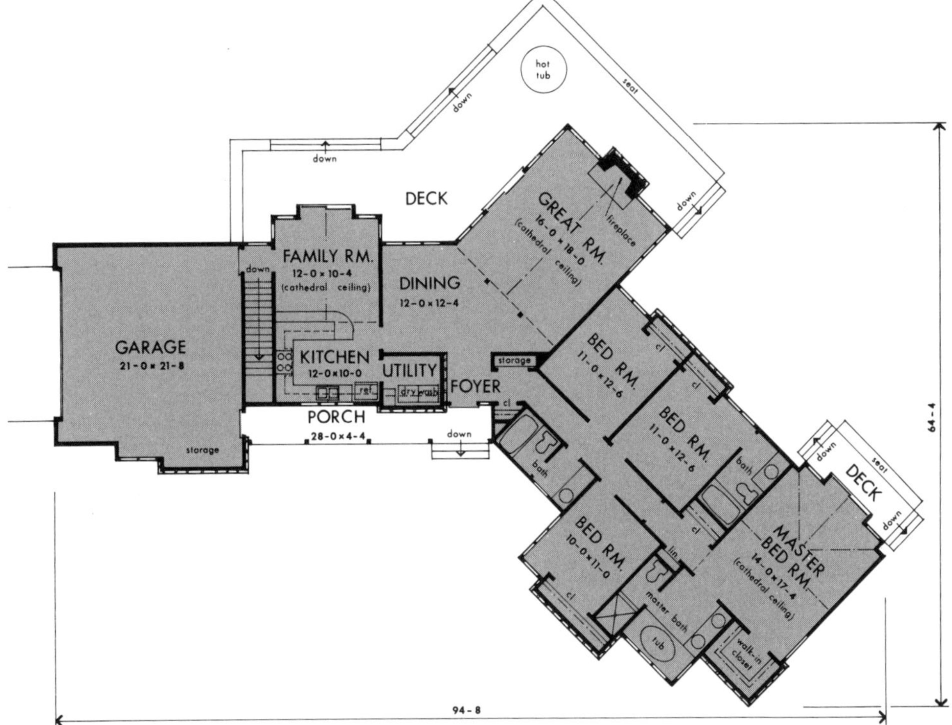

Design Q9601

Square Footage: 1,988

● This country-style ranch is the essence of excitement with its combination of exterior building materials and interesting shapes. Because it is angled, it allows for flexibility in design—the great room and/or the family room can be lengthened to meet family space requirements. The master bedroom has a cathedral ceiling, a walk-in closet, private deck and a spacious master bath with whirlpool tub. There are three family bedrooms, two of which share a full bath and one having a private bath. Expansive deck area with space for a hot tub wraps around interior family gathering areas. Both family room and great room have cathedral ceilings; the great room has a fireplace. For crawl-space foundation, order Design Q9601; for partial basement foundation, order Design Q9601-A.

Design by
Donald A. Gardner, Architect, Inc.

wood lattice above
seat
DECK
28-8 × 16-4
hot tub
down
MASTER BED RM.
13-4 × 16-0
fireplace
BED RM.
12-0 × 16-0
fireplace
skylights
KIT.
8-8 × 11-10
ref.
clerestory above
fireplace
tub
master bath
walk-in closet
GREAT RM.
20-0 × 21-0
exposed wood beams
cl
FOYER
lin.
wash
dry
walk-in closet
bath
PORCH
27-8 × 6-0
down
down
44-0
65-4

Design Q9607

Square Footage: 1,299

● Though rustic in appearance, this two-bedroom plan provides all the features sought after in today's well-planned home. A large central area includes a great room, entrance foyer and kitchen with serving and eating counter. Note the use of cathedral ceilings with exposed wood beams, skylights, clerestory windows and fireplace in this area. The master suite has an optional fireplace, walk-in closet, and whirlpool tub. The second bedroom also has an optional fireplace and a full bath. All rooms open to the rear deck, which supplies space for a hot tub.

REAR

Design by
Donald A. Gardner, Architect, Inc.

FRONT

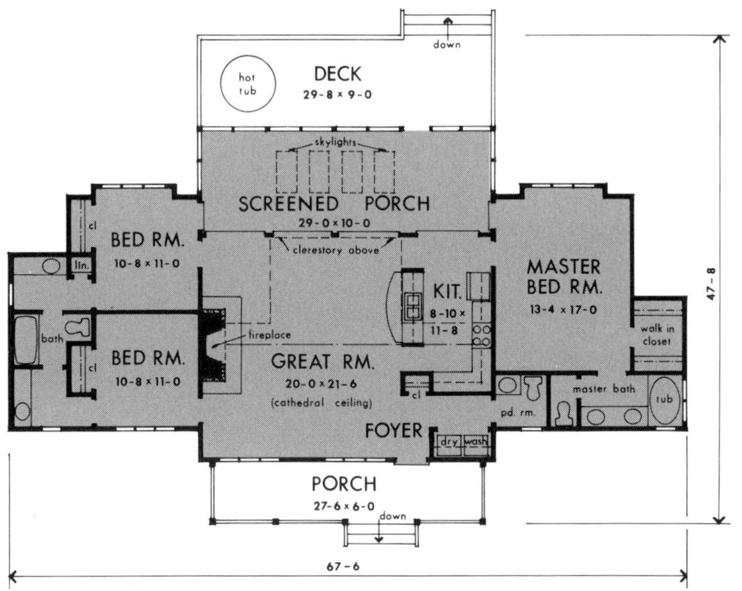

Design Q9609

Square Footage: 1,426

● Rustic charm abounds in this amenity-filled three-bedroom plan. From the central living area with cathedral ceiling and fireplace to the sumptuous master suite, there are few features omitted. Be sure to notice the large walk-in closet in the master bedroom, the pampering whirlpool tub, and separate water-closet compartment. Two other bedrooms have a connecting bath with single-bowl vanity for each. The house wraps around a screened porch with skylights — a grand place for eating and entertaining. The spacious rear deck has plenty of room for a hot tub.

REAR

Design by
Donald A. Gardner, Architect, Inc.

FRONT

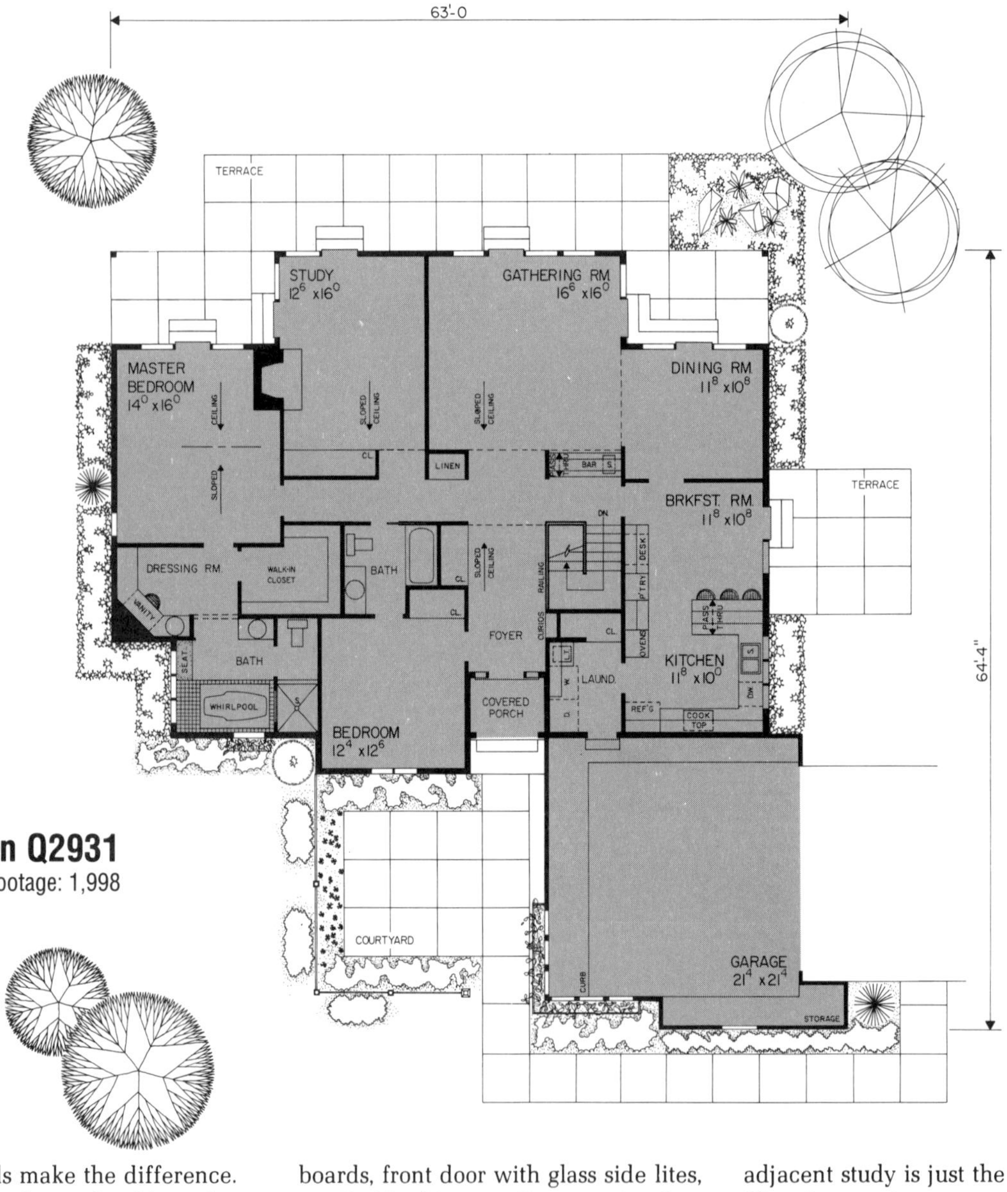

63'-0

TERRACE
STUDY 12⁶ x16⁰
GATHERING RM 16⁶ x16⁰
MASTER BEDROOM 14⁰ x16⁰
DINING RM 11⁸ x10⁸
LINEN
BAR
TERRACE
BRKFST. RM 11⁸ x10⁸
DRESSING RM.
WALK-IN CLOSET
BATH
FOYER
KITCHEN 11⁸ x10⁰
LAUND.
BATH
WHIRLPOOL
COVERED PORCH
BEDROOM 12⁴ x12⁶
COURTYARD
GARAGE 21⁴ x21⁴
STORAGE
64'-4"

Design Q2931

Square Footage: 1,998

Design by Home Planners, Inc.

● Little details make the difference. Consider these that make this such a charming showplace: Picket-fenced courtyard, carriage lamp, window boxes, shutters, muntined windows, multi-gabled roof, cornice returns, vertical and horizontal siding with corner boards, front door with glass side lites, etc. Inside this appealing exterior there is a truly outstanding floor plan for the small family or empty-nesters. The master bedroom suite is long on luxury, with a separate dressing room, private vanities, and whirlpool bath. An adjacent study is just the right retreat. There's room to move and — what a warm touch! — it has its own fireplace. Other attractions: roomy kitchen and breakfast area, spacious gathering room, rear and side terraces, and an attached two-car garage with storage.

Design by
Home Planners, Inc.

Design Q2947

Square Footage: 1,830

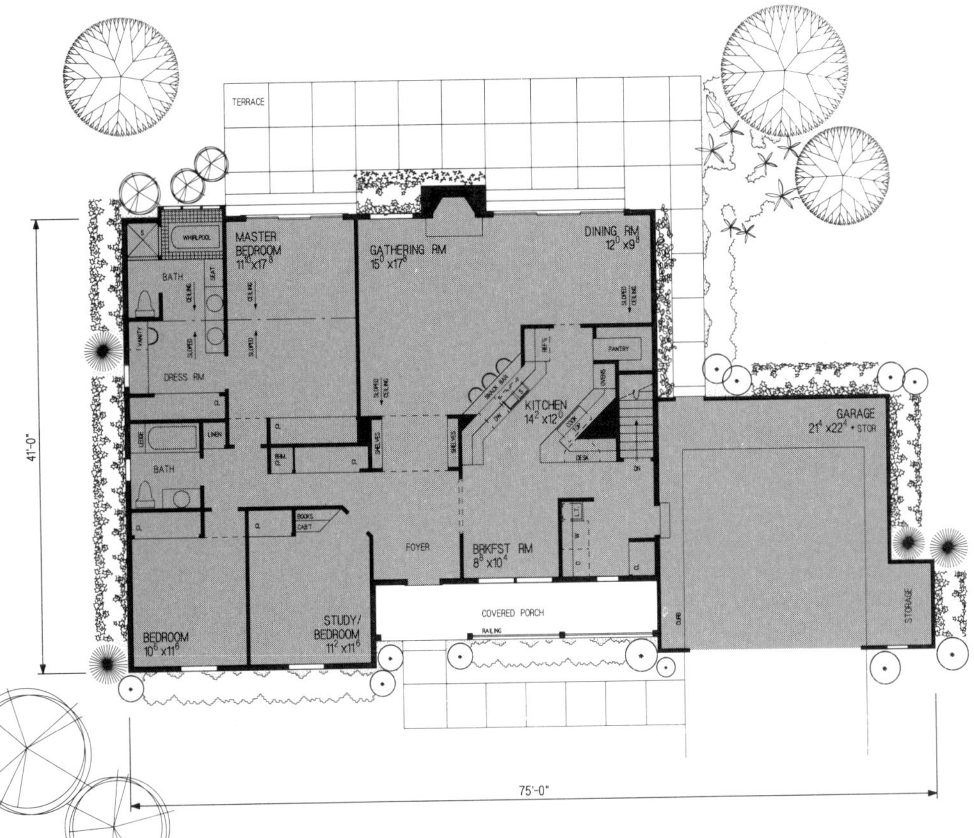

● This charming one-story Traditional home greets visitors with a covered porch. A galley-style kitchen shares a snack bar with the spacious gathering room where a fireplace is the focal point. An ample master suite includes a luxury bath with whirlpool tub and separate dressing room. Two additional bedrooms, one that could double as a study, are located at the front of the home.

When You're Ready To Order . . .

Let Us Show You Our Home Blueprint Package.

Building a home? Planning a home? Our Blueprint Package contains nearly everything you need to get the job done right, whether you're working on your own or with help from an architect, designer, builder or subcontractors. Each Blueprint Package is the result of many hours of work by licensed architects or professional designers.

QUALITY

Hundreds of hours of painstaking effort have gone into the development of your blueprint set. Each home has been quality-checked by professionals to insure accuracy and buildability.

VALUE

Because we sell in volume, you can buy professional-quality blueprints at a fraction of their development cost. With our plans, your dream home design costs only a few hundred dollars, not the thousands of dollars that custom architects charge.

SERVICE

Once you've chosen your favorite home plan, you'll receive fast efficient service whether you choose to mail your order to us or call us toll free at 1-800-521-6797.

SATISFACTION

Our years of service to satisfied home plan buyers provide us the experience and knowledge that guarantee your satisfaction with our product and performance.

ORDER TOLL FREE 1-800-521-6797

After you've studied our Blueprint Package and Important Extras on the following pages, simply mail the accompanying order form on page 221 or call toll free on our Blueprint Hotline: 1-800-521-6797. We're ready and eager to serve you.

Each set of blueprints is an interrelated collection of floor plans, interior and exterior elevations, dimensions, cross-sections, diagrams and notations showing precisely how your house is to be constructed.

Here's what you get:

Frontal Sheet

This artist's sketch of the exterior of the house, done in realistic perspective, gives you an idea of how the house will look when built and landscaped. Large ink-line floor plans show all levels of the house and provide a quick overview of your new home's livability, as well as a handy reference for studying furniture placement.

Foundation Plan

Drawn to 1/4-inch scale, this sheet shows the complete foundation layout including support

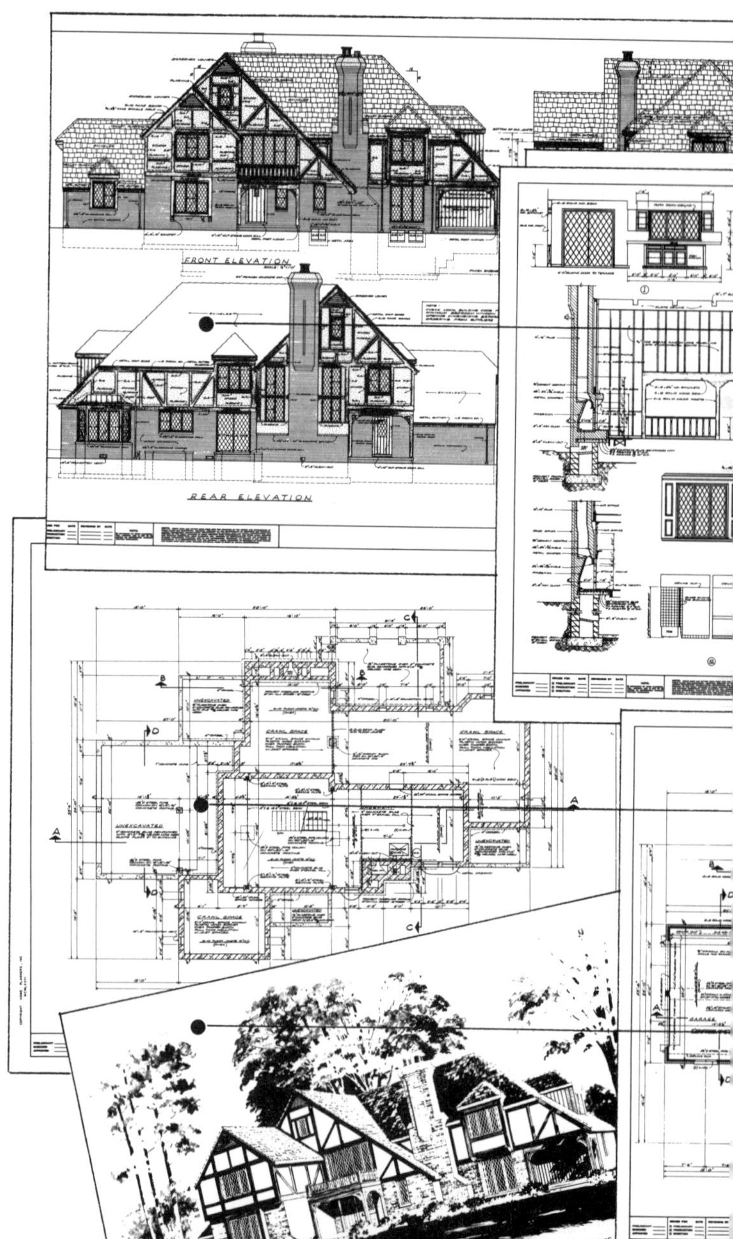

walls, excavated and unexcavated areas, if any, and foundation notes. If slab construction rather than basement, the plan shows footings and details for a monolithic slab. This page, or another in the set, also includes a sample plot plan for locating your house on a building site.

Detailed Floor Plans

Complete in 1/4-inch scale, these plans show the layout of each floor of the house. All rooms and interior spaces are carefully dimensioned and keys are provided for cross-section details given later in the plans. The positions of all electrical outlets and switches are clearly shown.

House Cross-Sections

Large-scale views, normally drawn at 3/8-inch equals 1 foot, show sections or cut-aways of the foundation, interior walls, exterior walls, floors, stairways and roof details. Additional cross-sections are given to show important changes in floor, ceiling or roof heights or the relationship of one level to another. Extremely valuable for construction, these sections show exactly how the various parts of the house fit together.

Interior Elevations

These large-scale drawings show the design and placement of kitchen and bathroom cabinets, laundry areas, fireplaces, bookcases and other built-ins. Little "extras," such as mantelpiece and wainscoting drawings, plus moulding sections, provide details that give your home that custom touch.

Exterior Elevations

Drawings in 1/4-inch scale show the front, rear and sides of your house and give necessary notes on exterior materials and finishes. Particular attention is given to cornice detail, brick and stone accents or other finish items that make your home distinctive.

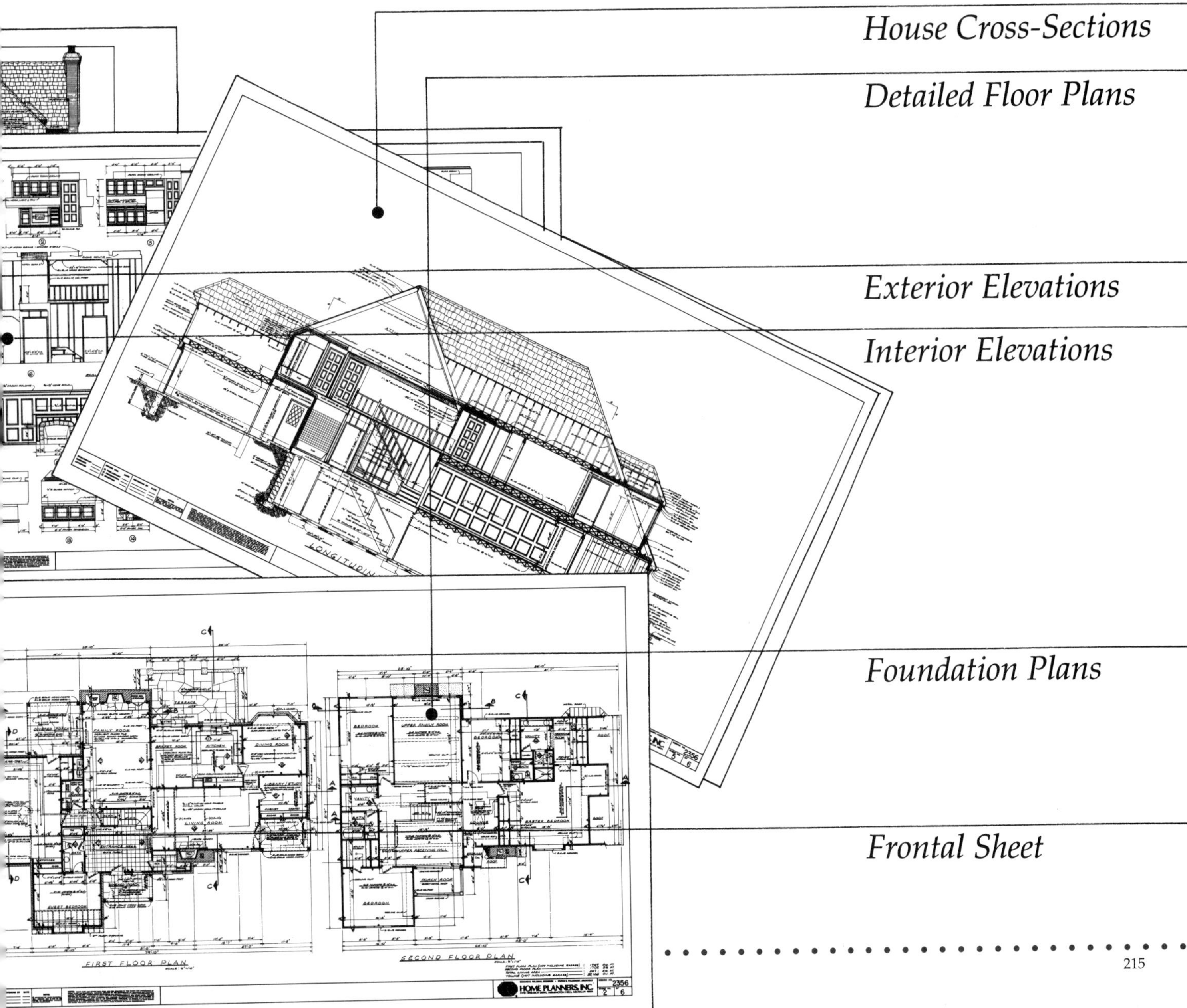

Important Extras To Do The Job Right!

Introducing six important planning and construction aids developed by our professionals to help you succeed in your home-building project.

Materials List

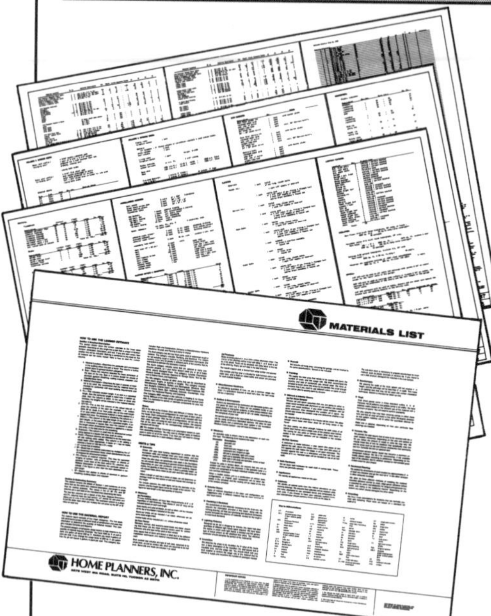

For many of the designs in our portfolio, we offer a customized materials take-off that is invaluable in planning and estimating the cost of your new home. This comprehensive list outlines the quantity, type and size of material needed to build your house (with the exception of mechanical system items). Included are:

- framing lumber
- roofing and sheet metal
- windows and doors
- exterior sheathing material and trim
- masonry, veneer and fireplace materials
- tile and flooring materials
- kitchen and bath cabinetry
- interior sheathing and trim
- rough and finish hardware
- many more items

This handy list helps you or your builder cost out materials and serves as a ready reference sheet when you're compiling bids. It also provides a cross-check against the materials specified by your builder and helps coordinate the substitution of items you may need to meet local codes.

(Note: Because of differing local codes, building methods, and availability of materials, our Materials Lists do not include mechanical materials. To obtain necessary take-offs and recommendations, consult heating, plumbing and electrical contractors. Materials Lists are not sold separately from the Blueprint Package.)

Specification Outline

This valuable 16-page document is critical to building your house correctly. Designed to be filled in by you or your builder, this booklet lists 166 stages or items crucial to the building process.

For the layman, it provides a comprehensive review of the construction process and helps in making the specific choices of materials, models and processes. For the builder, it serves as a guide to preparing a building quotation and forms the basis for the construction program.

Designed primarily as a reference for the homeowner, this Specification Outline can become a legally binding document. Once it is filled out and agreed upon by owner and builder, it becomes a complete Project Specification.

When combined with the blueprints, a signed contract and schedule, the Specification Outline becomes a legal document and record for the building of your home. Many home builders find it useful to order two of these outlines–one as a worksheet in formulating the specifications and another to be carefully completed as a legal document.

To Order, Call Toll Free 1-800-521-6797

To add these important extras to your Blueprint Package, simply indicate your choices on the order form on page 221 or call us Toll Free 1-800-521-6797 and we'll tell you more about these exciting products.

Detail Sheets

Because local codes and requirements vary greatly, we recommend that you obtain drawings and bids from licensed contractors to do your mechanical plans. However, if you want to know more about techniques — and deal more confidently with subcontractors — we offer these remarkably useful detail sheets. Each is an excellent tool that will enhance your understanding of these technical subjects.

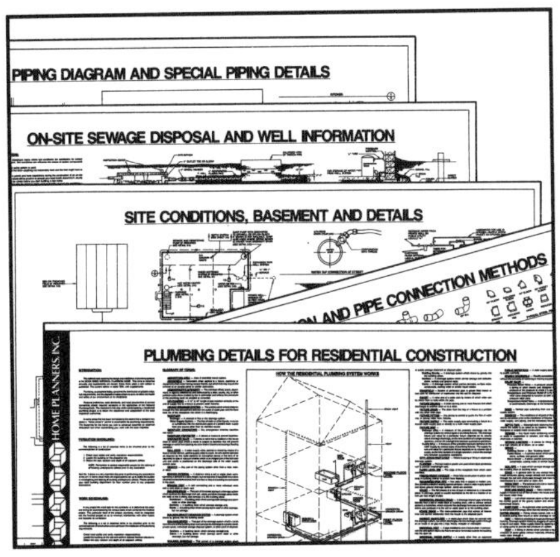

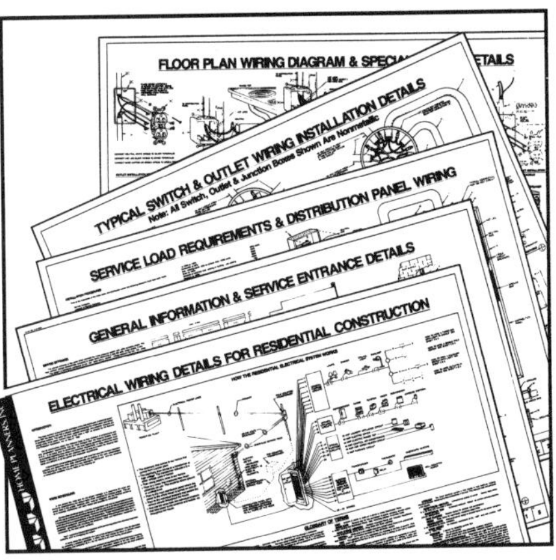

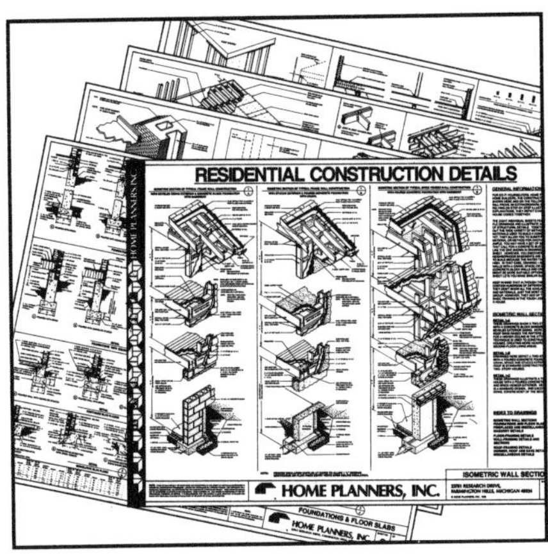

Plumbing

The Blueprint Package includes locations for all the plumbing fixtures in your new house, including sinks, lavatories, tubs, showers, toilets, laundry trays and water heaters. However, if you want to know more about the complete plumbing system, these 24x36-inch detail sheets will prove very useful. Prepared to meet requirements of the National Plumbing Code, these six fact-filled sheets give general information on pipe schedules, fittings, sump-pump details, water-softener hookups, septic system details and much more. Color-coded sheets include a glossary of terms.

Electrical

The locations for every electrical switch, plug and outlet are shown in your Blueprint Package. However, these Electrical Details go further to take the mystery out of household electrical systems. Prepared to meet requirements of the National Electrical Code, these comprehensive 24x36-inch drawings come packed with helpful information, including wire sizing, switch-installation schematics, cable-routing details, appliance wattage, door-bell hookups, typical service panel circuitry and much more. Six sheets are bound together and color-coded for easy reference. A glossary of terms is also included.

Construction

The Blueprint Package contains everything an experienced builder needs to construct a particular house. However, it doesn't show all the ways that houses can be built, nor does it explain alternate construction methods. To help you understand how your house will be built–and offer additional techniques–this set of drawings depicts the materials and methods used to build foundations, fireplaces, walls, floors and roofs. Where appropriate, the drawings show acceptable alternatives. These six sheets will answer questions for the advanced do-it-yourselfer or home planner.

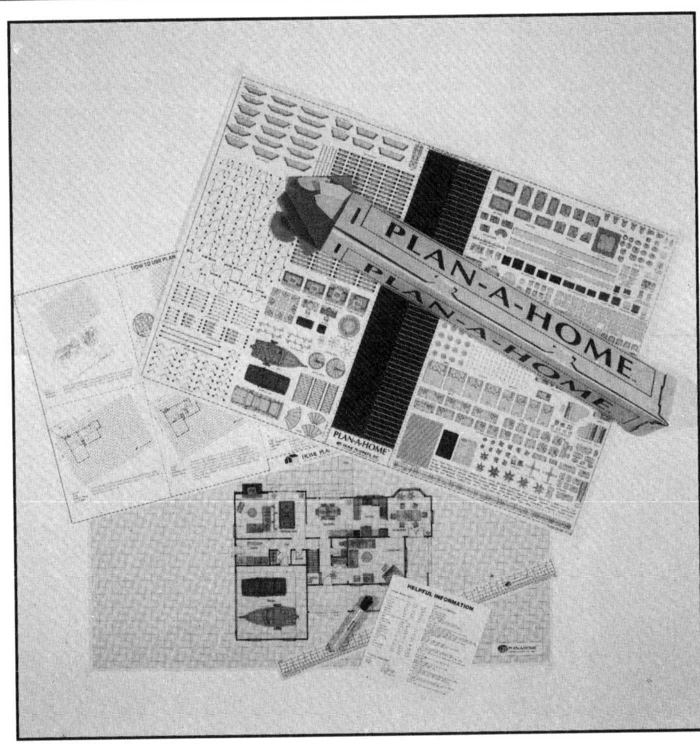

Plan-A-Home®

Plan-A-Home® is an easy-to-use tool that helps you design a new home, arrange furniture in a new or existing home, or plan a remodeling project. Each package contains:

- More than *700 peel-off planning symbols* on a self-stick vinyl sheet, including walls, windows, doors, all types of furniture, kitchen components, bath fixtures and many more. All are made of durable, peel-and-stick vinyl you can use over and over.
- A reusable, transparent, *1/4-inch scale planning grid* made of tough mylar that matches the scale of actual working drawings (1/4-inch equals 1 foot). This grid provides the basis for house layouts of up to 140x92 feet.
- *Tracing paper* and a protective sheet for copying or transferring your completed plan.
- A *felt-tip pen*, with water-soluble ink that wipes away quickly.

With Plan-A-Home®, you can make basic planning decisions for a new house or make modifications to an existing house. Use with your Blueprint Package to test modifications to rooms or to plan furniture arrangements before you build. Plan-A Home® lets you lay out areas as large as a 7,500 square foot, six-bedroom, seven-bath house.

House Blueprint Price Schedule and Plans Index

These pages contain all the information you need to price your blueprints. In general the larger and more complicated the house, the more it costs to design and thus the higher the price we must charge for the blueprints. Remember, however, that these prices are far less than you would normally pay for the services of a licensed architect or professional designer. Custom home designs and related architectural services often cost thousands of dollars, ranging from 5% to 15% of the cost of construction. By ordering our blueprints you are potentially saving enough money to afford a larger house, or to add those "extra" amenities such as a patio, deck, swimming pool or even an upgraded kitchen or luxurious master suite.

To use the Index below, refer to the design number listed in numerical order (a helpful page reference is also given). Note the price index letter and refer to the House Blueprint Price Schedule at right for the cost of one, four or eight sets of blueprints or the cost of a reproducible sepia. Additional prices are shown for identical and reverse blueprint sets, as well as a very useful Materials List for some of the plans.

House Blueprint Price Schedule

(Prices guaranteed through December 31, 1993)

	1-set Study Package	4-set Building Package	8-set Building Package	1-set Reproducible Sepias
Schedule A	$210	$270	$330	$420
Schedule B	$240	$300	$360	$480
Schedule C	$270	$330	$390	$540
Schedule D	$300	$360	$420	$600
Schedule E	$390	$450	$510	$660

Additional Identical Blueprints in same order ....$50 per set
Reverse Blueprints (mirror image) ....$50 per set
Specification Outlines....................$7 each
Materials Lists (for Home Planners', Design Basics', Alan Mascord's, and Donald Gardner's Plans only):

▲ Home Planners' Designs
- Schedule A-D $40
- Schedule E $50

† Design Basics' Designs....................$75
◆ Donald Gardner's Designs $40
✸ Alan Mascord's Designs $40

Exchanges....................$40 exchange fee for the first set; $10 for each additional set
$60 total exchange fee for 4 sets
$90 total exchange fee for 8 sets

To Order: Fill in and send the Order Form on page 221—or call us Toll Free 1-800-521-6797.

House Plan	Price	Page
† Q9206	C	178
† Q9212	D	18
† Q9214	D	17
† Q9215	D	29
† Q9219	D	181
† Q9230	D	16
† Q9232	D	82
† Q9235	C	199
† Q9239	D	106
† Q9242	E	20
† Q9247	C	179
† Q9251	D	92
† Q9252	C	83
† Q9260	C	198
† Q9267	C	133
† Q9269	D	94
† Q9274	D	21
† Q9289	C	19
† Q9297	E	43
† Q9298	D	42
† Q9299	D	116
† Q9300	C	98
† Q9301	D	99
† Q9302	D	111
† Q9303	D	110
† Q9304	C	131
† Q9305	C	130
† Q9306	D	132
† Q9307	C	158
† Q9308	D	159
† Q9309	C	180
† Q9310	C	193
† Q9311	C	192
† Q9312	D	194
† Q9313	D	195
† Q9314	E	28
✸Q9419	D	13
✸Q9420	D	70
✸Q9421	C	12
✸Q9430	B	164
✸Q9457	B	200
✸Q9458	D	201
✸Q9475	C	71
✸Q9476	C	165
✸Q9480	E	197
✸Q9481	C	196
◆Q9600	D	202
◆Q9601	C	209
◆Q9603	C	44
◆Q9604	C	207
◆Q9605	D	49
◆Q9606	C	11
◆Q9607	B	210
◆Q9608	C	168
◆Q9609	B	211
◆Q9616	D	55
◆Q9619	D	203
◆Q9620	B	151
◆Q9621	C	56
◆Q9623	D	52
◆Q9624	D	47
◆Q9625	D	45
◆Q9632	D	54
◆Q9636	D	65
◆Q9639	C	150
◆Q9643	D	15
◆Q9644	C	14
◆Q9645	C	23
◆Q9647	D	206
◆Q9654	D	22
◆Q9662	C	50
◆Q9666	C	169
◆Q9667	D	53
◆Q9668	D	57
◆Q9669	D	64
◆Q9670	D	208
◆Q9677	D	10
Q9850	D	62
Q9851	D	63
Q9852	C	80
Q9853	B	79
Q9854	C	78
Q9855	D	120
Q9856	D	121
Q9857	C	122
Q9858	D	123
Q9859	C	136
Q9860	D	137
Q9861	D	187
Q9862	C	186
Q9863	D	24
Q9864	C	25
Q9868	C	81
Q9869	D	119
Q9870	D	118

Before You Order . . .

Before completing the coupon at right or calling us on our Toll-Free Blueprint Hotline, you may be interested to learn more about our service and products. Here's some information you will find helpful.

Quick Turnaround
We process and ship every blueprint order from our office within 48 hours. On most orders, we do even better. Normally, if we receive your order by 5 p.m. Eastern Time, we'll process it the same day and ship it the following day. Because of this quick turnaround, we won't send a formal notice acknowledging receipt of your order.

Our Exchange Policy
Since blueprints are printed in response to your order, we cannot honor requests for refunds. However, we will exchange your entire first order for an equal number of blueprints plus the following exchange fees: $40 for the first set, $10 for each additional set; $60 total exchange fee for 4 sets; $90 total exchange fee for 8 sets.... *plus* the difference in cost if exchanging for a design in a higher price bracket, or *less* the difference in cost if exchanging for a design in a lower price bracket. (Sepias are not exchangeable.) All sets from the first order must be returned before the exchange can take place. Please add $8 for postage and handling via ground service; $20 via 2nd Day Air.

About Reverse Blueprints
If you want to build in reverse of the plan as shown, we will include an extra set of reversed blueprints (mirror image) for an additional fee of $50. Although lettering and dimensions appear backward, reverses will be a useful visual aid if you decide to flop the plan.

Modifying Our Plans
With such a great selection of homes, you are bound to find the one that suits you. However, if you need to make changes to the plans you have chosen, it may be easy for us to do this for you. Please ask for additional information when you place your order.

If you decide to revise plans significantly that are not customizable, we strongly suggest that you order reproducible sepias and consult a licensed architect or professional designer to help you redraw the plans.

Architectural and Engineering Seals
Some cities and states are now requiring that a licensed architect or engineer review and "seal" your blueprints prior to construction. This is often due to local or regional concerns over energy consumption, safety codes, seismic ratings, etc. For this reason, you may find it necessary to consult with a local professional to have your plans reviewed. This can normally be accomplished with minimum delays, for a nominal fee.

Compliance with Local Codes and Regulations
At the time of creation, our plans are drawn to specifications published by Building Officials Code Administrators (BOCA), the Southern Standard Building Code, or the Uniform Building Code and are designed to meet or exceed national building standards. Some states, counties and municipalities have their own codes, zoning requirements and building regulations. Before starting construction, consult with local building authorities and make sure you comply with local ordinances and codes, including obtaining any necessary permits or inspections as building progresses. In some cases, minor modifications to your plans by your builder, local architect or designer may be required to meet local conditions and requirements.

Foundation and Exterior Wall Changes
Most of our plans are drawn with either a full or partial basement foundation. Depending upon your specific climate or regional building practices, you may wish to convert this basement to a slab or crawlspace. Most professional contractors and builders can easily adapt your plans to alternate foundation types. Likewise, most can easily convert 2x4 wall construction to 2x6, or vice versa. If you need more guidance on these conversions, our handy Construction Detail Sheets, shown on page 217, describe how such conversions can be made.

How Many Blueprints Do You Need?
A single set of blueprints is sufficient to study a home in greater detail. However, if you are planning to obtain cost estimates from a contractor or subcontractors—or if you are planning to build immediately—you will need more sets. Because additional sets are cheaper when ordered in quantity with the original order, make sure you order enough blueprints to satisfy all requirements. The following checklist will help you determine how many you need:

_____Owner

_____Builder (generally requires at least three sets; one as a legal document, one to use during inspections, and at least one to give to subcontractors)

_____Local Building Department (often requires two sets)

_____Mortgage Lender (usually one set for a conventional loan; three sets for FHA or VA loans)

_____TOTAL NUMBER OF SETS

Toll Free 1-800-521-6797

Normal Office Hours:
8:00 a.m. to 8:00 p.m. Eastern Time
Monday through Friday
Our staff will gladly answer any questions during normal office hours. Our answering service can place orders after hours or on weekends.

If we receive your order by 5:00 p.m. Eastern, Time, Monday through Friday, we'll process it the same day and ship it the following business day. When ordering by phone, please have your charge card ready. We'll also ask you for the Order Form Key Number at the bottom of the coupon. Please use our Toll-Free number for blueprint and book orders only.

By FAX: Copy the Order Form on the next page and send it on our International FAX line: 1-602-297-6219.

Canadian Customers
Order Toll-Free 1-800-848-2550
For faster, more economical service, Canadian customers may now call in orders on our Toll-Free line. Or, complete the order form at right, and mail with your check indicating U.S. funds to:

Home Planners, Inc.
3275 W. Ina Road, Suite 110
Tucson, AZ 85741

By FAX: Copy the Order Form on the next page and send it on our International FAX line: 1-602-297-6219.

ORDER FORM

HOME PLANNERS, INC., 3275 WEST INA ROAD
SUITE 110, TUCSON, ARIZONA 85741

THE BASIC BLUEPRINT PACKAGE
Rush me the following (please refer to the Plans Index and Price Schedule in this section):

_____ Set(s) of blueprints for plan number(s) ___________. $________
_____ Set(s) of sepias for plan number(s) ___________. $________
_____ Additional identical blueprints in same order @ $50.00 per set. $________
_____ Reverse blueprints @ $50.00 per set. $________

IMPORTANT EXTRAS
Rush me the following:

_____ Materials List: Home Planners' Designs @ $40 Schedule A-D; $50 Schedule E; $75 Design Basics' Designs; $40 Alan Mascord's Designs; $40 Donald Gardner's Designs. $________
_____ Specification Outlines @ $7.00 each. $________
_____ Detail Sets @ $14.95 each; any two for $22.95; all three for $29.95 (save $14.90). $________
❑ Plumbing ❑ Electrical ❑ Construction
(These helpful details provide general construction advice and are not specific to any single plan.)

SUB-TOTAL $________
SALES TAX (Arizona residents add 5% sales tax; Michigan residents add 4% sales tax.) $________

POSTAGE AND HANDLING	**1-3 sets**	**4 or more sets**	
DELIVERY (Requires street address - No P.O. Boxes)			
•Regular Service Allow 4-6 days delivery	❑ $6.00	❑ $8.00	$________
•2nd Day Air Allow 2-3 days delivery	❑ $12.00	❑ $20.00	$________
•Next Day Air Allow 1 day delivery	❑ $22.00	❑ $30.00	$________
POST OFFICE DELIVERY If no street address available. Allow 4-6 days delivery	❑ $8.00	❑ $12.00	$________
OVERSEAS AIR MAIL DELIVERY	❑ $30.00	❑ $50.00	$________
Note: All delivery times are from date Blueprint Package is shipped.	❑ Send COD		

TOTAL (Sub-total, tax, and postage) $________

YOUR ADDRESS (please print)

Name ______________________________
Street ______________________________
City ______________ State ___________ Zip ___________
Daytime telephone number (______) ______________________

FOR CREDIT CARD ORDERS ONLY
Please fill in the information below:

Credit card number ______________________________
Exp. Date: Month/Year ______________
Check one ❑ Visa ❑ MasterCard ❑ Discover Card

Signature ______________________________

Order Form Key: TB26BP

Please check appropriate box:
❑ Licensed Builder-Contractor
❑ Home Owner

ORDER TOLL FREE
1-800-521-6797

ORDER FORM

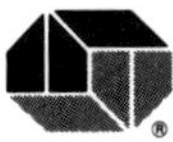

HOME PLANNERS, INC., 3275 WEST INA ROAD
SUITE 110, TUCSON, ARIZONA 85741

THE BASIC BLUEPRINT PACKAGE
Rush me the following (please refer to the Plans Index and Price Schedule in this section):

_____ Set(s) of blueprints for plan number(s) ___________. $________
_____ Set(s) of sepias for plan number(s) ___________. $________
_____ Additional identical blueprints in same order @ $50.00 per set. $________
_____ Reverse blueprints @ $50.00 per set. $________

IMPORTANT EXTRAS
Rush me the following:

_____ Materials List: Home Planners' Designs @ $40 Schedule A-D; $50 Schedule E; $75 Design Basics' Designs; $40 Alan Mascord's Designs; $40 Donald Gardner's Designs. $________
_____ Specification Outlines @ $7.00 each. $________
_____ Detail Sets @ $14.95 each; any two for $22.95; all three for $29.95 (save $14.90). $________
❑ Plumbing ❑ Electrical ❑ Construction
(These helpful details provide general construction advice and are not specific to any single plan.)

SUB-TOTAL $________
SALES TAX (Arizona residents add 5% sales tax; Michigan residents add 4% sales tax.) $________

POSTAGE AND HANDLING	**1-3 sets**	**4 or more sets**	
DELIVERY (Requires street address - No P.O. Boxes)			
•Regular Service Allow 4-6 days delivery	❑ $6.00	❑ $8.00	$________
•2nd Day Air Allow 2-3 days delivery	❑ $12.00	❑ $20.00	$________
•Next Day Air Allow 1 day delivery	❑ $22.00	❑ $30.00	$________
POST OFFICE DELIVERY If no street address available. Allow 4-6 days delivery	❑ $8.00	❑ $12.00	$________
OVERSEAS AIR MAIL DELIVERY	❑ $30.00	❑ $50.00	$________
Note: All delivery times are from date Blueprint Package is shipped.	❑ Send COD		

TOTAL (Sub-total, tax, and postage) $________

YOUR ADDRESS (please print)

Name ______________________________
Street ______________________________
City ______________ State ___________ Zip ___________
Daytime telephone number (______) ______________________

FOR CREDIT CARD ORDERS ONLY
Please fill in the information below:

Credit card number ______________________________
Exp. Date: Month/Year ______________
Check one ❑ Visa ❑ MasterCard ❑ Discover Card

Signature ______________________________

Order Form Key: TB26BP

Please check appropriate box:
❑ Licensed Builder-Contractor
❑ Home Owner

ORDER TOLL FREE
1-800-521-6797

Additional Plans Books

THE DESIGN CATEGORY SERIES

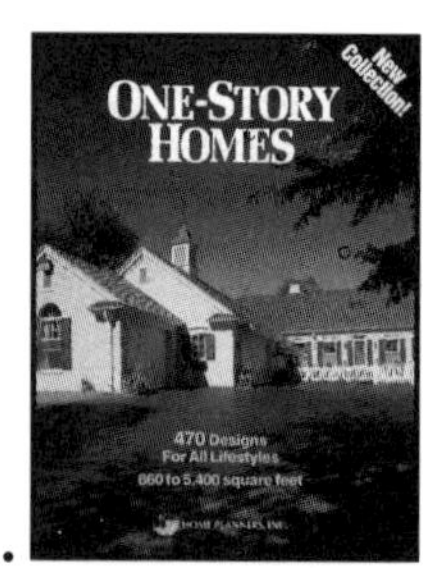

1. **ONE-STORY HOMES** A collection of 470 homes to suit a range of budgets in one-story living. All popular styles, including Cape Cod, Southwestern, Tudor and French. **384 pages. $8.95 ($10.95 Canada)**

2. **TWO-STORY HOMES** 478 plans for all budgets in a wealth of styles: Tudors, Saltboxes, Farmhouses, Victorians, Georgians, Contemporaries and more. **416 pages. $8.95 ($10.95 Canada)**

3. **MULTI-LEVEL AND HILLSIDE HOMES** 312 distinctive styles for both flat and sloping sites. Includes exposed lower levels, open staircases, balconies, decks and terraces. **320 pages. $6.95 ($8.95 Canada)**

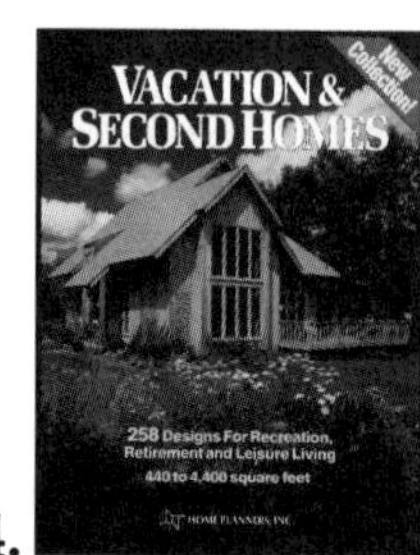

4. **VACATION AND SECOND HOMES** 258 ideal plans for a favorite vacation spot or perfect retirement or starter home. Includes cottages, chalets, and 1-, 1½-, 2-, and multi-levels. **256 pages. $5.95 ($7.50 Canada)**

THE EXTERIOR STYLE SERIES

9. **330 EARLY AMERICAN HOME PLANS** A heart-warming collection of the best in Early American architecture. Traces the style from Colonial structures to popular traditional versions. Includes a history of different styles. **304 pages. $9.95 ($11.95 Canada)**

10. **335 CONTEMPORARY HOME PLANS** Required reading for anyone interested in the clean-lined elegance of Contemporary design. Features plans of all sizes and types, as well as a history of this style. **304 pages. $9.95 ($11.95 Canada)**

11. **COLONIAL HOUSES** 161 history-inspired homes with up-to-date plans are featured along with 2-color interior illustrations and 4-color photographs. Included are many plans developed for *Colonial Homes'* History House Series. **208 pages. $10.95 ($12.95 Canada)**

12. **COUNTRY HOUSES** Shows off 80 country homes in three eye-catching styles: Cape Cods, Farmhouses and Center-Hall Colonials. Each features an architect's exterior rendering, artist's depiction of a furnished interior room, large floor plans, and planning tips. **208 pages. $10.95 ($12.95 Canada)**

PLAN PORTFOLIOS

MOST POPULAR HOME DESIGNS Our customers' favorite plans, including one-story, 1 ½-story, two-story, and multi-level homes in a variety of styles. Designs feature many of today's most popular amenities: lounges, clutter rooms, media rooms and more.

14. **272 pages. $8.95 ($10.95 Canada)**

AFFORDABLE HOME PLANS For the prospective home builder with a modest or medium budget. Features 430 one-, 1½-, two-story and multi-level homes in a wealth of styles. Included are cost saving ideas for the budget-conscious.

15. **320 pages. $8.95 ($10.95 Canada)**

LUXURY DREAM HOMES At last, the home you've waited for! A collection of 150 of the best luxury home plans from seven of the most highly regarded designers and architects in the United States. A dream come true for anyone interested in designing, building or remodeling a luxury home.

16. **192 pages. $14.95 ($17.95 Canada)**

NEW FROM HOME PLANNERS

5.

WESTERN HOME PLANS Over 215 home plans from Spanish Mission and Monterey to Northwest Chateau and San Francisco Victorian. Historical notes trace the background and geographical incidence of each style. **208 pages. $8.95 ($10.95 Canada)**

6.

DECK PLANNER 25 practical plans and details for decks the do-it-yourselfer can actually build. How-to data and project starters for a variety of decks. Construction details available separately. **112 pages. $7.95 ($9.95 Canada)**

7.

THE HOME LANDSCAPER 55 fabulous front- and backyard plans that even the do-it-yourselfer can master. Complete construction blueprints and regionalized plant lists available for each design. **208 pages. $12.95 ($15.95 Canada)**

8.

BACKYARD LANDSCAPER Sequel to the popular *Home Landscaper*, contains 40 professionally designed plans for backyards to do yourself or contract out. Complete construction blueprints and regionalized plant lists available. **160 pages. $12.95 ($15.95 Canada)**

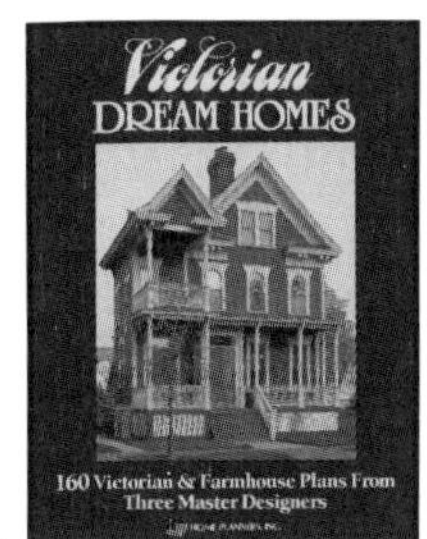

13.

VICTORIAN DREAM HOMES 160 Victorian and Farmhouse designs by three master designers. Victorian style from Second Empire homes through the Queen Anne and Folk Victorian era. Beautifully drawn renderings accompany the modern floor plans. **192 Pages. $12.95 ($15.95 Canada)**

17.

NEW ENCYCLOPEDIA OF HOME DESIGNS Our best collection of plans is now bigger and better than ever! Over 500 plans organized by architectural category including all types and styles and 269 brand-new plans. The most comprehensive plan book ever. **352 pages. $9.95 ($11.95 Canada)**

Please fill out the coupon below. We will process your order and ship it from our office within 48 hours. Send coupon and check for the total to:

HOME PLANNERS, INC.
3275 West Ina Road, Suite 110, Dept. BK
Tucson, Arizona 85741

THE DESIGN CATEGORY SERIES — A great series of books edited by design type. Complete collection features 1376 pages and 1273 home plans.

1. _____One-Story Homes @ $8.95 ($10.95 Canada) $ ________
2. _____Two-Story Homes @ $8.95 ($10.95 Canada) $ ________
3. _____Multi-Level & Hillside Homes @ $6.95 ($8.95 Canada) $ ________
4. _____Vacation & Second Homes @ $5.95 ($7.50 Canada) $ ________

NEW FROM HOME PLANNERS

5. _____Western Home Plans @ $8.95 ($10.95 Canada) $ ________
6. _____Deck Planner @ $7.95 ($9.95 Canada) $ ________
7. _____The Home Landscaper @ $12.95 ($15.95 Canada) $ ________
8. _____The Backyard Landscaper @ $12.95 ($15.95 Canada) $ ________

THE EXTERIOR STYLE SERIES

9. _____330 Early American Home Plans @ $9.95 ($11.95 Canada) $ ________
10. _____335 Contemporary Home Plans @ $9.95 ($11.95 Canada) $ ________
11. _____Colonial Houses @ $10.95 ($12.95 Canada) $ ________
12. _____Country Houses @ $10.95 ($12.95 Canada) $ ________
13. _____Victorian Dream Homes @ $12.95 ($15.95 Canada) $ ________

PLAN PORTFOLIOS

14. _____Most Popular Home Designs @ $8.95 ($10.95 Canada) $ ________
15. _____Affordable Home Plans @ $8.95 ($10.95 Canada) $ ________
16. _____Luxury Dream Homes @ $14.95 ($17.95 Canada) $ ________
17. _____New Encyclopedia of Home Designs @ $9.95 ($11.95 Canada) $ ________

Sub-Total $ ________
Arizona residents add 5% sales tax; Michigan residents add 4% sales tax $ ________
ADD Postage and Handling $ 3.00
TOTAL (Please enclose check) $ ________

Name (please print) ______________________________
Address ______________________________
City ______________ State ______________ Zip ______________

CANADIAN CUSTOMERS: Order books Toll-Free 1-800-848-2550. Or, complete the order form above, and mail with your check indicating U.S. funds to: Home Planners, Inc., 3275 W. Ina Road, Suite 110, Tucson, AZ 85741.

TO ORDER BOOKS BY PHONE CALL TOLL FREE 1-800-322-6797

TB26BK

INDEX